# Place Names

MW00787617

What are place names? From where do they originate? How are they structured? What do they signify? How important are they in our life? This groundbreaking book explores these compelling questions and more by providing a thorough introduction to the assumptions, theories, terminology, and methods in toponymy and toponomastics – the studies of place names, or toponyms. It is the first comprehensive resource on the topic in a single volume and explores the history and development of toponyms, focusing on the conceptual and methodological issues pertinent to the study of place names around the world. It presents a wide range of examples and case studies illustrating the structure, function, and importance of toponyms from ancient times to the present day. Wide-ranging yet accessible, it is an indispensable source of knowledge for students and scholars in linguistics, toponymy and toponomastics, onomastics, etymology, and historical linguistics.

FRANCESCO PERONO CACCIAFOCO is an associate professor in linguistics at Xi'an Jiaotong-Liverpool University. Before joining XJTLU, he was a senior lecturer in historical linguistics at Nanyang Technological University. He works on the etymology of Indo-European place names, on the study of Aegean scripts, on cryptography, on language deciphering, and on language documentation.

FRANCESCO CAVALLARO is an associate professor in linguistics at Nanyang Technological University. His research interests are in sociolinguistics and the social aspects of bilingualism, especially of minority groups in multilingual contexts.

# Place Names

*Approaches and Perspectives in Toponymy*
*and Toponomastics*

Francesco Perono Cacciafoco

*Xi'an Jiaotong-Liverpool University*

Francesco Cavallaro

*Nanyang Technological University*

Shaftesbury Road, Cambridge CB2 8EA, United Kingdom

One Liberty Plaza, 20th Floor, New York, NY 10006, USA

477 Williamstown Road, Port Melbourne, VIC 3207, Australia

314–321, 3rd Floor, Plot 3, Splendor Forum, Jasola District Centre, New Delhi – 110025, India

103 Penang Road, #05–06/07, Visioncrest Commercial, Singapore 238467

Cambridge University Press is part of Cambridge University Press & Assessment, a department of the University of Cambridge.

We share the University's mission to contribute to society through the pursuit of education, learning and research at the highest international levels of excellence.

www.cambridge.org
Information on this title: www.cambridge.org/9781108490160

DOI: 10.1017/9781108780384

First published 2023

*A catalogue record for this publication is available from the British Library.*

ISBN 978-1-108-49016-0 Hardback
ISBN 978-1-108-74824-7 Paperback

# Contents

# Figures

# Tables

# Preface

Since 1876, when the term *toponymy* was used for the first time in English (according to the *Oxford English Dictionary*), studies on place names have proliferated, covering the large majority of the areas of the world and investigating toponyms according to different, multifaceted approaches (intensive, extensive, qualitative, quantitative, etymological, geographical, statistical, critical, sociological, political, and so on) and through multidisciplinary and interdisciplinary perspectives.

The study of ancient place names can be configured as a sort of 'archaeology of language' that allows us to uncover many facets of our past' and even discover remote changes in population and settlement dynamics which date back to before any form of writing and written documentation was invented. The historical-linguistic, historical-phonetic, and etymological reconstruction of place names developed by toponymists can be compared to the patient detective work of archaeologists in excavation sites and on archaeological findings. Both involve the slow, careful, and meticulous uncovering of many prehistoric and historical layers, in order to understand when an artefact was made and, in the context of toponymy, when a place name was coined. The recovery of the different diachronic stages of the morphology of a toponym can be configured as a 'toponymic stratigraphy' that can lead us far back in time to its proto-form and root. Indeed, place names are among the few surviving vestiges of prehistoric human communities, and their study can help us to open a window through which we may view facets of their lives and events that happened before what is properly called history.

At the same time, the sociolinguistic and sociological study of toponyms allows us to understand the everyday relations between human beings and their places and place names. This synchronic view of toponyms enables us to analyse the many implications, at the cultural, social, political, societal, and, ultimately, personal/intimate levels, arising from the mutual interaction between people and their naming practices. Toponyms are part of the cultural identity of individuals and, hence, are affected by the social and linguistic changes people undergo. The naming practices human beings implement on places are, generally, aimed at safeguarding their memory, celebrating what they deem worthy, and commemorating important events and people. However, they can also have the opposite use, that is, to 'delete' history, and to make individuals and historical facts fall into forgetfulness.

The link to landscape, the identity-making and deep perception of a name of a place by local speakers, or the total loss of its origins and the stories generated around its possible explanation by the same local speakers, the pride connected with a toponym, or the simple familiarity with it have been 'always there' in the memory of individuals. They all are intangible components of the strength and value of place names, which go beyond their analytical and linguistic study and which ingenerate in human beings a sort of 'feeling of (or for) the places', which, in turn, becomes part of the cultural heritage of people and their collective memory.

This 'feeling of the places' reverberates in the intimate relationship between the landscape, its landmarks, and its names. This intimate relationship would not exist without the people who give names to the elements of their environment, the actual naming subjects. They are a necessary and fundamental social component that materially produces and perpetuates those names, in a naming process that is not only a natural 'linguistic procedure' – to give a name to what is still unnamed – but also reflects the deep, spontaneous, necessary, intellectual, and even sentimental connections between human beings, the territory and landscape, and land and places. Robert Macfarlane wonderfully describes these relations, among his other works, in his celebrated book *Landmarks* (2016), and we (as well as more or less everyone in the world, probably) have experienced the same feeling when, in our childhood, we were walking in the countryside with our grandparents, who were unveiling to us a whole world made of stories and memories connected with the names of the places and their landmarks – a heritage beautifully portrayed, among others, by Margaret Gelling and Ann Cole in their extraordinary book *The Landscape of Place-Names* (2000) and by Anna Pavord in her truly remarkable work titled *Landskipping* (2016). Heritage, memories, and place names, being intangible and largely undocumented, are cultural components which, every day, are at risk of being lost. However, while place names exist and are passed down from generation by generation by people, and studied and recorded by scholars, that heritage, those memories, and the attachment to the places will never be really lost, because they are (sometimes enigmatically) attested and preserved in the names themselves, the names of the places.

The task of all current and future toponymists starts exactly from there, from the need, which is configurable as a mission, to document and recover the origins and the stories of those names, to return them to the new generations, and, through them, to safeguard the 'feeling of the places', the intrinsic nature of the deep and ancestral relationship between human beings and their landscapes, lands, territories, landmarks, and the atavistic memories connected with them.

All this goes beyond linguistics, or history, or geography, and the analytical study of place names allows scholars to portray, or at least to draft, a more or less comprehensive picture and context of the toponyms. This context includes the culture of the human beings who coined those place names and of all the generations of individuals who, consciously or unconsciously, contributed to their survival, by passing them down over centuries and even millennia simply by using them, talking about them, and 'speaking' them.

The fact that, besides written records, place names are essentially 'told' and 'spoken' by people makes them pure linguistic entities shaped, over time, by the natural 'making of the language'. They are made by individuals, and this uninterrupted naming process connects all humans with each other. Toponyms change, in their morphology and semantics, over time exactly because they follow the path of human communication and the linguistic shifts that arise due to the diachronic evolution of languages. They are also sometimes 'fossils' because they do not always align with the historical development of the common lexical items of a language, and therefore they assume, somehow, their own typical and individual morphology, sometimes enigmatic, sometimes incompatible with the general sound laws regulating the diachronic changes of a language. The toponymic evolution they experience, nonetheless, is almost always produced by linguistic phenomena which are 'living', since place names are 'told' and 'spoken', and this therefore makes of them a very specific (or special) category of 'linguistic fossils'. Indeed, in a way, they are 'living' toponymic records, also because they are sometimes possibly the only surviving evidence of a remote past and of remote stages of a language. Very ancient place names are still in existence in our times, and this makes them very valuable linguistic relics.

Toponyms, actually, are not easy to define. A common phrase uttered in the classroom by Dr Francesco Perono Cacciafoco is, 'a place name is a place name', and this self-evident, very simple tautology is, perhaps, the best explanation of what a place name is, because a place name is everything we wrote above and a lot more. A toponym shows, in itself, a sort of cultural syncretism, which is unsuspected when we first start to deal with it. A place name, generally, is taken for granted, and rarely people wonder about its origins or original meaning or its histories or even the stories which surround it. Therefore, it is 'simple' because it is 'just a word' heard or used in everyday life. Being 'simple', there seems to be no reason to investigate it. However, we know that a place name is not simple at all, and that a true etymological reconstruction of a toponym could require a whole paper or a book in itself to explicate it. Everything is in the name, its history, its etymological origins, its original meaning, the stories connected with it, and its cultural impact. All, therefore, comes from the name.

Not many people realise that the historical-linguistic study of place names is one of the keys to cracking the code of the ancient origins of languages and to answer the fundamental question: 'what came before?'. What came before, throughout the different stages of our current languages and of the languages and proto-languages from which our languages derive? What came before our times and the times before ours, and before our ancestors and their ancestors? What do we know of the culture and beliefs of peoples so ancient that they left no written memory, because writing had not been invented in their times yet? What came before place names and before places got those names, in a time when the first humans with language started giving names to their world? Sometimes, the historical-linguistic study of toponyms allows us to 'feel' the auroral sensation of our most remote ancestors, who, in a possibly terrible and extremely dangerous existence, as life would have been in prehistoric times, nonetheless had the privilege, for the first time, of giving names to the features of their world. Indeed, ideally they, the above-mentioned first 'naming subjects', were at a specific point in time (of course, varying chronologically and geographically from place to place, and with varying dynamics of language disappearance and regeneration) the first ones to coin names for 'all things' and, indeed, for their places. They were the 'first namers'. Finding out who they were and the languages they were speaking is the focus, or the ultimate mission, of a historical linguist, as well as of a toponymist dealing with the historical-linguistic analysis of place names. That is, to try to reconstruct their names for places and to give us a sense of how the languages of those remote and long-forgotten ancestors sounded.

Convergently, the documentary study of place names, an important component of research in language documentation and field linguistics, enables scholars to work on toponyms at two different, but interrelated, levels. On one hand, a field linguist dealing with aboriginal and/or Indigenous toponymy in undocumented and endangered linguistic contexts gives an irreplaceable contribution to document and safeguard languages which are at high risk of disappearance. On the other hand, by studying local place names and documenting them, the field linguist is able not only to hypothesise and establish links among place names within the same language or within languages belonging to the same language family, but also has the possibility to outline a sort of 'diachronic stratigraphy' of those place names, and to infer theories on their relatedness and their development over time. Despite working with generally undocumented languages, the morphological comparison of place names and the assessment of their role in the general linguistic context of a newly documented language enable the researcher to establish internal relations and filiation processes among aboriginal and/or Indigenous place names (and also common lexical items). This can be done even when the place names do not allow for a precise and chronological reconstruction at the level of diachronic development, and generally the linguist is able to answer, at least partly, the fundamental above-mentioned question: 'what came before?'.

A sociological and sociolinguistic approach to the study of place names, such as those connected with critical toponymies and political toponymy, is essential in interpreting and analysing toponyms. In these approaches, the place names are not treated as prehistoric 'living fossils' or undocumented lexical items which can reveal significant elements of an ancient or an aboriginal and/ or Indigenous culture, but as 'living' linguistic elements actively or passively interacting with speakers *hic et nunc* or, at least, in modern and contemporary times. The sociological and sociolinguistic approach to the study of place names, therefore, enables the researchers to put their finger on the pulse of a community and to analyse toponyms in their dynamics connected both with modern and contemporary societies and their developments, and with the sociological aspects of their nature as 'linguistic items' in living languages. In this context, this study of toponymy could be defined as 'synchronic', even if it always contemplates a diachronic interpretation of societies and sociolinguistic elements.

The motivation for this book originated from a course in toponymy and toponomastics taught by Dr Perono Cacciafoco. The module was a successful and pioneering attempt to introduce topics in toponymy and toponomastics to undergraduate students through an interdisciplinary approach involving historical linguistics, etymology, language documentation, human geography, historical geography, urban geography, history, palaeoanthropology, archaeology, and sociology.

One main challenge in teaching that course was the lack of an authoritative and reliable text on toponymy and toponomastics. Without a single guiding reference, the module was based on the large scientific literature available, which was, unavoidably, somewhat dispersed. What was needed was, therefore, a general and comprehensive source to be used as an exact and timely reference on the discipline of toponymy in itself, with a standardisation of the specialised terminology and with a consistent apparatus of examples aimed at triggering and nurturing the interest of students and young scholars towards the study of place names. Hence, the idea of this book. An academic reference text in toponymy and toponomastics was born. A volume like this requires balance in the use of the sources and in the choice and explanation of examples. With this in mind, this book aims at being a solid and, at the same time, agile source and reference for students and scholars interested in place names, their history, and their analysis. Indeed, the goal of the large set of case studies provided in this volume is to enable readers to start their journey in toponymy as proactive researchers.

A book like this, by necessity, has to be 'general', both in its theoretical contents and in the comments and explanations of examples which it presents. 'General', nonetheless, does not mean 'simplistic' or 'generic'. Indeed, every academic reference text needs to be selective, and it was therefore not possible to include in this volume toponyms from all the language families of the world or examples from all the linguistic contexts. Nonetheless, readers can find well-documented case studies, which have been carefully chosen because of their paradigmatic nature, as they offer deeply founded methodological examples and patterns which can be applied (with the unavoidable required adjustments depending on their different contexts) to toponymic reconstructions from all over the world. Besides the academic and scientific rigour in delineating each context and the related case studies, this book also has the courage to deal with advanced topics in historical-linguistic and toponymic reconstruction, which, sometimes, are examined through experimental approaches. For instance, readers will be introduced to the notion of 'pre-language', which, in some aspects, is controversial or not considered fundamental in historical linguistics, but which is essential in the screening and assessment of the nature of very ancient place names. In this book, we will also grapple with the concept of 'language contact in prehistoric times', which is believed by some linguists to be problematic and difficult to prove for very remote eras. We take the stance that place names, in the absence of written records or material culture findings, can sometimes help us to hypothesise the existence of very ancient linguistic roots and proto-forms, and to reconstruct possible movements of populations and settlement dynamics.

One of the main contributions of this volume is to sort out a plethora of toponymic terms and definitions and, finally, lay out a definitive nomenclature for all the sub-disciplines and technical lexicons in toponomastics. Up to now, there have not been clear definitions given to the different approaches in the field, and the terminology has been vague and applied differently by different scholars. This has created somewhat of a confusing situation in toponymy. We may not be the first to have used labels such as 'historical toponomastics', 'diachronic toponymy', and 'synchronic toponymy'. However, in this volume, we finally give these terms their rightful place and importance in the field and eliminate the ambiguity and vagueness which characterised them. As such, in this book, we have clearly distinguished the sub-disciplines of toponymy and given all the technical terms out there their proper and logical explanations and place. For example, probably for the first time, 'historical toponomastics' is defined as the historical reconstruction of toponyms through the analysis of available written sources and documents, while 'diachronic toponymy' is the study of place names in the absence of written and documented records. 'Synchronic toponymy', in turn, is also clearly presented as the analysis of toponyms in the context of the *hic et nunc* (modern and contemporary times) at the cultural and sociological level. We also take the opportunity to explain very specific and interrelated contexts of the study of place names, by providing, for example, the clear definitions of key concepts and thematic areas.

Indeed, the development and establishment of notions and sub-disciplines in toponymy is part of our efforts to systematise epistemological contents and technical terminology in this field, and to provide students and scholars with a source which is accurate and complete not only at the level of details and examples, but also at the theoretical and terminological level. By formalising and standardising a technical lexicon in toponymy, we aim to express toponymic notions with exactness and clarity and to give substance to a toponymic vocabulary relevant to both students and scholars.

Examples are provided from a large range of languages, language families, cultural contexts, societal environments, and epistemological approaches. Of course, a volume like this should, ideally, deal with all the place names of the world, in a sort of hubris-project *à la Bouvard et Pécuchet*. However, that would be impossible for this book, or any book. Despite this, we have tried to provide readers with a significant number of consistent and exhaustive case studies which will accompany students and scholars through their journey into toponymy and which will enhance their understanding of the related theoretical notions and issues.

Toponymy is studied in this book according to a very comprehensive approach, both at the historical and historical-linguistic level and at the cultural and sociological level. Place names, therefore, are on the one hand reconstructed etymologically, with plenty of case studies and examples to help readers to follow etymological processes and theories, and on the other hand they are examined according to their relations with cultures, societies, and civilisations, in order to understand not only their historical and linguistic origins, but also the role they play in people's everyday life.

The book consists of ten chapters, generally associating a theoretical component with consistent examples or case studies. This provides readers not only with the necessary set of technical notions inherent in toponymy and toponomastics and the specific subtopics of each chapter, but also with detailed case studies that corroborate the theoretical concepts. The aim is to accompany readers through the study of the methodologies and the analyses of relevant examples. Methods applied are not only from linguistics (e.g., the comparative method and the use and/or reconstruction of sound laws in the historical interpretation of place names), but are derived from a mutual association of all the above-mentioned disciplines which are involved in the study of toponymy. The methodologies discussed in this book are, therefore, multidisciplinary in their nature and, sometimes, experimental.

Each chapter of the volume is focussed on a specific topic or conceptual macro-area. However, we have tried to make sure that each section is not a 'watertight compartment'. Each chapter, therefore, despite being aimed at introducing readers to specific notions and examples, makes reference and links to the relevant parts in other chapters and other significant sources, all according to an expressly designed progressive learning path. This is an integral component of the epistemological discourse of the book that takes readers by the hand in a journey into toponymy and toponomastics.

In particular, Chapter 1 is a general but comprehensive introduction to the basic concepts and terminology of toponymy and toponomastics and to the study of place names as a whole; Chapter 2 is a discussion of the study of toponymy under the lens of language change and introduces the notions of 'historical toponomastics', 'diachronic toponymy', and 'synchronic top-onymy'; Chapter 3 explores different aspects and epistemological elements of historical toponomastics; Chapter 4 illustrates how the study of toponymy can help linguists in reconstructing proto-languages and introduces the theor-etical dichotomy between the notions of 'pre-language' and 'proto-language'; Chapter 5 deals with topics and issues in diachronic toponymy and with how toponyms can be studied in communities in the absence of any historical document; Chapter 6 is focussed on the links between landscape, landscape sciences, and toponymy, and on how resources from these disciplines can be used to improve the etymological reconstruction of place names; Chapter 7 investigates the interaction between historical toponomastics and historical geography and, in particular, shows how evidence from historical-geographical resources aids the reconstruction of place names; Chapter 8 deals with the notion of 'synchronic toponymy', its methods, and its applications, and explores in detail sociopolitical factors in naming practices, presenting new and more current approaches to toponymy, such as critical toponymies and the notion of 'commodification of place names'; Chapter 9 examines the relation between place names and society and its sociological and sociolinguistic implications, dealing in particular with the power relations within communities and with how, in postcolonial times, Indigenous people have tried to reclaim their traditional place names; Chapter 10 focusses on the strong link between cartography and toponymy and on the relevance of toponymic data in historical cartography.

Throughout this book, scholars and students are therefore accompanied, step by step, through the analysis and reconstruction of the history and intrinsic elements of place names and, by following the unravelling of a linguistic and sometimes philological reasoning, they are able to ideally draw a sort of 'identikit' of those toponyms, and to unveil their stories. Place names, indeed, tell us stories which can often date back hundreds of thousands of years, and they do that just by carrying within themselves 'simple' phonemes or mor-phemes which are, on closer inspection, not that 'simple', or not 'simple' at all, and are in actual fact a whole universe.

All the contents of this volume show how toponymy is a multidisciplinary and interdisciplinary study in nature, and to what extent a specific expertise in different fields is necessary to the toponymist to conduct and develop a comprehensive and consistent research of place names. The practice of toponymy also requires competence in historical and philological studies, both at the level of archive investigation and at the textual interpretation level, especially so when the toponymist has to deal with written documents and (possibly ancient) manuscripts. Moreover, the capacity of being able to analyse literary works (with the required background of specific knowledge) is essential in interconnecting the study of toponymy with literature and with toponymic contents of texts which are artistically and culturally significant for human communities and human beings. A deep cultural sensitivity and a firm belief in the scientific mission of linguistic and anthropological investigations are indispensable in the practice of preserving undocumented languages, and these are the foundations of the field linguistics approach to toponymy. Indeed, aboriginal and/or Indigenous place names and their study are an essential component of the safeguarding and documentation of endangered cultural contexts.

The toponymists of the future should, possibly, become 'global toponymists', removing all political implications from the term 'global' and interpreting it as 'all-embracing', 'multifaceted', 'interdisciplinary', 'multidisciplinary', and 'polymathic'. This, of course, without losing their focus on the place names themselves, on the disciplinary goals, and on the scientific mission of toponymy.

This volume, therefore, aims at providing the toponymists and the toponymists of the future with what we feel is a useful tool to accompany them in a journey through the fields of toponymy and toponomastics and to guide them across the analytical study of place names. An academic book cannot ever replace the everyday practice of research and the experience gained through individual learning and progression in knowledge, but can provide readers with hermeneutic and epistemological instruments which can lay an indispensable foundation for their path. We hope that, along the way, they will encounter many discoveries and the unsuspected but pleasant surprises that toponymy can provide. All the parts of this work could surely be expanded, and they could definitely generate specific books in themselves. Nonetheless, we feel that a volume like this should be a solid and robust synthesis aimed at being a guide to students and scholars as a starting point and encouragement in research, and that it has to be necessarily 'self-contained' not in its purpose, but in its contents. It is the task of the toponymists of the future to possibly write the books originating from each chapter of this volume, and we wish them all the best in their endeavours, which will surely deeply enrich our knowledge of this wonderful field of study. Therefore, *sapere aude!*

As a parting note, we would like to remind our readers that toponyms are not 'just names'. As we have explained and will expand on in the book, these simple names are often anything but simple, and are able to survive for thousands of years, to overcome dramatic events, and to tell us unexpected tales and unveil unsuspected truths. It is enough to 'listen to' these names and, when 'listening' is not enough, to study and to investigate them, in a silent and uninterrupted dialogue with them. They will then reveal to us their unwritten stories and, in a way, allow us to give a voice back to our ancestors who crafted them.

Like the pilgrims on the route to Santiago de Compostela (the Camino de Santiago), we would like to close this book with the encouragement, for our readers: *ultreia et suseia!*

# Acknowledgements

We would like to thank those that contributed to making this book a reality: the anonymous reviewers, whose insightful and valuable comments helped to make this volume so much better; our research assistants, Ng You Ni Eunice, Phang Sean Jia Jun, Tan Zhi Xuan, Yom Samantha Jing Yi, and, in particular, Lim Shaun Tyan Gin, who helped us with a multitude of tasks and the final editing. Needless to say, any mistake or omission is our responsibility.

# 1    Introduction

## 1.1    What are Names and Toponyms?

Names, or more specifically proper nouns, are linguistic signs made up of single or multiple words that can denote a range of entities: from a person to groups of persons, to plants, animals, and other living beings, to landmarks such as rivers, buildings, settlements, and so on. George Redmonds' definition captures this function of names aptly; he describes names as 'special words that we use to identify a person, an animal, a place or a thing, and they all have a meaning. In many cases that meaning will lie concealed in the name's history, but in others it will still be transparent' (Redmonds, 2007, p. ix). The scientific study of all kinds of names is called onomastics and derives from the Ancient Greek word *ónoma* (ὄνομα) 'name'. Since onomastics is deeply connected with numerous other fields, including linguistics, history, geography, anthropology, and sociology, the study of place names is, naturally, very interdisciplinary. Onomastics is commonly known to have two principal branches:

(1) anthroponymy (or anthroponomastics): the study of personal names
(2) toponymy (or toponomastics): the study of place names, or toponyms

Other names investigated in different but related subfields are ethnonyms (the names of nationalities or ethnic groups) (Koopman, 2016) and glottonyms (the names of languages) (Bright, 2003).

A toponym (from Ancient Greek τόπος (*tópos*) 'place', and ὄνομα (*ónoma*) 'name') is a name given to a particular place, and toponymy and toponomastics refer to the discipline that studies place names. It is worth noting that although toponymy can be considered a synonym of toponomastics, the word 'toponymy' in itself can also be used to indicate and identify the set of place names belonging to a specific area. For example, Singapore toponomastics is the study of Singapore place names, while Singapore toponymy could be understood as a synonym of Singapore toponomastics, but can also be used to refer to the whole set of place names associated with Singapore. Thus, the term 'Singapore toponymy' can be used in the sentence: 'Singapore's toponymy reflects its sociopolitical history and make-up.' In this example, we cannot utilise the term 'toponomastics' in such a way.

Toponyms are linguistic signs denoting a space and place and are tied to the way humans conceptualise and organise spaces. Being geographical in nature, places and their toponyms are undeniably connected with the fields of geography, topography, cartography, geology, and landscape archaeology. Place names, furthermore, are part of the lexicon of human speech and follow the rules of a given language, reflecting the sounds, morphology, structure, and meanings of the language itself, its origins, and the changes that the language underwent in its development (see Chapter 2). All these make toponyms invaluable to linguists and philologists. Any sense of place is, thus, richly integrated with the interplay and connection of different contexts and disciplines, creating a multilayered entity ready to be uncovered and unpacked. The process of naming a place indicates that the place is important with regards to human activity and human society (Algeo and Algeo, 2000), and this importance will be explained in detail in this book.

Toponymy and toponomastics, as general terms, refer to the study of place names and their features, including, but not limited to, their origins, etymology, development and change over time, use, cultural and sociological characteristics, and their value in society. In the context of linguistics, they are usually considered to be part of the 'linguistic items' studied in etymology and sociolinguistics. Linguists usually seek to discover the etymology and meaning of a particular toponym (Coates, 2013), or they focus on how names are used.

In the sections that follow, we will first provide the definitions, with related discussions, of some of the subfields associated with toponymy and toponomastics, as well as of the technical approaches applied to the study of toponymy. We will then go into the ways in which scholars have previously classified toponyms, before looking at the structure of place names and at how groups of toponyms (known as toponymic systems) share the same roots and naming processes. We will then conclude this chapter with an explanation of how toponyms can be seen as linguistic fossils.

## 1.2     What are the Sub-Disciplines Connected with Toponymy?

Toponyms, at their core, are labels for places, whether they indicate natural features (e.g., mountains, rivers, forests) or man-made features (e.g., buildings, streets, cities). As humans, when we name or label something, it means that we have deemed it important and seek to make it noticeable in our conceptual schema by attaching a name to it. If a place is not named, it is not a place, but 'merely the distance between places, a place holder' (Algeo and Algeo, 2000, p. 272). With the constant expansion of human settlements and activities, geographical places that remain unnamed have become fewer and fewer, as more and more places accrue importance in the human schema. At the same time, as we continue to expand human occupation, there will virtually be no place left unnamed.

Toponymy and toponomastics categorise different types of place names and this has generated a number of different technical terms. These terms identify, classify, and differentiate the many different types of existing place names. Readers are directed to the website of the International Council of Onomastic Sciences (https://icosweb.net/) for a more exhaustive list.

- Toponyms: place names in general. From Ancient Greek *tópos* (*τόπος*) 'place', and *ónoma* (*ὄνομα*) 'name'.
- Hydronyms: the names of all kinds of water bodies, including rivers, streams, brooks, lakes, and seas. From Ancient Greek *hýdōr* (*ὕδωρ*) 'water', and *ónoma* (*ὄνομα*) 'name'. The discipline studying hydronyms is called hydronymy. Hydronymy can also indicate the set of specific hydronyms belonging to a specific area. A less used but more detailed categorisation of bodies of water includes the following.
  - Oceanonyms: the names of oceans. From Ancient Greek *Ōkeanós* (*Ὠκεανός*) *Oceanus* (a water deity) 'ocean'.
  - Pelagonyms: the names of seas. From Ancient Greek *pélagos* (*πέλαγος*) 'sea'.
  - Potamonyms: the names of rivers. From Ancient Greek *potamós* (*ποταμός*) 'river'.
  - Limnonyms: the names of lakes. From Ancient Greek *límnē* (*λίμνη*) 'lake'.
  - Micro-hydronyms: the names of smaller and more localised bodies of water, for example, brooks, springs, and wells.
- Oronyms: the names of mountains, hills, and hillocks. From Ancient Greek *óros* (*ὄρος*) 'mountain', and *ónoma* (*ὄνομα*) 'name'. The discipline studying oronyms is called oronymy. Oronymy can also mean the set of specific oronyms of a specific area.
- Speleonyms: the names of caves, chasms, grottoes, mines, and entire underground systems. From Ancient Greek *spélaion* (*σπήλαιον*) 'cave' and *ónoma* (*ὄνομα*) 'name'.
- Odonyms: the names of streets, avenues, boulevards, drives, lanes, and other denominations relating to inhabited areas. From Ancient Greek *hodós* (*ὁδός*) 'a way, path, track, road', and *ónoma* (*ὄνομα*) 'name'. The discipline studying odonyms is called odonymy. Odonymy can also mean the set of specific odonyms of a specific area.
- Urbanonyms: the names of urban elements, such as, streets, blocks, parks, avenues, drives, churches, buildings, and so on. These are all part of an urbanonymic system, also considered micro-toponyms, as they are usually only known by the local people living in the area (Urazmetova and Shamsutdinova, 2017). From Latin *urbs* 'city', and Ancient Greek *ónoma*

(ὄνομα) 'name'. With the rapid expansion of human settlements, more man-made places have been classified recently (Podolskaya, 1988, p. 14).

Finally, other less commonly used denominations of toponyms include the names of forests (dryonyms, from Ancient Greek *drýs* (δρῦς) 'tree', and *ónoma* (ὄνομα) 'name'), the names of islands (insulonyms, from Latin *insula* 'island' and *ónoma* (ὄνομα) 'name', or nesonyms, from Ancient Greek *νῆσος*, 'island', and *ónoma* (ὄνομα) 'name'), and the names of groups of people (inhabitants, natives, residents) connected with a particular polity (demonyms, from Ancient Greek *dêmos* (δῆμος) 'people', and *ónoma* (ὄνομα) 'name').

Place names can be studied according to different research approaches. In the next sections, we will present the most commonly used classification systems.

## 1.3     Strategies and Categories in Toponymic Research

A commonly used strategy in toponymic research is to classify toponyms into the broad categories of macro-toponyms and micro-toponyms. Macro-toponyms are names of larger or major geographical sites, such as countries, capitals, regions, and even major streets. Micro-toponyms are smaller places known to a smaller set of people (usually locals), for example, wells, gates, local streets, and brooks. Blair (2015, p. 2) lists three types of micro-toponyms; they are either names for small features, the placenames of a local area, or 'unofficial placenames that hardly anybody knows of'. Meanwhile, Tent (2015, p. 8) defines micro-toponyms as 'names of small geographic features – either natural or constructed – that are not officially recognised or gazetted, and do not generally appear on any published maps. They usually name a feature that is itself part of a larger named feature.' Scholars like Clark (2009, p. 208) also mention that micro-toponymy studies minor geographic features. Clark notes that studying micro-toponymy involves analysing 'the name for the bank on a lake, or for a feature on such a bank, or a waterhole in a river, or the name of a feature on the side of a mountain'. Miccoli (2019, p. 86) connects the 'macro-/micro-' difference to the level of knowledge regarding the places and the sources where these names can be found; macro-toponyms are usually well known and can be found in large-scale maps, guides, and atlases. Micro-toponyms, on the other hand, have limited spread of knowledge, are known only to specific people within a region, and, if official, are attested mostly in city plans. However, the boundary between these two categories can be blurred, depending on the perspective of the user(s) defining these places. For example, Singapore is a macro-toponym, for both locals and non-locals alike, but Orchard Road, being a tourist attraction in Singapore, can be a macro-toponym to those that know it and a micro-toponym to those that do not. Similarly, Jurong, a suburb in Singapore, can be a macro-toponym to local

Singaporeans, for it is a large and important region in the nation, but a micro-toponym to non-locals. Although there is no hard boundary between the two categories, another way to look at them is to think that macro-toponyms tend to be standardised and are unlikely to change, while micro-toponyms are relatively less stable and are subject to change (Urazmetova and Shamsutdinova, 2017).

Being 'micro' in its features does not make a micro-toponym 'micro' in its significance. Micro-toponyms deserve to be recorded and studied as well as place names of larger features. Often, micro-toponyms are coined by local speakers, and they not only serve as navigational markers, but also as markers of their identity. Many micro-toponyms are significant in oral traditions, appearing in foundation myths and legends.

Tent (2015) points out how The Australian National Placenames Survey (ANPS) adopted the terms 'intensive' and 'extensive toponymy' for toponymic study. Tent explains that intensive toponymic research involves 'writing a placename's "biography"'. This is done by answering the *wh-* questions: 'who', 'why', 'when' the place was named, 'what' is the meaning of the name, and 'where' the name comes from (Tent, 2015, pp. 67–8). He goes on to say that extensive toponymy 'is more straightforward to conduct than intensive toponymy'. This approach looks for patterns in a collection of place names, unearthing observations such as naming practices and distribution of geographical features and so on that may not be obvious if we only focus on discrete place names. Thus, at the heart of the extensive approach would be the search for toponymic patterns among toponymic datasets. While some forms of classification are useful, Tent cautions against an intensive/extensive dichotomy, arguing that the intensive approach often forms the basis of and precedes the extensive model (Tent, 2015, p. 70). Thus, knowledge of individual place names facilitates the identification of patterns and processes among numerous toponyms.

One other broad classification involves the semasiological/onomasiological distinction. The semasiological approach deals with what names or their elements mean or meant, while the onomasiological approach deals with how particular concepts are encoded linguistically. Coates (2013) states that the semasiological approach can be understood in the linguistic and historical senses, as in the question 'why and how did X come to be called X?', and the onomasiological approach looks to answer the question 'how do we, or should we, express terminologically the elements in system Y (and the relations among them)?' (Coates, 2013, p. 4316).

One final noteworthy classification is represented by the two categories of endonyms and exonyms (Kadmon, 2007). An endonym is the 'name of a geographical feature in one of the languages occurring in that area where the feature is situated', while an exonym is the 'name used in a specific language for a geographical feature situated outside the area where that language has official status, and differing in its form from the name used in the official language or languages of the area where the geographical feature is situated' (Kadmon, 2007, p. 10). *The Glossary of Toponymic Terms* by the United Nations Group of Experts on Geographical Names lists the pinyin (Hanyu Pinyin, or pinyin in short, is the Romanisation system for transliterating Mandarin Chinese) form Beijing as an endonym and Pekingas an exonym. Another example is the exonym Moscow, while Москва and the Romanised Moskva are both endonyms.

## 1.4     Different Approaches to Toponymy

The study of toponyms is carried through either of two approaches. One approach looks at places and place names over a long period of time (historical toponomastics and diachronic toponymy; see below and Chapters 3 and 5), while the other is concerned with the study of place names within a specific moment in time (synchronic toponymy; see below and Chapter 8).

The historical, diachronic, and etymological study of place names is mainly conducted according to two approaches which are commonly used, but which do not have universal accepted appellations and definitions. Aiming at a terminological systematisation and at a conceptual standardisation, we call them, in this book, diachronic toponymy and historical toponomastics.

As a general definition, we call diachronic toponymy the discipline which studies toponymy inherently in undocumented and endangered languages and language families (Perono Cacciafoco et al., 2015), that is, within linguistic contexts in the absence of written documents and records. The approach is conducted by applying to the study of generally aboriginal and/or Indigenous place names a traditional comparative methodology aimed at the reconstruction of consistent or regular sound changes affecting the language, enabling us to recover proto-forms and roots for the analysed place names (see Chapter 4). In some cases, by studying the 'story' or history of a place name or related place names, we are also able to reconstruct historical events that happened to minority and Indigenous groups, often foreshadowed by their local oral-traditional myths. In this context, the term 'diachronic' is interpreted literally as 'throughout time' (from Ancient Greek *diá* (διά) 'through', and *chrónos* (χρόνος) 'time'), because, in diachronic toponymy, due to the absence of historical documents and records, the linguist can try to reconstruct a place name only between two ideal points in time, from the currently attested toponym to the reconstructed proto-form recovered through the application of the comparative method to the target language, and possibly related languages. While the reconstruction of a proto-form and root is possible, in this context, it is very difficult to hypothesise an absolute chronology for those proto-forms and roots and, therefore, the ideal representation of this process is that of two points in time, generating a straight line from the currently attested form to the reconstructed proto-form, without the option of an accurate chronological documentation of the sequence of sound changes for the place name.

We call the other etymological approach to the study of toponymy historical toponomastics, namely the historical-linguistic practice of reconstructing the history (and prehistory) of place names by relying on available written (or otherwise documented) historical records and sources. This is more generally done in the context of well-studied and documented languages and language families (e.g., the Indo-European languages). Historical toponomastics is closely related to etymology (the study of the origins of words and their original meanings), and aims at reconstructing, through the application of the comparative method, the historical phonetics of place names (the diachronic development of sounds in a language and the relation of one sound to another in the same language, whose study allows us to reconstruct proto-forms and roots in an original proto-language from which the analysed language and its relatives in the same language family derive), their proto-forms and roots, and the sound laws generating them. The historical toponomastics approach allows the linguist to reconstruct a sort of 'chronological stratigraphy' of the place names, because the existence of historical documents and records enables scholars not only to etymologically recover proto-forms and roots for the toponyms they study, but also to collect, list, and analyse the diachronic variants of a place name and, therefore, to chronologically 'portray' its morphological development over time. In this process, there will be always a moment in which historical records are no longer available, because the linguistic investigation goes back to times predating the invention of writing. From that point in time, the comparative method, together with the recovery and application of sound laws intrinsic to the naming process, and the historical-phonetic reconstruction of forms and proto-forms mitigate the absence of historical records and allow for the completion of the etymological reconstruction of the examined place names.

As we have just illustrated, the diachronic and historical study of place names involves other disciplines and sub-disciplines of historical linguistics, such as etymology, historical phonetics, and historical semantics, all of which contribute to the correct interpretation of the origins of toponyms. Place names not only record elements of the civilisations of those who lived before us, but also depict the past landscape and the changes caused by human activity. Therefore, an effective chronological reconstruction needs to tap into historical geography, historical cartography, historical topography, landscape archaeology (David and Thomas, 2008; Cambi, 2011), geo-archaeology (Cremaschi, 2008), palaeo-anthropology (Facchini et al.,

1993), genetics (Beretta, 2003; Perono Cacciafoco, 2014). Data and approaches from these (sub-)disciplines can be useful to cross-check results from a linguistic analysis. This can be done, for example, by evaluating the changes in the hydro-geo-morphology of relevant territories and areas occupied by human settlements. Researchers can then investigate possible links between the toponyms and the actual landscape, thereby confirming or disproving etymological hypotheses (Gelling and Cole, 2000). The links and intersection of these fields with toponymy will be taken up throughout this book.

A non-etymological approach to the study of toponymy looks at place names in the context of a specific frame of time, that is, synchronically, even if in the study of languages almost nothing is properly 'synchronic', because language and its elements continuously change and develop over time and all the linguistic aspects are products of diachronic processes. Therefore, 'synchronic' indicates, in this context, a toponymic study concerned with place names as they exist at one specific point in time and within a limited time frame. We call this approach synchronic toponymy, which deals with the function of names in society and with the perception of names by members of society (Karpenko, 1964, cited in Belen'kaya, 1975, p. 315). Belen'kaya (1975, p. 320) notes the following: 'Synchronic analysis not only points up the relationship between place names in the over-all system of toponymics, but suggests the linkage between place names and objective reality, i.e., the way in which the population perceives the name and understands its content, regardless of whether this understanding corresponds to the original meaning of the word.'

This is a sociolinguistic discipline that accounts for societal factors in establishing, changing, conceiving, or understanding place names. These factors include changes in language planning and language policies, political or economic factors, and the sociopolitical influences that force people to shift away from the languages that they normally speak. This approach thus complements a diachronic/historical study of toponymy. The discussion on synchronic toponymy will be taken up in more detail in Chapter 8.

## 1.5    How do we Classify Toponyms? A Brief Outline of Toponymic Classification Systems

Place names can be classified into different systems. What follows is a discussion of the most commonly used classification systems. We will provide a brief overview of the types of toponymic classification systems that scholars have developed over the course of the last fifty to sixty years. These typologies span through different time periods and contexts and across different countries.

For years, scholars have sought to develop adequate typologies to classify place names. While we do not aim to list and analyse them all in this volume, we have included a few notable ones here. For a more comprehensive and exhaustive review of such toponymic classification systems, indispensable readings are Tent and Blair (2009; 2011).

As early as 1945, in his celebrated *Names on the Land* (Stewart, 1945), George R. Stewart began to categorise places in the USA in terms of their naming strategies. Stewart later developed a toponymic typology first published in 1954 (Stewart, 1954) and then refined in his book *Names on the Globe* (Stewart, 1975). He proposed ten categories of place names as summarised in Table 1.1.

Table 1.1 *Stewart's toponymic typology*

| Category | Sub-categories |
| --- | --- |
| *Descriptive names*<br>*Names that describe and characterise the qualities of a place* | 1. Sensory descriptives<br>2. Relative descriptives<br>3. Intellectual descriptives<br>4. Metaphorical descriptives<br>5. Subjective descriptives<br>6. Negative and ironic descriptives<br>7. Hortatory descriptives<br>8. Repetitive descriptives |
| *Associative names*<br>*Names that evoke associations with different objects* | |
| *Incident names*<br>*Names that associate a place with an incident at a particular time* | 1. Acts of God<br>2. Calendar names<br>3. Animal names<br>4. Names of human actions<br>5. Names from an event associated with a person<br>6. Names from feelings<br>7. Names from sayings |
| *Possessive names*<br>*Names that denote some idea of ownership or that a place is associated with something or someone* | |
| *Commemorative names*<br>*Names that commemorate a person, place, or event* | 1. Persons<br>2. Other places<br>3. Abstractions<br>4. Miscellaneous |
| *Commendatory names*<br>*Names given by some attractive peculiarities of a geographical object* | |

Table 1.1 (*cont.*)

| Category | Sub-categories |
|---|---|
| *Folk etymologies* | |
| *Names with false etymologies* | |
| *Manufactured names* | |
| *Names which are manufactured or coined from sounds, letters, or fragments of other words* | |
| *Mistake names* | |
| *Names which appeared from a mistake made in the transmission from one language to another, either from inaccurate hearing of what was said, or because of faulty rendering of the sounds in writing* | |
| *Shift names* | |
| *Names which have been moved from one location to another* | |

Stewart's development of this typology is based 'upon the proposition that all place-names arise from a single motivation, that is, the desire to distinguish and to separate a particular place from places in general' (Stewart, 1975, p. 86). Although there are many purposes in coming up with such systems to categorise place names, according to Stewart's system, the focus is not to reconstruct the origins or etymology of toponyms. Rather, Stewart hopes to explain the naming processes and differentiate one place name from another. Indeed, the system devised by Stewart allows a preliminary categorisation of place names, which can lead to observations of patterns on the settlement dynamics, history, landscape, and so on.

While this classification system (like more or less all classification systems) is a good attempt at classifying place names, it is far from perfect. Some of Stewart's categories have many sub-categories, making them relatively cumbersome for users. For example, there are eight sub-categories under 'descriptive' names, such as sensory descriptives, relative descriptives, intellectual descriptives, and metaphorical descriptives, among others, which make it confusing to classify place names and to discriminate one sub-category from another. Moreover, the boundaries between each category do not seem to be clear-cut, and a place name can be in two or more categories. Stewart (1954, p. 11) calls them 'border-line instances'. Some overlapping types include: descriptive-incident, where 'an incident, if recurring, may become characteristic and, therefore, descriptive'; and incident-possessive, 'since possessive names are so closely connected with associate-descriptive, they also are naturally connected with incident names' (Stewart, 1954, p. 11). However, as Tent and Blair note:

Stewart's resultant typology has several areas of overlap (e.g., 'commendatory names' and 'names from feelings'), and has classes that are too narrow (e.g., 'repetitive descriptives') and ones that are too broad (e.g., 'associative names'). Stewart's system is also inconsistent in that some main categories have unnecessarily detailed subcategories (e.g., 1 and 3), whilst others (e.g., 2, 8, 9, 10) require further partitioning. (Tent & Blair, 2011, p. 71)

Ideally, this classification would work with all kinds of place names. However, as Stewart worked primarily on place names of Indo-European languages (excluding languages of India), the system might not be suitable for place names in other parts of the world, especially those of non–Indo-European origins.

Another early attempt to classify place names was carried out by J. B. Rudnyćkyj, who sought to categorise Canadian and North American place names. Rudnyćkyj proposed three toponymic principles: historical, linguistic, and onomastic, as outlined in Table 1.2. He developed the linguistic and onomastic principles of classification in a 1949 paper published in Ukrainian, which was published in English in 1958.

Table 1.2 *Rudnyćkyj's typology (adapted from Tent and Blair, 2011, p. 72)*

| Category | Sub-categories |
| --- | --- |
| *Historical (H)* | 1. Indian names ('Indian period') |
| | 2. Descriptive names from Portuguese, Spanish, and French period of exploration |
| | 3. Names with religious character from French period of exploration |
| | 4. Names from British Loyalist period |
| | 5. Names from the modern or national period |
| *Linguistic (L)* | 1. Aboriginal Amerindian place names |
| | 2. Place names of Romance providence |
| |    a. Portuguese |
| |    b. Spanish |
| |    c. French |
| | 3. Place names of Germanic origin |
| |    a. Anglo-Saxon |
| |    b. German |
| |    c. Icelandic |
| |    d. Scandinavian |
| |    e. Other |
| | 4. Place names of Celtic origin |
| |    a. Scotch [sic] |
| |    b. Irish |
| | 5. Place names of Slavic origin |
| |    a. Ukrainian |
| |    b. Russian |
| |    c. Polish |
| |    d. Other |

Table 1.2 (*cont.*)

| Category | Sub-categories |
|---|---|
| | 6. Other place names |
| |   a. Hebrew |
| |   b. Grecised [sic] |
| |   c. Latinised |
| |   d. Other |
| |   e. Artificial neologisms |
| *Onomastic (O)* | 1. Autochthon (aboriginal) Amerindian names |
| | 2. Imported (European) place names |
| |   a. Transplaced |
| |   b. Transferred |
| | 3. Canadian toponymic neologisms |

He then proposed that each place name can be explained according to the formula:

$$PN = \frac{o}{H,L}$$

Where *PN* denotes the place name and *o*, *H*, and *L* refer to historical, linguistic, and onomastic. An example of how Rudnyćkyj envisaged the working of his formula can be seen in Tent and Blair's (2011, p. 72) application of it to the place name *Victoria*, which could be derived as follows (the numbers and lowercase letters refer to the sub-categories in Table 1.2).

$$PN = Victoria = \frac{o2b}{H5,L6c}$$

Tent and Blair (2011) levelled several criticisms against this typology. For instance, Rudnyćkyj does not explain why *o* is the numerator while *H* and *L* are the denominators. Furthermore, given that no mathematical processes are involved, a formula is redundant. Besides this, Tent and Blair note several other redundancies when the sub-categories are combined. For example, the first linguistic sub-category (aboriginal Amerindian place names) is identical to the first onomastic sub-category (autochthon (aboriginal) Amerindian names) and, thus, a place name like *Winnipeg* would appear in both. Similarly, the second onomastic sub-category (imported (European) place names) can cover almost all the linguistic sub-categories.

Another very complex classification is the effort by Zelinsky (2002) to develop an overarching typology of names. Sometimes, scholars aim to classify almost all possible place names, leading to a laundry list of categories and sub-categories, some of which might not even be related and relevant to the discussion. In a bid to account for almost all possible names, Zelinsky's effort to develop a typology of names, while laudable, is problematic on a few fronts. He makes an appeal for the systematic 'cataloguing and arranging [of] all the objects under investigation into some logical, coherent classificatory scheme' (Zelinsky, 2002, p. 248). To this end, he proposes eight categories: deities, biodata (humans, flora, and fauna), places, events, social entities, enterprises, artefacts, and unclassifiable, with each category having sub-categories. Place names fall under his third category, places. Within this, he includes a large list of sub-categories, including celestial objects and extra-terrestrial place names. As Tent and Blair (2011, p. 11) note: 'This schema is not a typology of toponyms but an *ad hoc* catalogue of geographic features and a seemingly unrelated conglomeration of natural and cultural themes.'

Another multilayered classification was produced by Rennick (2005). He first proposed to distinguish between 'place' as a human settlement, such as a community, town, or city, and 'feature' as a natural element, such as a lake or stream. 'Feature' also includes man-made structures, such as schools, churches, stations, and so on (Rennick, 2005, p. 291). His final classification can be seen in Table 1.3.

Table 1.3 *Rennick's toponymic typology (Rennick, 2005; adapted from Tent and Blair, 2011, p. 77)*

| Category | Sub-categories |
|---|---|
| *Personal names* | 1. Full names (family, given, nicknames, discoverers, first settlers, etc.) |
| | 2. Names of local people |
| | 3. Friends, relatives of early settlers |
| | 4. Non-local persons associated with the place |
| | 5. Prominent non-local persons (national leaders, historic figures, etc.) not having an association with the place |
| *Names taken from other places or features* | 1. Names imported from earlier residences of first settlers |
| | 2. Names transferred from nearby features |
| | 3. Names taken from other places with no association with place or residents |
| *Local or descriptive names* | 1. Location, direction, position, or distance in relation to other places or features |
| | 2. Shape, size, odour, colour |
| | 3. Names derived from some other feature or characteristic of the natural environment (landscape, terrain, topography; soil, minerals; water bodies; animals; plant life) |
| | 4. Names of approbation and disapprobation or otherwise suggestively descriptive or metaphoric |
| *Historic events* | 1. Non-local (commemorative) |
| | 2. Local (nearby, at a single point of time) |
| | 3. Local (nearby, recurring behaviour) |
| | 4. Exclamations (first words uttered at time of naming) |

Table 1.3 (*cont.*)

| Category | Sub-categories |
| --- | --- |
| *Subjective names* | 1. Inspirational and symbolic names (e.g., reflecting aspirations and ideals of early settlers)<br>2. Nicknames of the kinds of settlers (referring to their character or behaviour)<br>3. Literary, scriptural and names reflecting high culture, tastes, interests, or aspirations<br>4. Humorous names and miscellaneous oddities reminiscent of events/conditions at time of settlement/naming |
| *Mistake names* | |
| *Names from more than one source* | |
| *Underived names* | 1. Including those of unknown etymology |

After considering numerous typologies, including the aforementioned ones, Tent and Blair (2009; 2011) proposed a new, improved typology based on the 'intensive' and 'extensive' toponymy approaches discussed earlier in this chapter (Tent, 2015) and on what they term the '"mechanism" of the naming process' (Tent & Blair, 2009, p. 22; 2011, p. 85), as part of their work with the Australian National Placenames Survey (ANPS). This 'mechanism' accounts for, in the authors' words, 'the procedures, methods, strategies, motivation, original reference and/or referents of names' in order to ascertain the modus operandi of the naming process.

Tent and Blair (2009; 2011) applied their typology to the Australian place names given by English, Dutch, and French explorers from the seventeenth and eighteenth centuries. An analysis of the typology revealed that, apart from developing a toponymic classification system that suited the Australian colonial context, the motivation for the choices by the different nationalities varied considerably. All three groups of explorers applied the 'eponymous' category the most. However, this category was used more often by the French than by the Dutch and the English. The English used it the least, instead favouring 'topographical descriptives and names that recalled incidents or occasions associated with the naming' (Tent & Blair, 2011, p. 87).

More recently, Blair and Tent (2020; 2021) redefined their typology. They explain that, 'The initial typology was founded upon identifying "motivations" for naming a geographic feature or place. Over time, it became clear that this focus appeared to concentrate on the namer and the concomitant psychology underlying the naming of a feature, rather than the feature itself and its context. Such a view made the process of naming seem to be more deliberative than is often the case' (2021, p. 33). Their latest classification is illustrated in detail in Table 1.4.

Table 1.4 *Redefined classification by Blair and Tent (2021, pp. 41–3)*

| Toponym type | Explication | Examples |
| --- | --- | --- |
| 1 DESCRIPTIVE | Using a name denoting an inherent characteristic of the feature | |
| 1.1 Topographic | Denoting the physical appearance of a feature either literally or metaphorically | *Cape Manifold*, named due to the number of high hills over it; *Broken Bay*, named due to some broken land that appeared to form a bay |
| 1.2 Relational | Denoting a relationship between a feature and another feature nearby, either in time, space or dimensions | *Old Adaminaby*, current name for the original town of *Adaminaby*; *East Peak*, the easternmost of the two peaks of *Mount Cougal* |
| 1.3 Locational | Denoting the location or orientation of a feature | *Cape Capricorn*, lying directly on the Tropic of Capricorn |
| 1.4 Functional | Denoting the function of a feature | *Australian Capital Territory*, designated to provide the site for Australia's capital city, *Canberra*. The name is descriptive of the function; *Memorial Park*, a memorial to the servicemen who fought in the First World War. The name is descriptive of its function |
| 2 ASSOCIATIVE | Using a name denoting something associated with the feature or its context | |
| 2.1 Environment | Denoting something in the local natural environment which is seen with or associated with the feature | *Lizard Island*, because the only land animals seen were lizards; *Belrose*, which reflects the flora endemic to the area, the Christmas bell, and the bush rose (see also 7.2) |
| 2.2 Occupation/ activity | Denoting an occupation, habitual activity, or related artefact associated with the feature | *Observatory Hill*, the site of Sydney's original observatory; *Try Pot Beach*, because of try pots found there from the former sealing station |
| 2.3 Structure | Denoting a manufactured structure associated with the feature | *Telephone Gap*, a saddle over which a telephone line used to pass |
| 3 EVALUATIVE | Using a name reflecting the emotive reaction of the namer, or a strong connotation associated with the feature | |

Table 1.4 (*cont.*)

| Toponym type | Explication | Examples |
|---|---|---|
| 3.1 Commendatory | Reflecting/propounding a positive response to the feature | *Australia Felix*, a region named to distinguish it from the parched deserts of the interior country; *Hope Islands*, so named because of the high hopes of being able to reach them |
| 3.2 Condemnatory | Reflecting/propounding a negative response to the feature | *Worlds End*, because of the lonely and desolate nature of the area; *Mount Hopeless*, because a new and still more disheartening feature was seen from its summit |
| 4 OCCURRENT | Using a name recording an event, incident, occasion or date when the feature was named | |
| 4.1 Incident | Recording an event or incident which led to the naming of the feature | *Indian Head*, a headland where a group of Australian Indigenous people were seen to be assembled; *Mount Disappointment*, named due to the inability of being able to ascend it |
| 4.2 Occasion | Recognizing a time or date when the feature was named | *Whitsunday Passage*, after the day on which it was discovered; *Trinity Bay*, after the day on which it was discovered |
| 5 COPIED | Copying the name-form from another place or from another language | |
| 5.1 Locational | Using the name of a feature from another place | *River Derwent*, after the *River Derwent* in *Cumberland*, England; *Cape Dromedary*, from the nearby *Mount Dromedary* |
| 5.2 Linguistic | Using the name-form (or its calque) which the feature has in another language | *Groote Eylandt*, identified by that name on seventeenth-century Dutch charts; *Steep Point*, a calque of the original 'Steyle Houck' named by the seventeenth-century Dutch explorer Willem de Vlamingh |
| 6 EPONYMOUS | Using the name of a person or other named entity by using a proper name, title, or eponym substitute as a toponym | |
| 6.1 Human | Using the name of a person or of a group of people | |

Table 1.4 (*cont.*)

| Toponym type | Explication | Examples |
|---|---|---|
| 6.1.1 Namer | Using the namer's own name as the toponym | *Forster*, named by William Forster, premier of New South Wales (1859–60); *Tasman Island*, named by Abel Tasman |
| 6.1.2 Notable person | Using the name of an eminent person, patron, official, noble, politician etc., or the name of a group of such people | *Cape Byron*, after Captain John Byron of the HMS *Dolphin* (1764–6); *Gosford*, after the Earl of Gosford |
| 6.1.3 Colleague | Using the name of a member of an expedition or survey involved in the discovery or naming of the feature, or the name of the group so involved | *Point Hicks*, after crewmember Lieutenant Hicks on Cook's HMS *Endeavour*; *Cape Banks*, after Joseph Banks on Cook's HMS *Endeavour* |
| 6.1.4 Family member or friend | Using the name of a family member or friend of the namer | *Mount Eliza*, named by Captain Middleton after his wife Eliza; *Denmark River*, after naval surgeon Alexander Denmark |
| 6.1.5 Associated person | Using the name of a person or a group connected to the feature as, for example, a founder, builder, owner or local inhabitant | *Bennelong Point*, after an Indigenous man who lived on the point; *Frenchs Forest*, after James French, who set up sawmills in the area |
| 6.2 Other animate entity | Using the proper name of a non-human animate entity | *Norseman*, after the horse, Hardy Norseman; *Banana*, after a bullock, Banana |
| 6.3 Non-animate entity | Using the proper name of a non-animate entity | |
| 6.3.1 Notable abstract entity | Using the name of a notable occasion, entity or concept, such as a battle, a political association or other abstract category | *Admiralty Islands*, after the British Admiralty; *Staaten River*, after States General, the parliament of the *Dutch United Provinces* (1623) |
| 6.3.2 Named concrete entity | Using the name of an entity such as (a class of) a ship, train, or aircraft | *Catalina Bay*, a former base for Catalina Flying Boats during the Second World War; *Coolangatta Creek*, after the schooner *Coolangatta* wrecked there in 1846 |
| 6.3.3 Expedition vessel | Using the name of a vessel involved in the 'discovery' or naming of the feature | *Endeavour River*, after Cook's HMS *Endeavour*; *Mt Zeehan*, after Tasman's ship *Zeehaen* |
| 6.4 Literary, biblical, or mythical entities | Using the name of a figure or place from literature, the Bible, or mythology | *Ivanhoe*, after Sir Walter Scott's novel *Ivanhoe*; *Oberon*, after the King of the Fairies in Shakespeare's *Midsummer Night's Dream* |

Table 1.4 (*cont.*)

| Toponym type | Explication | Examples |
|---|---|---|
| 7 INNOVATIVE | Introducing a new linguistic form as a toponym | |
| 7.1 Humor | Using language play with humorous intent to create a new toponym | *Nangiloc*, after the neighbouring town, *Colignan*, spelt backwards; *Doo Town*, because houses in this town have house-names containing 'Doo', e.g., *Doo-little* |
| 7.2 Aptness | Creating a new linguistic form or importing a word from another language to produce a toponym of pleasing sound, positive connotation or appropriate meaning | *Orana*, from a Polynesian word, because of its euphonious sound and positive connotation; *Belrose*, a *Sydney* suburb named after flora endemic to the area, the Christmas bell and the bush rose (see also 2.1) |

This section has shown that people try to make sense of place names and, because names are part of our conceptual schema, it is typically human to try to classify them and to generate an organisation mechanism which would help in making them more recognisable and easier to sort.

## 1.6    How Are Toponyms Structured?

Not all place names have the same structure. However, it is more common to see a toponym formed of two parts: a geographic term, or the generic term that classifies the type of geographical territory of a place; and the name itself, or the specific name of a place. For example, in *Tweed River* and *Mount White* (Tent, 2020), we have the specific names 'Tweed' and 'White', and the generic names 'River' and 'Mount'. *Sungai Johor* is a major river in the state of *Johor* in *Malaysia*, and is another example of the specific + generic structure, with *Sungai* 'river' being the generic name that classifies the geographic object, and *Johor* 'precious stone, jewel' as the specific name of the river. Due to the specific + generic structure of the toponym, the morphology and semantics of the place name can, at times, be humorous. This can be observed in tautological place names, which usually result from the generic and specific names coming from different languages, and users being unaware of the similar meaning between the two. For example, the *Sahara Desert* in Arabic is called *Aṣ-ṣaḥrā' Al-kubrā*, which means 'The Great Desert'. In English, though, it took its name from the Arabic word for 'deserts', *ṣaḥārā*, rather than the word for 'Great'. Therefore,

*Sahara Desert* has the Arabic word for 'deserts' and the English word 'desert'. A more extreme example is *Nesoddtangen*, which applies to a peninsula in *Norway* and to a town at the tip of the peninsula. Each of the parts of this name are synonyms of 'peninsula' or 'promontory': *nes* means 'headland', *odd* means 'point', and *tangen* means 'spit', respectively.

## 1.7    Toponymic Systems

Thus far, we have been looking at individual toponyms. However, we commonly encounter groups of place names that share a common root (and the related meaning) and tend to be territorially located near to each other. This grouping constitutes a toponymic system: a set of place names that belong to a specific area and share the same etymological stem[1] (and related meaning) and/or the same naming process.

Among many others, a significant example of a toponymic system can be found in Abui, a Papuan language spoken by about 17,000 people on the island of *Alor*, in the *Alor-Pantar* archipelago in southeast *Indonesia* (Kratochvíl, Delpada, & Perono Cacciafoco, 2016). The word *muur* 'lemon' in Abui has become the naming source for four villages in northern *Alor*: *Muur Mea* 'lemon mango', *Muur Maasang* 'altar lemon', *Muurafang* 'old lemon village', and *Muur Meelang* 'lemon village'. From a field investigation in the area, it seems that the inclusion of the root *muur* 'lemon' derives from the lemons grown in the territory. Not only does this show and explain a common etymological stem among place names, but this case study also highlights a similar or common naming process, that is, that toponymic systems are connected because of specific relations to the landscape (Kratochvíl et al., 2016). The source is generally an 'object' that is fairly important or dominant in the sociogeography of the place and community, and is the motivation for the toponyms being named after it. These findings and conclusions can only be observed by collecting and investigating several toponyms, not just one, in the toponymic system within the area, and then uncovering the connections between them. This discussion will be taken up in more detail in later chapters.

It is worth noting that toponyms might have been, originally, common nouns that refer to natural objects in the landscape. As part of the general lexicon, the words comprising toponyms have meaning, and can refer to different objects (Poenaru-Girigan, 2013). Taking the Abui example again, we have seen that *muur* is the Abui word for 'lemon'. Another popular horticultural crop on *Alor Island* is *mea* 'mango' (Lim & Perono Cacciafoco, 2020a). Thus, the words *mea* and *muur* refer to any mango or lemon that Abui people may be talking about. However, at some stage in time, the word *mea* gained a specialised

---

[1] In this book, we use 'root' and 'stem' to refer to the same morphological unit.

meaning or value for the Abui and began identifying a particular place. It, thus, became a toponym. *Muur Mea* (English gloss 'lemon mango') is a village in northern *Alor*. To the Abui villagers, the combination *Muur Mea* no longer simply means 'lemon (and) mango', but is the name of the village where they now reside, separate from its direct semantic value. In other cases, the source (in this instance, *muur*) can become the basis for several toponyms, which then form the toponymic system arising from a common process of naming, as noted in the above paragraph. The formation of such a system also gives us a glimpse of how early humans organised their geographical landscape into an 'oral map' composed of place names.

Aside from landscape or specific objects, a toponymic system can also arise from the settlement dynamics of an area, connecting together several places. For example, the hamlet of *Squaneto* (see the discussion in Chapter 3), belonging to the village of *Spigno Monferrato*, is located on a ford of the *Valla* stream, flowing into the *Bormida River*, in lower *Piedmont*, northwest *Italy*, and, as will be explained in Chapter 3, its etymology may be connected with the notion of 'water', precisely of 'water place' (a place located on the water – on a ford, in this case). *Squagiato*, another hamlet of *Spigno Monferrato* located not far from *Squaneto*, may share with it the etymological origin. However, *Squagiato* is not located on the river, but on a hill overlooking the stream. While it might be difficult to connect these two names with the landscape, they do seem to share the same Indo-European root, $*s\text{-}ak^w(a)\text{-} > *squa\text{-}$, meaning 'water' ($*ak^w[a]\text{-}$, Latin *aqua*) (see a more detailed discussion of this and of the controversy surrounding this reconstruction in Chapter 3). Therefore, one possible explanation is that *Squagiato* was probably founded by the ancient Indo-European people who moved from the original *Squaneto*, which is on the riverbank, to the top of the hill, possibly to look for shelter. They then gave it a name very similar to where they had come from. This probably happened while other people belonging to the same community stayed in *Squaneto* when *Squagiato* was founded, or maybe the original settlement on the ford was repopulated at a later time by the people who had moved to *Squagiato* when there was no more need for a shelter on a hill. The analysis and reconstruction of this naming process gives us an insight into the settlement dynamics of this group of people hailing from *Squaneto*. While we cannot establish or prove the movement of people for sure (given that this happened thousands of years ago), looking at these two places, which are part of the same toponymic system, allows us to postulate that the ancient Indo-European people living in the two villages were somehow related and that there was a migration pattern from one to the other, in this case to find shelter in times of trouble.

Some toponyms belonging to the same toponymic system are linked because of historical events. In the Abui context, a local story (see Perono Cacciafoco & Cavallaro, 2017; Perono Cacciafoco & Cavallaro, 2018) connects eight places within the same area. The origins of the eight toponyms and micro-toponyms, although not all connected etymologically, derive from the same source – the story of the god *Lamòling*. In this sense, we see how a toponymic system might share an original naming process also in the absence of direct or comprehensive etymological links among its place names, a naming process which, according to the Abui, is connected with a cultural identity component and a collective memory represented by local oral-traditional stories. These myths and stories have been defined as the 'history/memory of the soul' of the Abui people (Perono Cacciafoco & Cavallaro, 2017, p. 53). The Abui people believe that the 'meta-history' depicted by their traditional myths and legends is true and 'historical', belonging to and representative of their original history. The *Lamòling* story is, indeed, regarded as history by the Abui people, and the places that are derived from it are, according to them, the real location of the events of the story and still exist today. The Abui people can even point out the exact location of these places and they know all their names. *Lamòling* was an Indigenous god that fell out of favour with the Abui people, competing with another 'newer' god called *Lahatàla*, and the story tells of *Lamòling's* appearance, relationship with the Abui people, and eventual downfall. The toponyms of the villages of *Takalelàng*, *Takpàla*, and *Lù Melàng*, the ceremonial houses *Kolwàt* and *Kanurwàt* in *Takpàla*, the 'altar' *Karilìk*, and the localities of *Lamòling Bèaka* and *Pakulàng Hièng* all come from the story itself. Taking the place name *Lamòling Bèaka*, meaning 'bad *Lamòling*' or '*Lamòling* the evil', as an example, this toponym was given to the place by the Abui people after the mythical event when *Lamòling* offered to the Abui people from *Takalelàng* and *Takpàla* a meal consisting of the body of a child who had gone missing. This led them to conclude that *Lamòling* was responsible for abducting and killing the child and the villagers plotted their revenge on the god. The Abui people can indicate the exact position of the place of the meal still today, a place which did not have a name before the event, and which was named in order to link the territory to the monstrous act which they believed really happened there. One cannot explain the origins of each place belonging to this toponymic system in isolation, as all of them arose from one common, intangible, and not properly linguistic origin, that is, the story. Uncovering such a toponymic system is akin to doing detective work; once you are able to unveil the origin of one of the place names belonging to the toponymic system, the reconstruction of the naming process of the entire set becomes easier.

It is necessary to note that toponymic systems can be investigated and recognised in both documented and undocumented languages. In the case of a documented language, we can point to the small toponymic system of *Squaneto*/*Squagiato* mentioned above as an example. In this case, there are available historical records and sources to aid our investigation of the categorisation of the toponyms coming from the root *squa-* (< *s-ak$^w$a-*) 'water'. Still within the Indo-European context, an example of a large toponymic system involves the toponymic type *alba*, with the many toponyms that originated from the *\*alb-* root throughout *Europe*. The *Alba* toponymic system, indeed, can be observed on a larger scale than the *\*squa-* toponymic system, and in this case we also have a significant amount of historical records and material. With these means, we can trace the source of the naming back to the Indo-European root *\*alb-* (with its variants), meaning 'water' and indicating, specifically, the property of the 'colour' of water, which is one of transparency and clearness (see Chapter 7 for a comprehensive analysis of this toponymic system). The *\*alb-* toponymic system is widespread all over *Europe* and involves border areas and includes different phonetic and phonological variations of the place names. On the other hand, Abui is an endangered language that is still largely undocumented. The Abui examples we have shown above illustrate toponymic systems in a context of a language at high risk of disappearance, where linguists can rely mostly on the collection of *tira* (Indigenous myths, legends, and other narratives) during field investigations conducted by hiking along traditional mountain trails, on maps drawn with the assistance of locals, and on stories elicited from consultants and native speakers. Investigating toponymic systems in the Indo-European context belongs to the disciplinary area of historical toponomastics. Researching the naming process in contexts like the Abui and the *Lamòling* example discussed above, where the story is the actual 'history' for the local speakers, belongs to the field of diachronic toponymy research.

## 1.8    Toponyms as Linguistic Fossils

The study of toponymy is arguably a multifaceted pursuit that blends diachronic/historical and synchronic approaches, along with the many inter-connected disciplines and fields, ultimately providing an interdisciplinary endeavour and grounding to the study of place names, a central theme that will be explored throughout this book.

At the core of toponymic research is the fact that place names are, often, very persistent and unchanged over time, even when a territory is characterised by population movements and language shift. As such, they can conserve elements of languages that have now disappeared. A special feature of place names is the fact that they are able to survive demographic changes and even dramatic and violent settlement dynamics (for instance, immigrations or invasions by people who speak different languages). Even if place names are modified because of a change in population, they frequently preserve some aspects of their original forms in their morphology, and they have been adapted to the linguistic system of new speakers without being completely removed or replaced. This is what allows us to reconstruct their roots. In some cases, the new speakers tend to consider the previous place names as prestigious linguistic forms of landscape descriptions, useful also for orientation and navigation, and have little or no interest in removing or changing them (unless they want a sort of *damnatio memoriæ* of the population they have defeated and/or subdued). Even if the new people do not understand their original meanings, place names are known reference points in the orientation system for the new people, and they provide them with a 'feeling' for the depth of time. Therefore, they do not require modification or renaming and any changes happen, over time, according to the natural and common language-change processes (see Chapter 2). As such, toponyms are regarded, in a way, as 'linguistic fossils' (Zhao et al., 2020) – stable entities that may be preserved over centuries and contain valuable information which may have been lost elsewhere when languages were forgotten or replaced, and thus can 'permit historical inferences about languages and the people who spoke them' (Campbell, 2013, p. 436). Indeed, on a general level, a geological/paleontological fossil is dead and provides us with a knowledge which is preserved in stone, while place names are atypical 'linguistic fossils', because in a way they are 'fossilised' in their morphology, carrying ancient roots and morphemes within themselves, but at the same time are still 'alive', because they are still being used and 'spoken' by people and therefore survive still in our times, even if their intrinsic, linguistic DNA can be extremely old. A geological/paleontological fossil comes to us as a document from the stone, while a place name comes to us through living languages and therefore is still 'alive', despite dating back to very remote times.

# 2    Language Change

## 2.1    What Is Language Change?

It is a well-known and documented fact that languages are constantly changing. Change is normal in the development of a language, and happens at every linguistic level: phonological, morphological, lexical, syntactic, and semantic. How and why languages change is the central concern of historical linguistics (Campbell & Mixco, 2007, p. 92). Historical linguistics also encompasses how languages relate to one another, for example, whether they are derived from a common origin or how language contact has affected them. Language change can account for language variation, which is one of the focuses of sociolinguistics. Language variation concerns itself with how languages vary across different regions and across social groupings such as age, gender, class, religion, ethnicity, occupation, and so on (Campbell & Mixco, 2007, p. 217). In some cases, the movement of people from different regions and across social classes leads to language change and, thus, language variation is important in our understanding of how languages change (Campbell & Mixco, 2007, p. 216).

As we pointed out in Chapter 1, in order to carry out a historical study of a language, we need a multidisciplinary approach incorporating disciplines other than linguistics. Evidence from the fields of paleo-anthropology, genetics, archaeology, and geography, among others, gives us insights into the habits, history, movements, and many other facets of prehistoric humans, which can lead to a better understanding of the archaic stages of a language and the relationship across languages (Kiparsky, 2014, p. 87). An interdisciplinary approach allows us to answer the questions of 'how' and 'why' languages change in more detail. At the same time, as a scholar of the field, Lyle Campbell, said, historical linguistics and its findings have enabled the solutions to historical issues outside of linguistics (Campbell, 2004, p. 1). Specifically, it can help us answer, among other queries, questions like: 'what were the earliest humans like?', 'what did they do?', and 'what did they speak?'.

Many of these concerns can also be addressed via a study of place names. It is thus no surprise that the diachronic study of language change, historical linguistics, has a core role in toponymy and toponomastics.

## 2.2     Language Change and Toponymy

The evaluation and study of language change phenomena is essential to the historical-linguistic reconstruction of place names and to the analysis of the naming processes which generate them. Languages change at the sound level, word level, sentence level, and meaning level. These changes can be due to either internal or external factors. Internal factors are those that occur within a speech community, generally among monolingual speakers, who adopt new ways of saying things according to social factors (e.g., age, gender, social class). Speakers may also enact structural changes to their language, for example, by removing marked features or regularising some grammatical aspects (e.g., British English 'learnt' became 'learned' in American English). Many of these changes are driven by issues of prestige and standardisation. External factors are those that are induced by contact with speakers of other languages. This phenomenon happens when coming into contact with other cultures and languages leads people to shift away from their traditional language and adopt the new language, especially when the latter has higher prestige. Other changes due to language contact are the borrowing of vocabulary and influences exerted by the new language at the structural level, that is, at the phonological, morphological, and syntactic levels. All communities naturally experience a continuous evolution of the lexicon and the structure of their languages (Campbell, 2013). This unstoppable change applies – with specific variations – also to place names, though they almost never evolve at the same rate and speed of change the common lexicon of a population sees.

Historically, languages change when a new group of people replaces or merges with another. If these two (or more) groups speak different languages, then there may be a period of multilingualism in the community, followed by the moment in which either one language replaces the other or a new contact language develops. An example of this was observed when the Roman Empire conquered most of *Europe*, and Latin became widespread. Local languages interacted with Latin and, from this interaction, the Romance languages developed in *Europe*. The example below, from the *Book of Exodus* (20:7), illustrates the changes from Latin to modern-day Romance languages (Burridge & Bergs, 2016, p. 4).

| | |
|---|---|
| Latin | non adsumes nomen Domini Dei tui in vanum nec enim habebit insontem Dominus eum qui adsumpserit nomen Domini Dei sui frustra. |
| French | Tu ne prendras point le nom de l'Eternel, ton Dieu, en vain; car l'Eternel ne laissera point impuni celui qui prendra son nom en vain. |
| Italian | Non usare il nome dell'Eterno, ch'è l'Iddio tuo, in vano; perché l'Eterno non terrà per innocente chi avrà usato il suo nome in vano. |

| | |
|---|---|
| Spanish | No tomarás el Nombre del SEÑOR tu Dios en vano; porque no dará por inocente el SEÑOR al que tomare su Nombre en vano. |
| Portuguese | Não tomarás o nome do Senhor teu Deus em vão; porque o Senhor não terá por inocente aquele que tomar o seu nome em vão. |
| English gloss | Thou shalt not take the name of the Lord thy God in vain; for the Lord will not hold him guiltless that taketh his name in vain. |

As we said in Chapter 1, toponyms can sometimes be considered 'linguistic fossils' because they remain relatively unchanged or stable over time, while the common lexicon of a community evolves naturally. However, toponyms are not impervious to all linguistic changes. The morphology of a place name can be heavily influenced by the changes happening to the languages around it. As a result, place names can have forms that are difficult to reconstruct because they derive from languages that were completely replaced by other possibly related, or even unrelated, languages. This situation is usually also accompanied by the local speakers' loss of linguistic knowledge necessary to understand the long-lost (previous) language (or languages).

Language change is, therefore, something all toponymists must consider very carefully in their investigations. In toponymic studies, it is necessary to analyse and document the different chronological steps of language change in place names through a thorough application of the comparative method (see the next section), and of the known phonetic and morphological laws (Kiparsky, 2014, pp. 64–102) inherent in the language(s) involved in the naming processes of the studied toponyms.

The strategy is to reconstruct a sort of 'stratigraphy' of place names, which can then be used to develop what we can call a historical 'identity card' of the place names themselves. 'Stratigraphy' is a notion borrowed from geology and archaeology, but applies well to the historical study of toponymy. This is because the linguistic study of place names can be configured as an 'archaeology of language', generally dealing with very ancient, sometimes prehistoric, appellations. By tracking the different historical-linguistic layers and stages of their diachronic development, we can reconstruct the origins and original meanings of toponyms and, therefore, their intrinsic naming processes. We are thus able to unearth and recover their original morphology, structure, and meaning from a time when writing was not yet invented, and are therefore able to document them in the absence of historical records and documents, very much like archaeologists do for prehistoric societies through the discovery and study of their material culture.

A historical-linguistic assessment and analysis of language change phenomena affecting place names, as well as the study of historical linguistics in general, pursues the dream of returning a voice to prehistoric people. The reconstruction of ancient toponyms is a painstakingly difficult task that must always face a necessary approximation. Over the years, we have observed huge progress being made in historical-linguistic procedures and methodologies to elaborate detailed historical-phonetic sequences and historical-phonological sets. Despite all this, a reconstructed language is always 'only' a reconstructed language, and the reconstructed forms and proto-forms (more on the notion of 'proto-' in Section 2.3 and in Chapter 4) of place names are always 'only' reconstructed forms and proto-forms. We cannot know absolutely if our postulations are correct because we do not have access to the original speakers (they lived in a very remote past) to either confirm or deny them. In fact, we do not even know for certain whether a proto-language was really spoken at a specific point in prehistoric times. Therefore, the proto-language we reconstruct can only be a theoretical and approximate reconstruction of a possible ancestral and common idiom spoken by our ancestors (Joseph & Janda, 2003).

The assessment of language change phenomena over time, through a process of diachronic language reconstruction, is fundamental to the study of the relations among attested languages. This is the only means we have at our disposal to shed light on the events that occurred in human communities before the introduction of writing systems, and before humans passed from prehistory to proto-history, and to the properly called historical times. Much like an arrowhead dating back to 40,000 years ago, linguistic roots and proto-forms are relics of the origins of humankind, and place names more so.

Language change also has a synchronic component, which involves the development and evolution of languages into different variants and dialects (Chambers, Trudgill, & Schilling, 2008). This is usually investigated in the study of language variation, or dialectology. Language variation also needs to be inherently considered in toponymy. Changes or variations in pronunciation of place names among local speakers in a specific territory and at a specific time can lead to dramatic changes, over centuries and millennia, in the morphology of toponyms, when the local speakers, because of the natural evolution of their languages, lose the knowledge of the original form and meaning of their place names. In this context, the synchronic element of variation affects and triggers the diachronic change of toponyms.

Language change is, therefore, configurable as the 'prime motor' of the diachronic change of place names over time, and only a thorough and careful study and analysis of this phenomenon, both at the historical-linguistic level and at the level of dialectological interpretation, can there be an accurate and plausible reconstruction of the original toponymic forms. This may, in a way, fulfil the dream and goal of giving a voice back to our prehistoric ancestors, people now lost in time, unable to speak to us except through linguistic traces they left behind and, indeed, in their place names.

## 2.3     The Comparative Method

In historical linguistics, the comparative method helps us to compare different languages in order to determine their relationships to one another. The comparative method is based on the principle of regular sound change, which holds that any change in the sounds of a language that happen over time occur in a prevalently regular way according to patterns (sound laws) that we can reconstruct, and thus can help us explain diachronic sound change phenomena over time. Languages are analysed using the comparative method to determine whether they are related and share a common mother language or proto-language, that is, a single language from which they evolved.

To determine whether languages are related, historical linguists look for regular sound correspondences between two (or more) languages and to the relevant lexemes, known as 'cognates'. We investigate words in different languages that look and sound alike, and search for consistent patterns of sounds in Language A that correspond to Language B, and so on. That is, we search for cognates, or words that descend from a single (or shared) source word (also known as a proto-form) in an ancestral language. Through the comparison of cognates and the reconstruction of the sound laws they foreshadow, we can trace the proto-language from which these forms (and proto-forms) and languages originated, while compiling a dictionary of roots of the proto-language itself. Table 2.1 shows some classical examples of Indo-European cognates.

Historical toponomastics (see Chapter 3) focusses on the reconstruction of the etymologies of toponyms. It can lead to the recovery of the origins of place names and highlights (a) the original naming process, (b) the possible, subsequent process of paretymology (or false etymology, see Chapter 3), and (c) the links and relationships of the place names to other place names or words from the general lexicon or onomastic vocabulary of the studied language or of related languages. The idea that many toponyms are 'linguistic fossils' depends on the tendency of their morphology to remain stable across time. This can be at both the lexical and grammatical levels. As mentioned in Chapter 1, the notion of 'linguistic fossils' means that there is information preserved in the toponyms that may have been lost elsewhere when languages were forgotten or replaced. Reconstructing the root of the toponyms can thus reveal linguistic features that, possibly, were once common in the most archaic form of the language (the proto-language) but have since disappeared from the lexicon of the daughter languages.

Table 2.1 *Examples of Indo-European cognates*

| Greek | Latin | English | Sanskrit |
|-------|-------|---------|----------|
| *phráter* | *fráter* | *brother* | *bhrātar-* |
| *nuktó* | *noctis* | *nights* | *naktasya* |
| *zugón* | *iugum* | *yoke* | *yugam* |
| *heptá* | *septem* | *seven* | *sapta* |

## 2.4 How Toponyms Are Affected by Language Change

As discussed earlier in this chapter, toponyms as linguistic resources are affected by language change, which is evident in place names across various language families and contexts. In his article 'Scottish place names as evidence for language change', Nicolaisen (1993) studies the phonological change affecting final consonants in unstressed syllables in Scottish toponyms (the languages spoken in *Scotland*, such as English, Scots, and Scottish Gaelic, are from the Indo-European language family). As an example, Nicolaisen highlights a change in Scottish place names from the final velar nasal [ŋ] to an alveolar nasal [n]. One famous place that follows this hypothesis is *Stirling*, which Nicolaisen claims is a toponym 'for which no reliable linguistic ascription or acceptable etymology has ever been suggested' and hence is a 'meaningless place name' (Nicolaisen, 1993, p. 307). Its earliest recorded form was *Striuelin* in the early twelfth century, and its most common name was *Striuelin(e)*. Note that it shows an -*n* ending. Until the middle of the sixteenth century, we see names like *Struelin* and *Striulin* in metathesis (i.e., when sounds or syllables switch places in a word) as *Stervlen and Styrvelyn*. Around this time, we see other less frequent but parallel forms like *Striueling* and *Strivling*, and later the metathesised *Steruelyng*, *Sterling*, and *Stirling*. The -*ling* forms, according to Nicolaisen, became more frequent and exclusively used in the middle of the seventeenth century. What we see in the case of *Stirling* is that there are two sets of spellings and pronunciations that happen side by side, -*lin* or -*lyn*, and -*ling* or -*lyng*. In the fifteenth century, the *i*-spelling was more common than the *y*-spelling. From the second half of the sixteenth century or the early seventeenth century, the -*ling* or -*lyng* spellings started to dominate and take over. As Nicolaisen (1993, p. 309) sums up, the growing number of -*ng* spellings in Scottish place names when they were previously spelt and pronounced as -*n* presupposes 'an underlying trend from -*n* to -*ng* in pronunciation at times when lexical material is either silent or, at least, not very eloquent on the subject'.

*Trinidad*, located in the *Caribbean*, was first occupied by the Spanish, and then the British. The island offers interesting insights into the complexities of linguistic diversity in place names. From a historical-linguistic perspective, it shows how linguistic contact between different languages, such as Spanish, French, French Creole, and English, resulted in linguistic changes to toponyms at different levels. Laurence (1975, p. 124) notes the following.

What seems strange at first glance is that, despite the fact that the island ceased to be a Spanish possession over 150 years ago, that during most of the modern period the official language of the island has been English, and that the island never was a French colony, there still remains in modern Trinidad such a plethora of Amerindian, Spanish and French toponyms which generally date to Pre-British days. This is an unusual situation, given the more generalised tendency in the English-speaking Caribbean for English toponyms to predominate, and more especially, for aboriginal names to disappear.

As an example, Laurence takes the modern names of two offshore islands, *Gasparee* and *Little Gasparee*. In early maps, *Gasparee* was known as *Gaspar* or *Gaspar Grande* '*Large/Big Gaspar*'. In these maps, a smaller island has the Spanish diminutive *-illo* and was known as *Gasparillo* '*Small/Little Gaspar*'. Over time, the linguistic changes on the island also affected these toponyms. *Gaspar* (or *Gaspar Grande*) became *Gasparil* and, later, owing to the deletion of the final *-l*, *Gasparee*. This word-final sound deletion is a phonetic change due to the characteristics of French Creole and is also found when French forms come into linguistic contact with Trinidadian English. The Spanish name *Gasparillo* is hypothesised by Laurence to be derived from the local inhabitants confusing it with the French plant *gasparil*, a type of forest wood. What we have then is that the linguistic contact between different languages over time has led to the Spanish *Gaspar Grande* becoming *Gasparee*, and the smaller island becoming *Little Gasparee*. Here, we also see that, due to linguistic contact and the diversity of languages spoken in *Trinidad*, local speakers sought to relate place names with more familiar terms in their languages, changing the meaning of the toponyms and creating toponymic paretymologies.

Reszegi (2010) notes that many oronyms (the names of mountains, hills, hillocks; see Chapter 1) in *Hungary* have been borrowed from Slavic languages. *Hungary* is not a Slavic nation, but is surrounded by Slavic countries, for instance, *Belarus*, *Russia*, *Ukraine*, *Czech Republic*, *Poland*, to name a few. An example of this phenomenon is the oronym *Makra*, likely a borrowing of the Slavic toponym *Mokra* (*Gora*) 'wet (mountain)'. Another instance is *Dobódél*, which can be traced back to the Slavic *Dubodiel* 'oaky mountain'. These examples show that toponyms and toponymic patterns have been borrowed and applied in a new context and are good instances of how language change due to contact can, in some cases, affect the naming process.

Nash (2009) conducted fieldwork on toponyms of *Nepean Island*, a small island located 800 metres south of *Norfolk Island*, an Australian territory in the *South Pacific*. The languages used on *Norfolk Island* are English and Norf'k. Norf'k is an English and Tahitian creole spoken by the descendants of the Pitcairners (Euronesian people of British and Tahitian descent), who arrived on *Norfolk Island* in 1856. Although Nash notes that Norf'k is used to name toponyms on *Nepean Island*, there is evidence of English influencing the Norf'k names, resulting in modifications to the original denominations. A place on *Nepean Island* is often referred to as *Em Steps*. *Em* is a short form of the Norf'k word *dem* 'them', 'those', 'they'. Pluralising the word 'step', as in *Em Steps*, is not typical of the Norf'k language, as the language does not pluralise nouns. Nash postulates that, because the original toponym was English, it was adopted into Norf'k and, thus, the 'Steps' of the original toponym was kept. This is a clear example of how a toponym went from the English original to being adapted to a new creole as it became more common on the island, but with some remnants of the original English name.

The case studies in this section show that any place name can be affected by language change, no matter its language family or context. Very often, though, the roots of the place name remain. This supports the hypothesis that a place name's linguistic form remains stable and unchanged across time (Mailhammer, 2016, p. 318; Wainwright, 1962, pp. 38–55). In some cases, linguistic contact and exchange phenomena generated the changes. Like in the Trinidadian case above, the meaning of two island names as the Spanish toponym *Gasparillo* was confused with the French dendronym (the name of a plant, from Ancient Greek *déndron* [δένδρον] 'tree, plant', and *ónoma* [ὄνομα] 'name') *gasparil*. On *Nepean Island*, they led to a Norf'k toponym keeping the original English morphological structure of pluralisation. A common trend observed in these examples is that of linguistic contact between speakers of two or more languages, resulting in toponymic changes due to the linguistic interaction between these languages. This notwithstanding, in many of these examples (like the word 'Steps' in *Em Steps* and the *Gaspar* root in *Gasparee* and *Little Gasparee*), a recurring theme is the stability of the root and morphology of the toponym. This not only allows us to reconstruct the etymology of the place name and gives us insights into the languages spoken in the locality in the past, but, as we will demonstrate in the next section, could facilitate the decipherment of a previously unknown language.

## 2.5    Toponymy and Language Decipherment

Writing is among the greatest inventions of humankind, and arguably a significant aspect of how we transitioned from prehistory to historical times, marking the evolution from oral cultures to written-word societies. Ancient civilisations developed many different writing systems, setting them in stone, clay, wood, and even rudimentary types of papery materials, not considering the fact that, one day in the future, these would be unearthed, studied, debated, and eventually deciphered. Archaeological excavations often yield clay tablets and slabs with inscriptions on them carved by civilisations long gone. Upon discovery, these unfamiliar symbols can baffle us, immediately raising numerous questions of such ancient writing systems. Are they actual writing and, in so doing, are they 'conveying a precise and unequivocal meaning' (Olivier, 1986, p. 377), or are they merely decorative? If they are, indeed, writing, what do they say? Are the symbols similar to any existing writing system? What language is transcribed by the inscription writing? Is the language known, or unknown? These symbols immediately become mysterious puzzles and involuntary ciphers (since, originally, they were invented for communication and not for concealing information), containing details seemingly impossible to retrieve, unless one cracks the code. What many people do not know is that place names have played an important role in the decipherment of ancient writing systems and languages.

To date, there are many scripts created in ancient times that still remain undeciphered. Some examples from all over the world include Linear A, Linear Elamite, Etruscan, Meroitic, and the Rongorongo Script. It is not for lack of trying that these writing systems remain undeciphered, as numerous people, among them linguists and non-linguists alike, have devoted themselves to cracking the code for many decades. A principal obstacle in order to begin deciphering an unknown writing system is having sufficient data available (i.e., enough clay tablets or epigraphs with the inscriptions). Understandably, it is almost impossible to decipher a writing system with very limited signs or symbols. An example is the Indus Script, which has text with an average of only five signs, and whose longest recorded text has only twenty signs (Robinson, 2009), and which will probably never be deciphered. One of the best ways of deciphering an unknown script is to link it with that of a known language. The existence of bilingual inscriptions like the Rosetta Stone (carved in Ancient Greek, which transcribes Ancient Greek, and in Ancient Egyptian, transcribed by both Ancient Egyptian Hieroglyphs and Demotic) quickened the process of deciphering the Egyptian Hieroglyphs, as Ancient Greek was well documented and studied beforehand. In this case, researchers could match the contents between the Ancient Greek text and the two Egyptian scripts, recognising proper nouns, in particular, and assigning phonetic values to symbols from the unknown scripts. Nonetheless, few documents contain bilingual writings in attested languages and systems, rendering the decipherment of undeciphered texts very difficult indeed.

How then does one find this linguistic link to known scripts and languages? The Rosetta Stone showed us that names (in that case, proper nouns) hold the key to uncovering the ancient secrets of a lost civilisation. Though written in scripts transcribing different languages, bilingual or multilingual inscriptions tend to transcribe proper names with little variation, keeping to some extent the original phonetics of the name, and adapting it to the linguistic system of the target languages. This allows the researcher to match names usually known in one of the languages in both scripts. Sounds can then be assigned to the corresponding symbols in words or clusters of characters in the unknown script, used to crack other sets of symbols, their phonetic values, and, ultimately, their meaning. Ancient Egyptian Hieroglyphs, along with their later versions, Hieratic and Demotic, began to be deciphered when proper nouns in Ancient Egyptian were identified in several 'cartouches' (oval figures that enclose a set of hieroglyphs) on the Rosetta Stone, and were matched with their equivalent in Ancient Greek. These names included those of Hellenic royal figures, such as Ptolemy and Cleopatra. In particular, Jean-François Champollion deciphered the rest of the hieroglyphics in 1822, after he was able to successfully identify the name of Pharaoh Ramses using the 's' phonetic value identified by him and Thomas Young from the name 'Ptolmis' (the Ancient Egyptian version of the Ancient Greek anthroponym Ptolemy). As we can see, the anthroponyms of long-lost kings, such as Cleopatra, Ptolemy, and Ramses himself, were instrumental in breaking the previously unfathomable code of the hieroglyphics. Similar conditions allowed for the decipherment of Sumerian Cuneiform. In this case, a breakthrough was made with the interpretation, by Henry Rawlinson, of the names of King Darius of Persia and his son Xerxes in the Old Persian section of the trilingual (Old Persian, Akkadian, and Elamite) Behistun Inscription from Iran, in the 1850s.

Other than anthroponyms, toponyms have also been key factors in allowing the connection between the known and hitherto undeciphered languages. Due to the simple fact, as we have argued in this volume, that toponyms are 'linguistic fossils' – stable entities that may be preserved over centuries – searching for place names in an unknown script has become a valid strategy in language decipherment. They are ubiquitous in human history, mentioned alongside historical records, marking historical events, and are intertwined with folklore and mythology. They might not be enough to crack the code entirely, but toponyms generally allow a substantial starting point to the deciphering process, which hopefully gains momentum. Linear B, a syllabic script that was used for writing Mycenaean Greek by the Mycenaeans, centuries before the Homeric poets, was deciphered by Michael Ventris in 1952 thanks to the identification of specific Cretan place names, even in the absence of any bilingual inscription or notion of what language was 'hidden' behind Linear B. As an example of the role of toponymy in language decipherment, we will discuss briefly how Linear B was deciphered through the discovery of place names in its documents.

## 2.6    Toponymy and the Decipherment of Linear B

In 1899, British archaeologist Sir Arthur Evans, while excavating the Cretan site of *Knossos* (where the palace of the mythical King Minos was located), unearthed a wooden chest full of small, inscribed clay tablets (see Figure 2.1). The writing was written originally on unbaked clay, which was inadvertently (but also fortunately) baked in the fire that destroyed the palace. Written with a stylus, the carvings were very clear and hence relatively easily read. Three sets of tablets were found in total, and together contained three unknown scripts.

Figure 2.1 Linear B tablet and transcription. Mycenaean tablet (MY Oe 106) from the House of the Oil Merchant. The tablet states the amount of wool to be dyed (adapted from Marsyas, 2005)

The three unknown scripts excavated in *Crete* by Evans were, as named by him: Cretan Hieroglyphic (4100–1700 BCE), Linear A (18000–1000 BCE), and Linear B (ca. 1450–1200 BCE). While Linear B is deciphered, Cretan Hieroglyphs and Linear A remain undeciphered.

Linear B resembled the Classical Cypriot Script, which was known to be a syllabary transcribing Ancient Greek, used between 600 and 200 BCE. Assuming this similarity, a comparison of the two scripts was carried out. The most common final consonant in Greek is *s* (sigma). If the two scripts were writing the same language, then the sigma character in the Cypriot Script would be expected to correspond with that of Linear B, at the final consonant position. Upon comparison, this character was found in Linear B, but not at the word-final position. The consensus, therefore, was that the script of Linear B evolved into the Cypriot Script, but that the language it was writing was not Ancient Greek.

Indeed, Sir Arthur Evans was adamantly against the hypothesis that Linear B transcribed Ancient Greek also for another reason. Evans believed Linear A was the script of the earlier civilisation of Minoans, while Linear B was the script used by the Mycenaeans, a powerful neighbour and rival who conquered the Minoans around 1400 BCE. It was his opinion that the Mycenaeans possibly based their own writing system on that of the conquered Minoans.

Sir Arthur Evans began the decipherment process of Linear B, but after his death most of the initial groundwork was laid by Emmett L. Bennett Jr and Alice Kober. It was only when their work was then taken up by Michael Ventris, with the cooperation of John Chadwick, that Linear B was deciphered in 1952. Of particular importance for us in the context of this book is how toponyms were the key sources of information that allowed Ventris to ultimately decipher Linear B.

Emmett L. Bennett Jr wrote his doctoral thesis on the Linear B tablets found in *Pylos, Crete*. In his publication on the *Pylos* tablets in 1951, he classified the Linear B signs and listed their variant forms, paving the way for statistical analyses of the Linear B signs and symbols that would ultimately lead to their decipherment. Bennett's irreplaceable contribution to the decipherment of Linear B was to have established a typographic standard for the writing system.

Alice Kober, a classicist from Brooklyn College, focussed on the structure of the language of the Linear B signs. She assigned a number to each sign, so that even though she could not associate a phonetic value to each sign, she was able to explicate the relationships between them. Kober then started the decipherment by assuming that the alphabet-equivalent of Linear B was made of syllables, not single phonemes. She did this by counting them. They were around ninety syllables, which is too few for a pictographic writing system and too many for an alphabetical writing system, but a perfect number for a syllabic script. Kober discovered that Linear B syllables consisted of either a vowel or a consonant, followed by a vowel. That is, she worked out that Linear B was organised as an 'open syllabary' where the syllables are not 'closed' by a consonant. A syllabary consists of different syllabic signs for combinations of consonants plus vowels, but, generally, also has 'special' signs which register only the vowels, with the possible addition of different signs which are not properly syllabic, but can be configured as ideograms or logograms. She also managed to reconstruct some rules of the undeciphered language with this systematic approach, by identifying the case system and several word combinations. The discovery of the cases allowed her to understand that Linear B was the script of a highly inflected language (comparable to Ancient Greek, Sanskrit, and Latin), possibly Indo-European. Her identification of the writing system as syllabic made possible the creation of classification tables, or grids (see Table 2.2). Unfortunately, Kober died of cancer in 1950, before she could crack the script.

Michael Ventris continued Kober's work in deciphering Linear B based on her discoveries. Kober had realised that each character in Linear B was a syllabogram, representing a consonant-vowel combination. Ventris took it a step further by testing what happens if the vowel appeared alone. He hypothesised that there had to be some instances where a vowel appeared 'alone' at the beginning of a word. He began by listing all these hypothetical connected signs in a grid (Table 2.2). Ventris' methodology, indeed, was not properly linguistic

Table 2.2 *Initial Linear B grid by Ventris (Chadwick, 1958, p. 58)*

| Vowels ... | I | II | III | IV | V |
|---|---|---|---|---|---|
| Pure vowels? | 61 | – | – | – | 08 |
| Semi-vowel? | – | – | – | 59 | 57 |
| Consonant I | 40 | 10 | 75 | 42 | 54 |
| II | 39 | 11 | – | – | 03 |
| III | | (14) | – | 51 | 01 |
| IV | 37 | 05 | – | | 66 |
| V | 41 | 12 | – | 55 | 31 |
| VI | 30 | 52 | – | 24 | 06 |
| VII | 73 | 15 | – | (72) | 80 |
| VII | 46 | 36 | – | – | – |
| IX | | 70 | – | 44 | (74) |
| X | 53 | – | (04) | 76 | 20 |
| XI | – | 70 | – | 44 | (74) |
| XI | 60 | 02 | 27 | 26 | 33 |
| XII | 28 | – | – | 38 | 77 |
| XIII | | 32 | 78 | – | – |
| XIV | 07 | – | – | – | – |
| XV | 67 | – | – | – | – |

or philological, but was based on a grid system grounded in his training and experience as a cryptanalyst for the Royal Air Force during the Second World War. He then noticed that some clusters of symbols (possible words) appeared over and over again. He guessed that these possible words could have been the names of important peoples (like kings) or of important cities (place names). For instance, he noted that the symbol he numbered as '08' was one of those syllabograms that frequently appeared at the beginning of a word, and his grid showed that '08' may represent a vowel.

The only Cretan town with a name known to begin with a vowel possibly important to the people of *Knossos* in Minoan times was the nearby port of *Amnisos*. Therefore, Ventris assigned the transcription A-MI-NI-SO to the cluster made up of the symbols 08-73-30-12 (without the final 'S'). His instinct showed promise as the symbols '73' and '30' were in the same column of the grid, indicating that they both possibly represented symbols ending with the same vowel, 'I'. From his grid, he could also deduce that the '12' representing 'SO' was in the same vowel column as symbols '70' and '52'. Thus, he inferred that these symbols were all syllables ending with an 'O' sound. By referring to the Cypriot Syllabary (which, as mentioned, was already deciphered and transcribed Ancient Greek), he compared the shape of symbol '30' in Linear B with a corresponding syllabogram in the Cypriot Syllabary, with the phonetic value of 'NI', and found them to be very similar. He then attributed the phonetic value of 'NI' to the Linear B symbol '30'. That was a perfect match with the solution A-MI-NI-SO. By applying his results thus far to another common cluster comprised of the symbols 70-52-12, he inferred that they would have to represent (?)O-(?)O-SO. Ventris asked himself whether (?)O-(?)O-SO represented the name of the city of *Knossos*. Hypothesising KO-NO-SO, Ventris was able to get two new consonantal sounds, 'K' and 'N', for his grid. Moreover, since '30' and '52' were in the same consonant row, he concluded that they represented the consonant 'N'. This was a match with 'NI' and 'NO' in the names he was working on, *Amnisos* and *Knossos*. Ventris then studied the cluster 69-53-12, where '53' was in the same vowel column as '73 – MI' and '30 – NI'. Following his initial results, the cluster 69-53-12 could then be (??)-(?)I-SO. This matched the toponym *Tylissos*, or *Tylisos* (TU-LI-SO). Ventris now had the phonetic values of eight signs which, through application of each one of these values to more and more clusters, which did not transcribe place names but common lexical items, gave rise to many others, and he arrived quickly at a more complete grid.

To be precise, deciphering the toponyms did not give any immediate evidence of what language was transcribed by Linear B. However, as shown in our brief recount above, the toponyms were the key to the initial decipherment. Ventris went on to decipher the clusters 05-31 as TO-SA and 05-12 as TO-SO, which were similar to the Ancient Greek terms for 'total', *tossos* (or *tosos*, τόσος) and *tossa* (or *tosa*, τόσα). This confirmed that Linear B was transcribing an archaic version of Ancient Greek, that is, Mycenaean Greek. Although Ventris was initially against the notion that Linear B was transcribing Ancient Greek, by 1 July 1952 he had changed his mind and he had deciphered the enigmatic writing system. The genius of some very skilled glyphbreakers and the discovery of place names allowed the decipherment of an unknown writing system transcribing an unknown language, one of the most exciting and important achievements in linguistics of the past century.

John Chadwick, an expert in Ancient Greek, then began collaborating with Ventris and helped him in deciphering the rest of the script and in documenting the grammar and vocabulary of Mycenaean Greek. The decipherment of Linear B was thus instrumental in discovering that the Mycenaeans were Greek, and that they spoke/wrote an archaic variety of Ancient Greek. Figure 2.2 presents the values for the Linear B syllabograms.

A central theme in this section is the usefulness of toponyms in deciphering an undeciphered writing system and its related unknown language. While this has not been documented, it is possible that Ventris knew how toponyms could be harnessed as tools for the decipherment process and, upon seeing an unknown cluster, hypothesised that it named an important place during a specific period of time (i.e., the port of *Amnisos* between Minoan and Mycenaean times) before attempting to make connections between the toponym and the cluster. He was also astute in linking another unknown cluster to the city of *Knossos*, which was the capital city of Minoan *Crete* and the main administrative centre on the island under the Mycenaean rule. We again can appreciate here how toponyms tend to remain stable over time even though the languages spoken and the populations occupying territories might change.

## 2.7     Toponymy in Minoan *Crete*: An Experimental Case Study

The Linear B example that we have just discussed has taught us that place names can be fundamental in deciphering undeciphered languages, especially in a context like the Mycenaean Greek one, in which we have the worst-case scenario in language decipherment: both the writing system (Linear B) as well as the underlying language are unknown to the glyphbreakers. In this section, as an expansion of our example concerning Linear B, we will briefly focus on Minoan toponymy from *Crete* in the light of the undeciphered Linear A documents, which represent one of the most significant unsolved puzzles in the context of writing systems.

The case study we propose below is highly experimental and works only at the theoretical level, but is an exciting example of how possible place names help linguists to infer interpretations of unknown languages 'hidden' behind

Figure 2.2 Linear B Syllabograms (elaboration by Francesco Perono Cacciafoco)

undeciphered scripts, of ancient populations dynamics, and of the origins of the peoples speaking those languages.

Linear A, as mentioned, is an undeciphered Aegean writing system used in the Bronze Age (ca. 3300–1200 BCE) in *Crete* by the Minoan civilisation and 'hides' the so-called, but unknown, 'Minoan language'. It predates the Linear B script discussed in the previous section and, in a way, is considered to be the script from which Linear B was generated when the Mycenaeans adopted the Minoan writing system. Being an undeciphered writing system, it is practically impossible to establish whether the phonetic clusters so far identified as possible place names in the Linear A documents (which consist mainly of small clay tablets) are real toponyms. Their transcription has, moreover, been proposed by applying the phonetic values of similar-looking Linear B syllabograms to their 'equivalent' symbols in Linear A. This procedure would work only if the language transcribed by Linear A was the same as that transcribed by Linear B (i.e., Mycenaean Greek), or if speakers of Mycenaean Greek decided to match the phonetic values of their language with analogous phonetic values of the language 'hidden' behind Linear A, even in the case that Minoan was unrelated to Mycenaean. Both solutions have not yet led to a decipherment of Linear A and, therefore, are evidence of the highly experimental and somehow speculative nature of this process. Any reconstructed place name in Minoan is, therefore, 'possible' only if we accept this transcription strategy. The other major assumption is that these clusters do indeed represent toponyms.

Thus far, all attempts to decipher Linear A as if it were transcribing an Indo-European language – Ancient Greek, *in primis*, based on Linear B, but also Luwian, Hittite, and many others – have failed. Similar results have been attained in attempts to reconstruct the language 'hidden' behind Linear A as being a Semitic or Afro-Asiatic language (Perono Cacciafoco, 2017).

Table 2.3 presents an example of an experimental etymological reconstruction of several possible Minoan place names according to an Indo-European key of interpretation, by applying historical-phonetic methodologies and the comparative method to the analysis of those toponyms. It is important to stress again the fact that the following etymological reconstructions are theoretical and are based on the above postulations, which are not proven (otherwise Linear A would be a deciphered writing system), but provide a proposal for discussion and debate and show how the etymological reconstruction of possibly Cretan place names may reveal that Minoan could have had Indo-European origins.

We do not think *a priori* that Linear A transcribes an Indo-European language, but the toponyms are here reconstructed as if they were Indo-European in their origins and as if they had, therefore, an Indo-European etymology. This was done in order to test the Indo-European option linguistically, and to either

Table 2.3 Possible Minoan place names and their reconstructions (adapted from Younger, 2020, 10c)

| Linear A | Ancient Greek (Indo-European) | Proto-Indo-European | Possible parallels | Possible meanings |
|---|---|---|---|---|
| DI-KI-TE | $Δίκτη$ | < *$Dĭk̑$-$tḗs$ | Ancient Indian $diktás$ 'from sky's regions'. Includes the idea of 'moving away from the centre'. | 'Border of the sky' |
| I-DA | $Ἴδη$, Doric $Ἴδα$ | < *$H_a í$-$h_a íd$-$á·h_a$ | The first element is the Indo-European *$H_a í$-$h_a íd$-$ā́$, meaning 'strong'. The second element, *$h_a$, means 'mountain,' or 'something that comes up from the soil'. A possible parallel, almost an homonym, is the name of a mountain in Asia Minor, near ancient Troy ($Kaz\ Dağı$ in Turkish), the mount $Ἴδη$ ($Idē/Ida$) in Ancient Greek, and $Ida$, $Idē$ in Latin. This is an unexceptionable parallel, with the same meaning and possibly the same Indo-European etymology. | 'Strong mountain, strong high ground' |
| PA-I-TO | $Φαιστός$ | < *$Bʰáh_a$-$ĭ$-$sth_2$-$ó$-$s$ | The first element, compatible with Ancient Indian $^2bʰa$- (Monier-Williams 1899, p. 750) ~ *$Bʰáh_a$-, means 'light, clarity, splendor, Sun'. The second element, $ĭ$-$sth_2$-$ó$-$s$, matches the -$stum$ and -$stom$ elements in Hispano-Celtic $Bergistum$ and Celtiberian $Boustom$. We can see an association of both elements in the Cretan place name $Phaistos$. It indicates a place that is not covered or a place which is under the sun. The practice of naming places that are directly under the sun is not rare in Indo-European languages. An example would be the Italian place name $Solaro$. There is no etymological connection, but there is a link at the historical-semantic level in the related naming process. Another instance can be provided by the Brittonic $Greenogue$-type place names. | 'Place in the sun' |

Table 2.3 (cont.)

| Linear A | Ancient Greek (Indo-European) | Proto-Indo-European | Possible parallels | Possible meanings |
|---|---|---|---|---|
| ⊡⅄⅃ SU-KI-RI-TA | (*SU-QI-RI-TA ~ Σύβριτα?) = Σύβριτα | < *[H₁]sū́-ĝritā́·hₐ | The first element is the Indo-European *h₁sú-. It can be associated with 'well', evident in the Ancient Greek eu-, Latin eu-, as in the English word euphemism and in the Italian word eufemismo. The second element, -ĝritā·hₐ, is connected with the description of an action, and with the meaning of 'stretched out'. It generally refers to the 'planimetry' of a place on its landscape, i.e., 'well (spatially) distributed on the territory'. | 'Well stretched out' |
| ⊞⅄ TU-RI-SA | Τύλισος f. | < *Túl(hₐ)-lĭ-hₐsŏ-s, *Tŭl(hₐ)-lĭ-hₐsā́·hₐ | The first element is the Prehistoric Indo-European appellative *tūlŏ-, *tūlŏ-, meaning 'height', or 'to be tall'. The second element, *-lĭ-hₐsŏ-, is compatible with an Anatolian descriptive suffix with the meaning of 'characterised by', or 'provided with'. The Polcevera Table (or Sententia Minuciorum), an ancient bronze inscription dating back to the year 117 BCE, contains a decree of the Roman Senate, with several place names listed on it. Among them is Tuledonem (accusative masculine singular), is a mountain in Liguria, Italy, and is a plausible parallel for TU-RI-SA. | 'Provided with height' |
| ⅄Λ꙰Υ I-TI-NI-SA | Nῖσα/Nίσα | < *H₁ĭ-tĭ-nĭ-nm-s-ā́·hₐ | The first element is compatible with Ancient Indian ĭtĭ- 'to go'. The second element is comparable to Ancient Greek Nῖσα/Nίσα 'wandering life'. A hypothetical correspondence for this place name is Itanos, which, in ancient Crete, was an important city and port in the east of the island. | 'Intensive pastures along the way' |

| Sign | Reconstruction | Description | Gloss |
|---|---|---|---|
| **KU-NI-SU** | < *K̂un-h₁/₄iŝh̯ₐ-ŭ-s | The first element is the Indo-European *k̂un- 'dog'. The second element may be associated with the Brittonic *Isu[rium]. A parallel, at the historical-semantic level, and in the context of the naming process, is the Italian place name *El Paradis di can* [Il Paradiso dei cani], 'Dogs' Heaven', in *Valtellina (Lombardy)*. | 'Dogs' Shrine' |
| **SE-TO-I-JA** | < *Sĕnt-ŏ-h₁ĭ-iǐ̯ā·hₐ | First element: Celtic *sĕntŭ- 'path'. The root and suffix of the second element mirror the Lithuanian *pérėja* 'passage, mountain pass'. In Lithuanian, which is a conservative Indo-European language, *-eja* derives from *-h₁ĭ-iǐ̯ā·hₐ*. Hypothetical correspondences for this place name are *Archanes* or *Ioukhtas*. The possible connection with *Archanes* was initially proposed by Owens (1994), who found that the high recurrence of the string of symbols was accompanied by a high amount of trade activity. *Archanes* has ancient roads which lead to *Ioukhtas* (now more commonly known as *Mount Juktas*), a mountain in north-central *Crete*, one of the most important peak sanctuaries in the Minoan world. | 'Passage with path', or 'mountain pass' |
| **SA-RA** | < *Sₑh₃-ǎ·hₐ | *Sₑh₃-, as well as *war-/*uar-/*var-, means 'to flow', and is connected with the 'description' of watercourses. There are several *vara-*, as well as several *sar-/sara*-type rivers, in *Europe*. A parallel is the French hydronym *Saire*. | 'Flowing' |

ascertain or disprove the transcriptions of these syllabic segments through the phonetic values or Linear B.

The main linguistic and epistemological problems the toponymists have to take into account in this context are as follows.

- It is not granted that the phonetic clusters listed below are place names. Linear A documents are undeciphered and, therefore, all interpretations of clusters of symbols are highly hypothetical and not confirmed. The clusters in Table 2.3 are thought to be place names because, in some cases, their phonetic transcription seems to match up with Ancient Greek place names from *Crete* or because their morphology is compatible with the morphology of Indo-European place names as is shown in the table (but see the following point), and because of the position where they appear on the Linear A tablets. That is, these clusters/segments often appear in initial positions in the Linear A tablets and they occupy more or less the same spaces the deciphered place names occupy in the Linear B tablets. See our discussion of A-MI-NI-SO and KO-NO-SO in the previous section.

- It is not granted that the phonetic clusters listed below can be read correctly according to the given transcriptions, because the transcriptions themselves, as mentioned above, are based on the idea of a phonetic and phonological equivalence between Linear A and Linear B (or between Minoan and Mycenaean). That is, the Linear A symbols are, arbitrarily, given the phonetic values of the equivalent Linear B syllabograms. If Linear A is transcribing a language incompatible with Linear B, for example, a Semitic language or an Afro-Asiatic language (cf. Linear B transcribes Mycenaean Greek, an Indo-European language), the reconstruction of these phonetic clusters is simply wrong.

If we accept, for the sake of completing the experiment and testing linguistically the Indo-European option, that the analysed clusters are (or could be) place names, and if we accept that they have (or could have) an Indo-European origin, we can try to reconstruct their etymologies, through a historical and comparative approach. This is a method commonly used in other Indo-European contexts, possibly enabling a new perspective in the quest to decipher Linear A, as well as a starting point for discussion and debate.

The possible Linear A syllabograms have been transcribed according to the phonetic values of the corresponding Linear B symbols in the first column. Where possible, an equivalent in Ancient Greek has been listed in the second column. The toponym, then, has been historically-phonetically reconstructed in Proto-Indo-European (third column). In the last column, a possible gloss has been assessed and listed, as well as plausible parallels (both at the level of etymology/historical morphology and at the level of semantics) with other (attested) Indo-European place names.

At the etymological and eminently theoretical level, these nine possibly Minoan place names could all have relatively solid Indo-European etymological reconstructions, which are consistent not only linguistically, but also semantically. This, in turn, may even help in identifying the locations of those places in *Crete* through the hydro-geo-morphology implied in the toponyms. However, Linear A is still an undeciphered writing system, and the Indo-European toponymy of Minoan *Crete* is and remains just a fascinating hypothesis which adds to our knowledge and understanding of this absolutely enigmatic script, with the hope that in the future it could contribute to its decipherment.

## 2.8    Summary

In some sense, there appears to be a paradox; while place names are susceptible to language change at various levels, toponyms are also relatively stable and the roots in toponyms can be from a language that has been replaced and subsequently lost due to population shifts and migrations. However, what we know is that these roots remain within the place names, making them 'linguistic relics', which are tremendously valuable in helping linguists to shed light on the nature of past languages and proto-languages or undeciphered writing systems such as Linear B, and possibly still-undeciphered ones such as Linear A.

How, then, can we be sure whether the explanation for the root of a toponym is accurate? In the next chapter, we will turn our attention to one of the core areas in toponymic research, aimed specifically at answering this pertinent question: historical toponomastics.

# 3    Historical Toponomastics

## 3.1    Historical Approaches to Toponymy

As mentioned in Chapter 1, toponymy and toponomastics can be approached from multiple points of view. Place names in a specific area can be studied in a specific moment in time (synchronic toponymy) or over a period of time (diachronic toponymy and historical toponomastics). The topic of synchronic toponymy will be covered in Chapter 8. The focus of this chapter will instead be on studying place names and their changes over time. We will elaborate more on historical toponomastics in this chapter, and on diachronic toponymy in Chapter 4.

As just mentioned, historical toponomastics and diachronic toponymy both deal with place names over time. Although they both involve studying place names through time, they differ on two fronts: (a) the context in which they work, and (b) the available sources that they rely on. As stated in Chapter 1, both disciplines fall under and relate closely to historical linguistics, the study of language change over time. The terms diachronic and historical entail, indeed, a historical investigation. In the process of reconstructing the origins of place names, toponymists avail themselves of records or other physical evidence from related fields such as:

- history – historical records, such as chronicles and ancient manuscripts
- epigraphy – writings engraved on clay or stone
- geo-archaeology – locations of ancient, inhabited centres, evidence of the stratigraphic development of sites through geological processes, and evidence of material culture, which are dated through geological methods (Cremaschi, 2008)
- historical geography, historical cartography, historical topography – ancient maps, topographic maps, military maps (David & Thomas, 2008; Cambi, 2011)
- landscape archaeology and archaeology – items and objects found when excavating an ancient place and dated according to different methodologies (David & Thomas, 2008; Cambi, 2011)
- palaeontology and paleo-anthropology – skeletal remains, bone fragments, footprints, cultural evidence like stone tools and artefacts collected from the localities under investigation (Facchini, Beltrán, & Broglio, 1993)

- genetics – paleo-anthropological remains through the analysis of their mito-chondrial DNA, which allows the reconstruction of population movements and settlement dynamics in very remote times, and the connected development of prehistoric inhabited centres and possible related toponymy (Cavalli-Sforza, Menozzi, & Piazza 1994; Cavalli-Sforza, 2001; Beretta, 2003)
- historical semantics – diachronic semantic change involving place names over time, due to changes in population in a specific area or to the loss, by speakers, of the original meaning of a toponym (Beretta, 2003; Perono Cacciafoco, 2014)

## 3.2    Historical Toponomastics

Historical toponomastics refers to the study of how to reconstruct the remote etymology of place names (a) in the context of well-known languages and language families, and (b) in the presence of available physical historical records and sources. Because of the availability of such records, as just mentioned, this kind of study usually involves well-known language families (e.g., Indo-European). Historical toponomastics is closely related to etymology, which is the study of the original structures and original meanings of words. A historical-toponomastic analysis, therefore, aims to provide documented and reliable etymologies for place names by reconstructing their historical morphology until the recovery of their proto-forms and, ultimately, their roots, is achieved. These, in turn, can shed light on prehistoric naming processes and on remote (in time) and undocumented population movements and settlement dynamics. So far, this approach has mostly been applied to the well-documented languages in *Europe*, with some applications also to Austronesian languages (Blust, 1984–5).

The etymological study of place names is one way to conduct toponymic research. A toponym is encoded with several layers of information: its literal meaning, its referent, its cultural connotations, its archaic/diachronic linguistic features, and its etymology, both true and false (Nash & Simpson, 2012, p. 395). A false etymology is known as 'paretymology' and it occurs when local speakers try to explain words in their language through their often limited linguistic knowledge. When this happens in the context of place names, it is called 'toponymic paretymology', which will be discussed in detail later in this chapter.

Thanks to the information encoded in a place name and through the available historical records, studying the etymology of a place name enables the toponymist to reconstruct its history and origins. Some scholars, like Coates (2013), suggest that etymological reconstruction is the most important procedure in toponymic research, as all names were once meaningful, when created. Other scholars disagree. However, even those scholars that disagree may also adopt part of the etymological framework (see Tent, 2015a). Tent (2015a, pp. 67–70) describes an intensive approach (which is, ultimately, qualitative and etymological) to toponymy as the process of writing a place name's 'biography' (the 'who', 'when', 'why', 'what', and 'where', regarding the naming process). He adds that this is only possible with the availability of reliable documentation.

As mentioned in Chapter 1, place names are, generally, linguistic evidence left by past civilisations and the onomastic elements they carry often depict the landscape as it was at the time of their naming and, possibly, the subsequent changes caused by human activity. Therefore, in order to arrive at a correct interpretation of the origin of a place name, an effective chronological reconstruction needs to tap into a number of disciplines. The study of historical toponomastics, indeed, is not strictly focussed on the linguistic and etymological reconstructions in themselves, but, rather, also takes into account the historical, geo-morphological, and archaeological characteristics of the studied sites. This would mean focussing our attention not only on the etymology *stricto sensu* of a place name, but also on the verisimilitude of the linguistic reconstruction in relationship with the real and physical data from the territory and with the clues provided by other related sciences connected with landscape. Data and methodologies from these disciplines can then be useful to cross-check and to confirm or disprove the results of the linguistic analysis. For example, if a place name contains a morpheme meaning 'water' (or if 'water' is the main meaning of its root), but, currently, there are no water sources in the vicinity, the toponymist would have to evaluate the possible changes in the hydro-geo-morphology of the relevant landscape and the whole area, to investigate possible links between the toponym and the actual territory – was there water nearby, in the past? Is there evidence of a river changing course or of the draining of a lake or swamp? Is there evidence of the movement of people? This verification, which involves the diachronic analysis of the hydro-geo-morphology of the area where the place name is located, could endorse or refute the etymological hypotheses (Gelling & Cole, 2000), even in the case in which the etymological reconstructions were (apparently) linguistically unexceptionable. Only in this way are we able to reconstruct the most possible accurate etymology of a place name.

A historical-toponomastic approach to place names can be described as an 'archaeology of language' and, as mentioned in Chapter 1, enables the toponymist to delineate a 'diachronic stratigraphy' of the toponyms. A continuous and well-studied documentation of the languages spoken in a specific area and the abundance of historical documents and records allow not only an accurate etymological reconstruction, in the linguistic context, but also to chronologically highlight the different stages of development of a place name, at the morphological level, and in connection with the physical elements of the territory, its geology in general, and, at the level of landscape, its hydro-geo-morphology. The linguistic reconstruction is essential to recover toponymic roots and proto-forms, which go beyond the historically documented time, because the historical-linguistic analysis moves, necessarily, towards a time predating the invention of writing. Nonetheless, those roots and proto-forms etymologically reconstructed through the comparative method and the analysis of the historical-phonetic developments of toponyms are always connected with the physical element of the territory where the place names appear. Etymology, landscape sciences, paleo-anthropology, geo-archaeology, and geology find, therefore, their successful synthesis in the context of historical toponomastics.

## 3.3    Methodologies in Historical Toponomastics

The methods involved in historical toponomastics, along with that of the intensive model outlined by Tent (2015a), are akin to writing a toponym's 'biography'. To do so, the scholar answers a set of *wh*-questions associated with the place name (Tent, 2015a, p. 68).

- *Who* named the place? *Who* lived there?
- *When* was the place named?
- *Why* was the place given this particular name?
- *What* is the meaning of the toponym? *What* were the previous names of the place, if any? *What* kind of geographical features (physical and human) surround this place?
- *Where* is this place?

In addition to these, there are the usual etymological questions to be answered, which we define as follows.

- *What* is the original form of the place name?
- *What* is the root or proto-form of the place name?
- *What* language and language family does the place name belong to?

As explained above, in the context of historical toponomastics, because we are dealing with names in well-documented languages (e.g., the already mentioned Indo-European language family), there is often access to records and documentation. These include epigraphs, ancient manuscripts, chronicles, general dictionaries, journals, letters, maps, gazetteers, and toponymic dictionaries that mention place names and their possible origins. With the aid of these records, scholars can try to answer some of the *wh*-questions. In addition to written and even pictorial sources, a lot of data can be obtained from the analysis of historical geography and landscape archaeology sources inherent in specific areas. It is, therefore, possible, in the context of a historical toponomastics approach, to work convergently with other disciplines like history, geography, archaeology, landscape studies, and so on, as we have previously explained.

At the eminently linguistic (and, therefore, etymological) level, the historical-linguistic reconstruction of a place name is developed through the application of the comparative method and the reconstruction and use of sounds laws which govern the morphological development of lexical items (in our case, toponyms) over time. The analysis and recovery of the historical-phonetic changes in the diachronic evolution of a place name allows us to go back in time to its proto-form and root and, through them, to assess and establish not only its original form (or, at least, the linguistic stem/'matrix' from which the place name derives from), but also its original meaning. The linguistic reconstruction of a place name, therefore, always associates etymology in itself with historical semantics (the study of the changes in the meaning of words or expressions over a period of time), and the target is always the recovery not only of the original (historical) morphology of a toponym, but also of its original meaning.

A step-by-step method in a historical toponomastics analysis is outlined in Table 3.1. These *wh*-questions are by no means exhaustive. However, they are a good indication of some of the hermeneutic tools that guide the scholar as they reconstruct the origins and meanings of place names. This does not mean that all the answers for a question such as 'who lived there?' or 'what were the previous names of the place, if any?' can always be found in written records. They may come, rather, from visual representations or other sources as well, or even through an extra-linguistic (geological, for example) study of the place name and its surroundings. What is more important, however, is that these questions guide the process of the historical toponomastics investigation. In some cases, the answer to *wh*-questions like 'when was the place named?' can be found in both written and visual representations, owing to the fact that these documents often are accompanied by the year in which they were produced or published, which, in turn, allows us to know what the toponym was at a particular time.

## 3.4     Case Studies in Historical Toponomastics

### 3.4.1     Sessame

This section details an example of how the step-by-step process outlined above might be applied in a real toponymic investigation. For this case study, we will analyse the place name of the small village of *Sessame*, located in the province of *Asti*, in the Italian region of *Piedmont* (Figure 3.1).

The first step of the analysis is to gather data of the place name. Studying written records of the toponym, Perono Cacciafoco (2016a; 2016b) found only one form for this denomination, *Sexamus*, from an Italian toponymic dictionary (Gasca Queirazza et al., 1999). The dictionary reports that the name was attested in the year 1127. Perono Cacciafoco then conducted a linguistic

Table 3.1 *A step-by-step guide to historical toponomastics*

| Step 1: Gathering the data of the place name | |
|---|---|
| Source | Aims |
| *Written records*<br>*E.g., dictionaries, journals, letters,*<br>   *manuscripts, chronicles,*<br>   *toponymic dictionaries* | • Who named the place? Who is the author?<br>• Who lived there?<br>• When was the place named? When was it written (i.e.,<br>  the first time the place name has been attested in<br>  a written form)?<br>• What were the previous names of the place, if any? |
| *Visual representations*<br>*E.g., maps, gazetteers, photos* | • Who named the place? Who is the author?<br>• When was the place named? When was it drawn or<br>  published (i.e., the first time the place name has been<br>  attested in a pictorial form)?<br>• What kind of geographical features (physical and<br>  human) surround this place?<br>• Where is this place? |
| **Step 2: Linguistic analysis of the place name** | |
| *Written records*<br>*E.g., literature review from other*<br>   *scholars, toponymic dictionaries*<br>   *explaining the etymology of place*<br>   *names* | • What are the roots or proto-forms of the place name that<br>  we can reconstruct through actual attested forms?<br>• What do the roots or proto-forms mean?<br>• How might the roots or proto-forms be pronounced?<br>• Are there any words in other languages (or proto-<br>  languages) that can be connected with the same roots?<br>  What are these languages (or proto-languages)?<br>• How have others explained the roots or proto-forms of<br>  the place name? |
| **Step 3: Extra-linguistic analysis of the place name** | |
| *Historical geography*<br>*E.g., historical maps* | • Are there any other places with the same root? Is there<br>  a toponymic system connected with this root?<br>• What kind of geographical features (physical and<br>  human) surround these places (e.g., warm water, hot<br>  springs, fire, stones, caves, tools etc.)? What do we<br>  know about the hydro-geo-morphological features of<br>  these places?<br>• Do these maps show them to be at their current location? |
| *Landscape archaeology*<br>*Previous excavations and their*<br>   *findings* | • Who lived there?<br>• When is the earliest sign of habitation?<br>• Were there any dominant trades or activities carried out?<br>• Is there any material evidence of geographical features<br>  (physical or human)? |
| **Step 4: Putting it all together** | |
| *Summary* | • Societal data: Who named the place? Who lived<br>  there? What did they do? Do we know anything |

Table 3.1 (*cont.*)

| Step 4: Putting it all together | |
| --- | --- |
| *To reconstruct the remote origins of a place name, we have to take into account the following* | about the 'age' of the place based on the name (i.e., when was the place named)? This is because the most ancient people tended to name places according to primary needs for survival and to the existing hydro-geo-morphology of the places. Hence, a place which is called 'pasture of the flowers trail' is probably not the most ancient or remote of the names, as its denomination is a sort of 'poetic description' of its landscape and is not connected with indispensable primary goods needed for survival. |
| | • Etymological data: what is the original form of the place name? What is the meaning of the toponym? Why was the place given this particular name? What are its root and proto-form? What language (or proto-language) does it belong to? |
| | • Historical geography and landscape archaeology: where is this place located? Where are other places with similar names? Is there a toponymic system connected with it? What kind of geographical features (physical and human) surround this place? |

analysis on all previous research carried out on this toponym. These include what has been concluded about the possible roots and proto-forms of the place name and all the literature written by other scholars on the previous versions of the name and possible etymological elements of *Sessame*. For instance, Giovanni Martina interpreted the form *Sexamus* as deriving from the Latin expression *(ad) sexagesimum lapidem*. This would be a spatial and distal marker that indicates the distance of *Sessame* from *Turin* (*il sessagesimo miglio dal capoluogo piemontese* 'the sixtieth mile from the Piedmontese administrative centre', i.e., *Turin*) (Martina, 1951, p. 122). Another scholar, Goffredo Casalis, noted that *Sessame* is located very close to where the two branches of the *Bormida River* converge, and that the actual place where the convergence happens is called 'the unions' (*le giunte*). He posited that *Sessame* could have come from the German expression *sich sammeln*, meaning 'to gather'. It could also mean 'junction' (Casalis, 1833–56, p. 10). In some ways, this gives us a clue about the fact that the original *Sessame* was located near or along the *Bormida River*, a fact which still remains valid today, as confirmed by Perono Cacciafoco after checking the maps of the area and making a fieldwork trip to the village. An explanation which tried to reconstruct the roots of the place

Figure 3.1 Location of *Sessame* (adapted from d-maps, 2021)

name was carried out by Dante Olivieri in his *Dizionario di toponomastica piemontese* (*Piedmontese Toponomastics' Dictionary*). Olivieri postulates that *Sessame* could derive from the Proto-Indo-European root *\*sal(s)-* 'salt', or 'brackish water' (from which other words, like the Latin *sāl*, Italian *sale*, and Ancient Greek ἅλς [*háls*] derive), justifying this by noting the presence of sulphurous and salty springs in *Sessame*. He, therefore, links the possible root and meaning of *Sessame* to its hydro-geo-morphological features (Olivieri, 1965, p. 321).

All these hypotheses are incomplete or substantially questionable and require more research. The next step, therefore, involves a comprehensive extra-linguistic analysis of *Sessame* and its surrounding area. Through looking at maps of *Sessame* (and its nearby territories) and the names of its hamlets, and, as mentioned above, after a fieldwork trip in the area, Perono Cacciafoco (2016a; 2016b) identified two toponyms that are particularly interesting: *Gringàvoli*, where the two branches of the *Bormida River* converge at the border with *Bistagno* (cf. Chapter 7), and *Caldana*, where a sulphurous spring is found. The finding of these two place names could give credibility to Olivieri's explanation. Furthermore, as mentioned, maps also show that the *Bormida River* flows in *Sessame*'s territory and that the two branches of the watercourse do, in fact, 'join' where the town of *Sessame* is located. As we will explain in Chapter 7, we know that the river is named after the possibly Pre-Indo-European root *\*borm-*, meaning 'hot water', or 'warm water', and might have gotten its name from the many hot springs found along its course.

However, evidence from paleo-anthropological research conducted in the area surrounding *Sessame* includes several prehistoric tools, such as stone axes, flint arrowheads and knives, and other Stone Age instruments that have been found all along the *Bormida River* course, including in the *Acqui Terme* (an ancient Roman spa town located in the nearby province of *Alessandria*) terri-tory, where *Sessame* and *Bistagno* are ubicated. This probably means that, in prehistoric times (surely during the Neolithic, but, plausibly, as far back as the Upper Palaeolithic), stone-cutting and tool-making activities were carried out in the area (Perono Cacciafoco, 2011). As mentioned, the tools found around *Sessame* date back at least to the Neolithic, making it possible to speculate that a village where the current *Sessame* is located has existed since the Stone Age. Apparently, the stone tools are not directly linked to the practice of agriculture, but they are connected with carpentry and hunting, as the most common tools used during the Neolithic era for agriculture were the scythe and the sickle, rather than the tools mentioned above (among them were also ritual axes that, because of their weight, were not usable in everyday life and were used only in rituals).

After gathering data of the earliest historical (written) attestations of *Sessame*, investigating possible explanations of the origins of the name (from the work of earlier scholars), as well as accounting for any extra-linguistic factors, that is, historical maps, names and features of its hamlets, the presence of the river that flows in the territory, and findings from Paleo-anthropology, Perono Cacciafoco (2016a; 2016b) suggested two possible explanations for the etymology of *Sessame*. He proposes that the place name could have been derived from:

1. the Proto-Indo-European root *sĕk-, meaning 'to cut', or 'section', or 'to dissect' (Pokorny, 1969, pp. 895–6). This solution is linked to the paleo-anthropological findings from the area, like the above-mentioned axes and knives. If *sĕk-, in *Sessame*, is interpreted as 'cutting tool', the toponym could have been linked to prehistoric stone axes and knives found in the area, and to the activity of cutting stone to produce tools. Those utensils, because of their nature and function, would be connected with woodwork-ing and hunting (and, as mentioned earlier, not with agriculture). *sĕk- would mean, in this case, 'to cut stone (to produce tool)', or 'to cut (wood)', or 'woodworking' (the stem generated words like the Latin verb *sĕcāre* 'to cut', or 'to cut off', Italian *segare* 'to cut with a saw', and the Ancient High German *sah* 'knife'), which can show how the lexicon (and place names) of Indo-European languages embedded the notion of cutting stone to produce tools and to use those stone tools to chop wood or other objects.

2. the Proto-Indo-European root *sag-, meaning 'to seek', or 'to track', or 'trail', or 'to follow a scent'. This is in connection with the flint arrowheads and knives found in the area of the *Bormida River* near *Sessame*. *sag- is at the origins of a number of words such as the terms for 'thunderbolt' in Breton, *saez* or *seaz*, in Welsh, *saeth*, in Latin, *sagitta*, and in Italian, *saetta*. All these words mean or have clear links to 'arrow' (Pokorny, 1969, pp. 876–7). The root *sag- could also be the stem of the name of *Sagunto*, a historical town located in eastern *Spain*, in the province of *Valencia*.

This case study provides an example of how historical toponomastics might proceed through the collection of available data on a toponym using both written records or visual sources, like maps (whose dates of publication might give us a window on what the toponym was known as in the distant past), before combining linguistic and extra-linguistic analyses of a place name. The linguistic analysis involves studying the roots and proto-forms of the toponym and an in-depth literature review of how other scholars have explained the denomination and have tried to reconstruct its roots and proto-forms. Yet, it is imperative that we do not simply believe what other scholars, or even locals, state or write about a place name. What is important, besides the etymological study, is to look for extra-linguistic clues provided by the contexts of historical geography, landscape archaeology, and paleo-anthropology. These disciplines help the scholar to investigate the links between the linguistic aspects of a place name and the physical and/or human landscape. Simultaneously, the toponymist can investigate if, in the same area, there are any other places with the same possible root and if they can be part of a common toponymic system. Then all the information from linguistics, history, geography, landscape archaeology, and paleo-anthropology is pieced together before proposing a possible reconstruction or supporting elements of an existing hypothesis about the origins of the place name.

### 3.4.2    Squaneto

Another example of how a multidisciplinary approach leads to new ways of analysing the etymology of place names can be seen in the case study of *Squaneto* (cf. Chapter 1). *Squaneto* is a hamlet of the *Spigno Monferrato* village, located in northwest *Italy*, lower *Piedmont*, in the province of *Alessandria* (Figure 3.2). The reconstruction of this place name has proven to be somewhat problematic. Two possible etymological processes, based on the restitution of plausible historical-phonetic sequences, reconstruct the place name in a way that translates into 'territory renowned for flowers'[1] and 'pasture of the flowers' trail'[2] (Perono Cacciafoco, 2014).

At this point, it is important to highlight a very interesting aspect of naming that we need to keep in mind. If people need water, and the main feature of a particular area is water, these people will probably name the area using 'water' as the main part of the place name. This is, at least, what happened in prehistoric times, when the primary natural goods were indispensable to prehistoric peoples for their survival, and the place names were not only names, but represented 'directions' for the orientation and access to primary goods in the mental (unwritten and undrawn) map that those peoples had of their territories. This is because the priorities of the earliest settlers would have been to develop and give specific names to places with food, water, and other vital necessities. Such directional indicators enabled them to survive and orientate themselves to places with resources (i.e., places to go) and dangers (i.e., places to avoid), and would constitute what is known as one of the most important components of the original 'naming process' in prehistoric times (Facchini et al., 1993). In a second stage, when people are already organised in primordial societies and have relatively safe access to water and other primary

---

[1]  A detailed reconstruction, kindly provided by Dr Guido Borghi, is as follows. Indo-European *$skuto$-$h_1yah_2no$-$peiHtu$-$s* 'pasture of the flowers' trail' > Celtic *$skutaanoeetus$ > Latin *$Scutanoetus$ > dialect *Squanèi* = *Squaneto* = 'territory renowned for flowers'.

[2]  A more detailed reconstruction, also kindly provided by Dr Guido Borghi, is as follows. Indo-European *$skutah_{2/4}$ > Celtic *$skutaa$* > m. Irl. Scoth. f. 'spike' (root *$skeut$- 'to cut'), *$h1yah_2no$-$s* > Celt. *$jaanos$ > Irl. a:n 'noble' (root *$h1yah_{2/4}$- 'to go'), *$peiHtu$-$s* > Celt. *$eetus$ > Irl. iath. 'territory, pasture' (root *$peiH$- 'to feed') = *Squaneto* = 'pasture of the flowers' trail'.

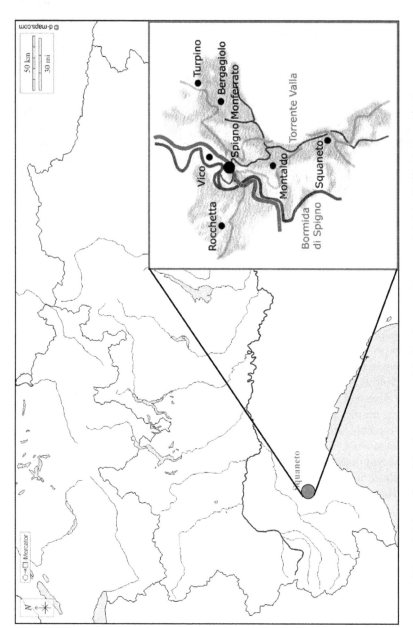

Figure 3.2 Location of the *Squaneto* municipality (sources: Comune di Spigno, 2004; d-maps, 2021)

goods, they may 'intellectualise' the landscape and produce 'descriptive interpretations' of places. What this means is that, because people's basic needs
have been met, they then choose a name that describes the (possible) beauty of
a place or that highlights features that are not directly connected with the
primary goods that are found in that locality. In this sense, place names given
by prehistoric people within primordial organised societies are indicatively less
ancient than place names given by prehistoric people from more remote times,
when survival was the main, if not the only, aim.

The two reconstructions of *Squaneto* as 'territory renowned for flowers' and
'pasture of the flowers' trail' appear to belong to the 'second stage' of the
naming process; they describe the landscape in 'poetic' terms and highlight
aesthetic features of the territory. This could mean that the toponym is ancient,
but not connected with the first stage of the naming process, as it implies an
'intellectualisation' of the landscape, by describing the beauty and features of
the place, and is not connected with the primary goods needed for survival.
Thus, if we try to trace back a more ancient and original explanation for the
name, the related reconstruction will most probably yield simpler lexical and
conceptual referents linked to primary goods. The sequences reported above
were carried out purely at an etymological level and did not take into account
any analysis of the hydro-geo-morphology of the territory. A more comprehensive approach, as outlined in this chapter, would include a thorough examination of the physical morphology of the areas under investigation. This would
allow us to link a place name to its landscape (see also the discussion of
*Borgomale*, later in this chapter), and even to ascertain whether dramatic
hydro-geo-physical changes, for example, a flood or an earthquake, occurred
in the past (Ucko & Layton, 2005).

Taking all this into account, we know that *Squaneto* is located on a ford of the
*Valla* stream. The *Valla* stream, in turn, is a tributary of the *Bormida River*,
flowing nearby. This ford has always played an important territorial role in the
area, possibly already from the Upper Palaeolithic, as it allowed people (and
goods) to cross from one side of the *Valla* (a stream which is difficult to cross
elsewhere) to the other, an importance that would definitely have been valued
in prehistoric times, when survival in a hostile environment was of the essence.
The *Valla* creek was indispensable to the Stone Age inhabitants of the small
valley, therefore, both because the watercourse was a source of good water and
because the ford was a safe and strategic place to found a village. A plausible
assumption deriving from these considerations would be to interpret the
inhabited centre of *Squaneto* as a *vicus ad aquam* 'water place', and to
hypothesise that the place was named after the notion of 'water', as this was
the salient feature of the place in the ideal, mental map of the prehistoric people
living in the area. This, indeed, would have been the case even before the
arrival of the Indo-Europeans in *Europe* (see Chapter 4). This close connection

with water, in turn, would be encased in the place name. Hence, another possible reconstruction, based on the assessment of the hydro-geo-morphological features of the place, in conjunction with an alternative etymo-logical analysis, can be proposed.

The new etymological analysis begins with a parsing, or segmentation, of the toponym and an attempt to account for all its components: *s-qua-n-eto*.

The *-n-* can be interpreted as a euphonic particle inserted by the local speakers possibly to avoid the difficulty or ambiguity in pronunciation due to the proximity of two vowels producing a hiatus (Perono Cacciafoco, 2014). This feature, with others, is representative of the complicated and multifaceted processes of language change, where the original form and meaning of a place name might be lost and local speakers add parts to the morphology of the toponym to relate it to other more 'transparent' names in their linguistic system, or 'contemporary' lexicon, or to better match the features of the local dialect(s). The suffix *-eto* is common in many Italian place names and indicates, seman-tically, a 'place' or a 'village'. It comes from Latin *-etum*, referring to the notion of 'place'. The Italian forms *-eto* and its Latin antecedent *-etum* are suffixes, productive for phytonymic 'collectives'. They generally refer to 'woods'. Over time, in Italian toponymy, *-eto* lost, semantically, the basic connection with 'woods' and started to indicate 'place' or 'village'. At the level of semantic content, therefore, Latin *-etum*, does refer also to 'grove', but this is not common in Italian toponomastics for the derived suffix *-eto*. Indeed, there are many examples of Italian (< Latin) place names, such as *Noceto* (< *Nocetum*) or *Pruneto* / *Prunet(t)o* (< *Prunetum*), surely connected with trees, but that do not refer directly to 'groves'. *Noceto* and *Prunet(t)o* have probably never repre-sented 'groves', in their diachronic toponymic development, although they are connected with the notions of 'walnut trees' (Italian *noce*, masculine = 'walnut tree') or 'plum trees' (Italian *pruno* = 'plum tree', also 'blackthorn'). Indeed, *Nocetum* > *Noceto* is not 'walnut grove', but 'walnut village/place' or 'village of the walnut trees', and *Prunetum* > *Prunet(t)o* is not 'plum (or blackthorn) grove', but 'plum (or blackthorn) village/place' or 'village of the plum trees/ village of the blackthorns'. Originally and at the ideal level, they may have been villages characterized by the presence of those trees. However, despite the presence of trees and the references to trees in the names, the suffix *-eto* (< *-etum*), means, in this context, 'place' or 'village'. Therefore, throughout the manuscript, we utilise *-etum* > *-eto* to indicate 'place' in Italian place names, which is the widespread toponymic use of the suffix in Italian.

If we accept the argument made earlier, according to which the place was named after something connected with an indispensable natural resource, that is, water, then a possible derivation for the *\*-qua-* component of the *Squaneto* denomination can be from one of the Proto-Indo-European stems for 'water', precisely, *$ak^w$-. This is the root from which Latin *aqua*, Italian *acqua*, French *eau*, Spanish *agua*, among others, derive from.

If this is the case, accounting for the initial *$s$- of the place name constitutes the biggest morphological issue, because the consonant is in the 'root position', but, according to this reconstruction, it would not be part of the root. This problem has been and is a source of controversy in the field. It is possible to try to segment the root of the place name, *$squa$-, as *$s$-$ak^w$-$(a)$-, which seems to give a clear match with the Indo-European root *$ak^w$-$(a)$- and provides a simple and effective etymological explanation. However, the segmentation of the *$squa$- root as *$s$-$ak^w$-$(a)$- is not conventional and does not take into account, in this case, the importance of the consonant, *$s$-, which is in the root position. As a matter of fact, a root like *$squa$- should, conventionally, be analysed as if it were a single morphemic unit including its first element. It should, therefore, be segmented as *$sakwa$- (or *$sak^wa$-). However, separating the initial *$s$- and considering it as a 'juxtaposed consonant' allows us to hypothesise *$ak^w$-$(a)$- as the root of the toponym, which seems convincing and solves the issue of the etymological obscurity of the place name. Nonetheless, as mentioned, it is not conventional and is problematic at the historical-phonetic and historical-phonological levels. Indeed, an approach considering the possible historical-phonetic nature of the denomination would not 'cut' a consonant from the root, that is, *$s$-, and would consider the stem as *$sakwa$- (or *$sak^wa$-) and not as *$s$-$ak^w$-$(a)$-. To be clearer, the segmentation process allows the solving of many etymological issues, but it is risky (and sometimes arbitrary), in that it cannot provide accurate and plausible historical-phonetic and historical-phonological reconstructions. It is, therefore, by definition, an experimental method.

An explanation of *$s$-, which, as outlined above, is not universally accepted, is that it was possibly added by speakers in a time more recent than the original naming process and, therefore, it could be defined as a 'juxtaposed consonant', probably derived from linguistic 'overlapping' due to the misunderstanding of the original form and meaning of the place name by local speakers over time. The 'overlapping' is produced by the speakers themselves, in an attempt to link the name to the phonology or morphology of the local language/dialect in a specific moment in time, when locals need to explain the place name but have lost the direct knowledge of its origins. The explanation postulating a 'juxtaposed consonant' has a parallel in Italian etymology, with several examples of this phenomenon from the general lexicon of the Italian language. For instance, the Italian word for 'sword', *spada*, provides an example of a lexeme in which the apparent root consonant, *$s$-, is not properly the root consonant in itself. The Italian term *spada* (French *épée*, Provençal, Catalan, Portuguese, and Spanish *espada*) comes from Latin *spátha*, equivalent to Ancient Greek σπάθη (*spáthē*) ~ Modern Greek σπαθί (*spathí*), possibly from proto-Ellenic *$spát^hā$. All these forms come, in turn, from the Indo-European proto-form $*ph_2\text{-}d^hh_1\text{-}éh_2 \sim *(s)ph_2\text{-}d^hh_1\text{-}éh_2$, which comes from the root $*peh_2$ $\sim *(s)peh_2\text{-}$, meaning 'to draw', plus $*d^heh_1\text{-}$, 'to put', 'to do', plus a feminine ending, $*\text{-}eh_2$. The $*s\text{-}$ component, in the original stem, is presumably not the root consonant, which, conversely, should be $*p\text{-}$, and does not directly constitute an original morphological element of the word. Nonetheless, over time, the same $*s\text{-}$ component in the beginning of the forms for 'sword' has become widespread (and 'accepted' as a non-original root consonant) and has been used by speakers to pronounce the attested lexemes in the above-mentioned Indo-European languages (even in French, where its 'absence' can be easily explained) (Beekes, 2010). The same etymological reconstruction can be applied to the Italian words for 'spatula', *spatola*, and 'brush', *spazzola*. Both derive from *spáthula*, a Latin derivative of *spátha*, and, as we discussed for 'sword', *spada*, above, the $*s\text{-}$ component was added, in their morphology, at a much later time than their original roots in Proto-Indo-European. If, as argued above, *Squaneto* can be considered a *vicus ad aquam*, it is possible to postulate that the initial $*s\text{-}$ of the place name could have had a similar origin.

A visual representation of the naming process could, therefore, be as follows:

$$Squaneto = s\text{-}qua\text{-}n\text{-}eto$$
$$\downarrow$$

$$Squa\text{-} = s \text{-} qua = s\text{-}qua \qquad\qquad < \qquad\qquad *s\text{-} + *ak^{W}a = *sak^{W}a$$
$$\downarrow$$
$$*sak^{W}a$$
$$\downarrow$$

$$*s\text{-} + \;\; \rightarrow \;\; *sak^{W}a\text{-} \;\; \rightarrow \;\; *sakua\text{-} \;\; \rightarrow \;\; *saqua\text{-} \;\; \rightarrow \;\; *s(a)qua\text{-} \;\; \rightarrow \;\; *squa$$
$$*ak^{W}a\text{-}$$
$$\downarrow$$

$$*squa\text{-} (< *s\text{-} + *ak^{W}\text{-}/ak^{W}a) + \text{-}n\text{-} + \text{-}eto\ (< \text{Latin } \text{-}etum) = squa\text{-}n\text{-}eto$$
$$\downarrow$$
$$Squaneto\ (< *s\text{-}ak^{W}a\text{-}n\text{-}eto)$$

The etymological connection of *Squaneto* with the Indo-European root $*ak^{W}\text{-}$ (which gave origin, among others, to the Latin form *aqua*) seems also to be corroborated by attested variants of the place name in Late/Medieval Latin. At those times, *Squaneto* was known as *Exaquanetum* (*ex-aqua-n-etum*) and *Subaquanetum* (*sub-aqua-n-etum*), showing a clear presence of *aqua* ($< *ak^{W}\text{-}$), 'water', preceded by the prepositions *ex-* 'from' and *sub-* 'under', 'beneath', which could provide a morphological support for the initial $*s\text{-}$ – $*ex\text{-} > *(e)x\text{-} > *x\text{-} > (*cs\text{-}) > (*[c]s\text{-}) > *s\text{-}$ and/or $*sub\text{-} > *su(b)\text{-} > *s(u)\text{-} > *s\text{-}$ of the Italian toponym, *Squaneto*, or which could represent a reinterpretation of the place name in Late Roman and/or Medieval times. Both forms, *Exaquanetum* and *Subaquanetum*, could be considered as two *ex post* explanations or paretymological attempts by speakers to connect, in the way they pronounced it, the place name with new phonological features of their changing language (possibly in the stage between Vernacular Latin and Archaic Italian) and could show how an *s- element (here represented by the addition of the prepositions *ex* and *sub*), which did not belong to the original root (*$ak^W$-) or to the original proto-type in *aqua-* of the place name (*aquanetum*), was added to try to make sense of the toponym and/or to 'make' it closer to the 'current' (in those times) pronunciation. This change was implemented without completely losing the connection with the notion of 'water' (*aqua*), because the preposition *ex* indicates movement from one place ('from') and the preposition *sub* a position/location under/beneath something, in this case 'from water' or 'under water', or, specifically, 'from the water place (*ex-aquanetum*)' or 'under the water place (*sub-aquanetum*)', a possible reference to the ford and occasional floods. Therefore, both Latin forms would have been still connected with the notion of 'water' and the interpretation of the place as a *vicus ad aquam*. Two prepositions like these, in any case, are evidently not original parts of a possible root, but are used as 'prefixes' and are later and/or paretymological additions to a more original and more ancient form which, in the case of *Squaneto*, is closely linked to the notion of 'water' and to the Indo-European stem *$ak^W$- (Bosio, 1972).

It is also useful to highlight the fact that *Squaneto* is not the only Italian place name showing this possible phenomenon affecting the root. *Squagiato* and *Saquana* are the names of two villages located in the same geographical area. If we accept that they share the same possible etymology (outlined above), they form, with *Squaneto*, a local toponymic system (cf. Chapter 1). *Saquana*, in fact, could represent a sort of intermediate form in this possible 'toponymic chain', because it preserves, in its current, contemporary morphology, the type *(-)aqua-*, 'water', preceded by *s-*, which is, evidently, a 'juxtaposed consonant'. The *s-* is, in all probability, a late phonetic and morphological addition, and is not a 'root consonant'. *Saquana* (*s-aqua-na* or *s-aqua-n-a*) is a sort of 'fossil evidence' of the fact that both *Squaneto* and *Squagiato* may originate etymologically from the proto-type *aqua-* (< *$ak^W$-*), in forms which we can segment as *s-(a)qua-n-eto* and *s-(a)qua-giato*. Moreover, while the ending of *Squaneto* is clearly represented by -*etum* (> -*eto*, 'place', 'village'), *Squagiato*'s ending should come from the root *$h_2ag$'*-, 'to lead' ~ *$h_1yah_2tu$-s* > Celtic *jaatus* > Irish *a:th*, 'ford' (< root *$h1yah_{2/4}$-*, 'to go'), which would describe perfectly the nature of these villages, 'water places' located on a ford.

Moreover, this approach may also help to explain another problematic toponym from the same geographical area. *Spigno* is the name of a village located in northwest *Italy*, *Piedmont*, in the province of *Alessandria*, not far from *Squaneto*. There are claims according to which *Spigno* derives from Latin *spineus* 'thorny' (from Latin *spina* 'thorn'), in reference to the possible existence of 'thorny bushes' dotting its territory. However, this is a false reconstruction, or a paretymological explanation, which connects the origins of the place name with a Latin linguistic layer and with an 'easy' referent, not taking into account the most ancient *strata* of the toponym. *Spigno* is a very ancient village (the settlement dates back at least to the Neolithic) located on the *Bormida River*, along which also *Squaneto* is situated, and, thus, should be considered a *vicus ad aquam* 'water place'. An assessment and analysis of the hydro-geo-morphology of the territory could suggest, therefore, to connect the toponym with the Indo-European root *\*ang-/\*-agn-* 'water', or 'flowing water' (cf. Chapter 7). Similar to the challenge we highlighted with *Squaneto*, several issues need to be accounted for. If we segment *Spigno* as *\*s-p-agn*, the 'p' could have been added for euphonic or paretymological reasons, that is, to avoid vocalic mispronunciation or to 'model' the place name on the late referents *spineus* and *spina*. The raising of the low and central vowel, /a/, in the possible root *\*-agn-*, to a frontal and high vowel, /i/, as attested in *Spigno*, may be a result of the phonetic and phonological changes produced by the local speakers, to assimilate the form to their dialect. Finally, the operation of separating the initial *\*s-* from the possible root and considering it, as we did for *Squaneto*, as a 'juxtaposed consonant' allows us to hypothesise *\*agn-* as the main root. This etymological reconstruction is highly experimental and would need further evidence and discussion, but allows the restitution of a surely prehistoric name for a prehistoric village, to overcome the simplistic interpretation of the toponym as originally Latin.

All in all, these etymological reconstructions show not only how the place name *Squaneto* has undergone language change, but, perhaps more importantly, how an analysis of the hydro-geo-morphology of the territory, combined with the etymological reconstruction, might unveil, or at least suggest, *Squaneto*'s nature of *vicus ad aquam* and the importance of 'water' in its naming process. This reconstruction would match up both with linguistic requirements and with the analysis of the landscape and would also be consistent with the earliest stages of the naming process of places by humans, one which is connected with possibly the most important primary good for survival, 'water'. However, this reconstruction also highlights some of the challenges facing us in the journey towards the achievement of the final etymological results, such as taking into account the possibility of the existence of 'juxtaposed (root) consonants', which would not have been an integral and original part of toponymic stems and are still the subject of heated debate.

The example used a historical-toponomastics lens to reconstruct the place name *Squaneto* and aimed to show that a more effective analytical strategy, in etymological reconstruction, involves the adoption of a multidisciplinary approach that is much more capable of shedding light on place names than the approaches relying on linguistic elements only. However, as pointed out, this is not without its challenges.

## 3.5     Dealing with Paretymologies in Historical Toponomastics

It is worth cautioning that, in the study of toponyms, scholars often come across accompanying stories from local speakers behind the toponyms, which generally carry within their paretymologies traditional contents and 'fanciful' explanations for the origins of the place names. We must be wary of the presence of such paretymologies, which on the one hand can add complexity and stratigraphy to the toponyms, but on the other can derail any attempt at an accurate etymological reconstruction.

Toponymic paretymologies, or the linguistic misinterpretations of place names, occur when the original morphology and/or the original meaning of toponyms are lost. After this loss, local speakers tend to reconstruct the etymology of a toponym on the basis of their local linguistic variety, or on the basis of lexemes that belong to their contemporary dialect or language. In other words, not being historical linguists and not having the linguistic competence to allow them to go through the different developmental stages of their language or of the languages that were spoken in their area before their current language, local speakers try to give a linguistic reason for names of places, which have become obscure and impenetrable to them. They do so by looking for analogical forms in their common and contemporary lexicon, or by referring (when not generating them) to local oral-traditional stories which could explain the legendary or meta-historical origins of the names of these places. This kind of paretymology is defined as *bona fide* paretymology, because it is generally unbiased, and the only genuine aim by the local speakers is to provide an explanation for their place names. When, conversely, the etymology is produced because scholars have not accounted for all the historical evidence or the lack of evidence to support their claim, or perhaps because they may have ulterior motives or biases – that is, to 'ennoble' a place or to 'belittle' it by enhancing or decreasing local 'prestige', to provide false evidence for a genealogy, for example, by connecting a place name with a family name, to remove references to previous inhabitants, to tendentiously prove linguistic or academic theories, or to flatter powerful people – this paretymology, which is generally produced by scholars or erudite people, is called scholarly paretymology.

In general, then, toponymic paretymology happens when the original meaning of a place name has been lost over time. The speakers, therefore, try to find a parallelism in the sounds or the meaning, for that place name, in the language they currently use, without going back in time to previous linguistic stages and without having the knowledge necessary to do that. This kind of phenomenon is due, generally, to a change in the population (through immigration or invasion) or to the loss of the original morphology and/or original meaning of the place name due to (internal) language change over time (cf. Chapter 2). In this section (and see also the example of *Pareto* in Chapter 5), we will detail two cases of toponymic paretymology. The first is an example of a scholarly paretymology. The second is of a *bona fide* paretymology.

### 3.5.1 Franciacorta

The Italian place name *Franciacorta*, from *Lombardy*, north-central *Italy*, in the province of *Brescia*, provides a good example of how speakers, and even scholars, might misinterpret the etymology of a toponym. The popular belief on *Franciacorta* stems from its literal and transparent meaning. In Italian, *Franciacorta* literally means 'short' (from the Italian word *corta*) and *France* (*Francia* is the Italian name for the country of *France*). Its first attestation probably dates back to 1277, in the *Statuta Communis Civitatis Brixiae* (Odorici, 1856, pp. 258, 324; Valentini, 1898, pp. 5, 98). However, the place is located in *Italy*, and, being a territory with a significant number of cities, towns, villages, and hamlets, the usage of 'short', as a spatial indicator, is not applicable. Speakers, therefore, after having lost the knowledge of the origins and original meaning of the denomination, were soon puzzled by the name, and sought to explain the denomination via linking it to either 'short Frenchmen' or to someone with ties to *France* having stayed in the area for a short time.

Researchers themselves produced scholarly paretymologies when they engaged in forced interpretations of the origins of *Franciacorta* and of its original meaning. One such explanation for *Franciacorta* was offered by Jacopo Malvezzi, a fifteenth-century doctor and historiographer from *Brescia*. Malvezzi proposed that the name *Franciacorta* was coined after a pseudo-historical event connected with Charles the Great,[3] the emperor of the Holy Roman Empire, who was also known as *Charlemagne* or *Carlo Magno* (Rampoldi, 1833, pp. 117–18; Sabatti, 1807, pp. 73–6). In 774, Charles the Great and his Frankish army invaded *Italy* and entered *Lombardy* to fight against the Lombards. They then established a base at *Rodengo Saiano*, a village located within the territory of *Franciacorta*. According to the above-mentioned historian, on the eve of a Parisian religious festival, the feast day of St Denis, which Charles the Great had previously promised to spend in *Paris*, he proclaimed, '*questa terra è una piccola Francia*' ('This land is a small *France*'), so that he and his army could spend the festive day on 'French' soil.

---

[3] Charles the Great (748–814) was king of the Franks (a Germanic people who invaded the Western Roman Empire in the fifth century) and, among others, defeated the Lombards (a Germanic population who ruled a large area of the Italian peninsula between the sixth and eighth centuries). Under his rule, the majority of territories in *West* and *Central Europe* were united under what was known as the Carolingian Empire, or the Holy Roman Empire. Parts of his empire formed the basis of *France* and *Germany* today.

In this case, *piccola* 'small' would be the equivalent of *corta* 'short' and, hence, the 'small *France*' as proclaimed by Charles the Great would be the 'short *France*' that *Franciacorta* is parsed as. This paretymology, while sticking to a historical fact that Charles the Great and the Franks came to the *Brescia* territory, is speculative, because there are no historical sources attesting Charles the Great making this proclamation.

Another scholarly paretymology of *Franciacorta* involves Charles I of *Anjou* (Rampoldi, 1833, pp. 117–18; Sacchi, 1852, pp. 115–17; Odorici, 1856, pp. 181–2). The Italian writer Gabriele Rosa reports that Charles I of *Anjou* and his French troops entered *Italy* and passed through *Lombardy* on the way to fight Manfred, king of *Sicily*, in 1265. The troops settled down and rested in the area of *Rovato*, a village in the *Franciacorta* area. Locals and scholars alike believe that the French upset the women of the surrounding villages, resulting in a riot by the local people (Odorici, 1856; Cocchetti, 1859; Cantù, 1858; Racheli, 1894). The inhabitants of *Rovato* and its nearby villages, like *Erbusco* and *Capriolo*, rebelled against the soldiers of Charles of *Anjou*, shouting '*Francese fuori! Qui la Francia sarà corta!*' ('Out with the French! Here French rule will be short!'). Charles I of Anjou and his troops were driven out by the insurrection. The 'short' in this quote, and by extension the 'short' in 'Short France'/*Franciacorta*, refers to the short period of occupation by the French of the *Franciacorta* territory and is directly attributed to the exclamation by the local insurrectionists. Like for the previous paretymology, there is no historical evidence to prove the credibility of this rebellion and of the French being driven out by a local popular insurrection.

While taking note of how locals and some scholars explain the meaning and origins of the place name, it is crucial to take into account only what can be historically and officially documented and only the records that are available to us. Even when these resources do not provide all the evidence necessary to completely solve the puzzle, nonetheless, they can offer to us verified elements, which help to shed light on all the different facts and perspectives. In the case of *Franciacorta*, historical maps and especially local official documents, such as notarial deeds, acts of donations to local abbeys, and historical chronicles that date back to the High Middle Ages (from 1000 to 1250 CE), provide us with a relatively clear picture of both the physical landscape and the human activities of the territory and its borders. An analysis of these records shows us that *Franciacorta* could actually derive from the expression *curtes francae* 'carriage-free/duty free courts' (Guerrini, 1969, pp. 814, 880; 1986, p. 168). Indeed, around the eighth century, the *Brescia* area, where *Franciacorta* is located, was the residence of Benedictine and Cluniac monks. These monks had significant religious power and social prestige, and were responsible for overseeing and cultivating the surrounding lands. These lands were generally exempted from tax payments by the political rulers of *Brescia*. *Franciacorta*, as a territory, was part of these lands exempted from paying local taxes and it was, therefore, a *franca curtis*, a 'duty-free court'. To explain the present-day morphology, we need to see that it is indeed a paretymology. In this case, the 'use' and 'nature' of *franca curtis* or *curtis franca* were lost to the local people and they no longer connected the place with a 'duty-free court', but with the commonly known country *Francia* 'France' and the adjective *corta* 'short'. We also know that, in Italian, *Franciacorta* 'sounds' much better than *\*CortaFrancia*. Therefore, for the local speakers, it was no longer *franca curtis* or *curtis franca*, but *Franciacorta*.

### 3.5.2  Borgomale

An analysis of the place name *Borgomale*, the denomination of a small village located in northwest *Italy*, southern *Piedmont*, in the *Cuneo* province (Figure 3.3), is a good example of how disciplines outside linguistics can be used to analyse not only the etymology of the name, but also the historical, cultural, and landscape changes that have happened over time in a territory. The place name *Borgomale* can be broken down, in Italian, into *borgo* 'village', or 'hamlet', and *male* 'bad', or 'evil'. This is why the village is currently known as the 'bad village', or 'village of evil'. Inhabitants of the village had difficulties to accept this 'bad name' and had to look for possible explanations for it. Some of them say that the denomination came about because, in the past, the villagers were evil and the village was punished by God. They try to provide a religious or historical reason connected with the 'punishment by God' by making reference to how the population in *Borgomale* almost disappeared during the different waves of the Black Death and has remained very small ever since. However, an investigation of records kept by the local churches (in *Italy*, churches normally preserve historical records of births and deaths in their localities, and this practice can be traced back at least to the Middle Ages) shows that the number of inhabitants in the village has, in fact, historically been stable and, in contrast to what the inhabitants believe, did not vary even during the various waves of the Black Death. It is, therefore, clear that despite the local speakers' attempt to motivate it historically, this explanation for the name is a *bona fide* paretymology.

Taking a look at the emblem and/or coat of arms of *Borgomale* (which dates back to the Middle Ages[4]) (see Figure 3.3), we see a row of trees on a hill. A more detailed scrutiny of historical records connected with the territory

[4] The Middle Ages lasted approximately from the fifth century to the late fifteenth century (from 476 CE, the collapse of the Western Roman Empire, to 1492 CE, the 'discovery' of *America* by Christopher Columbus).

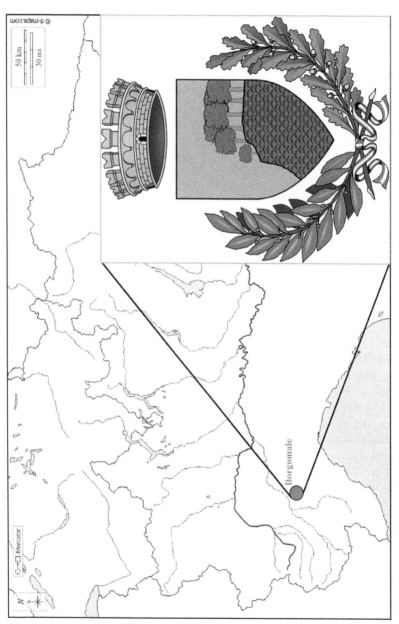

Figure 3.3  Position and coat of arms of the *Borgomale* municipality (adapted from d-maps, 2021; Vale93b, 2019)

reveals that apple orchards have existed in *Borgomale* and the surrounding area since the Middle Ages and even in the Modern Age.[5] In relatively recent times, all the hills have been planted with grape vines, and the extensive change in the agricultural landscape has contributed to the loss of the memory that the apple trees and apple orchards were once cultivated locally. If we assume that, indeed, the trees depicted on the coat of arms of the village are apple trees, this gives us a more transparent reason for the place name, one which accounts for this fact, as well as the linguistic changes the name underwent (both in terms of its morphology and meaning).

Why is a village with apple trees called 'bad village', or 'village of evil'? Surely, there is more to how the villagers explain the place name. The answer, after our analysis of the coat of arms and the historical records attesting apple trees in the area, can be found by looking at the linguistic elements of the toponym.

We can start by analysing the Latin and Italian forms of both *borgo* and *male*. The Italian *borgo* comes from the Latin *burgus* 'village', or 'hamlet', while the Italian *male* comes from the Latin *mālum* (genitive *māli*) 'evil'. Further linguistic analysis, however, shows that the Italian *male* can be traced back to two forms of the Latin word *malum*, differentiated only by the length of the vowel /a/. One is the Latin word *mălum* (pronounced with the short vowel *ă*), which means 'bad', or 'evil'. The corresponding Italian forms are *male* (noun, 'evil') and *malo* (adjective, 'bad'). The other form is the Latin *mālum* (pronounced with the long vowel *ā*), and means 'apple', or 'apple tree'. Its corresponding forms in Italian are *mela* 'apple', and *melo* 'apple tree'. Therefore, in this case, in the passage between Late Latin and Vernacular Italian, the Latin /ă/ became the Italian /a/, *mălum* > *male/malo*, while the Latin /ā/ became the Italian /e/, *mālum* > *melo/mela*.

As mentioned above, the name *Borgomale* is traditionally (and wrongly) believed to have come from the Latin expression *Burgus Mali* 'village of evil'. However, as we explained above, a study of historical documents, such as the emblem of the municipality and the church records, as well as an analysis of elements of the historical landscape, revealed the existence of apple orchards in *Borgomale* since the Middle Ages. This, together with an indispensable linguistic analysis of the name, allowed us to conclude that, since apple orchards were documented in *Borgomale*'s territory in the past, it can be proven that *Borgomale* came from the Latin *Burgus Māli* 'village of the apple tree', or 'village of the apple'. The correct reconstructed form in modern Italian should, therefore, be *\*Borgomelo*, or *\*Borgo Melo* 'the village of the apple tree'.

---

[5] The Modern Age lasted from the end of the Middle Ages to the beginning of the nineteenth century (from 1492 CE, the 'discovery' of *America* by Christopher Columbus, to 1815, the end of the Congress of *Vienna*).

The reason why it was re-coined by local speakers, in the passage between Late Latin and Vernacular Italian, as *Borgomale* 'bad village', or 'village of evil', is due to the fact that the local speakers had lost the quantitative nature of the vowels in Latin (Latin is a quantitative language, at the level of vowels, while Italian, despite being a neo-Latin language, is not appreciably quantitative in its vowels), in particular of the phoneme /a/, which, in the passage between Latin and Italian, as described above, was treated differently according to the quantitative length of the vowel itself. This ingenerated the process producing the *Borgomale* false etymology/toponymic paretymology.

To be even more precise, to explain the possible misconstruction of the meaning of *Borgomale*, we need to understand that in Latin pronunciation plays an important role in distinguishing the meaning of words such as *malum*. However, as mentioned, this linguistic aspect of Latin was lost when Latin started its vernacular phase towards the neo-Latin stages and eventually evolved into the Romance languages of *Europe*, like Italian, which is spoken by the villagers of *Borgomale* today. Given that these villagers do not know Latin, they are unable to differentiate or perceive this difference in pronunciation and are, thus, unaware of the actual origins of the toponym. Therefore, they try to explain the place name through their limited linguistic competence, unaware of the evolution of Latin and its transition to Italian. To asseverate the reasons of the name, they even went as far as inventing the story of the Black Death to justify the association of 'bad' with the village (Perono Cacciafoco, Cavallaro, & Kratochvíl, 2015).

Several themes emerge from the toponymic case study of *Borgomale*. The first shows an example of paretymology in historical toponomastics. The current villagers of *Borgomale*, in order to explain the place name, having lost the original link of the toponym to Latin *mālum* 'apple', or 'apple tree', reinterpreted its semantics and invented an oral-traditional story about the Black Death that nearly exterminated the entire village. This led the village to be known as the 'bad village', or 'village of evil'. The second and more important insight from this example in historical toponomastics is how linguistics intersects with other disciplines to reconstruct the etymology of place names. Through historical-linguistic and historical-phonetic knowledge, we understand that Latin has different vocalic quantities than Italian, and this quantitative difference affects the meaning of words (Perono Cacciafoco, 2015a), a fact here witnessed by the two forms of *malum*, *mălum* (short vowel *ă*) and *mālum* (long vowel *ā*), which allowed the Latin speakers to distinguish the lexemes and their meanings. As the difference in vocalic quantity was lost in Italian, the two words were differentiated, always in Italian, by two independent vowels, /a/ and /e/, therefore *male* 'bad' or 'evil', and *mela* 'apple'. Such a small vocalic change can produce dramatic etymological and linguistic consequences.

In studying the etymology of *Borgomale*, we have drawn upon the landscape features of the municipality, specifically investigating what trees/crops were grown and are growing there. At the same time historical aspects connected with the human settlement were also examined. This was done by searching through local historical records, such as church documents that recorded births and deaths in the community over time, and the coat of arms of *Borgomale*. All these steps were taken with the objective of correlating the relationship of the toponym and its meaning to the environmental and anthropic features of the territory of *Borgomale*. In the process, we have been able to linguistically correct the toponymic paretymology put forth by the speakers and, indeed, reconstruct an accurate etymology of the place name.

### 3.5.3    Bailu Zhou, *'The Egret Island'*

Sources and documentation in historical toponomastics can come in many forms. In this section, we see how ancient maps, and even ancient poems, can serve as visual and written attestations of place names in their oldest forms. The example draws from the research of Xu (2016), which illustrates the historical toponymy and historical topography of two river islands, an older island located in the *Yangtze River* and another with the same name currently found in the *Qinhuai River*, both in the territory of *Nanjing*, the capital of *Jiangsu* province, southeast *China*. At the same time, this serves as an excellent case study on historical toponomastics in a non-Indo-European context, and of how paretymologies are not always and purely linguistic in nature.

In the southern part of *Nanjing*, there is a garden called *Bailu Zhou* 白鹭. It surrounds a river island with the same name, that is, *Bailu Zhou*, situated in the *Qinhuai River*, which is a tributary of the *Yangtze River*. An analysis of available written records, as the first step in historical toponymic methodology, shows that the island was mentioned already in the eighth century, when the famous Chinese poet Li Bai (701–762 CE) wrote a poem entitled *Deng Jin Ling Feng Huang Tai* 登金陵凤凰台 'The Phoenix Bird Tower'. In this poem, *Bailu Zhou* appears, as evidenced in the verse: *Er Shui Zhong Fen Bai Lu Zhou* 二水中分白鹭洲 'And the river divides in two streams, holding the *White Heron Island* between' (Obata, 1928, p. 114). The *White Heron Island* (白鹭洲) could be *Bailu Zhou*, and was the site that inspired Li Bai to compose this poem. It is worth noting, however, that, despite Shingeyoshi Obata's translation of *bailu* (Li, 1928) into 'white heron', a more accurate rendition of this Chinese word would be 'white egret' and, therefore, the place could be known as 'The Egret Island'.

An extra-linguistic analysis of the place name (the second step in historical-toponomastic methodology), however, tells us that the current *Bailu Zhou*, with the garden, is not the one mentioned in the poem. The island from the poem was located outside the *Jiang Dong Men* 江东门 gate, in *Nanjing*. This gate is known as 'The Gate at the East Side of the *Yangtze River*'. In other words, *Bailu Zhou*, in its most ancient form and location, was ubicated outside a gate of the *Yangtze River* rather than in the *Qinhuai River*, where the current *Bailu Zhou* is located. The extra-linguistic analysis, in this case, involved an in-depth search for and study of ancient maps, and Xu (2016) was able to find several such cartographic documents in Chen Yi's book on the historical geography of *Nanjing*, *Sunwu Du Jianye Tu* 孙吴都建邺图. The book has a historical map (see Figure 3.4a) of the capital city of the *Wu* Kingdom (229–280 CE), *Jianye*, which is one of the ancient names of *Nanjing* (Chen, 1516, p. 8). On this map, we find the earliest record of the ancient *Bailu Zhou*.

In a second historical map (Figure 3.4b) of *Jiankang* (another ancient name of *Nanjing*) in *Dongjin Du Jiankang Tu* 东晋都建康图, from the *Sun Wu* period (222–280 CE), the island appears to have expanded and is now very close to the riverbank (Chen, 1516, p. 22). This is due to the erosion of river sands on the banks of the watercourse and the accumulation of debris on the bank located in front of *Nanjing* (Xu, 2016, pp. 48–9). Figure 3.4c shows that, in another map from the *Song* period (960–1279 CE), the islet was part of a much larger island right against the riverbank, and a new island had formed close to where *Bailu Zhou* used to be. In yet another map from the *Ming* period (1368–1644 CE), shown in Figure 3.4d, we see that even the name of *Bailu Zhou* had disappeared (Chen, 1516, pp. 24–7).

The ancient *Bailu Zhou* remains more or less topographically constant until the *South Tang* Dynasty (937–976 CE), a conclusion that can, once again, be drawn through a study of historical maps. In the map representing *Jiankang* in the *Song* Dynasty (960–1279 CE), shown in Figure 3.4c, the island is divided into three constituents: *Bailu Zhou*, *Ruzhou Xiang* 汝州乡 'The Ruzhou County',[6] and *Shanyu Kou* 鳝鱼口 'The Eel Port' (Chen, 1516, p. 20). Finally, in the *Ming* Dynasty (1368–1644 CE), because of the geological process of debris accumulation, the island joined the riverbank to become a peninsula and was no longer in its original shape or form (Chen, 1516, p. 24) (see Figure 3.4d). In this map, the ancient *Bailu Zhou* is nowhere to be seen. The analysis of the historical maps of the area shows that *Bailu Zhou*, as stated in Li Bai's poem, was actually at a different place from the current location.

Turning our discussion back to the garden and island of *Bailu Zhou* that is located on the *Qinhuai River*, historical records show that the garden may have been one of the private gardens of Xu Da (1332–1385 CE), a famous general who lived during the *Ming* Dynasty. His son, Xu Huizu (1368–1407 CE),

---

[6] *Ruzhou* is a city in *Henan* province and lends its name to a district in *Bailu Zhou* during the *Song* Dynasty.

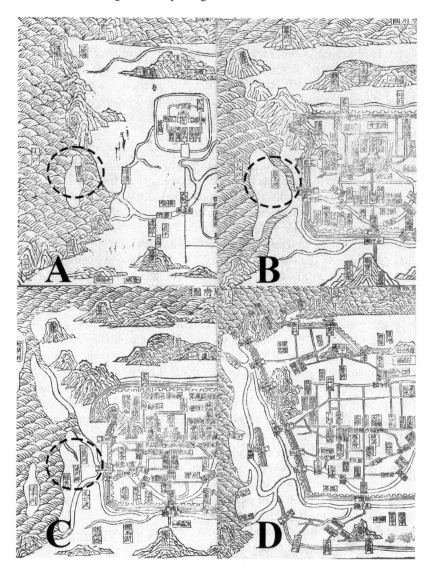

Figure 3.4 Historical maps showing the location of *Bailu Zhou* (adapted from Chen, 1516)

expanded the garden and named it *Dong Yuan* 'The East Garden', which became a popular meeting place for intellectuals and celebrities (see, for instance, Wang, 1577/1773, pp. 2–3). A study of the physical landscape of the current *Bailu Zhou* on the *Qinhuai River* shows the growth of reeds in the shallows around the island. These reeds attract egrets in the autumn season, a particular that explains how the island and its garden became associated with egrets. Furthermore, a visual analysis of modern maps of the province where *Bailu Zhou* is located shows a propensity to name places after local ornithonyms (i.e., names of birds, from Ancient Greek *órnis* [ὄρνις] 'bird', and *ónoma* [ὄνομα] 'name'). Examples of such toponyms are the oronym *Yanzi Ji* 燕子矶 'The Swallow's Promontory' on the *Yangtze River*, and a village in the western part of *Nanjing* called *Bailu* 'Egret'.

Today, *Bailu Zhou* on the *Qinhuai River* constitutes a prestigious resort which is well known for its natural scenery and its rich history, and its physical landscape appears to mirror the literary descriptions of the historic *Bailu Zhou* on the *Yangtze River*. For this reason, people connect it with the *Bailu Zhou* in Li Bai's poem. At the same time, locals and even the authorities behind the garden's restoration believe that the name was taken from Li Bai's poem. Evidence of this can be seen on signs from the 1930s found in the garden that state: *Qi Ming Chu Tai Bai Yi Shi* 其名出太白一诗 'The name comes from Li Bai's poem' (Xie & Xie, 2007, p. 221). We can guess, then, that the current island is not the original island, but was named by analogy and association with the *Bailu Zhou* islet on the *Yangtze River* in Li Bai's poem.

Several methodological themes emerge from the *Bailu Zhou* case study. The first concerns the use of written and visual sources in gathering data of place names. Xu (2016) shows that even ancient poetry can contain information about the names of places, coupled with evidence from the material landscape – in this case, that of wooden signs found in the garden. Such evidence can be utilised to postulate the original (and current) forms of the place names, explanations for the naming process, and even possible reasons for the transfer of the name from one island to another. The second theme involves the linguistic analysis of the name, and it shows how the *Bailu Zhou* in Li Bai's poem was explained as either a 'White Heron Island' or 'The Egret Island'. This name is supported by the real presence of egrets around the island. This evidence could only have been provided by an extra-linguistic analysis of the actual place through a field trip to the current site of the islet. The extra-linguistic analysis forms, indeed, the third theme in this research. As well as the fieldwork, Xu's study draws from Chen (1516), which contains numerous historical maps, which were utilised as primary sources. To sum up, by studying these maps in the *Sunwu Du Jianye Tu* 孙吴都建邺图, Xu (2016), as mentioned, reached the conclusion that the *Bailu Zhou* mentioned in Li Bai's poem was located outside *Jiang Dong Men* 江东门, a gate in *Nanjing*, whereas *Bailu Zhou* in its current form is located on the *Qinhuai River*.

We can consider this as an example of a particular type of toponymic paretymology. Normally, paretymology involves a 'misunderstanding', by contemporary speakers, of the original form and meaning of a place name.

We saw this in the *Borgomale* and the *Franciacorta* case studies above. These examples are linguistic in nature. The case of *Bailu Zhou*, instead, stems from the speakers' limited awareness of the hydro-geo-morphological processes and physical geography of the area and their misunderstanding inherent in the location of the original *Bailu Zhou*, which has since disappeared. Due to the flow of the river, soil erosion, and other hydro-geo-morphological processes, *Bailu Zhou* shifted, over time, towards the mouth of the watercourse. These changes can be inferred by studying historical maps such as those in Figure 3.4. *Bailu Zhou* eventually changed its shape and position, reaching a point where it joined with the riverbank, and the original shape and structure of the island is now no longer observable, leading speakers to confuse other islands that they can see for the island that they know through Li Bai's ancient poem, and, thereby, mistakenly transferring the name of the ancient *Bailu Zhou* to an island on the *Qinhuai River*. In this sense, toponymic paretymology might not always be purely linguistic in nature, but it can be, as it were, 'geographic' and 'geological' as well. As previously mentioned, it is only through a holistic approach that accounts for not just the linguistic elements but also the historical geography and landscape archaeology of a territory that we are able to determine the accuracy of any reconstruction.

## 3.6 A Paradigm for Contact Etymology

In the previous two sections we saw that, by applying a historical toponomastics approach, we can successfully reconstruct the possible root for a place name, as we saw in the analysis of *Sessame* earlier, or, as we ascertained in the discussion of *Bailu Zhou*, we can reconstruct or derive the original name and the naming practices that created the name itself. One other step we can consider is whether a study of any possible contact scenarios, especially among speakers of different languages, could contribute to a better understanding of the place name's etymology. This would involve investigating whether it is possible that language contact and borrowing phenomena could have happened among different groups of speakers or, in some cases, among several prehistoric peoples speaking different languages or proto-languages. As we will see in Chapter 4, the Proto-Indo-European *\*kar-/\*kal-* root could have potentially (and, in a way, paradoxically) existed prior to its proto-language phase. Language contact between speakers of a possible pre-language (Pre-Indo-European/non-Indo-European) and speakers of the reconstructed proto-language (Proto-Indo-European) could have ultimately modified the root to fit the language system of the proto-language speakers, while retaining certain atypical (and linguistically remote) morphological features (e.g., the reduplication of the root in the place name *Carcare*).

It is generally accepted that there are two categories of toponyms. (1) A place name is created by speakers of a language and then passed down to newer generations of speakers of the same language. In this case, the word undergoes the same processes of change as the language itself (see Chapter 2). (2) The place name was introduced by speakers of another language through language contact. The latter category of toponyms is referred to as potentially having a possible 'contact etymology'. Mailhammer likens it to:

a game of Chinese Whispers: every time a little bit of the message is changed, but considerably more so each time one layer has no or little command of the language of the message. While native transmission can often display surprising results and does not always follow completely regular patterns, this is all the more true for contact transmission, where not only unexpected sound substitutions and unexpected ways of reanalysis occur, but where there can be a great amount of inconsistency involved. (Mailhammer, 2013, pp. 9–10)

Mailhammer (2013) also proposes a three-step framework for dealing with words derived from language contact. The aim of this framework is to allow us to reconstruct and understand the possible contact situation that resulted in language borrowing, find the contact languages, and identify the feature(s) of the word(s) that seem 'peculiar' to the presumed proto-language, and, therefore, the features that may originate from another language. The contact etymologies proposed may then be able to shed light on the origins of words and toponyms that might seem obscure. Below, we outline schematically the different stages of this procedure.

### 3.6.1   Step 1: Contact Scenario

In this step, we describe in detail the contact situation where words can be transferred from one language to another. This includes answering questions such as the following.

- What is the type of contact situation (e.g., borrowing, imposition, mixed language)?
- Why was a foreign word adopted by native speakers (e.g., factors of usefulness of the foreign language or privilege of the foreign group)?
- What is the relationship between the communities speaking the different languages (e.g., militarily or economically) dominant, dominated, or neither?
- What are the characteristics of the communities speaking the different languages (e.g., tight-knit or loose; open or closed)?
- What is the degree of bilingualism or multilingualism in the community?

Mailhammer (2013, pp. 19–20) believes that extra-linguistic evidence (e.g., archaeological, genetic evidence) of contact is not crucial in the reconstruction of the contact scenario, although it can help to support the contact etymology. He believes that a linguistic explanation 'shows how that item was transferred from one language to the other' (p. 20) and is more important. He also says that a detailed enough reconstruction demonstrating how a toponym shows influences from another language is enough proof of contact etymology.

### 3.6.2    Step 2: Contact Language

The next step is to find the possible language(s) that came into contact with the speakers of a locality. This task is not easy and sometimes we may only have an indication of the language family or what the language is not. The important thing here is not to be vague. Mailhammer (2013, p. 20) warns that 'Vague statements, such as "a non-Indo-European language" or the name of a language family, or simply "unknown substratum", can sometimes be all that can be said about a word, but it is obvious that this can hardly be called an etymology.' Insufficient data frequently hinder the identification of the contact language, and we can only ascribe the features identified in the word to a hypothesised language (Mailhammer, 2013, p. 21). The contact language can be speculated by the analysis of features of the word in question. The word may exhibit characteristics that are uncommon in the recipient language. We might then hypothesise that this feature is borrowing or another influence from the contact language. When such a situation arises, it is useful to find languages and/or language families in which this feature is prominent.

### 3.6.3    Step 3: Contact Structure

After the two steps of establishing a contact scenario and a contact language, we then locate the contact structure. Under this process, we first identify the source word or feature and explain the changes that have occurred in the linguistic contact between the contact language and the recipient language. Working out the linguistic changes involves considering the social and linguistic contact situation, for instance, whether the borrowing or imposition of the foreign word retained its phonology from the contact language (perhaps due to prestige factors), or if it was incorporated into the linguistic system of the recipient language and its original sounds were changed. Mailhammer makes a distinction between contact and 'conventional' etymology.

What makes or breaks a contact explanation, of course, is the account of the point at which the word or structure is transferred from one language into the other. After establishing the situation and the contact language, it is necessary to pin down the source word or structure and explain any changes on the way into the receiving language. What happens after the item has come into the language falls then again within the domain of conventional etymology. (Mailhammer, 2013, p. 22)

A simple example of this is the English word *cockroach*. It is thought to have been borrowed from the Spanish *cucaracha*, and its initial English form was *cacarootch*. In this case, contact etymology concerns itself with the original meaning of the lexeme and how the language contact enabled the word to come into the English language. The study of 'the modern form is handled by conventional etymology' (Mailhammer, 2013, p. 22).

In the toponymic context, an emblematic example is provided by multilingual place names from southern *Africa* (Möller, 2019), which:

reveal cultural and language contact between Bushmen (San), Khoikhoi, Bantu and European language speakers over many thousands of years. These toponyms reflect the diversity of languages that had an influence on words and common names used by local people speaking different languages. Many of these place names are complex and their origins and meanings can only be explained by tracing onymic (naming) formatives in components from cognate words appearing in other languages, often only by deciphering the phonological, orthographic and morphological adaptations that they underwent, or through translated names elucidating the meanings. (Möller, 2019, p. 5)

One instance of this is connected with the common practice, by speakers of different languages, to name places after the cries of local animals. This can be observed in the different names for 'lion' in southern *Africa*. One of the denominations of the animal in the /Xam and Hie languages is *hou:m*, which is an onomatopoeic form that appears in the name of the *Houms River*. In the /Nu//en and !O!kung languages, 'lion' is *xam*, or *gam*. In Afrikaans, the animal is called *leeu*. All these languages belong to different language families and contexts and are spoken in a relatively large geographical area. They have been interacting for centuries and have produced interesting contact-linguistic phenomena. One illustration of this is how the Khoikhoi hydronym *Gamka* 'lion river', was translated into Afrikaans, as *Leeuwenrivier*, keeping the same meaning of 'lion river'. One other example is the place name *Leeu-Gamka*, which consists of the Afrikaans word for 'lion', *leeu*, and the Khoikhoi term for 'lion river', *gamka*, making it a tautological toponym, as it literally translates as 'lion-lion river'. Raper, Möller, and Du Plessis (2014) state that the town got its name from being located where the *Leeu* ('Lion') *River* flows into the *Gamka* ('Lion River'). This is a good example of marked language contact in toponymic context, with a possibly connected etymological/semantic misunderstanding (Möller, 2019, pp. 8–9).

Möller (2019, p. 5) states that, while analysing a place name in a specific language, it is not always easy to identify what has been borrowed from unrelated languages. She cites the example of the Bushman word for the hyena, *goaan*, which has been borrowed from the /Xam language. The zoonym (from Ancient Greek ζῷον [*zô[i]on*] 'animal', and ὄνομα [*ónoma*] 'name') has, subsequently, been adapted in other linguistic contexts and can be identified in a number of hybrid Nama/Afrikaans place names, such as *Guaapvlakte* 'Guaap Flats' and *Gwaapseberg* 'Gwaap Mountain' (Raper et al., 2014). Möller (2019, p. 5) also says that the appellative 'hyena' was the motivation for the hydronym *Wolf River* (with an apparent substitution between animals). In addition, the name for the call that hippopotami emit is, in some Bushman languages, *kubu* or *nguvu*. This term was adapted to *imvubu* in Zulu and can be seen in the hydronym *Umzimvubu*, and, in Venda, gave origin to the connected place name *Levubu*.

These toponyms display the different linguistic and cultural contexts from which they were generated and are evidence of a prolonged language contact among speakers. Indeed, contact phenomena led to the assimilation and reuse of lexemes which, then, triggered the naming processes for these local place names. Contact etymology can explain which languages participated in the generation, establishment, and acceptance of these place names among the related communities over time.

## 3.7   Summary

In this chapter, we have presented how historical toponomastics makes use of readily available data from historical and well-documented sources to reconstruct possible roots and proto-forms and, ultimately, the origins and the original meanings of place names. The reconstructions derived from this approach are compatible with the general lexicon of the local and current languages and consistent with the historical phonetics of the possible related previous diachronic stages of those languages and their proto-languages. As seen in the case studies, there is also reliance on resources from outside of linguistics, such as historical maps and documents, population records, and evidence of the crops found in each locality. This showcases the interdisciplinarity of toponymy and how we can combine both linguistic and extra-linguistic factors in studying place names.

The questions that may be asked at this stage are: 'how far back in time can we go with our reconstructions?' and/or 'what happens when we try to go back in time to a period from which we do not have any historical records?' We will try to answer these questions in the next chapter, where we will take up the discussion of pre-languages and proto-languages.

# 4    Toponymy and the Historical-Linguistic Reconstruction of Proto-Languages

We have already mentioned in this volume the importance of the historical toponomastics approach to the historical-linguistic reconstruction of place names. Toponyms, in turn, can provide indispensable clues for the study of the diachronic developmental stages of the languages to which the analysed toponyms belong to, and of the proto-languages from which those languages derive. Indeed, through the reconstruction of place names it is possible to postulate settlement dynamics and population movements that are not recorded by historical sources because they occurred prior to the invention of writing, and therefore in prehistoric times. Toponyms can even be used as clues to decipher an ancient language, as in the case of Mycenaean Greek and Linear B, explained in Chapter 2. The focus of this chapter is to provide an outline of how toponymy can help us to uncover archaic linguistic features of proto-languages and even of postulated pre-languages, which are, by definition, unattested and reconstructed. Pre-languages are languages that were lost a long time before proto-languages began to differentiate into historical, attested languages. In the field of historical toponomastics, this is accomplished mainly through etymological reconstructions of ancient place names.

The essential question that governs all diachronic reconstructions in historical linguistics is: 'what people were there before, and what language(s) did they speak?'. Unavoidably, this question, at the etymological level, must stop at the stage of the reconstruction of proto-forms and roots. These are the basic, most remote, and abstract components of a proto-language, and they are therefore the last possibly reconstructable lexical and morphological items.

A number of issues affect a comprehensive historical-toponomastic approach to ancient toponymy. First, how far back in time can we go with our reconstructions? At some stage, we will run out of written documentation or artefacts that may substantiate our findings. That is, once we go far enough back in time, namely in prehistoric times, we will not have any historical records to refer to, because writing was not invented yet at that developmental stage of mankind. We can then only hypothesise and not discuss our results with certainty. At the same time, the goal of our analysis is to linguistically recover the most ancient proto-forms and roots of place names. This means that, in specific cases, we need to postulate the existence of a pre-language that predates a proto-language.

These issues open a theoretical debate on the notions of 'pre-language' and 'proto-language', which will be briefly discussed below.

Ancient stems, derived from the reconstruction of place names, can be used to recover the general lexicon of a proto-language. These roots are 'ancient' by definition, because they represent the most remote reconstructable lexical units of a proto-language, to the point of being relatively theoretical and abstract linguistic elements, always unattested, in themselves, and reconstructed. Indeed, it is because they are basic morphological components of prehistoric toponyms that they are so important in the context of historical toponomastics. This is because they not only allow the toponymist to reconstruct the remote forms of place names, but they also enable linguists to connect them with the most ancient developmental stages of prehistoric proto-languages. As mentioned in earlier chapters, extremely ancient toponyms were named prevalently after primary goods and aspects of everyday life (e.g., water, edible crops, animals, shelters, fire, stone, dangers) by prehistoric peoples, or referred to the hydro-geo-morphology of the landscape (e.g., flowing waters, mountains, cliffs, caves, fords, swamps, glades). Place names functioned as intangible aids to the earliest settlers to establish a mental and ideal map of their territories, and to help them to orientate around the landscape, in what can be defined as 'primordial natural navigation'.

## 4.1 Pre-Languages and Proto-Languages

At the level of definition, a proto-language is an unattested, remote, abstract, and hypothetical language spoken in the distant past and in the absence of writing or of any other form of historical documentation, by prehistoric individuals belonging to the genus *Homo*. The proto-language is reconstructed, through the comparative method, on the basis of the attested (still living or already dead) and therefore historically documented languages which derive from it. A proto-language represents a linguistic stage predating the differentiation of the languages which have been generated from it when the communities speaking that proto-language became geographically separated and their ways of speaking, through the normal process of language change (cf. Chapter 2), evolved into different languages that are historically attested. All these (new) languages belong to the same language family which, generally, assumes the name of the proto-language. An example is English, which is an Indo-European language derived from the (Proto-)Germanic branch of Indo-European. The languages in a language family share lexical items (with their related meanings) and morphological and syntactic structures. In Chapter 2, we showed how, by applying the comparative method and through a reconstruction of sound laws, it is possible to reconstruct the proto-language from which all the languages belonging to a language family derive. A classic example of this is Proto-Indo-European, the proto-language at the origins of the so-called Indo-European languages. It has been reconstructed on the basis of the comparison and analysis of the attested Indo-European languages themselves, both still living (e.g., Albanian, Lithuanian, Italian, and Modern Greek) and already dead (e.g., Ancient Greek, Latin, Gothic). Through the analysis of the Indo-European languages and the recovery of the original proto-language, moreover, we can reconstruct 'second-generation proto-languages', like Proto-Germanic, derived from Proto-Indo-European and at the origins of the Indo-European Germanic languages, and Proto-Celtic, derived from Proto-Indo-European and at the origins of the Indo-European Celtic languages, and so on (Figure 4.1). Moreover, among Indo-European languages, we can make a distinction between a 'first stage' of attested (historical) Indo-European languages, at the level of 'seniority', for example, Sanskrit, Ancient Greek, and Latin, and a 'second stage' of attested (historical) Indo-European languages, derived from some of the 'first stage' Indo-European languages, like, for example, Modern Greek and Romance (Neo-Latin) languages like Italian, French, Romanian, Spanish, and Portuguese.

A pre-language, conversely, is (at the theoretical level) a language[1] spoken in a specific territory by peoples who pre-existed the new settlers (i.e., speakers of a new language). When a pre-language and a proto-language, which are both unattested by definition, are involved in language contact, that means that the dynamics between an old population and a new one happened in very remote times. The new settlers, by occupying the same territory of the old inhabitants at a later time, replace the previous peoples and their language. They are, indeed, bearers of a new language (or family of languages) not related to and incompatible with the language(s) of the previous inhabitants. A pre-language, therefore, by definition comes before a proto-language. In the case that the speakers of the proto-language completely erase linguistically the pre-language layer and erase ethnically the speakers of the pre-language, in the absence of any written record, the pre-language becomes lost forever.

To be clearer, a proto-language can be reconstructed, while a pre-language is purely 'theoretical' and, unfortunately, we cannot reconstruct it. We know it existed, because we have evidence (as documented by the material culture of the people speaking it and, literally, by their bones and genes) of populations inhabiting specific areas before the arrival of the proto-language speakers. These people possibly lived in these areas for thousands of years, but their

---

[1] Note that when we say 'language' in this context we don't really know whether we are talking of one language or a set of related languages. It may have been a language family, or a set of unrelated languages and/or language families.

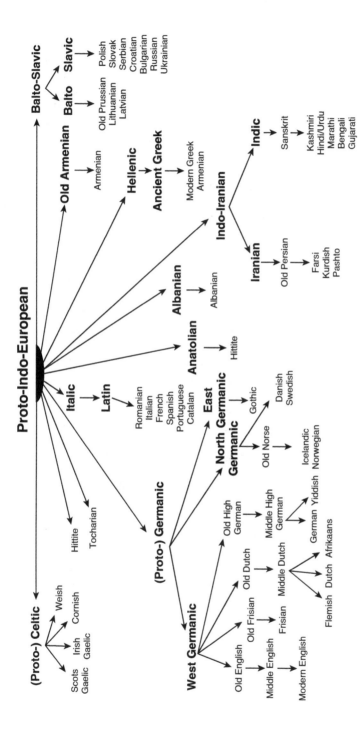

Figure 4.1 A family tree showing some of the 144 languages within the Indo-European language family

unattested and unrecorded language or languages have been irremediably lost. Using the Indo-European context as an example, we know that *Europe*, before the possible arrival of the Indo-Europeans (who were the linguistic bearers of Proto-Indo-European), was inhabited for tens of thousands of years by other peoples belonging to the genus *Homo*. These people surely were speaking a variety of (Pre-Indo-European) languages, which were all erased with the arrival of the Indo-Europeans, and which were superseded by Proto-Indo-European.

Generally, a proto-language and a pre-language, even if spoken in the same area, are not considered to be connected or related to each other. 'Proto-Indo-European' therefore indicates what possibly was the common prehistoric Indo-European (proto-)language before branching out to the 'second-generation' proto-languages derived from it and in the attested historical Indo-European languages. 'Pre-Indo-European', conversely, despite containing the notion of 'Indo-European' in its name, was probably a non-Indo-European language (or set of languages) in its intrinsic nature, and *pre-* in its name means exclusively that it was pre-existing and predating (Proto-)Indo-European.

In current scholarship, as mentioned earlier in this book, a proto-language usually consists of a collection of reconstructed roots and proto-forms which have been recovered by analysing cognates belonging to all the languages derived from it through the application of the comparative method (cf. Chapter 2). This method also allows us to understand which branches of a language family developed earlier or later, over time. While a proto-language can be reconstructed with the sound laws regulating its development into the 'second-generation' proto-languages and the attested historical languages derived from it (as seen in Chapter 2) through the comparative method, a pre-language can only be hypothesised. Indeed, the existence of very remote civilisations speaking pre-languages can only be inferred through the analysis of physical evidence from the fields of (prehistoric) archaeology and paleo-anthropology. For example, the existence of a Pre-Indo-European culture seems widely attested by the numerous prehistoric sculptures of the pregnant Venus-type found across *Europe* by archaeologists like Gimbutas (1974; 1989; 1991; 1999). Those artefacts seem to attest to the existence of a strongly matriarchal society (or societies)[2] occupying the *Old Continent* (i.e., *Europe*) way before the possible arrival of the Indo-Europeans (and the Indo-European languages). This society (or societies) would have had its own language (or languages), which was then supplanted by Proto-Indo-European and the derived Indo-European languages.

---

[2]  In contrast, the Indo-Europeans were bearers of a patriarchal model of society, with a composite *pantheon* of gods, which then became widespread in the *Old Continent*. An example of this is the 'set' of Ancient Greek deities.

The only possible way to reconstruct plausible 'linguistic fossils' of pre-languages is the analysis of presumably prehistoric place names. Toponyms, indeed, could indirectly preserve some traces of the languages spoken before the arrival of speakers of a proto-language. This is because, as we have already mentioned, ancient place names tend to be stable over time. Even with possible morphological modifications, they are not (drastically) changed by new people, especially in their roots. This applies not only to *Europe*, but, more or less, to linguistic contexts all over the world, from prehistoric ages, and also in more recent times. This is also true in aboriginal and/or Indigenous environments, within communities inhabiting remote territories, and in isolated areas where writing is not used or has not been developed yet.

To sum up, a pre-language is generally considered unrelated to a proto-language that replaced it and was spoken before the arrival of the speakers of that proto-language. The existence of a pre-language can only be hypothesised due to the massive lack, or total absence, of documented evidence. However, toponyms may be the missing linguistic links we need to prove its existence and to ideally give back the voice to its very ancient speakers. This is only a simplified representation, but it emblematically underlines the theoretical differences between the notions of 'pre-language' and 'proto-language'.

Moreover, it is possible that, because of cultural contact between the speakers of a pre-language and the speakers of a proto-language, some lexemes from the former were transferred into the linguistic system of the latter. Those lexemes, despite being adapted to the phonetic, phonological, and morphological standards of the 'new' proto-language, may retain some of their original features. An analysis of these possible linguistic 'anomalies' can generate the hypothesis according to which these 'contact features' are not 'native' to the proto-language, but derive from the pre-language that pre-existed it.

Later in this chapter, we will discuss three toponymic systems that could shed light on the relations between the notions of 'proto-language' and 'pre-language' and Toponymy. These examples will postulate the existence of roots belonging to a Pre-Indo-European *stratum*, which survived the possible arrival of the Indo-Europeans and which were reused and re-functionalised[3] in the Indo-European phonetic, phonological, and morphological systems.

Before we go on, it is worth briefly outlining some theoretical positions about the notions of 'Pre-Indo-European' and 'Proto-Indo-European'. A discussion on pre-languages and proto-languages, indeed, can only be conducted

---

[3] Re-functionalisation is the process according to which a linguistic form that is borrowed/imported from a language is incorporated in the linguistic system of another, possibly unrelated, language. It is a concept from classical philology and historical linguistics and describes the process by which a linguistic construction, such as a word or a grammatical form, 'acquires a new meaning' (Pato, 2018, p. 1) or 'a new discourse-pragmatic function other than its original function' (Rosemeyer, 2018, p. 1).

in the context of well-researched and documented language families and, to date, the best candidate is still the Indo-European context. Indo-European languages are very well-researched, but that does not imply that all scholars are in agreement about their origins. We will briefly introduce here, therefore, some well-known theories on who were the speakers of Proto-Indo-European and their possible relation to Pre-Indo-European civilisations. Some of these positions are dated and obsolete, or have been the object of quite heated debates. However, in order to provide our readers with a multifaceted perspective on the issue of the Indo-European origins, we feel it is worth summarising them here. We will, convergently, also focus on the theories in which the notion of 'pre-language' can be relevant to toponymy. The aim of this chapter is not to provide an exhaustive discussion on these theories (which is beyond the scope of this book), but to highlight the role that toponymy plays in the studies of Indo-European languages, and to show how some European place names are possible evidence of the presumable existence of Pre-Indo-European language(s) and can be gateways to a better (and unbiased) understanding of prehistoric *Europe*.

## 4.2    Giacomo Devoto's 'Mediterranean Theory'

In language-contact contexts, when pre-existing peoples are subjugated by other (new) ethnic and linguistic groups, or when people speaking different languages (and/or languages belonging to different language families) merge into one community, one of the results of the process is that the descendants of both groups generally end up speaking a single language. While the resulting language will most likely be a variant/development of the language spoken by the new people, it will probably also include features belonging to the old language. An Indigenous or local language that provides features (lexical, phonetic, syntactic, etc.) to the language of the people who invade and impose their language on the local population is referred to as 'linguistic substrate'. This language leaves discernible traces in the new language spoken by all the 'merged' people in a specific area. In the European prehistoric context, with the possible arrival of the Indo-Europeans, the Pre-Indo-Europeans were overrun by the newcomers. The end result of this process was a replacement of the Pre-Indo-European languages by the new Proto-Indo-European language (or already differentiated (proto-)languages spoken by the Indo-Europeans). However, despite the linguistic change, some features of the previously spoken language(s) could have been adopted by, or incorporated into, the new language(s). The hypothetical existence of a Pre-Indo-European linguistic substrate seems to emerge from some very ancient European place names.

Giacomo Devoto hypothesised that the Indo-Europeans, particularly the (proto-) speakers of Ancient Greek and Latin, came from northern and/or central *Europe* (Devoto, 1962). They then would have settled in the Mediterranean area that spans across three modern continents (*Europe*, northern *Africa*, and the *Middle East*), where non-Indo-Europeans (or Pre-Indo-European) communities were already living for a long time.

Devoto used the term 'Mediterranean substratum' to reflect possible linguistic traces of the hypothesised Pre-Indo-European language(s) in (Proto-)Indo-European and in the Indo-European languages. He utilised the notion of 'Mediterranean' and extended it also to other regions, such as *Anatolia, Iran,* and *India*. Devoto's theory was popular at the time because it gave a justified relevance to the Celtic element of the Indo-European linguistic layer, by connecting it with the 'original moment' of the settlement of the Indo-Europeans in *Europe*. Despite being influential, and still being used sometimes as a reference to the possible *Urheimat* ('homeland') of the Indo-Europeans, his approach has over time become relatively obsolete.

## 4.3    Marija Gimbutas' '*Kurgan* Hypothesis'

Marija Gimbutas developed the so-called '*Kurgan* Hypothesis', also known as the '*Kurgan* Theory', '*Kurgan* Model', or 'Steppe Theory', on the origins of the Indo-Europeans. This theory is still one of the mainstream positions on the identification of the possible *Urheimat* of the Indo-Europeans themselves. She proposed her hypothesis based on very significant archaeological findings, and provided a largely acceptable proposal identifying the possible homeland from where the Indo-Europeans and their languages spread throughout *Europe*, *Eurasia*, and parts of *Asia*. Her position describes the hypothesised arrival of the Indo-Europeans in their new territories at around 4500 to 1000 BCE, in different stages, or 'waves'. Gimbutas postulated this by diachronically 'following' various facets of the so-called *Kurgan* culture she had contributed to unearthing, especially the routes from the east to the west of the burial and funerary traditions (the Turkic term *kurgan* means 'burial') belonging to that culture (Gimbutas, 1974; 1989; 1991; 1999). These burial sites were accompanied by specific types of pottery and other cultural artefacts. In Gimbutas' view, what we know as 'Indo-European' could, actually, be a (proto-)language, or a set of languages, resulting from the merging of the Indo-Europeans (which the archaeologist identified as *Kurgan* people) with the Indigenous Old Europeans (Gimbutas, 1974; 1989; 1991; 1999), who were possibly non-Indo-European (Pre-Indo-European) people.

This hypothetical language, or set of unattested remote languages that we can reconstruct only in the shape of a proto-language, is referred to as 'Common Indo-European'. This is a sort of synonym of 'Proto-Indo-European', and the prefix *proto-* indicates, as mentioned above, that: (a) it was, theoretically, the language that was commonly spoken by the original

Indo-Europeans, who migrated into *Europe* and all the way to *India*, before they were separated from each other, with the consequent development of the different Indo-European languages; and (b) we do not have any documents or records of this unattested, hypothetical language, and it can only be reconstructed through the comparative method on the basis of the attested Indo-European languages.

## 4.4     Hans Krahe's 'Old European Hydronymy'

In 1963–4, the German linguist and philologist Hans Krahe conducted a comprehensive analysis of many hydronyms in central and western *Europe*, from the *Baltic* to the *Iberian Peninsula* (Figures 4.2 and 4.3).

These watercourse names constituted what he deemed as the 'Old European Hydronymy' (in German, *Alteuropäische Hydronymie*) (Krahe, 1962; 1964). According to the scholar, these hydronyms contained roots that could belong to a very ancient linguistic layer of *Europe*. The roots *\*var-/\*ver-*, *\*al-/\*alm-*, and *\*sal-/\*salm-*, which occur repeatedly in the river names he analysed, and the recurring endings in *\*-a* seemed to foreshadow a remote pattern in the prehistoric European toponymic naming processes (Krahe, 1962; Vennemann, 1994). According to Krahe, these hydronymic occurrences suggested that a language (or a few languages belonging to the same linguistic system and possibly sharing basic lexicon and typological features) was prevalent in a large part of *Europe* in prehistoric times (Mailhammer, 2015; Vennemann, 2003).

It should be noted that the wording 'Old European', according to Krahe, refers to a very old layer of European hydronymic lexemes, which is different from the definition given by Gimbutas (1989), who would have identified this layer with a non-Indo-European (and/or Pre-Indo-European) Neolithic linguistic context. Krahe (1964) postulated that the language giving rise to the 'Old European Hydronymy' cannot be detected anymore. Nonetheless, by comparatively using Indo-European roots and historical-phonetic procedures to analyse the 'Old European' hydronyms, Krahe came to the conclusion that these names were not generated from the 'mother tongue', or single language, from which all the Indo-European languages came, but belonged to an intermediate Western Indo-European layer that gave rise to most of the West European languages, such as Germanic, Celtic, Italic, and so on.

The linguistic homogeneity observed in the 'Old European Hydronymy' led researchers to debate on whether prehistoric *Europe* was in fact linguistically homogeneous or not. Mitochondrial DNA evidence seems to show that the Indo-Europeans were not very different, genetically, from the populations possibly pre-existing them, whom they subsequently displaced (Anthony, 1995; Bentley, Chikhi, & Price, 2003; Haak et al., 2005; Nichols, 1998; Schlerath, 1973; 1981; Schrijver, 2001). However, authoritative scholars like

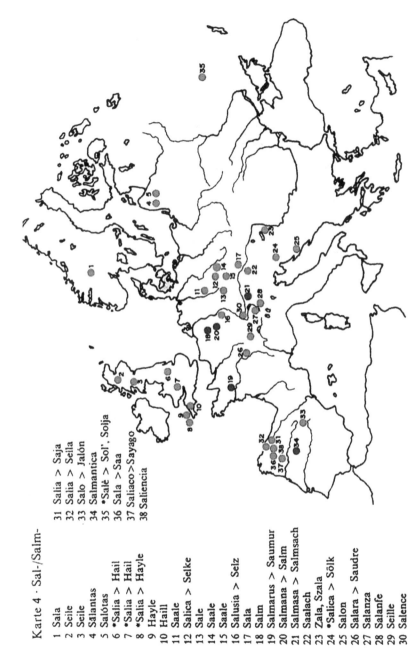

Karte 4 · Sal-/Salm-

| | |
|---|---|
| 1 Sala | 31 Salia > Saja |
| 2 Seile | 32 Salia > Sella |
| 3 Seile | 33 Salo > Jalón |
| 4 Salantas | 34 Salmantica |
| 5 Salótas | 35 *Salē > Sol', Solja |
| 6 *Salia > Hail | 36 Sala >Saa |
| 7 *Salia > Hail | 37 Saliaco>Sayago |
| 8 *Salia > Hayle | 38 Saliencia |
| 9 Hayle | |
| 10 Haill | |
| 11 Saale | |
| 12 Salica > Selke | |
| 13 Sale | |
| 14 Saale | |
| 15 Saale | |
| 16 Salusia > Selz | |
| 17 Sala | |
| 18 Salm | |
| 19 Salmarus > Saumur | |
| 20 Salmana > Salm | |
| 21 Salmasa > Salmsach | |
| 22 Saalach | |
| 23 Zala, Szala | |
| 24 *Salica > Sölk | |
| 25 Salon | |
| 26 Salara > Saudre | |
| 27 Salanza | |
| 28 Salanfe | |
| 29 Seille | |
| 30 Salence | |

Figure 4.2 Krahe's list of Old European hydronyms for the root *sal-/*salm- (adapted from Ras67, 2017a)

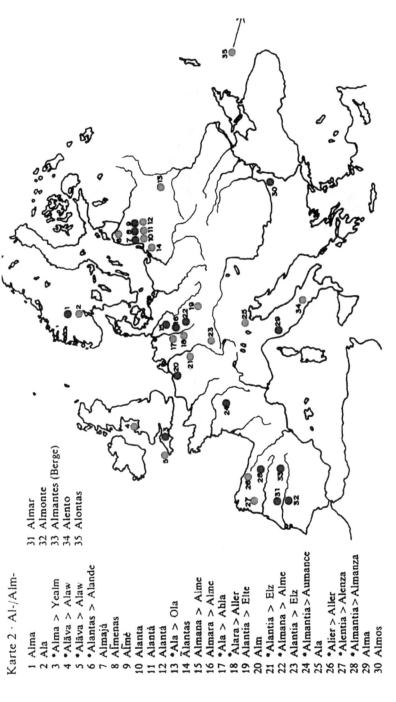

Karte 2 · Al-/Alm-

1   Alma
2   Ala
3   *Alma > Yealm
4   *Alāva > Alaw
5   *Alāva > Alaw
6   *Alantas > Alande
7   Almajā
8   Almenas
9   Almé
10  Alanta
11  Alantā
12  Alantā
13  *Ala > Ola
14  Ālantas
15  Almana > Alme
16  Almara > Alme
17  *Ala > Abla
18  *Alara > Aller
19  Alantia > Elte
20  Alm
21  *Alantia > Elz
22  *Almana > Alme
23  Alantia > Elz
24  *Almantia > Aumance
25  Ala
26  *Alier > Aller
27  *Alentia > Alenza
28  *Almantia > Almanza
29  Alma
30  Almos

31  Almar
32  Almonte
33  Almantes (Berge)
34  Alento
35  Alontas

Figure 4.3  Krahe's list of Old European hydronyms for the root *al-/*alm- (adapted from Ras67, 2017b)

Trask (1997, p. 364) opt for a view of '*Old Europe*' as a land with a diversified set of languages, 'large and small, some related, some not'. In this context of prehistoric multilingualism, possibly involving the interaction between different (proto-)language families, Basque (the language Trask studied in depth) – or proto-Basque – would represent an almost unique 'relic' of that situation and, according to this position, it is plausible to think that languages connected with Basque were more common in *Europe* (the so-called '*Old Europe*') before the Indo-European languages replaced them. Basque, therefore, would be a remnant of a diachronic stage preceding Indo-European in *Europe*, in a moment in which the linguistic situation of the *Old Continent* was quite fluid. Apparently, no living languages are related to Basque, which is a language that is quite different, in all aspects, from Indo-European languages (despite a long interaction with them, especially with Spanish). Other long-extinct languages, possibly Pre-Indo-European, could have been related to Basque, for instance Aquitanian, but this connection would date back to a time predating the Indo-European settlements in the *Old Continent*. Therefore, Basque speakers were possibly the original inhabitants of the *Iberian Peninsula*, way before the place was occupied by the Celts and then by the Romans. The existence of the Basque language would, therefore, be evidence of the diversified linguistic situation of *Europe* Trask was referring to.

However, the debate on the nature of '*Old Europe*', on the existence of a language or set of languages that can be defined 'Pre-Indo-European', and on Basque itself as evidence of a linguistic layer predating Indo-European in general is still ongoing.

Independently from the exactness of the ethnographic reconstruction, Krahe's work on 'Old European Hydronymy' is still a very valuable reference on the ancient names of European bodies of water, at the linguistic and toponymic level, especially in the context of the analytical investigation of hydronyms. Krahe's research is still fundamental in the debate on Indo-European origins and on the settlement dynamics of *Europe* between the so-called 'last Ice Age'[4] and the Neolithic.

Most scholars of Indo-European agree with Krahe's analysis according to which the hydronyms he analysed belonged to a remote component of the Indo-European family of languages, and this, with the unavoidable variants, remains the mainstream view. One of the most famous and controversial theories opposing this position is Theo Vennemann's (2003) 'Vasconic Substrate Hypothesis'. Vennemann's main argument is that the hydronyms analysed by

---

[4] The Late Cenozoic Ice Age began around 34 million years ago. The Quaternary glaciation, its last stage, is currently in progress, and started 2.58 million years ago. Our planet is going through an interglacial period (Holocene epoch) of the Quaternary glaciation. The last glacial period of the Quaternary glaciation finished approximately 11,700 years ago. This last 'cold period', called also 'last glacial' and, improperly, the 'last Ice Age', began about 115,000 years ago.

Krahe belonged not to an ancient layer of Indo-European, but to a Pre-Indo-European language family called, by him, 'Vasconic', of which the only surviving language in modern times would be Basque. Venneman's theory is a *unicum* in the context of studies on Pre-Indo-European *Europe*, being divergent from all other approaches so far produced. For this reason and due to several debatable assertions and postulations (i.e., the chronology of the origins and development of Vasconic languages, the notion of a 'Vasconic language family' in itself, and the related toponymy), it is extremely original, but also considerably controversial.

## 4.5     Theo Vennemann's 'Vasconic Substratum Theory'

Vennemann (1994) focusses on the role of Afro-Asiatic (or Semitic) and Vasconic (e.g., Basque) languages in the prehistoric development of the languages of *Europe*. His theory is proposed in a series of works that the researcher wrote over the years and is mainly presented in his famous book *Europa Vasconica – Europa Semitica*, a collection of 27 essays. Vennemann argues that, after the so-called 'last Ice Age', most areas of central and western *Europe* were inhabited by speakers of a family of languages which he calls 'Vasconic', of which the only survivor today, according to him, is Basque. Vasconic speakers formed a very ancient substrate of Indo-European. Vennemann draws his primary evidence for the presence of elements of what he defines 'Vasconic' throughout much of *Europe* from the above-mentioned 'Old European' hydronyms collected and analysed by Hans Krahe (Krahe, 1962; 1964). He re-analyses these hydronyms according to a new perspective, and interprets them as 'Vasconic'. According to the scholar, this toponymic evidence leads to the hypothesis that Basque, generally considered a language isolate with no living related languages, is the only survivor of a larger Pre-Indo-European ('Vasconic') language family. He argues that this Pre-Indo-European family of languages once (in very remote times) extended throughout most of *Europe*, and that it also had some influence on the later Indo-European languages (Vennemann, 2003).

Vennemann's theory ingenerated heated debates, and many scholars discussed it widely. Among them, Peter Kitson (1996) wrote an important paper challenging the 'Vasconic Hypothesis' and developed a thorough re-analysis and discussion of Krahe's 'Old European Hydronymy'. He problematised the notions of 'Pre-Indo-European' and '*Old Europe*', suggesting that nearly all of the examples provided by Vennemann were erroneously segmented. He then provided a comprehensive Indo-European interpretation of the ancient European Hydronymy. This not only challenged the theoretical premises and assumptions of the theory proposed by Vennemann (1994; 2003), but also provided a more up-to-date reassessment of Krahe's findings. According to Kitson (1996), all the unusual structures observed in the so-called 'Old European Hydronymy' have Indo-European roots. In his effort to explain those place names according to an Indo-European key of interpretation, he also connected words for water bodies of ancient Indo-European languages (e.g., Hittite and Old Iranian) with Krahe's 'Old European Hydronymy', showing, therefore, that the 'Old European Hydronymy' in itself could not have been 'Pre-Indo-European', because it intrinsically and essentially belonged to the Proto-Indo-European context. His critique of Vennemann is summarised in the following passages.

The Indo-Europeanness of *alteuropäisch* names was obvious to Krahe and his colleagues from the beginning. Occasional attempts to prove otherwise depend on ignoring a lot of evidence presented above and falsifying some of it. A recent such exercise, that of Vennemann (1994), parades a technical linguistic (specifically morphological) virtuosity that may mislead the unwary but lacks proper control in several directions. (Kitson, 1996, p. 95)

Still Vennemann deserves thanks for supplying what had been a gap in the literature and showing us what a seriously worked up attempt to analyse the *alteuropäisch* linguistic material as non-Indo-European would look like. It is reassuringly much less coherent than the traditional Indo-European versions. (Kitson, 1996, pp. 97–8)

Kitson concludes his critique by stating that 'The linguistic material of the *alteuropäisch* river names is Indo-European, and they must be analysed rationally on that basis' (Kitson, 1996, p. 113).

The scholar thus disagrees with Vennemann's hypothesis of the 'Vasconic' linguistic layer by affirming that it is morphologically incorrect, before reminding us of the essentially Indo-European nature of Krahe's 'Old European Hydronymy'. As mentioned, Kitson (1996) was not alone in his opposition to Vennemann. In more recent publications on the notion of 'Old European Hydronymy', Harald Bichlmeier (2012) and Jürgen Untermann (2009), among others, also support the Indo-European origins of European river names. Bichlmeier (2012), for example, refutes the comparison of ancient 'Old European' place names with elements of modern Basque (Bichlmeier, 2012, p. 424). Moreover, Untermann, an authoritative scholar in the field of Paleo-Hispanic languages (and one of Krahe's former students), provides further linguistic proofs for the Indo-European origins of the 'Old European Hydronymy', with unexceptionable examples mainly belonging to the *Iberian Peninsula* context (Untermann, 2009).

## 4.6    Mario Alinei's 'Palaeolithic Continuity Theory', or the 'Palaeolithic Continuity Paradigm'

Another significant approach to the interpretation of the origins of the languages of (prehistoric) *Europe* is the so-called 'Palaeolithic Continuity

Theory' (PCT), or 'Palaeolithic Continuity Paradigm' (PCP), known in Italian as *Teoria della Continuità*. The PCP was developed, in the mid-1990s, by Mario Alinei and his international work-group (Alinei, 1996; 2000). This theory is based on the postulation that what we call '(Proto-) Indo-European' was already spoken in *Europe* from the Upper Palaeolithic, with the first inhabitants of the *Old Continent* belonging to the *Homo sapiens* species, at least around 40,000 years ago (therefore, with the migration of *Homo sapiens* in *Europe*). This would place the possible arrival of what we call 'the Indo-Europeans' at a much earlier time than the currently accepted mainstream notion.

The timeline proposed by the PCP, with its consequent linguistic implications, enables a number of problematic etymologies of seemingly morphologically obscure Indo-European common lexical items and place names to be solved and, in a way, explained. An example of this is given by the terms for *eel* in Indo-European languages, which are difficult to be reconstructed with a traditional approach. The English word *eel* in itself, indeed, has a relatively obscure etymology, as well as its cognates in other Indo-European languages. These words include, among others, German *aal*, Old High German and Old Saxon *āl*, Old Frisian *ēl*, Dutch *aal*, Old Icelandic *āll*, and Danish and Swedish *ål*. According to the PCP, the Proto-Indo-European *\*al-* (and *\*alb-*) root can effectively explain the etymology of *eel*. *\*al-*, in Indo-European, is connected with the meaning of 'feed', or 'nourish', detectable, among others, in the Latin verb *alō* 'I feed', or 'I nourish', in the Old Irish verb *alim* 'I nourish', and in the Old Icelandic form *ala* '(to) feed'. The notion of 'feed', or 'nourish', in turn was originally closely linked to the concept of 'water', and specifically to one of its products, 'fish'. The *eel* is a 'fish' that lives in the 'water', and was part of the diet of prehistoric European people, who by eating it were obtaining a form of nourishment coming from the water. By expanding on this reconstruction, it is therefore possible to hypothesise a close relationship between the Indo-European roots *\*al-* and *\*alb-*, and the possibly equivalent Indo-European stem *\*albh-* 'water' discussed later in this chapter. The two roots are probably etymologically and historical-phonetically related, and their connection is made stronger by their semantic link to the notion of 'water' and of the 'nourishment' which could come from water. The PCP postulates the existence of variants of a single basic root referable to a concept, like 'water', and to a toponymic indication of a place situated close to a watercourse or to the sea (represented, in Indo-European, by the etymological *alba*-type). The theory dismisses the mainstream '*Kurgan* Hypothesis' proposed by Marija Gimbutas, highlighting the fact that, apparently, there are no genetic and archaeological traces of invasions of different populations in *Europe* after the so-called 'last Ice Age' (therefore, the movements of the *Kurgan* people would have represented an 'internal migration'). The PCP supporters claim that this lack of archaeological evidence strengthens the idea of an uninterrupted cultural continuity from the Palaeolithic to Neolithic times.

Despite the active participation of other distinguished linguists, such as Guido Borghi and Xaverio Ballester, in the development of this theory (see also Ballester & Benozzo, 2018), the PCP is not universally accepted and is conversely also rejected by several scholars who do not share the concept of 'continuity'. The PCP has been criticised on a number of methodological and epistemological issues. For example, at the linguistic level, by pushing back the 'epoch' of the presence of the Indo-Europeans in *Europe*, the PCP assumes that it took a tremendous amount of time for Indo-European to split and differentiate into different branches, and that in Neolithic times the different Indo-European languages had already been consolidated. This point is seen as very problematic by many scholars. Moreover, the etymologies reconstructed through the PCP's methodology cannot be confirmed generally according to the traditional application of sound laws and historical-phonetic criteria.

## 4.7    Pre-Languages, Proto-Languages, and Toponymy

The notion of 'pre-language' we discussed above is unavoidably problematic. Staying with the European example, no matter what theory is proposed, it is a fact that, before the possible arrival of the Indo-Europeans, *Europe* was already inhabited, and had been for a very long time, by individuals belonging to the genus *Homo*. These people spoke their own language (or languages), which are forever lost.

- The literature, generally, refers to 'Indo-European', 'Common Indo-European', and 'Proto-Indo-European' as being the same Indo-European (proto-)language, that is, the unattested, reconstructed (proto-)language theoretically spoken by all the original Indo-European people(s) before its differentiation into second-stage Indo-European proto-languages (e.g., Proto-Germanic, Proto-Italic, Proto-Hellenic) and the attested historical Indo-European languages (e.g., Gothic, Latin, Ancient Greek). This proto-language would include, by definition, etymologies traceable back only to Indo-European itself (not to other language families or proto-languages) and reconstructed up to the level of roots, as, for example, in the *Proto-Indo-European Etymological Lexicon* by Julius Pokorny (1969), without taking into consideration possible language contact, in prehistoric times, by the Indo-Europeans during their journey(s) towards *Europe*.

- We can, at the theoretical level, add to this set another term, 'Pre-Proto-Indo-European', which refers to the more ancient variety of Indo-European spoken by the Indo-Europeans before they spread across *Europe*, indeed, before their possible arrival in the *Old Continent*, that is, a possible, theoretical stage of Indo-European predating what is called 'Proto-Indo-European' or 'Common

Indo-European', representing a more ancient layer of the development of Indo-European in itself.

• We use, conversely, 'Pre-Indo-European' to refer to the (plausibly) non-Indo-European languages spoken in *Europe* before the arrival of the Indo-Europeans, that is, the possible linguistic stage, in *Europe*, before the 'arrival' of the Indo-Europeans, which was 'erased' by the arrival of the Indo-Europeans themselves.

In this section, we will move our discussion to the role of toponymic research in the discussion of pre- and proto-languages. Though limited to their lexical context, etymological reconstructions of toponyms are still important in the postulation of pre-languages. As mentioned above, we have, indeed, very little linguistic evidence (or no evidence at all) of the existence of pre-languages, except probably for some place names that have survived till today and that could carry within themselves traces of those long-lost languages. Ancient toponyms, as we have mentioned thus far, are somehow stable in their basic linguistic morphology over time, and they tend to preserve their roots even when speakers have completely lost the knowledge of their origins and original meanings. This makes them, as we said in Chapter 1, 'linguistic fossils' or 'linguistic relics' of previous stages of languages spoken by populations which have been superseded by other peoples speaking different languages. For this reason, they can theoretically survive across time, when all other aspects of the languages around them have completely changed. They can, therefore, provide us with some insights into the dynamics and notions of 'pre-' and 'proto-languages'. The etymological reconstruction of place names allows us, therefore, to postulate the existence of roots that originated from pre-languages.

Because pre-languages and proto-languages are by definition different and theoretically unrelated, they cannot be matched phonetically or phonologically. As a result, we have to expect that a toponym coined by speakers of a postulated pre-language should be phonetically and phonologically modified, during the passage between the pre-language context to the new proto-language reality, to be adapted to the new proto-language. Therefore, the pronunciation of the toponyms should be equated to the standard linguistic features of the proto-language itself. However, place names are not common lexical items but 'special' linguistic entities that generally do not to follow the 'normal' dynamics of diachronic language change. Therefore, it is possible to expect that, despite the unavoidable phonetic and phonological changes, the roots of these toponyms would tend to be preserved.

It is also worth remembering that although toponyms may be relatively stable in their form, their meanings are subject to change and, over time, their original semes, or the original semantics of their roots, may be forgotten by the speakers of a language or by new speakers of another language. Local speakers would try, then, to relate the names that have become 'obscure' to more familiar terms in their language and to change linguistic elements of the original toponyms to match them with more familiar lexical items. As a result, they can generate toponymic paretymologies (as discussed in Chapter 3). This is a sort of paradox; while, generally, ancient toponyms are relatively stable and tend to retain their original roots, they are also susceptible to change, especially due to population shifts and contact with other languages. It is up to the toponymist, then, to reconstruct the correct etymology of the place names, uncovering their original morphological forms and meanings.

In the next section, we will present and discuss three specific examples of language change in possible contact contexts, and of how toponyms, while generally retaining their roots, experience shifts in their phonetics, phonology, morphology, semantics, and sometimes orthography.

## 4.8    The Notion of 'Pre-Proto-Indo-European': The Case of the *$h_a$albh-/*alb- Toponymic System

Language change, as mentioned in Chapter 2, can happen at a number of linguistic levels: phonological, morphological, lexical, syntactic, and semantic. In Chapter 3 (see also *Spigno*, in Chapter 7), the case study of *Squaneto*, in particular, demonstrated a possible phonetic and phonological shift in which speakers could have combined the *s- and *-n- sounds to the root of the place name, $ak^w$- 'water', with the addition of the suffix -eto (< Latin -etum) indicating the notion of 'place', or 'village'. The phoneme *s- was possibly added as a 'formant consonant' and did not belong to the original root of the toponym. The phoneme *-n- was added as a euphonic particle, possibly to avoid the contact of the two vowels 'a' and 'e' in the name *Squaneto*, which would have made its pronunciation less easy. The etymology of *Squaneto*, then, may be confirmed also by the comparison with other place names (and their naming processes) etymologically and geographically related, like *Squagiato* and *Saquana* (see also Chapter 6). If we accept this reconstruction, then we can say that these toponyms all belong to a consistent toponymic system.

In this section, we turn our attention to another very interesting (and problematic) toponymic system, which seems to show a large number of places in *Europe* deriving their names from a single root, *alb- (Table 4.1).

Here, it may be appropriate to briefly recap the definition of the notion of 'toponymic system' from Chapter 1. Toponymic systems are sets of place names of any type that belong to a specific geographic area and share the same etymological stem and/or the same original naming process. Places that date back to prehistoric times probably had originally very simple names, with the same name possibly repeated for different places, when that name was indicating 'something important' for the local prehistoric speakers. Places in a specific area, therefore, probably shared the same names or had very similar denominations, connected with the primary goods for survival and differentiated only by linguistic features that indicated characteristics of the toponym's localities, such as a specific geo-morphology and/or very important natural resources. For these reasons, toponymic systems can provide evidence of how early (prehistoric) humans organised their geographical landscape into an 'ideal, intangible map', in the absence of written languages and/or records.

The toponymic type *alba* is the basis for the names of many places in *Europe* (and also in parts of northern *Africa* and the *Middle East*), constituting a large toponymic system. These toponyms are derived, possibly, from the Proto-Indo-European root *alb-/*albh-. Its original meaning is connected with the notion of 'water' (Perono Cacciafoco, 2013), with some semantic differences when compared to the Indo-European stem $*ak^w$-, which simply means 'water' (in itself). $*ak^w$- is, indeed, a sort of 'pan-Indo-European' root for 'water', and many Indo-European languages have lexical items derived from it. From this root, for example, the words *aqua* in Latin, *acqua* in Italian, *eau* in French, *agua* in Spanish, and so on, are derived. Conversely, *alb-* is an Indo-European root also meaning 'water', but its semantics is more specialised, being connected with a 'quality' (or 'colour') of water, namely its 'transparency'.

At the theoretical level, the Proto-Indo-European root *alb-* could be interpreted as deriving from a hypothetical Pre-Proto-Indo-European stem $*h_aalbh$-, also meaning 'water'. While the notion of 'Pre-Proto-Indo-European' (as defined by us above) is disputed, in the field of historical linguistics, it could be considered plausible in this reconstruction.

Perono Cacciafoco (2013) uses the notion of 'Pre-Proto-Indo-European' as a terminological postulate for a diachronic analysis of the *alb-* toponymic and hydronymic system. Elements of this system can also be found along what could be possible migration routes (including territories located outside of the *Old Continent*) taken by the original Indo-Europeans in their migrations from outside *Europe*. Since the notion of 'Pre-Proto-Indo-European' is only theoretical, this is indeed an experimental reconstruction. In this context, this concept can be used to postulate a stage of Indo-European before language contact with other prehistoric (proto-)languages and/or language families. Within this framework, Perono Cacciafoco postulates the existence of a Pre-Proto-Indo-European root, $*h_aalbh$-, etymologically more ancient than *alb-/*albh-, which would have generated the Proto-Indo-European stem (*alb-/*albh-). This could have happened during the Indo-Europeans' movements towards their historical venues and before their possible arrival in their historical territories. The root, therefore, would have developed due to language contact with other (proto-)languages or language families during the Indo-European migrations. The stem, at the same time, would have been at the origins of the development of the above-mentioned toponymic system, documented also by the related roots and proto-forms *olbh- and its own variants *olb- and *orb- (Gasca Queirazza et al., 1999; Pellegrini, 2008), *albhā- (a late Indo-European form meaning 'city located on the water', or 'town located on the water' and later simply 'city', or 'town'), and *albho- 'white' (> Latin albus). These will be discussed in more detail below.

Actually, stems and lexemes could have been borrowed from non-Indo-European languages by the Indo-Europeans and reused and re-functionalised in their linguistic system during their journeys before their possible arrival in Europe and India. In particular, the stem *$h_a$albh-, despite being in its nature Indo-European, could be compatible with non-Indo-European lexemes like the Sumerian word ḫalbia, from which the Akkadian ḫalpium would have derived, with both lexemes meaning 'spring, well, water mass, water hole'. The geographical point of contact between non-Indo-European linguistic contexts (Semitic, in the case of Akkadian) and Indo-European with the development of the root *$h_a$albh- could have been Anatolia, and could be linguistically (at the level of attested lexemes) represented by the Hittite (Indo-European) term alpa-s, meaning 'cloud' (and, by extension, 'rainwater'). According to this theoretical reconstruction, therefore, the Pre-Proto-Indo-European root *$h_a$albh- would have been adopted by the Indo-European speakers in their linguistic system, producing the normalised form *alb- (~ *albh-).

The postulated Pre-Proto-Indo-European root *$h_a$albh- and the Indo-European stems *alb- and *albh- are indeed equivalent to each other and originally all indicated the notion of 'water'. Moreover, as seen from the list of place names in the toponymic system represented in Table 4.1, they were very productive in toponymy and, as names of places, used to indicate the notions of 'place located on the water' and 'place bordering a water body'. That is, they are metonyms, names for inhabited places with a primary etymological sense of 'water'.

To account for the variants of *alb- that begin with /o/, for example, Olbia, the oldest colony of Miletus, on the Black Sea, it is possible to hypothesise that the root underwent a sort of vocalic ablaut (apophony) of the initial vowel /a/ into /o/. The *olb- variant is found in many place names in Europe, such as the other multiple occurrences of the olbia-type outlined in Table 4.1. There are also place names belonging to this type, such as Orba and Orbicella, in which the phoneme /l/ changed into /r/ in postvocalic contexts and before bilabial consonants. Such a linguistic phenomenon is relatively common in the area of ancient Liguria, Italy, which is now located between the lower Piedmont and the contemporary Liguria region, where a number of these toponyms are found.

The root *olb- is, therefore, equivalent to the Ligurian stem *orb-, as witnessed, for example, in the name of the Orba River. The first known attestation of the hydronym dates back to 1137, with the form Urba (VV. AA., 1899–, CXIII, 38, 53). In 1176, it was indicated by the denomination Urbae (VV.AA., 1899–, XXIX, 74, 94). The common etymological

Table 4.1 *The* \*alb- *toponymic system. The listed toponyms derive from the root* \*alb- *and its associated variants*

| Root | Examples of toponyms |
| --- | --- |
| *alb-*<br>*albh-* | • *Alba* (*Alba Pompeia*), Piedmont, *Cuneo* province, *Italy*<br>• *Alba Heluorum, Provence, France*<br>• *Alba* (now *Arjona*), Spain<br>• *Albenga, Savona* province, *Liguria, Italy* (from Latin *Albingaunum* < *Album Ingaunum*)<br>• *Albera Ligure, Piedmont, Alessandria* province, *Italy*<br>• *Albiōn*, the original name of *Britain*<br>• *Albis*, the *nomen* of the *Elbe River, Germany*<br>• *Albisola* and *Albissola, Savona* province, *Liguria, Italy*<br>• *Albona, Istria, Croatia*<br>• *Albuca* (in ancient contexts, like *Gaul* and *Aquitaine*)<br>• *Albula*, the ancient name of the Italian river *Tevere* (Latin *Tiberis*)<br>• *Ventimiglia, Imperia* province, *Liguria, Italy* (from Latin *Albintimilium* < *Album Intimilium*) |
| *olbh-*<br>*olb-*<br>*orb-* | • *Olbia*, the oldest colony of *Miletus*, on the *Black Sea*<br>• *Olbia*, in *Britain*<br>• *Olbia*, on the right bank of the *Bug River* (in *Ukraine*)<br>• *Olbia*, in *Hellespont, Turkey*<br>• *Olbia*, in *Lycia, Turkey*<br>• *Olbia*, in *Provence, France*<br>• *Olbia*, in *Sardinia, Italy*<br>• *Olbicella, Alessandria* province, northwest *Italy*<br>• *Orba River, Alessandria* province, *Italy*. It flows in the territory of *Olbicella* and flows into the *Bormida River*<br>• *Orbicella*, an affluent of the *Orba River* and a variant of *Olbicella*<br>• *Martina d'Olba, Urbe* municipality, *Savona* province, *Italy*<br>• *San Pietro d'Olba, Urbe* municipality, *Savona* province, *Italy* |

explanation of this hydronym is that it derives from the Latin word *urbs*, meaning 'city', or 'town'. However, as explained in this volume, many reconstructions of (peripheral) place names have been carried out without taking into consideration historical-linguistic factors and only by linking toponyms to a contemporary stage of the local language or to its immediately preceding stage. The name of the river is clearly connected with the notion of 'water' and, therefore, the medieval form *Urba* is a paretymological variant, produced by the speakers to connect the hydronym with a 'safe' (but wrong) referent, the Latin word *urbs*. Nonetheless, the river name clearly derives from the root *alb-*, meaning 'water', in its variant *olb-/*orb-*. Another hydronym that shows the link between the variants *olb-* and *orb-*, and the stem *alb-*, is *Orbicella*, the denomination of a stream which flows in the territory of the village of *Olbicella* (which has the same name as the hydronym, just with the variant *olb-) and is an affluent of the *Orba River*. The hydronym itself is further linguistic evidence proving the equivalence of the roots *olb- and *orb- (< *alb-), and illustrates the coherence of the sound change from /l/ to /r/. A similar reasoning can be used to account for the name of the *Urbe* municipality, located in the valley of the *Orba River*. The place name is paretymologically connected, by the local speakers, with the Latin word *urbs* 'city'. This was probably due to the perception that the name was associated with the more 'prestigious' *Urbs*, with a capital 'u', that is, *Rome* itself, therefore meaning 'the City'. The denomination instead etymologically coincides with the hydronym *Orba* and derives from the same root (therefore, *Urbe* = *Orba* < *olb-/ *orb- < *alb-) and not from Latin *urbs* (Gasca Queirazza et al., 1999).

The stratification of the meaning of the root *alb- can be seen happening in late Indo-European, with place names not directly associated with 'water' but, in fact, connected with the Indo-European proto-forms *albo(-), *albio(-), and *alba(-), with the meaning of 'city', or 'town'. This can be seen, for example, in the names of three towns from northwest *Italy*, *Albera Ligure* (where the *Albirola* stream, another hydronym derived from *alb-, flows), *Albenga* (in Latin *Album Ingaunum*), and *Ventimiglia* (in Latin *Album Intimilium*). The *alba/album* component, in these place names, comes from the root *alb-, but is not connected anymore (primarily) with the notion of 'water', meaning rather 'city', or 'town', or 'inhabited centre'. These toponyms, in association with human settlements, therefore underwent the semantic transition of the seme of the root, from the meaning of 'water' to 'place located in the closeness of water' (because these inhabited centres were and are located, for self-evident reasons, in proximity of water) and then to a more generic meaning of 'place', 'city', or 'town'. This phenomenon can be observed in a number of toponyms across *Europe* belonging to the *alb- toponymic system. The proximity to waterways and water bodies has always been fundamental to the birth and development of villages, towns, and civilisations in general.

In the context of the semantic shift connected with the *alb- toponymic system, Perono Cacciafoco (2013) notes that another phenomenon of meaning change can be highlighted through the analysis of the late-Indo-European adjective *albho(-) 'light', or 'white'. This proto-form also derives from the root *alb- (~ *albh-) 'water', but its meaning indicates a colour and no longer the primary resource (water). However, its origin has to be still connected with a characteristic of the water, specifically its 'colour' or, better, its qualities of 'transparency' and 'purity' (i.e., 'clear water', 'white water'). The root, therefore, underwent another semantic change in the development of this proto-form, from 'water' to 'white', in the late Indo-European proto-form *albho(-) for 'light/clear/white water', in the equivalent proto-form *albha(-). This reconstruction, involving the generation of place names and common lexical items from the root *alb-, suggests a diachronic stratification of different meanings for the same root. Below, we outline the semantic transition that led to this, in the passage from ancient and remote phases of Indo-European to late Indo-European.

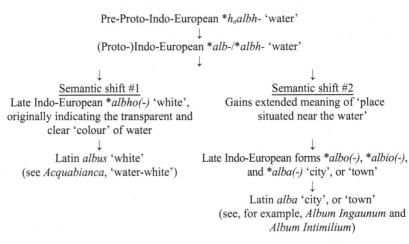

Pre-Proto-Indo-European *$h_a$albh- 'water'
↓
(Proto-)Indo-European *alb-/*albh- 'water'
↓

|  |  |
| --- | --- |
| ↓ | ↓ |
| Semantic shift #1 | Semantic shift #2 |
| Late Indo-European *albho(-) 'white', originally indicating the transparent and clear 'colour' of water | Gains extended meaning of 'place situated near the water' |
| ↓ | ↓ |
| Latin albus 'white' (see Acquabianca, 'water-white') | Late Indo-European forms *albo(-), *albio(-), and *alba(-) 'city', or 'town' |
|  | ↓ |
|  | Latin alba 'city', or 'town' (see, for example, Album Ingaunum and Album Intimilium) |

Another point worth noting is that place names derived from the root *alb- are also part of a series of toponyms, from different Indo-European contexts, that relate to other water-roots (different from *alb-), which are radicals with the original seme of 'water'. These other roots are semantically specialised according to specific meanings, such as *war- 'water', 'flowing water', or 'river', or 'rain', *pal- 'stagnant water', 'puddle', or 'backwater', *mar- 'lagoon', or 'sea'. Some of them indicate characteristics or qualities of water or of water currents, such as, for example, *tar- 'strong', or 'penetrating', and *ais- 'fast' (Villar, 1996, p. 117), like in, for example, Tarleton, in northwest England, and Aix-en-Provence (Ais, in Mistralian, Aquae Sextiae, in Latin) and Aix-les-Bains (Aquae Gratianae, in Latin), in France.

All these roots, in general, are at the origins of toponymic systems, naturally connected with hydronymy. If we analyse, for example, the *war- root, we can find toponymic examples in two hamlets of the Urbe municipality called Vara Inferiore and Vara Superiore, both associated with this root (Vara means 'flowing water', and comes from the root *war-, while Inferiore means 'lower' and Superiore means 'upper'). The root is also the basis for a number of hydronyms, such as the Vara River, the longest watercourse flowing in Liguria, Italy, and the Varàita River, flowing in the province of Cuneo, Piedmont, in northwest Italy. As is evident from this little sample of the toponymic system connected with *war-, the notion of 'water' was always present as an important naming component of place names from ancient times, always highlighting the importance of this primary good that makes life possible.

An interesting case suggesting the persistence of the meaning in the naming process is represented by *Acquabianca*, the name of a hamlet belonging to the above-mentioned *Urbe* municipality. The toponym, *Acquabianca*, is a compound which literally means 'white (*bianca*) water (*acqua*)', and comes from two forms independent from the root *alb-. *Acqua* is the Italian word for 'water' and derives from the above-mentioned Indo-European root generically meaning 'water', *$ak^w$-, which developed into Latin *aqua*, which consequently generated the Italian *acqua*. On the other hand, *bianca* (*bianc-o*, 'white', masculine singular; in Italian, the ending -*a* marks the feminine singular form) comes from Old High German *blanch* 'white', which then became the Modern High German form *blank* 'bright' or 'shiny'. The Germanic word was introduced in the Latin/Italian lexicon in the High Middle Ages. Despite the name *Acquabianca* not being connected etymologically with *alb- and its toponymic system, its meaning is linked to the 'colour' of water, the 'white'/'transparent' colour semantically indicated by the *alb- root. Independently from the historical morphology of the name, the cognitive and semantic components of its naming process are the same as the other place names derived from *alb-. That is, even as they are different at the morphological level, they are all connected by the notion of the 'white' ('transparent') colour of the water. This would indicate, therefore, a semantically equivalent naming process produced by the speakers at the cognitive level by using different morphological units.

In summary, we have reviewed a number of toponyms that are all connected with each other by the Proto-Indo-European root *alb- (~ *albh-) 'water' (with the variants *olbh-, *olb-, and *orb-). The *alb- toponymic system consists of place names (town names, village names, hamlet names, and hydronyms) that are characterised by very similar or even the same names. Our discussion highlighted not only the existence of this toponymic system, but also the semantic shifts involving the root *alb- in two directions, over time. One change follows the sequence:

'water' → 'place situated near the water or located on water' → 'city', or 'town',

while the other change, instead, follows the sequence:

'water' → 'white/transparent water' (from its 'colour') → 'white'.

This case study provides us with an excellent example which highlights the importance of waterways in the development of prehistoric settlements and which reconstructs a very ancient naming strategy based on the relationship between place names and the natural features of their locations. At the same time, it also shows the effects of language change over toponyms and lexemes belonging to the common vocabulary of languages, particularly the strength of semantic change.

## 4.9    The Toponymic Persistence of Prehistoric Stems: The Case of the *kar- Root

Perono Cacciafoco (2015a) provides a consistent discussion on what can be called the 'toponymic persistence' of linguistic roots and stems from very remote times. He does so through the study of the Proto-Indo-European root *kar- (with its possible variant *kal-), meaning 'stone', or 'rock', found in prehistoric European toponyms. Indeed, numerous hydronyms and toponyms connected with the *kar- root exist in *Europe*. These include, among many others, *Harund* (*Scandinavia*), *Carron, Cart Water*, and *Cary* (*Great Britain*), *Carad* (*Ireland*), *Harste* (*Germany*), *Chiers* (*Belgium*), *Charentonne, Cher, Charante* (*France*), *Carusa* (*Italy*), *Carranzo, Carranza, Carisa*, and *Carantó* (*Spain*). These place names, according to Antonio Tovar, are all believed to be derived from the proto-form *kar(r)a* (< *kar-*) 'stone', or 'rock' (Tovar, 1977; 1982). Francisco Villar adds another famous denomination to this possible toponymic system, that is, *Carrara* (central *Italy, Tuscany,* in the province of *Massa-Carrara*), the name of a town well known for its celebrated marble (Villar, 1997, p. 126). Additionally, Coates (2020) recently explored the possible link of a number of Croatian toponyms to the *kar-/*kal-root. All these place names (and many others) are associated with the root *kar- and with the notion of an important primary resource, 'stone' (or 'rock'). While these names are Indo-European in their reconstructable forms and origins, some of them can be hypothesised to date back to Pre-Indo-European times, because they indicate places that were inhabited in extremely remote times.

As we saw with the *alb- root in the previous section, it is a theoretical possibility that some Indo-European toponymic roots could belong to a Pre-Indo-European linguistic layer of *Europe*. These stems, involved in the making of toponyms, over time and following the possible arrival of Indo-European people in the *Old Continent*, would have been incorporated into the Indo-European linguistic system and therefore phonetically, phonologically, morphologically, and semantically reused and re-functionalised by the Indo-Europeans. One such root is *kar- (and see the discussion of *borm-, Section 4.10). To avoid any kind of misunderstanding, all the *kar- place names mentioned above are unmistakably phonetically Indo-European. However, they are so ancient and so widespread all over Europe that they allow us, as mentioned, to hypothesise that they existed before Proto-Indo-European times, that is, before the possible arrival in *Europe* of the Indo-

Europeans, and therefore to postulate that these names could have been originally Pre-Indo-European.

The root *kar-* is productive not only at the toponymic level, but also at the
level of general lexicon. Examples include the Indo-European proto-form
*kartu(-)*, which is at the origin of the Ancient Greek adjective κρατύς
(*kratýs*) 'strong', and of the verb καρτύνω (*kartýnô*), or κρατύνω (*kratýnô*),
'to strengthen', of Gothic *hardus* 'hard', and of Latin *ardŭus* 'hard'. From these
instances, we can see that *kar-*, along with its derived forms, has the complementary meaning of '(being) hard', which is a typical property of the stone, that
is, the hardness of the stone, which is linguistically indicated by *kar-*
(Benveniste, 2001).

The *kar-* root has a presumably Ligurian[5] variant, *kal-*, which is attested,
for example, in the Italian word *calanco*. Scholars Giacomo Devoto and Gian
Carlo Oli define *calanco* as a 'narrow and deep erosion's furrow with many
ramifications, limited by thin ridges, generally devoid of vegetation; it is
a phenomenon from predominantly clay soils, produced by runoff and/or
washing out waters' (Devoto & Oli, 1975, p. 406). *Calanco*, in its plural
form *calanchi*, refers specifically to sedimentary rocks and soils that have
been eroded by wind and water. The *calanchi* are widespread, among other
places, in the *Appennino Emiliano-Romagnolo* (a mountain range in north-
central *Italy*) (Devoto & Oli, 1975, p. 406), as well as in much of the *Liguria*
region and in the lower quadrant of *Piedmont*, where many toponyms derived
from *kal-* can be recorded (Perono Cacciafoco, 2015a). Thus, it is generally
accepted that the term *calanchi* is directly related to these particular hydro-geo-
morphological features prevalent in lower *Piedmont*, *Liguria*, and *Emilia
Romagna* (northern and north-central *Italy*). Devoto and Oli believed that the
word *calanco* derives from a possibly Pre-Indo-European (or 'Mediterranean',
as discussed above) word *cala* (from *kal-* or *kar-*) (Devoto & Oli, 1975,
p. 404), with the Pre-Indo-European (then Ligurian) suffix *-anco*. Another
scholar, Tristano Bolelli, writes about the possibly Pre-Indo-European origins
of the term *cala* (Bolelli, 1995, p. 74). These elements depict the 'oscillations'
in the interpretations of the Pre-Indo-European versus Proto-Indo-European
nature of the root(s) *kar-*/*kal-*. However, as Perono Cacciafoco (2015a, p. 38)
notes, 'nothing is known (with the exception of the hypothesis of their existence) about the languages possibly spoken in the whole Neolithic *Europe* (and
also in more ancient and remote times, starting, at least, from the Upper

---

[5] The Ligurians were a prehistoric population of *Europe* who gave their name to *Liguria*, a region
in northern *Italy*. In ancient times, it was much larger than the current region, located in northwest
*Italy*. The Old Ligurian language has been considered, over time, as a possible Pre-Indo-
European language or as an Indo-European language of the Italic and/or Celtic group (Walman
& Mason, 2006). Some scholars, indeed, posit the existence of two Ligurians, a non-Indo-
European one and an Indo-European one.

Palaeolithic) and about their mutual relationships'. Instead, what is known about these languages comes from possible loan-words or loan-roots, like *kar-/*kal- in Indo-European, if we think that *kar- and *kal- came from a Pre-Indo-European substrate.

The connection of *kal- with common lexemes in Indo-European languages indicating different kinds of stones and their properties is further evidence of the association of *kar- with *kal- and of their semantic and cognitive link to the notion of 'stone'. This is highlighted, among others, by the Latin forms calx 'lime' and calcārĭus 'calcareous', the Ancient Greek word χάλιξ (chálix) 'pebble, stone dissolving in water, gravel, lime, limestone', and the Italian term calcare 'limestone' (Devoto & Oli, 1975, p. 408; Bolelli, 1995, p. 75). According to Perono Cacciafoco (2015a, p. 48), 'the root *kar-/*kal- seems to be, therefore, a single root expressed by two equivalent and homologous variants'. Through his research on this issue, Perono Cacciafoco was able to add at least nine other toponyms connected with the *kar-/*kal- root to a list of place names constituting the related toponymic system. Among them, the scholar reconstructed the etymology of two Ligurian toponyms, Carcare and Cairo Montenotte, which are the names of places surrounded by the massive presence of calanchi, the hydro-geological phenomena outlined above that have characterised (among other localities) Liguria from prehistoric times.

Carcare and Cairo Montenotte are located in Liguria, northwest Italy (Savona province). They are two towns belonging to the so-called Bormida Valley, which has its name from the Bormida River (the name of this river and the significance of its root, *borm-, will be covered in the next section).

Carcare is located at an important road junction along the route connecting southern Piedmont with the Ligurian seacoast, in the Ligurian hinterland. Historical sources show that one of the oldest versions of Carcare's name was Carcaris. This was a Late Latin plural ablative attested in a document of the year 1111. Another document also mentions Carcaris in 1179 (Gasca Queirazza et al., 1999). A prehistoric settlement in Carcare's territory is attested from the Neolithic. Carcare, therefore, was already inhabited from remote ages, and it is possible to hypothesise human presence in its area probably from the Upper Palaeolithic (Biagi, 1980; Guidi & Piperno, 2005). The toponym could be explained in connection with the hydro-geo-morphology of its territory, characterised by the presence of calanchi and rocky hills, and by hypothesising the reduplication of the *kar- root from which the place name derives.

What makes the toponym Carcare so important is that the phenomenon of reduplication is not common in Indo-European, and therefore is not morphologically productive (Perono Cacciafoco, 2015a, p. 40). Nonetheless, because the reduplication in Carcare's toponymic form is undeniable, it is possible to postulate that this phenomenon could come from a conceivable Pre-Indo-European morphological pattern. Therefore, the root *kar-, which is undeniably Indo-European, could hypothetically have Pre-Indo-European origins, identifiable through the phenomenon of reduplication detectable in *Carcare*'s name. That is, a morphological feature not common in Indo-European. This, of course, happens not at the level of etymology, but at the level of 'morphological treatment' of the stem. The location where *Carcare* is ubicated is, as mentioned, surrounded by 'stony' hills characterised by the widespread presence of *calanchi*, which could have been the original motivation for its name. Perhaps the possible reduplication of the root of the toponym sought to emphasise the large amount of *calanchi* that surrounded *Carcare* and, if it were so, this would generate a non-Indo-European morphological phenomenon. Indeed, the fact that the reduplication of a root is not a common feature of the Indo-European historical morphology suggests that *Carcare* could have been part of its geographical and toponymic landscape already in Pre-Indo-European times. Then, after the Indo-Europeans 'arrived' and settled in *Liguria*, they assimilated the root into their linguistic system and, eventually, the radical became a Proto-Indo-European root. However, the stem still retained some of its original morphological properties (e.g., the reduplication) even when it was adapted into the linguistic system of the new speakers.

*Cairo Montenotte* is a town located near *Carcare,* in *Liguria*, in the province of *Savona*. The toponym has been continuously attested since the Middle Ages (Perono Cacciafoco, 2015a, p. 42). Planimetries of the village from the archives of the *Diocesi di Acqui Terme* 'Roman Catholic Diocese of *Acqui Terme*' and of the *Diocesi di Savona-Noli* 'Diocese of *Savona-Noli*' drawn in the tenth century show a medieval town centre installed into the rectangular construction plan typical of feudal planned villages. Meanwhile, *Montenotte* is the name of a small hamlet belonging to the municipality, famous for a Napoleonic battle that was fought there in 1796. The first attested written records of *Cairo Montenotte* are from the year 967, as *Carium*, derived from the root *kar- and therefore linked to the notion of 'stone', 'cliff', or 'rock' (Gasca Queirazza et al., 1999, p. 114), and as *Carius* (Ravera, Tasca, & V., 1997, p. 70), with the same meaning. In its original form, *Carium/Carius*, the place name *Cairo (Montenotte)* derives from *car(i)- < *kar- (with *kar- being the original stem). The toponym, in the form *Cario*, is later attested in the year 991, in the *Charta di fondazione e donazione dell'Abbazia di San Quintino in Spigno* (the 'Founding and Donation *Charta* of the Saint Quentin's Abbey in *Spigno Monferrato*') (Bosio, 1972). This is the *Charta* outlining the donation of a large amount of land for the founding of the *Abbazia di San Quintino* 'Saint Quentin's Abbey', located in *Spigno Monferrato* (Bosio, 1972, pp. 140–2). Both the abbey and *Spigno Monferrato* are not far from *Cairo Montenotte*, on the route from lower *Piedmont* to *Savona*. The tracing of *Cairo Montenotte*'s etymology to the *kar-/*kal- root is supported by the hydro-geo-morphology of its territory, characterised by the presence of *calanchi*, and by the existence of a 'parallel oronym' (at the etymological level, even if quite distant geographically), *Monte Cairo* 'Cairo Mountain', a calcareous mount that rises north of the town of *Cassino* in the *Lazio* region, central *Italy*, which shares with *Cairo Montenotte* the same etymology derived from the root *\*kar-*. Moreover, the geological structure of *Monte Cairo* is composed of limestone rock, which semantically matches with some of the Ancient Greek, Latin, and Italian words we have listed above, derived from the *\*kar-/\*kal-* root. The oronym *Monte Cairo*, hence, is indirect evidence of the connection of the root *\*kar-/\*kal-* with the toponym *Cairo* (*Montenotte*).

Aside from *Carcare* and *Cairo Montenotte*, many other place names in *Italy* (particularly from *Piedmont*, *Liguria*, and *Tuscany*) and in *Europe* in general (as listed above) are derived from the same *\*kar-/\*kal-* root. They possibly form a large toponymic system. Such places include, among many others, *Carretto*, hamlet of *Cairo Montenotte*, the ancient village of *Calizzano*, in *Liguria*, in the province of *Savona*, *Carezzano* and *Caranzano*, in southern *Piedmont*, *Calasca*, in northern *Piedmont*, *Charance*, an Alpine locality in the *Gap* municipality, *France*, and *Calci* and *Carrara*, in *Tuscany*. Of these toponyms, *Charance* might appear at first sight atypical in the *\*kar-/\*kal-* system. Yet, Perono Cacciafoco (2015a, p. 47) explains that the toponym also derives from the root *\*kar-/\*kal-*. Specifically, he notes, the original stem for *Charance* is an Alpine root *\*cal-* (< *\*kar-/\*kal-*) and can be traced back to ancient Ligurian word *kalanco* or *kalanca* 'steep stony descent that serves as a channel for avalanches', or *calanco*. The meaning of *Charance* can be, therefore, 'site of the avalanche of stones', or 'place of the stony landslide', and hence is always connected with the notions of 'stone' and 'rock', represented by the root *\*kar-/\*kal-*.

In this historical reconstruction of two place names in the Ligurian hinterland, *Carcare* and *Cairo Montenotte*, we see how toponymy can help us to hypothesise the possible existence of pre-languages. We first analysed the possibility of an interesting reduplication process of the *\*kar-/\*kal-* root, extremely uncommon in Indo-European, in the place name *Carcare*. This morphological structure can, hence, be regarded as a 'linguistic fossil' showing that the root could have preserved some of its Pre-Indo-European features even in Indo-European times. We then saw how the root *\*kar-/\*kal-* shows its persistence and pervasiveness, in Indo-European context, in the toponym *Cairo* (*Montenotte*) and in a large number of Italian and European place names. Indeed, the notions of 'stone' and 'rock', and the relationship with hydro-geo-morphological features like the *calanchi* that are widespread in *Liguria* and elsewhere, are almost always at the origins of the place names derived from the root *\*kar-/\*kal-* discussed in this section.

### 4.10    From Pre-Language to Proto-Language: The Case of the *borm- Root

We just saw, in our analysis of the *kar-/*kal- root, that Indo-European stems could have theoretically been Pre-Indo-European in their origins, and then assimilated over time by Indo-European speakers to become properly Indo-European. The following example is inherent in another place name which could provide some clues on the possible existence of a pre-language (Pre-Indo-European) and of linguistic contact between speakers of that pre-language (Pre-Indo-European) and speakers of a proto-language (Indo-European), when the former language was replaced by the latter.

The hydronym under study in this section is *Bormida* (see Figure 4.4), the name of an Italian river flowing in northwest *Italy*, between the regions of *Liguria* and *Piedmont*. The denomination is derived from the root *borm- (> *bormo-), meaning 'warm', or 'hot', or 'warm water', or 'hot water', and could specifically refer to the waters of the river being 'warm', or 'hot'. Although the waters of the *Bormida* are not hot, the course of the river is dotted by hot springs, which could have been at the origins of the meaning 'hot waters'. The stem *borm- (> *bormo-) could possibly also be considered Pre-Indo-European in its origins, or at least 'more ancient' than Indo-European (and therefore non-Indo-European), as we will argue below. At the same time, the root also generates an extensive meaning connected with the notion of 'hot spring(s)'. The *Bormida River* has two main branches, *La Bormida di Spigno* and *La Bormida di Millesimo*, which join near the village of *Bistagno*, but in the territory under the jurisdiction of the inhabited centre of *Sessame*.

The *borm- root is attested not only in the hydronym, but also in a number of other place names, all of which are associated with the notion of 'hot water', or 'warm water'. One of them is *Bormio*, the name of a town located in *Lombardy*, northwest *Italy*, in the province of *Sondrio*. *Bormio* has been renowned from ancient times for its thermal springs.

Place names associated with the *borm- root include, among others, *Burmu*, a hamlet of *Pigna*, *Liguria*, northwest *Italy*, in the province of *Imperia*. Giulia Petracco Sicardi studied *Burmu*, meaning 'big spring' (Petracco Sicardi, 1962, p. 63). As stated above, the root *borm- could have an extended meaning connected with the notion of 'spring'. Meanwhile, Perono Cacciafoco (2015b) lists two place names, *Bormida*, a village located in *Liguria*, in the province of *Savona* (which gets its name directly from the hydronym, being ubicated along the river), and *Worms* (a famous and ancient city located in the *Rhineland-Palatinate* area, *Germany*, on the *Upper Rhine*), both of which derive from *borm-. It is important to note that the original (Romanised) attested Celtic name of *Worms* was *Borbetomagus*, or *Bormetomagus*, meaning 'town located in a territory rich in (warm) waters'. The centre, whose official Roman name

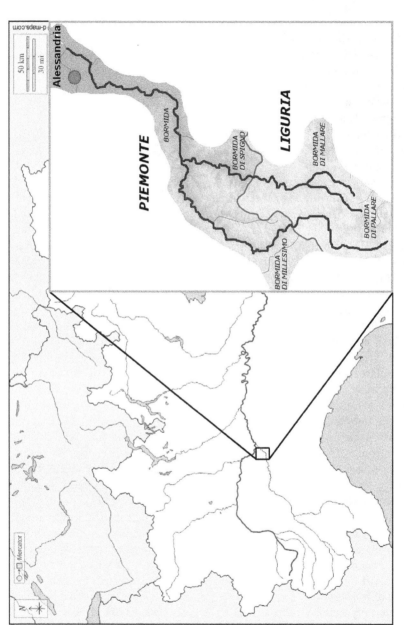

Figure 4.4 Location of the *Bormida River* (adapted from Ceragioli, 2014; d-maps, 2021)

was *Augusta Vangionum*, was then called *Vormatia*, later *Wormatia* or *Wormazia*, and the latter name has been in use since the sixth century. From the sixteenth century, the name appeared in the form *Wormbs*, which leads to the current denomination being attested from possibly at least the nineteenth century.

The hydronym *Bormida* appears in written sources as *Burmia*, in line 12 of the above-mentioned *Founding and Donation Charta of the Saint Quentin's Abbey in Spigno Monferrato*, drawn up on 4 May 991 (Bosio, 1972, pp. 18, 30, 138–40). *Burmia* is also in an 1137 document (VV.AA., 1899–), and is transcribed as *Burmea* in 1182 (Olivieri, 1965, p. 97). One of the most ancient attestations of the toponym *Bormio* is *Burmis*, from 822 (Gasca Queirazza et al., 1999). Going back further in time, Cassiodorus, in his work *Variae*, which was published in 538, mentions two toponyms, *Aquae Bormiae* and *Aqu(a)e Bormidae* (Cassiodorus, 1583). Perono Cacciafoco (2015b, p. 347) writes that these two places are difficult to locate and identify, but that both are related to the *borm- root and, hence, connected with either the place name *Bormio* and/or the hydronym *Bormida*. Despite the names being geographically difficult to pinpoint, Cassiodorus links *Aquae Bormiae* to a hot-water spring that can cure gout. Given that *Bormio* has very renowned thermal springs, this could be a significant clue for the possible association of *Aquae Bormiae* with *Bormio*. The name can also be referring to the *Bormida River*, since the watercourse flows through the city of *Acqui Terme* (*Piedmont*, northwest *Italy*, in the province of *Alessandria*), a small town renowned already in Roman times for its thermal waters (and for its hot, sulphurous spring called *La Bollente* 'The Boiling'). The meaning of the *borm- root is connected with the notions of 'warm', or 'hot' (in Proto-Indo-European $*g^{wh}erm\acute{o}$-/$*g^{wh}ormo$-) and thus could be extended to mean 'warm water(s)', or 'hot water(s)', because of the hot springs which surround the river in a large portion of its course. Getting back to *Aquae Bormiae* and *Aqu(a)e Bormida*, these names could therefore definitely be explained as 'warm waters', or 'hot waters'. Agreeing with the fact that *Aquae Bormiae* and *Bormida* stem from *borm-, Giacomo Devoto translated *Bormida* into 'the hot waters river', linking his interpretation of *borm- to *Aquae Bormiae* and the Latin term *formus*, meaning 'warm' (Devoto, 1962, p. 199). The *Bormida River* could also be linked to the names of the Celtic and Lusitanian gods *Bormō* and *Bormānus*, both associated with healing and (hot) springs. Variants of these names, such as *Borūs*, *Borvō*, *Bormō*, and *Bormānus*, are based on the *borm- (> *bormo-) root and on a connected stem *boru-. The stem *boru- could derive, in turn, from the *borm- root, and is considered a variant of the Proto-Celtic root *beru- 'to boil' (Pokorny, 1969).

The *borm- (> *bormo-) root could also be an equivalent of the Proto-Indo-European stem *bhreue- (and its variants *bher-, or *bhor-) (Pokorny, 1969, pp. 171–2), which means 'to bubble', or 'to boil', and is connected with words like Ancient Greek φρέαρ (*phréār*) 'well', or 'spring', Latin *fervēre* 'to boil', or 'to foam', and Gaulish *boruo* 'bubbling spring', or 'hot spring'. The root *\*bhreue-* (and its variants *\*bher-*, or *\*bhor-*) is also attested in some toponyms in the *\*borm-* toponymic system. Olivieri links the hydronym *Borbèra*, the name of a stream flowing in the homonymous *Borbèra Valley* (*Piedmont*, northwest *Italy*, in the province of *Alessandria*) to the root *\*borb-* (which is an equivalent of *\*borm-*, like in *Bormetomagus/Borbetomagus*), 'noise of the waters'. This is an onomatopoeic expression connected with the typical gurgling of a (hot) water spring or watercourse, and in turn can be linked to *\*bhreue-* (and its variants *\*bher-*, or *\*bhor-*) 'to bubble', or 'to boil', a process that produces the typical noise and, hence, the onomatopoeic expression (Olivieri, 1965, p. 95).

The *\*borm-* root (as well as the standard equivalent Indo-European stems *$\*g^{wh}ermó$-/$\*g^{wh}ormo$-*) also has a role in the 'making' of lexical items, in Indo-European languages, connected with the notions of 'hot' and 'warm', such as the already-mentioned Latin term *formus* 'warm', which can be traced back to the Proto-Indo-European proto-form *$\*g^{wh}ermos(-)$*. In this proto-form, the voiced aspirate labiovelar consonant /$g^{wh}$/ replaces the voiced bilabial /b/. Indeed, the root *\*borm-* (> *\*bormo-*) and the stems *$\*g^{wh}ermó$-/$\*g^{wh}ormo$-* are both Indo-European and are almost equivalent in their meaning and in their morphology. The difference in the root consonant (/b/ vs. /$g^{wh}$/) nonetheless seems quite relevant, as well as the slight semantic variation ('hot water'/ 'warm water' vs. 'hot'/'warm') and the fact that the *\*borm-* root seems more productive at the level of toponymy. Indeed, it is involved mainly in the 'making' of place names, while the *$\*g^{wh}ermó$-/$\*g^{wh}ormo$-* stems are connected with terms from the general Indo-European lexicon. These differences, therefore, allow us to hypothesise that the *\*borm-* (> *\*bormo-*) root is connected with the specific notion of 'water' ('warm water', or 'hot water', or, extensively, 'hot spring') and to a very ancient layer of the toponymy and hydronymy of *Europe*. Hence, we can postulate that it has Pre-Indo-European origins, and it would have been transferred into the Proto-Indo-European linguistic system through a process of reuse and re-functionalisation operated by Indo-European speakers once they settled in their historical territories in *Europe*. The root would have then been 'equated' by the typically Proto-Indo-European forms *$\*g^{wh}ermó$-* and *$\*g^{wh}ormo$-*, in a more generic and extensive meaning of 'warm', or 'hot'. The (Proto-)Indo-European roots *$\*g^{wh}ermó$-/$\*g^{wh}ormo$-*, as well as the possibly more ancient (and originally Pre-Indo-European?) *\*bhreue-* (and its variants *\*bher-/\*bhor-*), could have been later linked to *Bormida* and *Bormio* (and to their original root, *\*borm-* (> *\*bormo-*)), possibly also through Lepontic (or Celtic-Ligurian), an epigraphic Indo-European language and variety of Celtic. Lepontic is an ancient Alpine language that was spoken in parts of

*Rhaetia* and *Cisalpine Gaul* (what is now northern *Italy*) between 550 and 100 BCE and that could have inherited the two analogous stems from the possibly Pre-Indo-European root *\*borm-* (> *\*bormo-*) (Gasca Queirazza et al., 1999, p. 92; Pellegrini, 1981, p. 38).

In conclusion, the stem *\*borm-* (> *\*bormo-*) could have theoretically been widespread in *Europe* before the possible arrival of the Indo-Europeans. The phonetic treatment of the root consonant /b/ of *\*borm-* seems not to be immediately attributable to the (Proto-)Indo-European historical phonetics and the root would have been incorporated, over time, by the Indo-Europeans into their linguistic system. The stem was then reused and re-functionalised, becoming 'Indo-Europeanised' through the stem $*g^{wh}ermó-/*g^{wh}ormo-$, meaning, generically, 'warm', or 'hot'.

## 4.11    Summary

In this chapter, we have explored the differences between the notions of 'pre-language' and 'proto-language' and, by using examples from the Pre-Indo-European and Proto-Indo-European contexts, we have shown how the study of toponymy can be very relevant in reconstructing forms that can provide us with some important clues on the existence of pre-languages in prehistoric times.

The three toponymic systems analysed, the *\*alb-* (~ *\*albh-*), *\*kar-/\*kal-*, and *\*borm-* (> *\*bormo-*) systems, have allowed us to assess the possibilities of language-contact phenomena in prehistoric ages among speakers from different language families, in the dynamics of Indo-European versus non-Indo-European and/or of Proto-Indo-European versus Pre-Indo-European.

We have also been able to focus on the important notions of 'reuse' and 're-functionalisation' of roots and proto-forms in remote times, which are phenomena characteristic of linguistic contact. Due to the interaction among different speakers, a root or a lexeme in general acquires different meanings, morphology, and functions in the languages of the new speakers. This phenomenon can be prevalently reconstructed through the study and etymological analysis of ancient toponyms. Place names are, therefore, one of the few 'windows' we have to observe a linguistic world that is lost.

In the next chapter, we will turn our attention to contexts that do not have well-documented historical sources. This happens mainly in the case of undocumented languages and language families.

# 5     Diachronic Toponymy

## 5.1     What Is Diachronic Toponymy?

Diachronic toponymy (or, in some cases, diachronic toponomastics) is the discipline studying toponymy in the context of undocumented and/or endangered languages. Diachronic toponymy is concerned with reconstructing the possible origins of a place name (a) in undocumented languages, and (b) in the absence of historical records. At the linguistic and ethnic level, we are talking about language and place names belonging to aboriginal and/or Indigenous peoples anywhere in the world.

As the adjective *diachronic* entails, the chronological study of a toponym goes from one point in time to another, describing the 'passage' of a toponym, over time, from point A in (the possibly original form) to point B (the current, attested form of the place name). Diachronic toponymy, in terms of analysing the structure of a toponym, relies on an application of the comparative method based mainly on the assessment of diachronic phonetic changes. Through this study of place names, it is sometimes possible not only to reconstruct the etymology of toponyms, but also historical and unattested events that occurred to minority and Indigenous groups in the absence of written and/or historical records. This can be accomplished by analysing oral-traditional stories connected with a place name, as we have described in the *Lamòling* example in Chapter 1. This legend recounts the (hi)story of the Abui 'fallen god', *Lamòling*, documenting the passage from animism to polytheism and later to Christianity on *Alor Island*, in the Abui community (Perono Cacciafoco & Cavallaro, 2017; 2018). Eight local place names are connected with this tale and can be 'extracted' from it at the level of toponymic documentation, and this is a good example of how toponyms can be explained in linguistically undocumented contexts by analysing local oral traditions.

The term 'diachronic' in diachronic toponymy means, literally, 'through time' (from Ancient Greek *diá* [διά] 'through', and *chrónos* [χρόνος] 'time'). The practice of diachronic toponymy has to deal with contexts in which the absence of historical documents and records is often significant, and in which the etymological recovery of a place name is possible only between two ideal points in time, from (A), the currently attested toponym, to (B), the reconstructed proto-form obtained through application of the comparative method. This may need to be done by also comparing the languages spoken in a specific area that are possibly related to the language that is currently being analysed. This, in turn, produces the ideal 'image' of the diachronic toponymy reconstruction process as a movement that touches two points in time, through a straight line, with a starting point which is located *hic et nunc*, that is, the current attested toponym, and an ending point which is represented by a form which comes from a chronologically undefinable past (i.e., the reconstructed proto-form or root). However, while it is possible to reconstruct proto-forms and roots in this way, and we can therefore get back to the probable etymological origins of toponyms, the absence of written records makes it almost impossible to establish an exact chronology for the etymological forms. That is, we cannot define a detailed linguistic 'stratigraphy' for the place names.

Aboriginal and/or Indigenous peoples speaking undocumented languages, often in the absence of a mature and widespread written language, normally pass down their place names and the oral-traditional stories associated with them from generation to generation, according to a storytelling process which defines their cultural identity. By conducting language documentation fieldwork, and through interviews with local speakers, we can document the oral traditions and ancestral stories of the inhabited areas and collect data on the places under investigation. Afterwards, we can attempt to reconstruct the phonetic and phonological origins of the place names by, for example, comparing these toponyms with possible parallels in the common lexicon of both the target language and, if available, of neighbouring languages, especially those that possibly belong to the same language family.

## 5.2    Methodologies in Diachronic Toponymy

As discussed earlier, the main issue in dealing with diachronic toponymy is the need to conduct our linguistic analyses within largely undocumented and endangered languages. Unlike the context of historical toponomastics, in which we work with well-documented languages and with plenty of historical records, the languages analysed in diachronic toponymy usually do not have a writing system. If they do, it may not be widely used and most likely does not have a long tradition. This means that the explanations for the names of places are often passed down orally, through local myths and legends. Hence, rather than relying on written records (as we might do in historical toponomastics), the toponymist must make use of anthropological-linguistic procedures from language documentation and field linguistics, such as interviews with the inhabitants of the places.

Very similar to the step-by-step guide in historical toponomastics outlined in Table 3.1, diachronic toponymy also involves answering the already-mentioned *wh*-questions. The main difference can be seen in the column outlining the sources of data needed to analyse the place names. Importantly, to complement what the local inhabitants say to the researchers during their field interviews, significant details can still be drawn from the disciplines of physical geography and landscape studies on the area under scrutiny. A step-by-step guide to the approach applied when conducting research in diachronic toponymy can be found in Table 5.1.

Table 5.1 *A step-by-step guide to diachronic toponymy*

| Step 1: Gathering the data of the place name | |
| --- | --- |
| Sources | Aims |
| *Oral records*<br>*E.g., legends, myths, interviews*<br>    *with locals* | • Who named the place?<br>• Who lived there?<br>• When was the place named?<br>• What were the previous names of the place, if any?<br>• Are there any oral stories connected with the place? (These oral traditions may give us clues on when the place could have been named and the previous names of the place, if any.)<br>• What are the names of the toponyms surrounding this place? |
| *Visual representations*<br>*E.g., maps or sketches arising from*<br>    *oral interviews with locals and*<br>    *from a visual inspection of the*<br>    *place* | • What kind of geographical features (physical and human) surround this place? Is there a special primary good located in/around the area of the place name (e.g., water, good wood, agricultural or horticultural sources, fire, stones, caves, tools, etc.)?<br>• Where is this place located, in relation to the places identified from the oral records? |
| Step 2: Linguistic analysis of the place name | |
| *Linguistic and toponymic analysis*<br>    *of the place name* | • What is the onomastic source of the place name (landscape features, proper nouns, ceremonial locations, significant trees, etc.)?<br>• What is the primary and basic structure of the place name (simple or compound)?<br>• What is the morphology of the place name (e.g., if it shows morphological reduplication or if it has specific prefixes and/or suffixes)?<br>• What is the frequency of the structural/morphological components of the place name in the toponymic system (e.g., if they are isolated or if their roots are found in other place names)?<br>• What does the place name mean? Is its meaning linked to the hydro-geo-morphology of the territory? |

Table 5.1 *(cont.)*

| **Step 3: Extra-linguistic analysis of the place name** | |
| --- | --- |
| *Physical geography*<br>*E.g., physical inspections of the locality by walking through it, sketching the landscape and environment, making mental and physical maps of the territory* | • Are there any other places with the same root? Is there a toponymic system connected with this root?<br>• What kind of geographical features (physical and human) surround these places? What do we know about the hydro-geo-morphological features of these places?<br>• Where are they located? |
| *Landscape studies*<br>*E.g., inspections and excavations, oral interviews with locals* | • Who lived/lives there?<br>• Were/are there any dominant trades or activities carried out?<br>• Was/is there any material evidence of physical or significant geographical or human features (e.g., cliffs, settlements)? |
| **Step 4: Putting it all together** | |
| *Summary*<br>*To reconstruct the remote origins of a place name, we have to take into account the following* | • Societal data: who named the place? Who lived there? What did they do? Do we know anything about the 'age' of the place based on the oral stories connected with the name? This is because the oral-word societies often tell stories on how a place name, in its oldest form, could have been derived. At the same time, it is important to note that the most ancient names also tend to reflect the primary goods available in the area and the hydro-geo-morphology of the territory. Hence, a place which is called 'pasture of the flowers' trail' is probably not the most ancient or remote name, as this represents a sort of 'poetic' interpretation of the landscape.<br>• Linguistic data: what is the onomastic source of the place name? What is the primary and basic structure of the place name? What is the morphology of the place name? What is the frequency of the structural/morphological components of the place name in the toponymic system? What does the place name mean? Is it linked to the hydro-geo-morphology of the territory?<br>• Physical geography and landscape studies: where is this place? Where are other places with similar names? Is there a toponymic system connected with it? What kind of geographical features (physical and human) surround this place? |

## 5.3     A Diachronic Toponymy Case Study: Abui

How this step-by-step process might be utilised in a real scenario is demonstrated in a study of the toponymic systems composed of Abui place names. Abui was, until recently, a largely undocumented Papuan language spoken on the island of *Alor*, in southeast *Indonesia* (*Alor-Pantar* archipelago, *Timor* area). Abui is now better documented thanks to the efforts of scholars, such as Marian Klamer, Gary Holton, Antoinette Schapper, and František Kratochvíl, studying this language in the past twenty years. The language belongs to the Alor family of the Alor-Pantar languages, a family of clearly related Papuan languages spoken on the islands of the *Alor-Pantar* archipelago and derived from a common ancestor, Proto-Alor-Pantar. The language family is conventionally divided into two branches, the Alor branch and the Pantar branch, spoken on the islands of *Alor* and *Pantar*, respectively (see Figure 5.1).

In this section, we will analyse and discuss, using criteria from diachronic toponymy, two case studies of toponymic systems found on the island of *Alor*.

### 5.3.1     *The Abui Toponymic System of* Lamang Tāha, Lamang Uwo, Lalamang, *and* Laaling

We will focus now on the toponymic system composed of the Abui place names *Lamang Tāha*, *Lamang Uwo*, *Lalamang*, and *Laaling*, from *Alor Island*. This discussion draws from an earlier study by Perono Cacciafoco, Cavallaro, and Kratochvíl (2015), and the toponymic system highlighted here provides an excellent case study on how diachronic toponymy might be conducted and

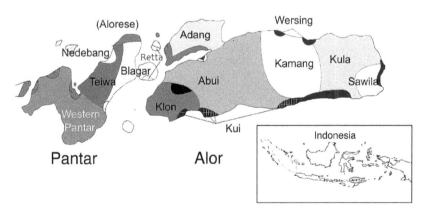

Figure 5.1  Map of the Alor-Pantar languages spoken in the *Alor* archipelago (adapted from Holton, 2009)

trialled in an oral-word society characterised by the presence of endangered and/or undocumented languages.

Two villages whose names are surely linked, *Lamang Tāha* and *Lamang Uwo*, are located on *Alor Island*, in the north-central territory of the Abui area. The first step to analyse them is to gather as much data as possible on the toponyms and on the areas where they are located. An illustration of how this first step can be carried out as shown in Table 5.2.

Table 5.2 *An example of step 1 in a diachronic toponymy study of four Abui place names*

| | |
|---|---|
| *Who named the places?* *Who lived there?* | **Abui people, who share family ties, live in these villages. They not only share family ties, but are organised according to a specific social system inherent in the management and use of the natural resources in their villages. These resources are normally managed, in turn, by each village, with each village regulating and deciding on the sharing of the local natural goods and resources for one year.** |
| *When were the places named?* | In these contexts, the researchers have no idea of when the places where named. Clearly, the toponymic system of *\*la-* was generated 'all together', since the speakers belong to the same enlarged community. However, it is impossible even to say which village, chronologically, came before or after. |
| *What were the previous names of the places, if any?* | Oral narratives only go back so far. Therefore, there is no record of any previous name, as far as we know. |
| *Are there any oral stories connected with the places? (These oral traditions may give us clues on when the places could have been named and the previous names of the places, if any.)* | So far, we have also not been able to collect any oral-traditional stories on these places, but we hypothesise that they do exist. |
| *What are the names of the toponyms surrounding these places?* | The place names around the four villages are (apparently) etymologically unrelated to them, e.g., *Lelawi*, which is connected with the notion of 'stone' (because of the 'rocky' nature of the landscape), *Lilafang*, which has an (apparently) obscure etymology, *Mafui/ Mafii*, which means 'flat village' (because its territory is located on a plateau), *Fulful*, which can be translated as 'tricky village' (linked to a local oral-traditional story), and the hamlet, *Hane Alo*, which means 'his name is Alo' (linked to another local oral-traditional story). |

Table 5.2 (*cont.*)

| What kind of geographical features (physical and human) surround these places? Is there a special primary good located in/around the area of the places (e.g., water, good wood, agricultural or horticultural sources, fire, stones, caves, tools, etc.)? | *Alor* is a mountainous island, and most of its villages are located on steep hills. However, these *la-/*lala-* villages are ubicated on a plateau, making their landscape relatively flat. This means that one of the main features of the landscape is the flat terrain, as it permits the cultivation of several varieties of trees which are considered 'good wood for houses'. Sometimes, the trees and the plants growing spontaneously there are burned to fertilise the territory and to grow better trees. |
| Where are these places in relation to the places identified from the oral records? | The villages, as mentioned, are located in the north-central area of the Abui territory, on *Alor Island*. |

From the information gathered in step 1, we know that the toponymic lexeme *lamang*, in *Lamang Tāha* and *Lamang Uwo*, at the point of time when the fieldwork was conducted (i.e., in June 2015), was considered, also by the local speakers, unclear in its meaning, while the meaning of the words *tāha* and *uwo* was clear, and refers to the positions 'above' and 'below', respectively. Based on the landscape features and hydro-geo-morphology of the places, these two terms express very transparent spatial indications of the villages, identifying the locations of these two inhabited centres relative to another village, *Lalamang*, also from the same area, and whose name the locals translate as 'the village of the good wood for houses'. By geographically and toponymically associating *Lamang Tāha* and *Lamang Uwo* with *Lalamang*, and by ascertaining that the second morphological parts of *Lamang Tāha* and *Lamang Uwo* refer to their spatial orientation in relation to *Lalamang*, we are able to postulate and map out the existence of a toponymic system, involving and including *Lamang Tāha*, *Lamang Uwo*, and *Lalamang*. The initial oral interviews with native speakers revealed that *lamang* was considered obscure. Nonetheless, after further investigations and after talking with them about the possible root *la-*, and the eventuality of it being reduplicated in *lala-*, as witnessed in *Lalamang*, the locals recognised in *la-* the notion of 'good wood', or 'good wood for houses'. A follow-up visual inspection showed that the trees in the area, that is, the main feature of the landscape of that plateau, are indeed considered to produce good wood, and that the wood of those trees is the one used to build houses. This provides a confirmation of the fact that the villages in this toponymic system have been named after a renewable natural resource, that is, that specific 'good wood'.

The second step involves the linguistic and toponymic analysis of the place names. As mentioned, *tāha* and *uwo* denote the transparent spatial indicators 'below' and 'above' of the places they name (with reference to their position in relation to *Lalamang*), and the \**la-* in *lamang* refers to the landscape feature of 'good wood for building houses'. A morphological analysis of these place names shows that, in their element *lamang*, they have a common stem, *la-*, as well as a common suffix, *-mang* (this will be detailed below).

Interestingly, *Lalamang* 'the village of the good wood for houses' can be parsed into \**la-*, \**-la*, and \**mang*, making it possible to speculate the reduplication of \**la-* before the suffix \**-mang* 'village'. *Lalamang* shows a common process in Abui toponymy in which the original root of a place name is reduplicated, a linguistic feature shared with a number of other Papuan and Austronesian[1] languages. This kind of reduplication always adds to a word a semantic 'nuance' of excellence, and raises an adjective to its superlative degree. Therefore, while \**la-* means 'good wood for houses', \**lala-* means 'very good wood for houses', or 'excellent wood for houses'. It is possible, following this, to recognise a sort of hierarchy between *Lalamang* and *Lamang Tāha* and *Lamang Uwo*, with *Lalamang* as the central and more important village, whose territory is characterised by the presence of the 'best/excellent wood for houses', and the two *lamang(s)* as two 'satellite villages', where the good wood for houses is good, but not of the same high quality as the wood in *Lalamang*.

As mentioned above, the etymological solution for the *lamang*-type place names did not come from the two *lamang(s)* and their root \**la-*, but from *Lalamang* and its reduplicated root \**lala-*. Apparently, the local speakers were unable to recognise the meaning of 'good wood for houses' in the simple, segmented root \**la-* in *Lamang Tāha* and *Lamang Uwo*, but they were able to retrieve it in its superlative form, \**lala-*, from *Lalamang*. When asked about the possible association of the (reduplicated) \**la-* root from *Lalamang* with the 'normal' root \**la-* from the two *Lamang* toponyms, the speakers were able to confirm that the three place names did share the same root, with the meaning of 'good wood for houses' but at different levels of quality, and that \**lala-* was a reduplicated, 'emphatic' form of \**la-*. This process can provide the readers with an idea of how the techniques of diachronic toponymy in the field of language documentation work; they function in a continuous interaction and dialogue with the speakers and in the collection of parts of a difficult linguistic puzzle that begins to make sense only in the end.

Further fieldwork investigations, moreover, revealed the existence of another Abui place name geographically and etymologically connected with the two *lamang(s)* and *Lalamang*, of the village of *Laaling*. This inhabited centre is not far from where *Lalamang* is located and likewise is characterised by the presence

---

[1] Personal comment by Gérard Diffloth.

of large treed areas. *Laaling* was translated by the Abui native speakers as 'place after burning'. If segmented as *Laa-ling*, the suffix of the place name could be connected with the Abui verb *tōlāling*, meaning 'to spread a fire everywhere'. *Laaling*'s territory, on the same plateau as *Lamang Tāha*, *Lamang Uwo*, and *Lalamang*, has also traditionally been used for the production of the 'good wood for houses'. In particular, in *Laaling*, a massive burning of the vegetation is periodically conducted to fertilise the soil and facilitate the growing of the trees. The root of this place name could be explained, therefore, by taking into account the meaning of the root *\*la-* in the names of the other three villages, as outlined above, that is, 'good wood for houses'. Nonetheless, the stem in *Laaling*, *\*laa-*, shows a lengthening of the vowel /a/, which makes it 'quantitatively' different (because it is longer) from the /a/ in the *\*la-* root of the other three villages. Despite this, when interviewed, the native speakers recognise in this *\*lā-* root the same morphology and meaning of the common *\*la-* root that we have talked about so far, indicating 'good wood for houses'. However, when asked to translate it, they gloss it as 'the best/excellent wood for houses', just as they did with the *\*lala-* reduplicated form of *Lalamang*. This is because, over time, this root was reduplicated, just like the stem in *Lalamang*, but because of phonetic and phonological changes that we cannot date the /l/ sound in the second *\*-la-* part of the *\*lala-* root was dropped. This produced two consecutive /a/ sounds from *\*la(-l-)a-* and therefore they merged into one phoneme, /a/, with the characteristic of its quantitatively longer vowel still evident in the Abui pronunciation of the place name, and in its perceived meaning, that is, as a superlative having 'the best/excellent wood for houses'. According to this reconstruction, the toponym *Laaling* could be mapped as follows.

*La-* + *-la-* (reduplication) + *-ling* (possibly from *tōlāling* 'to spread a fire everywhere', or 'to burn trees and plants to fertilise the terrain')

↓

*Lala-ling*

↓

*La(-l-)a-ling*

↓

*La-a-ling*

↓

*Laaling* (or *Lāling*, due to the presence of the double sound /a/ in the root)

An interpretation of the place name *Laaling* associates it with the practice of clearing the land by burning vegetation, in order, as mentioned, to fertilise the soil and facilitate the growing of trees which provide the wood suitable to build houses. This interpretation was made possible by drawing together the hydro-geo-morphology of the territory, with particular reference to its natural and human landscape, in this case the presence of varieties of trees that are good for building houses, or the burning process to fertilise the soil to allow them to grow, and the derived meaning of the root *la-. Further evidence is provided by the connection with the above-mentioned Abui verb *tōlāling*, which could be translated as 'to burn trees and plants to fertilise the terrain' and in Abui is used also as a noun or as an adjective meaning 'something burned', or 'all burned', or 'burnt'. According to some of the locals, *Laaling* was also the place where firewood was collected. *Laaling*, therefore, both because of its territorial location, that is, it is located at the same area of the villages of *Lamang Tāha, Lamang Uwo*, and *Lalamang*, and because of its etymology can be safely considered another place name belonging to the *la-toponymic system in Abui, characterised by inhabited centres which share the same etymology (the root *la-) and the same features from the natural landscape.

In this case study, we have seen how, in the absence of written records, methods from field linguistics and language documentation were used in the collection and analysis of toponymic data. This was done through interviews with native speakers and a physical inspection of the landscape during field-work. This research led to the discovery of a toponymic system on *Alor Island* consisting of a set of place names related to each other. The four place names are all linked to the Abui root *la-, meaning 'good wood for houses', and *Lamang Tāha, Lamang Uwo*, and *Lalamang* are also related to the toponymic and onomastic source of the notion of 'village' as expressed by the suffix *-mang*. We have said throughout this book that, besides their linguistic nature, place names must always be considered through an interpretation of the extra-linguistic elements that substantiate them, for example, the hydro-geo-morphology of their territories and the presence of primary goods available in their areas.

## 5.4    Diachronic Toponymy and Historical Semantics

Apart from analysing phonetic and phonological changes, as mentioned above, the interpretation and evaluation of place names can also go into more depth by assessing them through additional criteria considering their historical semantics. Some of these criteria are outlined in Table 5.3.

Thus, diachronic toponymy, through the application of etymological and semantic analyses, can lead to the reconstruction of a possible developmental path for a place name. Thereafter, after reconstructing a sort of preliminary 'identity card' of the denomination, the scholar can further compare the toponym with words from the general lexicon of the target language to confirm or disprove the possible reconstructed proto-form and root for the place name in question.

Table 5.3 *A summary of historical semantics criteria that can complement the historical-linguistic and anthropological-linguistic study of place names (Perono Cacciafoco et al., 2015)*

| Criteria/questions | Rationale |
|---|---|
| 1. *Is the place name transparent/self-evident (e.g., can be translated into literally something like 'village on the river', 'village located on the top of the mountain') or unclear?* | This question allows the toponymist to ascertain if the place name corresponds to the hydro-geo-morphological structure of the surrounding landscape. |
| 2. *Is the place name related to the primary goods used/sold/eaten by the people in the territory (e.g., water, food, animals, stone, fire, etc.)?* | Given that people in the ancient past tended to name things after primary goods, this question allows researchers to infer if the place name and its etymology is potentially more ancient or recent in origin. It also facilitates a study on the possible onomastic changes of the toponym over time. |
| 3. *Is the place name inherent in a physical feature of the territory? This can come in two forms, a 'poetic'/descriptively imaginative interpretation of the landscape (e.g., 'village of the flowery meadows') or a directional and spatial description of the settlement (e.g., 'upper village')?* | This question allows the toponymist to infer the possible 'age' of the toponym, because the 'poetic'/descriptively imaginative interpretation of the landscape and the directional spatial description of the settlement could mean that a place name is less ancient than those linked to primary goods for survival. A toponym with a 'poetic'/descriptively imaginative interpretation of the landscape may, possibly, imply the 'intellectualisation' of the landscape by speakers, where the magnificence and features of a place are described through metaphors, 'poetic' images, 'imaginative' adjectives, and other 'intellectualised' descriptors. |
| 4. *Is the place name a compound (e.g., 'big village')?* | The eminent compound structure of a place name helps the researcher to conclude whether the toponym is generally transparent in meaning (see question 1 above). |
| 5. *Is the place name semantically ambiguous?* | If the answer to this question is 'yes', it becomes important to reconstruct the original meaning of the place name by comparing it with other words and toponyms from the general vocabulary or the toponymic lexicon of its language and other related languages. |
| 6. *Does the place name (or its root) show a semantic specialisation (i.e., the narrowing of its meaning) over time (e.g., from 'town' as a 'generic town' to 'a specific part of a town or locality')?* | This criterion allows the toponymist to highlight the phenomena of semantic shift in place names over time and to assess if and how that semantic shift unveils any naming dynamics among connected toponyms in a specific area. It also helps the researcher uncover the possible relationship between names with settlement dynamics, movements of populations, natural catastrophes, natural phenomena, or historical events. |

An example of this process can be appreciated by applying it to the toponym *Afena Hapong*, another Papuan place name from the Abui territory of *Alor Island*. Following the above indicators, the procedure is illustrated in Table 5.4.

In summary, a deep knowledge of the lexicon and morpho-phonemics of the undocumented or endangered language under scrutiny goes a long way in helping the scholar to reconstruct the etymology of a place name.

Table 5.4 *A linguistic/toponymic analysis of* Afena Hapong *(Perono Cacciafoco* et al.*, 2015, p. 41)*

| Linguistic/toponymic analysis in diachronic toponomy | | Historical-semantic classification | |
|---|---|---|---|
| The onomastic source | *hapong* 'in front of' (landscape feature) + village; *afena* 'village'? | The place name is self-evident or unclear | *hapong* is clear and easily explainable at the etymological level; *afena* is clear and fully explainable only after the etymological reconstruction and the assessment of its semantic shift |
| The primary and basic structure of the name | Compound, two lexemes | The place name is related to the primary goods for survival | No |
| The 'morphology' of the name | 'Free morphemes' | The place name is inherent or not inherent in a physical feature of the territory | Spatial description |
| The frequency in the toponymic system of the language | High (*afena* is common in the language – it is a widespread word in the general lexicon and in other toponyms, generating at least one toponymic system) | The place name is a compound with clear semantic contents for each of its components | Yes |
| The semantics and the links with hydro-geomorphology | *Afena Hapong* 'a hamlet located in front of a village' (with, partially, the same name) – clear spatial indicator | The place name (or its root, or at least one of its lexical components) shows a possible 'semantic specialisation' | Yes |

The numerous toponyms in Abui that contain the element *afena* attracted the attention of researchers, who then extended the analysis to how *afena* is used as a normal lexical item (i.e., not in a place name), and to its cognates in other Alor-Pantar languages. Perono Cacciafoco et al. (2015) were able to confirm the sound law according to which in the Abui language the original Proto-Alor-Pantar sound *-*b*- becomes -*f*-. In the Abui context, therefore, *afena*, as well as its equivalent *afeng*, are two words belonging both to the general lexicon of the language and to its toponymic vocabulary. Both words mean 'village' and come from a Proto-Alor-Pantar proto-form *\*haban* 'village'.

The important aspect to highlight here is that the reconstruction of the sound change in these languages was boosted by the toponymic relevance of *afena*. While the sound change would most likely have been reconstructed independently from toponymy, there is no denying the fact that the study of *afena* as a toponymic element focussed the attention of field linguists on the term and its cognates. This led researchers to conclude that the Proto-Alor-Pantar bilabial phoneme /b/ is represented in Abui by the labiodental fricative sound /f/, and thus *afena* in Abui comes from *\*haban* in Proto-Alor-Pantar (Perono Cacciafoco et al., 2015). This reconstruction was made possible by applying the comparative method to numerous sets of cognates from the common lexicon shared by Abui with its neighbouring and related Papuan languages from *Alor Island*, such as Kamang (Woisika), Kui, Adang/Kabola, Klon, Kafoa (Jafoo), Sawila (Tanglapui), Kula/Lamtoka (Tanglapui), and Wersing/Kolana. The analysis of their phonetic and phonological similarities and changes, which is the basis of the comparative method, highlighted a regular sound change according to which almost every time the sound /b/ appears in Papuan languages on *Alor* it is changed into /f/ in Abui (and its Papuna variant). These languages have a prevalence of the /b/ sound (as seen in *\*haban*), while Abui uses /f/ (as seen in *afena* and *afeng*). Because (Due to the fact that) /b/ is widespread in the Alor-Pantar languages, this phoneme can be considered the original one. Therefore, /f/ in Abui can be defined as an innovation. *\*haban*, as a proto-form, belongs to the Proto-Alor-Pantar proto-language.

This has quite significant implications not only at the level of the etymological reconstructions of the common lexemes of Abui and of the assessment of the sound laws governing the Alor-Pantar languages, but also at the level of recovering the correct etymology of the proto-forms and roots of local place names.

### 5.4.1    *The Abui Toponymic System of* Afena Hapong, Afena Hietang, *and* Afena Poming

This case study focusses on the Abui village names *Afena Hapong*, *Afena Hietang*, and *Afena Poming*. Together, they constitute a toponymic system. As mentioned above, the main lexemes used in Abui to refer to the notion of 'village' are *afena*, *afeng*, as well as another lexeme, *melang*. In the previous section, we showed that both *afena* and *afeng* derive from the Proto-Alor-Pantar[2] (Proto-Alor sub-branch) form *\*haban*, which has been reconstructed by comparing Abui words with cognates of other Papuan languages belonging to the Alor branch.

The second elements of the toponyms, *hapong*, *hietang*, and *poming*, depict a spatial/directional aspect of the villages. The term *hapong* derives from the stem *\*(-)pong-*, with *\*ha-* as a prefix, and the compound means 'in front of'; *hietang* comes from the stem *\*(-)tang-*, with *\*hie-* as a prefix, meaning 'below'; and *poming* (prefix *\*po-* + stem *\*[-]ming*) in Abui means 'above', and is a spatial/directional indication opposed to *hietang* 'below'. Therefore, the place names have the meanings of 'village' (*afena*) 'in front of' (*hapong*), 'village' (*afena*) 'below' (*hietang*), and 'village' (*afena*) 'above (*poming*). Thus, *Afena Hapong* would mean 'place (located) in front of the village', or 'village (located) in front of another/the village', or simply 'village in front of'; *Afena Hietang* would mean 'place (located) below the village', or 'village (located) below a village', or simply 'village below'/'lower village'; and *Afena Poming* would mean 'place (located) above the village', or 'village (located) above another/the village', or simply 'village above'.

While *afena* and *afeng* sound pretty similar and are essentially the same word, our fieldwork trips revealed that the word *afena* is normally utilised to define hamlets or minor villages, while *afeng* has a more generalised use, depicting all kinds of villages. The inference we can make is that *Afena Hapong* is an inhabited centre subordinate to another village, and the spatial/ directional indication in its name ('in front of') refers to the larger village to which it belongs. As mentioned, *afeng* is prevalently used to indicate relatively bigger or 'major' villages, for example, among many others, *Fuung Afeng* 'peak village'. Moreover, according to the local speakers, *afena* seems to be used more often in the composition of place names than *afeng*, while *afeng* is a more common lexical item in the everyday speech of Abui speakers for the word 'village', when the term is used generically and not in toponyms. Therefore, *afena* seems to be a 'more toponymic' form, while *afeng* (while still appearing in Abui toponymy) appears to be a term more diffused in the Abui common lexicon (Perono Cacciafoco et al., 2015, p. 42). Indeed, *afeng* can be used to indicate a generic village or hamlet, without needing to specify the exact place name. Besides *afena* and *afeng*, the other word that Abui people commonly use to indicate a village is *melang*, for instance, *Muur Meelang* 'lemon village'. This shows that the terminology for 'village' in Abui has become multifaceted over time, going from generic terms for 'village', *afeng* and *melang*, used both in the general lexicon and in

---

[2] Proto-Alor-Pantar is the unattested and reconstructed 'mother language' from which all the Alor-Pantar languages, like Abui, derive.

local toponymy, to more specific notions like 'hamlet', 'subdivision', 'locality', 'part of a village', and 'area around a village', represented by *afena*.

While *afena* and *afeng* are actually two variants of the same word and come from the Proto-Alor-Pantar proto-form *\*haban*, the reconstruction of the etymology of *melang* is more problematic. According to some scholars (among others, Holton et al., 2012), *melang* could also derive from the proto-form *\*haban*. However, it is not easily reconstructed and it can only be done when we consider the lexicon of a related language, Kamang. The Kamang lexemes that are possibly involved in the 'making' of the word *melang* are *mane* and *komang*, which indicate 'a place where somebody lives' and/or 'fireplace' (Perono Cacciafoco et al., 2015, p. 43). However, this etymological reconstruction is not confirmed yet and at the moment is still at a hypothetical level.

Local speakers confirmed that the three villages were not independent or 'villages in themselves', but that in the past they developed around a 'major' village whose name was simply *Afena*, without any specific toponymic element or marker, meaning essentially 'village'. Nonetheless, in this toponymic system, what *Afena* would have meant in the perceptions of the local speakers was not just 'village', but 'the village' ('the main village'), while the other three *afena(s)* would have been three hamlets of the main village, specifically *Afena Hapong*, 'the hamlet located in front of the main village (*Afena*)', *Afena Hietang*, 'the hamlet located below the main village (*Afena*)', and *Afena Poming*, 'the hamlet located above the main village (*Afena*)'. Like for the *\*la-* toponymic system described above, language documentation techniques, with the etymological procedures applicable in diachronic toponymy, allow us to reconstruct the descriptive strategies used by local people to give names to their places and to understand their perceptions of their environment. Moreover, we are able to delineate how aboriginal and/or Indigenous peoples represent their world through the names they provide their places with.

The two case studies outlined in this section illustrate how research in diachronic toponymy can be supported by the analysis of reconstructed phonetic and phonological features of the languages under examination and of the assessment of the spatial description strategies by the local speakers. The second case study showed how this approach also revealed that an important semantic specialisation of toponymic terms had occurred over time. The approach of diachronic toponymy enables the researchers to investigate the origins and etymology of place names in endangered and undocumented contexts, and to see how aboriginal and/or Indigenous people perceive the space and their landscape, which are 'encoded' in their languages and toponymic terminologies.

Etymological methods in diachronic toponymy are indispensable in reconstructing roots and proto-forms. This can be done by comparing lexemes from the target language to cognates in related languages belonging to the same language family, as shown, for example, in the discussion on the word *melang*.

This allows the toponymist to attempt an etymological reconstruction of lexemes and place names in the absence of readily available historical and written sources. Furthermore, the assessment of any possible diachronic semantic shift can also help to analyse place names by ascertaining their transparency in meaning or their association with natural goods and/or physical features of the landscape.

In the context of diachronic toponymy, the ultimate aim of the toponymist is the reconstruction of what may be the original morphological structure and meaning of place names. That is, we try to arrive at the moment when the place was given its first name and uncover the possible reasons for its original naming process. As we have shown in this chapter so far, this is usually done by combining the etymological reconstruction with an assessment of any diachronic semantic shift(s) in place names, as well as by relying on all the information obtainable from the physical geography, hydro-geo-morphology, and landscape features of the territories. However, as we also said earlier, without any written records, we do not have the possibility of reconstructing the place name chronologically, step-by-step. It is worth remembering that the analysis of the hydro-geo-morphology of the places under investigation must be diachronic, and need to take into account the changes of the landscape over time (see Chapter 6 for a discussion of landscape archaeology). Not only does this allow the toponymist to uncover or make educated guesses about the most 'ancient' origins of place names in the absence of written and historical records, but it also allows the researcher to reconstruct people's movements and settlement dynamics over time, as well as important societal changes in the communities. For example, the documentation of the *Lamòling* legend and of the place-naming process associated with it permitted Perono Cacciafoco and Cavallaro (2017) to reconstruct social and cultural changes brought about by the introduction of Christianity on *Alor Island*.

## 5.5 Oral Stories as Toponymic Data

Given that diachronic toponymy works in the context of undocumented and endangered languages, where historical records and written sources are generally not readily available, the collection and analysis of oral-traditional myths and legends, and folklore in general, become indispensable in a linguistic and toponymic study. This is because, in these contexts, oral-traditional tales and stories are often associated with place names, and are transmitted from generation to generation only orally, and in the absence of written records. Therefore, an anthropological-linguistic attention to this intangible heritage of aboriginal and/or Indigenous people is always required and can provide the researchers with a great contribution not only in documenting endangered languages, but also in reconstructing undocumented toponymy. At the level of diachronic toponymy, the process involves the collection, preferably through audio or video recordings, and then the transcription of oral traditions connected with local place names from local speakers. This procedure, as mentioned, allows the researchers to collect and list place names through myths, legends, tales, and stories concerning local toponyms, and more generally enables field linguists to document the languages and cultures of their speakers. What we just described is best exemplified by the discovery and documentation of the *Lamòling* story mentioned in Chapter 1 (Perono Cacciafoco & Cavallaro, 2017). It was only through numerous interviews with local speakers and with the story's traditional 'owners', that is, the people who are the official and 'authorised' storytellers of the community, that the Abui legend and its associated toponyms and micro-toponyms could be reconstructed. More importantly, this foundation myth, which the Abui people believe is core to their identity, once discovered, allowed the researchers to better document not only the cultural identity and intangible heritage of these aboriginal people, but also their local toponymy.

Scholars, using methods from language documentation and anthropological linguistics, collect local stories and oral-traditional tales in order to answer the questions 'who named the place?', or 'what does the place name mean?'. In Indigenous societies, where languages are undocumented and/or endangered, Tucker and Rose-Redwood (2015, p. 198) note that toponymy is heavily intertwined with oral traditions.

Indigenous place naming is not solely a cartographic endeavour alone; rather, the invocation of place names by Indigenous peoples is generally part of a broader ensemble of performative practices that links the present with the past through storytelling, song, ceremony, oral history, and political protest.

As a result, by paying particular attention to oral traditions and/or oral histories of the territory, scholars have been able to document toponyms from minority or Indigenous languages. Research on this topic includes, among others, the Hopi in northern *America* (Hedquist et al., 2014), the Harvaqtuuq in *Nunavik, Canada* (Keith & Scottie, 1997), the Athapaskan in *Yukon Territory, Canada* (Cruikshank, 1981), the Sami in *Jokkmok*, northern *Sweden* (Cogos, Roué, & Roturier, 2017), the Western Apache in *Cibecue, Arizona* (Basso, 1988), and the Samoan in the *Pacific Islands* (Lilomaiava-Doktor, 2020).

An example of a story explaining a place name comes from the *Ulun Lampung* people, who live in *Lampung*, an Indonesian province located at the far south of *Sumatra*. They speak Had Lampung and use a local writing system (Pain, 1989). The oral-traditional myth explaining the place name, *Lampung*, is recounted below.

A volcanic eruption damaged the area of *Tapanoeli* (possibly the current Central *Tapanuli* Regency, located in North *Sumatra*). This natural phenomenon is also believed, according to the myth, to be responsible for creating the famous *Lake Toba* in Indonesia. The few people who managed to save themselves from the disaster were four siblings: *Ompung Silamponga, Ompung Silitonga, Ompung Silatoa*, and *Ompung Sintalaga*. They rode on a raft along the western coast of the *Swarnadwipa Island*, now known as *Sumatra* (*Swarnadwipa* means 'island of gold', or 'golden island'). One day, *Ompung Silamponga* fell ill. However, he still wanted to continue the journey. Nevertheless, his siblings felt tired, and decided to stop sailing. They alighted on an unnamed island and decided to let the sick *Ompung Silamponga* continue the journey on his own. They pushed his raft into the sea and, slowly, the craft was washed further and further away. The sick *Ompung Silamponga* drifted for a very long time, and, eventually, became unconscious. He woke up when the raft suddenly ran aground on an unexplored island, where he was surprised to find himself on a beach surrounded by calm waves, and he no longer felt ill. He got off and, because he liked the place, decided to settle there. According to this and other versions of this story, this place is the current site of *Krui*, a town in *West Lampung Regency*. After settling there for quite some time, *Ompung Silamponga* decided to explore the island further. He walked into a forest and climbed the mountains, and arrived at a mountain peak, which was possibly *Mount Pesagi* (*Lampung*'s highest peak, at 2,262 m above sea level). While overlooking the landscape and vast ocean, he was impressed by the beautiful scenery and shouted: '*Lappung! Lappung! Lappung!*'. *Lappung* means 'wide', or 'vast', in the local language. (Perono Cacciafoco, Binte Adzman, & Binte Sharin, 2017)

Some native speakers, therefore, believe that *Lampung* derives from the exclamation *lappung*, uttered by *Ompung Silamponga* when he stood on *Mount Pesagi* (with the consonantal passage of the first /p/ into /m/). Other locals connect the name *Lampung* with the anthroponym *Ompung Silamponga*, with a sort of 'macro-metathesis' between \*-*pung*, from *Ompung*, and \*-*lam(p)*-, from *Silamponga*, and others from the name *Silamponga*, parsed as *Si-lampong-a*, although fieldwork interviews with local informants have only been able to confirm the former reconstruction.

Yi (2016) conducted interesting research on how Indigenous place names are produced via oral narratives across numerous nations and geographical regions in the Americas. Through oral traditions, the land and its place names are metaphorically 'inscribed' by a 'voice', often that of the storytellers, who, alongside handing down historical and cultural aspects of the local peoples, spaces, and lands, narrate how places got their names. The role of the story-tellers in the Indigenous communities is essential in ensuring that cultural knowledge is transmitted from one generation to another. Yi studied the oral narratives of a number of Indigenous groups, such as oral-traditional elements from the Mayan (*Popol Vuh*) and Algonkian, Western Apache, Hopi, Haudenosaunee/Iroquois, and Laguna Pueblo myths and legends.

Yi (2016) explains how the toponyms of the Western Apache people of *Cibecue, Arizona*, 'are invested with the breath and story of ancestral story-tellers, the names are traces of their presence; places, in being called their given names, remember their namers' (p. 4). Yi then continues.

The breath of storytellers continually construct the past, making verbal marks on the land that define it as a place. These place-names are a form of 'footprints' or 'tracks' that invest the land with Western Apache history and culture, creating a kind of map that renders the 'path' of the past visible in the postcolonial present. (Yi, 2016, p. 5)

Yi also makes reference to Basso (1996) and to how he mispronounced the Apache name for the place they were touring. He tried to apologise, by saying that 'it didn't matter', because he had recorded it. His Apache guide made it very clear that:

'It's [does] matter,' Charles says softly to me in English. And then, turning to speak to Morley, he addresses him in Western Apache: What he's doing isn't right. It's not good. He seems to be in a hurry. Why is he in a hurry? It's disrespectful. Our ancestors made this name. They made it just as it is. They made it for a reason. They spoke it first, a long time ago! He's repeating the speech of our ancestors. He doesn't know that. Tell him he's repeating the speech of our ancestors! (Basso, 1996, p. 10)

Through oral stories, the land ideally remembers its namers. Toponyms also, in Yi's words, keep an 'oral record' of natural and man-made changes on the land itself (Yi, 2016, p. 9). Through the telling of stories, storytellers explain how physical-geographical phenomena and human modifications to the landscape came about. This is especially poignant as Basso (1996, p. 14) recounted the example of *Tliish Bi Tú'é* 'Snakes Water', an inactive spring located a few miles west of *Cibecue*. The Apache storyteller, Charles, blamed the disappearance of the water to 'an absence of fit (a "lack of match" is what he says in Apache) between the place itself and the way its name describes it. The name it was given a long time ago shows that it has changed. *Snake's Water*, as anyone can see, is no longer the way it was when the ancestors saw it first and made it their own with words.' He then stated that 'The names do not lie. [. . .] They show what is different and what is still the same' (Basso, 1996, p. 16).

## 5.6    Summary

The last two chapters have provided a comprehensive explanation of how historical toponomastics and diachronic toponymy work. These two approaches, basically, study place names across time. Crucially, they vary in terms of the language contexts and available sources that they rely on, as summarised in Table 5.5.

Notwithstanding the differences between the two approaches, the aim of diachronic toponymy and historical toponomastics is the same: to explain the possible development of a place name and of its naming process over time. The difference between the two approaches is that one does so without a robust amount of historical documentation, while the other can rely on

Table 5.5 *Diachronic toponymy and historical toponomastics*

|  | Diachronic toponymy | Historical toponomastics |
|---|---|---|
| Language contexts | Undocumented and/or endangered languages | Well-known languages and language families |
|  | E.g., Abui, a Papuan language | E.g., the Indo-European language family |
| Available sources | Documented/reconstructed (after long language documentation campaigns) lexicon from target language and other related languages in the same language family, interviews with the speakers, cooperation of local native consultants, intangible cultural heritage, oral traditions | Historical records and written sources, like epigraphs, manuscripts, chronicles, archival documentation, (historical) maps, dictionaries, lexicons of well-known language families, items, and objects from material culture (archaeology), paleo-anthropological findings, like skeletal remains, bones, stone tools, footprints, genetic documentation (DNA), etc. |

plenty of historical records. In the case of diachronic toponymy, due to the absence of historical sources within the culture connected with the undocu-mented language under examination, the methods of reconstruction differ from the ones of historical toponomastics. The researcher has to deal directly with the local people in a specific area, interviewing them, collecting their (oral) knowledge, and, from a linguistic perspective, comparing their pronun-ciation of their toponyms and the morphological structure of their place names with lexical items from the general lexicon of their language and of other related languages belonging to the same language family. Thus, dia-chronic toponymy is closely connected with the practices of field linguistics and language documentation developed, when possible, with a historical-linguistic approach. In the absence of writing and historical records of a language and its associated culture, toponyms offer valuable data for the analysis of that language.

Moreover, we have also seen in the last two chapters that extra-linguistic resources and perspectives are important in determining the accuracy of the toponymic reconstructions. One important component to consider is the land-scape, as place names are often named after landscape features. With this in mind, in the next chapter we will turn our attention to the links between toponymy and landscape.

# 6    Landscape and Toponymy

## 6.1    What Is Landscape?

In trying to define the notion of 'landscape', several options emerge. Crystal (1990) defines 'landscape' as the natural, visual features of an area of land such as mountains, trees, rocks, lakes, rivers, sand, grass, and so on. These features may not have been significantly changed by human activity and, thus, constitute the landscape for centuries (Crystal, 1990, p. 412). In such a definition, the landscape is the visual manifestation and observation of territories and territorial identities. Another theme that arises when we try to define the concept of 'landscape' is that landscapes are seen as the backdrop to which human activities occur in. For instance, Reed (1990) defines landscape as 'the external world in which men and women have carried on the everyday business of their lives from the remotest periods of pre-history down to the present' (Reed, 1990, p. xii). From this definition, it is evident that landscapes reflect the interrelationships between people and their environments over the course of human history. Landscapes provide, therefore, the backdrop to which people live their lives.

The intersection between nature and man is also evident in the definition provided by the European Landscape Convention (ELC), which was the first international treaty to be exclusively devoted to the European landscape. The ELC defines landscape as 'an area, as perceived by people, whose character is the result of the action and interaction of natural and/or human factors' (Council of Europe, 2000, p. 12). This definition, as Dejeant-Pons (2006) argues, is a holistic view and ultimately links the landscape to the advancement of four elements of sustainable development: nature, culture, society, and economy. Extending beyond the realm of just physical characteristics of a space, Antrop (2013) notes that the word 'landscape' has also become a metaphor to describe many human activities today, as in the case of media landscape or political landscape. 'Landscape' can also have adjectives attached to it, for instance, natural landscape or cultural landscape, and urban landscape or rural landscape. Because of the multiple meanings and different focuses of scholars studying the landscape, it is no surprise that 'the approaches to landscape are very broad and not always clearly defined', especially when people occupying the same piece of land 'see different landscapes' (Antrop, 2013, p. 13). The meaning of 'landscape' thus varies according to the background and contexts of the people who inhabit it. Due to the relationships that human beings have with the landscape, we are not only able to study it using objective and scientific methods, but we also can apply approaches taking into account subjective aspects, and delve into the feelings, perceptions, and meanings people associate with landscapes (Hendriks & Stobbelaar, 2003; Tilley, 2006; Taylor, 2012; Moore & Whelan, 2016).

'Landscape' does not just refer to the characteristics of the physical or geographical environment. David and Thomas (2008, p. 35) argued that, from the mid- to late 1980s, 'landscape' began to be seen as something more than 'environment', and scholars began to take into account the fact that humans engaged with their physical surroundings socially and culturally as much as environmentally[1]. Any research on landscape would, then, involve not just the visible features of the physical land, but also 'the spirits of the land and the waters and the skies that others may not know' (David & Thomas, 2008, p. 35). The landscape is, therefore, not just a setting in which we live our lives, but also a social and cultural creation in which we exist. A holistic assessment of the landscape enables us to see how social identity may be forged in that space. The landscape, therefore, has social and cultural values on top of its physical characteristics, and has to be treated and studied as such. Torrence (2002, p. 766) summarises the all-encompassing nature of landscape as follows.

[B]y definition, the term 'landscape' takes in all physical and natural components of the terrestrial environment. [. . .] it should be combined with 'seascape' [. . .] to encompass adequately the settings where human behaviour took place. Adding 'cultural' to land- and seascapes emphasises the role of the individuals who conceptualised these spaces and actively created and modified them in culturally specific ways.

The landscape is a meaningful place to the people that live in it. A socioculturally constructed landscape may or may not contain any visible human artefactual remains or prominent natural features. Nonetheless, it is an important space and place for the local society, because locals engage socially with it. The significance of a place, therefore, lies not only in the physical features, but also in the associated social, cultural, or even spiritual values of the place itself.

In toponymy, the relationship between place names and the landscape is very strong, especially for ancient toponyms. As we have discussed in earlier

---

[1] An early attempt to include the sociocultural perspective in studying the landscape is found in (Hodder, 1978), who adopted a more socially oriented assessment of landscape based on ideas about the social construction of space and its related practices, meanings, attitudes, and values.

chapters, places, in prehistoric times, were generally named after specific features of the landscape, such as natural resources (i.e., water, food, animals, stone, etc.) and the hydro-geo-morphological structure of the landscape encompassing the places themselves. Examples of the latter include the location of caves to be used as shelters or places with good water, essential to the survival of people. Conversely, places were also named after the bad or swampy water attested there, in order to avoid them. The discussion of *Squaneto* in Chapter 3[2] and the **alb*- toponymic system analysed in Chapter 4[3] illustrate very clearly how early people named places according to primary goods for survival, such as water. Toponyms, by alluding to and describing the related landscapes, helped people to orientate themselves in these spaces and, in the absence of drawing tools and writing systems, facilitated the sketching of a mental, oral, and ideal map of their territory. Prehistoric place names allowed the Stone Age people to navigate around their surroundings and to refer to them with precision and accuracy. Humans also adapted to their environment through the practice of naming places after real features of the landscape, which ultimately helped them to navigate the uncharted prehistoric world. Ucko and Layton (2005) argued that the relationship between landscape and humans is that landscape is usually represented as an ecological system 'to which human behaviour must adapt' (p. 8). The christening of places after natural resources and salient attributes of the landscape can be considered as a linguistic and geographic adaptation to the surroundings, and helped humans to stay alive in prehistoric times.

In this chapter, we will show how the landscape, and some of the disciplines studying it, particularly landscape archaeology, are useful to the reconstruction of the origins of toponyms. In particular, the analysis of elements and features

---

[2]  As mentioned in Chapter 3, the denominations of places from *Squaneto*'s area are also inherent in the notion of 'water'. For instance, located near *Squaneto* on the hill overlooking the *Valla* stream is a hamlet called *Squagiato*. *Squagiato* could be an imported place name (due to the migration of part of the population of *Squaneto* from the ford on the *Valla* creek to the hill above). *Squagiato* could be parsed into *$s$-$ak^{w}a$-$g(-)iato$, which follows the etymon of *Squaneto* ($s$-$ak^{w}a$-$n$-$eto$). Not far from *Squaneto* and *Squagiato* is the small hamlet of *Saquana*, on the course of the *Erro* stream. The toponym can be parsed, in the same way as *Squaneto* and *Squagiato*, into *$s$-$ak^{w}a$-$n$-$a$. All three examples confirm the strength of the Proto-Indo-European *$ak^{w}$-$(a)$- root, which means 'water', and are located besides water bodies. They are clear examples of how prehistoric place names were generally named after primary goods for survival, like water.

[3]  The **alb*- toponymic system, as we saw in Chapter 4, involves many places in Europe named after the Proto-Indo-European **alb*- root, meaning 'water', and semantically specialised in describing the 'transparency' of water. Some of those places had and have the same name, like the many *Alba*(s) and *Olbia*(s) spread all over the *Old Continent*. This shows that the very early function of toponyms (relatively different from today) was not to distinguish different places, but rather toponyms were coined to indicate the main characteristics of the lands they named (in the case of the **alb*- toponymic system, they were named after watercourses that flowed alongside them or after the seas). This served both to have a precise understanding of the hydro-geo-morphology of a specific area, for matters of survival, and to have a clear mental picture of the locations of available resources.

of the landscape enables the toponymist to confirm or disprove the possible etymologies of prehistoric place names. Moreover, we will show how interdisciplinary approaches in studying the landscape, combining the physical, natural environment, and sometimes even the spiritual domain, enrich our understanding of toponymy and also of the communities and cultures.

## 6.2 Landscape Archaeology and Toponymy

Research on the landscape can involve many disciplines, just as the study of toponyms does. Common fields associated with the landscape include landscape archaeology, landscape architecture, landscape ecology, geology, physical geography, human geography, cultural geography, historical geography, history, urban planning, cartography, topography, and, increasingly, the use and practice of geographic information systems (GIS) (cf. Chapters 7 and 10). Landscape archaeology is the study of the past use of the landscape, determined by archaeological findings. Some scholars have argued that the study of landscape archaeology could have begun with the discipline of archaeology itself (Maschner & Marler, 2008, p. 109), because the space in which we find archaeological remains would always constitute the landscape.[4] The discipline tries to interpret the excavated factual remains, which are material traces left behind by past civilisations, and to use these interpretations as the basis for understanding what the landscape was like or how it was used in the past. The notion of 'landscape archaeology' was perhaps first delineated and mentioned by the British scholars Mick Aston and Trevor Rowley in 1974. Both authors recognise that the landscape is not just a natural 'scenery', but an artefact rich in history and layering.

The landscape is a palimpsest on to which each generation inscribed its own impressions and removes some of the marks of earlier generations. Constructions of one age are often overlain, modified or erased by the work of another. The present patchwork nature of settlement and patterns of agriculture has evolved as a result of thousands of years of human endeavour, producing a landscape which possesses not only a beauty associated with long and slow development, but an inexhaustible store of information about many kinds of human activities in the past. (Aston & Rowley, 1974, p. 14)

As seen from this quote, the landscape features of the past may not be visible today. They may have been eroded away, buried, or modified either by natural hydro-geo-morphological processes (e.g., coastal erosion, alluviation) or by human activities (e.g., the flattening of a hill, deforestation). Yet, the

---

[4] The area where artefacts are found (and, thus, the 'landscape' in question) may be as small as a single household or a garden, or as large as an empire, but, importantly, that area shows that the landscape was (once) inhabited and/or used by humans, and the discovery of archaeological artefacts (which are evidence of previous civilisations) enables us to study the landscape itself and the material culture of the people who occupied it.

archaeological remains in the landscape can help us to reconstruct its development over time, and to understand the structure of past human settlements (and the related activities) in a specific area. Conversely, there are also cases in which there is a lack of archaeological findings in a particular landscape. In this context, a useful reading can be found in Ilves (2006), who writes about maritime landing sites in the Estonian-Swedish landscape (located along the coast of northwest *Estonia*, where a sizeable Swedish population lived for years before the Second World War). As Ilves notes, maritime landing sites, or passage points between land and water, are, like many other sites in landscape archaeology, 'relatively invisible' (Ilves, 2006, p. 95). To this end, the scholar proposes the use of toponyms in providing clues on archaeological sites located along coasts, a method that was up till then uncommon in Estonian maritime archaeology. Ilves details a number of maritime places in the Estonian-Swedish landscape that served as landing sites, grouping them into categories such as place names indicating former landing sites (and whose use and related meanings later changed), toponyms marking coastal locations for landing, and what she terms as 'chapel' names (Ilves, 2006, p. 97), that is, place names that allude to the sea and seafaring generally rather than specifically and might have been close to coasts where the ships landed.

Landscape archaeology is, naturally, a field related to historical geography, which also deals with changes to the landscape over time. It is worth noting that contemporary historical geography is more concerned with the recent past (Jones, 2004), as opposed to the possibly prehistoric and long-term focus of landscape archaeology. Historical geography, by definition, often relies on historical data (i.e., written documents, archival sources), and it focusses mainly on urban contexts, while landscape archaeology focusses on archaeological findings (such as monuments, buildings, houses, writings on stones or walls, jewellery, and other artefacts) and more (but not exclusively) on rural contexts. Historical geography studies the economic, social, and political forces determining geographical (and political-geographical) changes, for example, how the shift of government from colonial times to modern-day *Singapore* has affected the street names of the city, or how certain political motivations modify the geography of a region (see more in Chapters 7 and 8) (Branton, 2009). What this means is that landscape archaeology and its approaches investigate the connections between past human behaviours (which can be inferred through excavated remains) and the physical (and sometimes social) spaces in which they occurred.

In relation to toponymy, landscape archaeology is particularly useful in contributing to the analysis of places with a remote (or even prehistoric) name, some of which do not exist anymore. Unearthing possible archaeological and paleo-anthropological remains of a prehistoric settlement is essential in highlighting the diachronic development of the landscape features and/or hydro-geo-morphological aspects that can help confirm or disprove etymological hypotheses on the place name from that particular area.

## 6.3 Landscape Archaeology and Toponymy Case Studies

### 6.3.1 Pareto

A very interesting case study detailing how the application of landscape archaeology is particularly useful in toponymy is the name of the village of *Pareto*, located in *Piedmont*, northwest *Italy*, in the province of *Alessandria* (see Figure 6.1). *Pareto*, as a place name, has been incorrectly reconstructed, over time, by both local speakers and scholars, who falsely believed that the name could be explained as *Pareto* < Italian *Pereto* < Late Latin *Peretum/Piretum* < Late Latin *Peretus/Piretus* < Latin *pĭrus* ('pear tree') + *-etum* (suffix used in toponyms to mean 'village', or 'place') 'the village of the pear trees', or 'the place of the pear trees'. The reconstruction is based on the assumption that the name derives from the Latin *pĭrus* 'pear tree', and the Italian *pero* 'pear tree'. Speakers and scholars postulate that a possible dialectal change occurred, over time, from *-er-* to *-ar-*, probably in the passage between Late Latin and Vernacular Italian, and thus *Pereto* changed into *Pareto* to 'fit in' with the local dialect (DTI, 1999, cited in Perono Cacciafoco, 2014, p. 92). Nonetheless, this postulation may be wrong because, as we'll see in a moment, the *-ar-* segment could be considered the original one (belonging to the original root of the toponym and actually preserved in the current form of the name) and not a dialectal innovation, while the *-er-* segment, as well as the connection with the notion of 'pear tree', could represent a paretymological explanation. Indeed, the etymological reconstruction connected with Latin *pĭrus* and Italian *pero* is configurable as a *bona fide* toponymic paretymology (cf. Chapter 3) and also has an attestation of its influence and acceptance, over time, on the coat of arms of the village, which depicts a pear tree alongside a medieval tower (Figure 6.1). A careful examination of the historical landscape of the place provides, instead, evidence for a landscape-informed etymology of the toponym.

Landscape archaeology research in the area and an analysis of local historical archival documents and chronicles show that orchards of pear trees have never been attested in *Pareto*. Moreover, the village is located at the top of a steep hill dominating the surrounding territory, and its microclimate is not favourable for the growth of pear trees. Conversely, the place was used (according to archaeological and paleo-anthropological relics found in the area) by humans in prehistoric times as a shelter from dangerous animals, possibly bears and wolves. It is precisely from this geo-morphological characteristic that *Pareto* took its name. The toponym derives from a reference to the altitude of the village and to its 'stony nature', given that the village is located

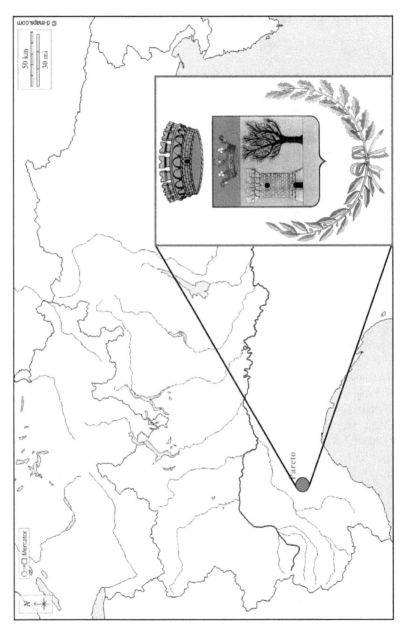

Figure 6.1 Position and coat of arms of the *Pareto* municipality (adapted from Comune di Pareto, 2017; d-maps, 2021)

on a steep hill. This relationship to 'stone' and to the 'impervious faces of the hill' is indicated through the Proto-Indo European (then (Proto-)Celtic) root of the place name, *br-, or *bar-, which means 'rock, mountain, cliff, hill, face of a mount' and which, over time, shifted to *par-. This interpretation would not have been possible without the assessment of evidence provided by the findings from landscape studies. Hence, a more accurate etymological reconstruction of the place name *Pareto*, based on its geo-morphology, is as follows.

*Pareto*
Possible original proto-form (Proto-Indo-European, then (Proto-)Celtic):
*Br-et(o) or *Bar-et(o)*

|  *Br-/*Bar-* | -et(o) |
|---|---|
| Proto-Indo European (then (Proto-Celtic)) root *br-/*bar-*, 'rock', or 'mountain', or 'cliff', or 'hill', or 'face of a mount' | Suffix, possibly (originally) Celtic = Latin -*etum* 'place', or 'village' |
| ↓ | ↓ |
| Latin and Italian *par-* | Italian *-eto* |

↓
Italian
*Par-eto*
'place located on a hill/cliff'

The toponymic reconstruction of the name *Pareto* involves the change of the initial voiced bilabial stop, *b-, to the voiceless bilabial stop, *p-*. The passage from *b-* to *p-* happened over time and is already attested in Latin, for example, in the word *pariēs*, 'rock face/wall', or 'rock', and the Italian word *parete*, 'rock face', or 'wall' (the reflex of the Latin form), which derives from the root *br-/*bar-*. This provides a confirmation inherent in the derivation of <u>Pareto</u> from the root *br-/*bar-* (which later became *par-* in some Indo-European languages, meaning 'rock', or 'mountain', or, 'cliff' or 'hill', or 'face of a mount'). Additional evidence that supports this reconstruction of *Pareto* as 'place located on a hill/cliff' is derived from the comparison with other Italian place names etymologically connected with the root *br-/*bar*, such as *Parétola*, a hamlet of the *Zeri* municipality (*Tuscany*, central *Italy*), whose denomination derives from Latin *pariēs* 'steep terrain, sheer rock or overhanging cliff' (Pellegrini, 2008, p. 194). Thus, among others, *Parétola*, like *Pareto*, has its etymological origins in the prehistoric and pre-Latin root of *br-/*bar-*, which indicates the 'rocky' nature of a cliff or hill.

Nonetheless, over time, speakers were involved in a linguistic misunderstanding about the possible origins of the place name *Pareto* and did not make, in their limited linguistic competence, the right connection between the place name and the Italian word *parete* ('rock face', or 'wall'), possibly because *Pareto* is in Italian a masculine singular name, while *parete* is a feminine singular word, and the speakers did not connect the two lexemes. People took, therefore, the route of another erroneous interpretation-based onanalogy of the Italian word *pero* 'pear tree', which, according to them, was phonetically compatible with *Pareto*, despite the difference in the root vowel (/e/ vs. /a/), and which is, like *Pareto*, a masculine singular word (while in Latin *pĭrus* is a feminine singular word). Conversely, they did not consider the geo-morphological characteristics of the territory and the landscape of the area, which corroborate the reconstruction of the prehistoric, pre-Latin (Celtic and, ultimately, Proto-Indo-European) linguistic layer linked to the root *\*br-/\*bar-*, describing, in the case of *Pareto*, the altitude and position of the village on the top of its hill and not connected with a phytonym (from Ancient Greek *phytón* [φυτόν] 'plant', and *ónoma* [ὄνομα] 'name').

The diachronic analysis of a landscape and the historical assessment of the developments of a territory over time, therefore, enable us to ascertain or at least to corroborate the exactness of the etymological reconstructions of place names. In the case of *Pareto*, we found that the notion of the presence of pear orchards or pear trees in the locality and thus the gloss of the place name as 'the village of the pear trees' are incorrect and, at the toponymic level, they produce an evident paretymology. This led us to search for a more accurate and plausible explanation of the place name and to etymologically reconstruct its root as being *\*br-/\*bar-*. This stem reflects the hydro-geo-morphology of the landscape of the place and, in particular, the characteristic of the village of being located at the top of a hill (which is 'stony' in nature). This is an example of how the geo-morphology of the landscape, in this case 'rocky' and 'stony', has provided the place with its name (at the etymological and semantic levels), and the name itself, *Pareto*, indicates something connected with 'rock', or 'stone', derived from the Indo-European root *\*br-/\*bar-*.

### 6.3.2    *Igbominaland* and *Badagry*

Aleru and Alabi (2010) provide an interesting example from the African context on how a study of the local toponymy can inform 'cultural, historical and archaeological reconstructions' (p. 151), facilitating therefore the analysis of past uses of the landscape and the customs of the people living in a specific territory. The scholars draw on their ethnographic and archaeological investi-gations from two areas in *Yorubaland*, in southwest *Nigeria*: *Igbominaland* and the *Badagry* coastal area (see Figure 6.2).

The authors, through an analysis of a number of settlements and based on past oral accounts and archaeological surveys, found that people in these areas engaged in a number of different economic activities, like farming, hunting, iron working, weaving, dyeing, bronze casting, and bead-making. These activ-ities, and their related trades, were reflected in local place names. For example,

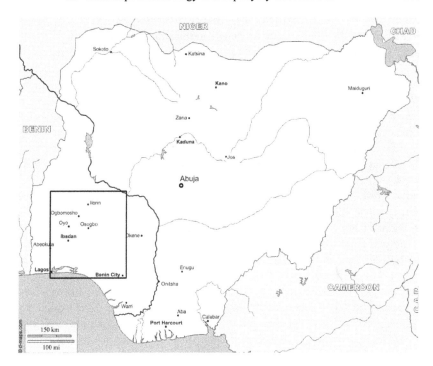

Figure 6.2 Map of *Nigeria* showing the area of the study by Aleru and Alabi (2010) (adapted from d-maps, 2021)

*Odó Ide* 'bronze mortar', a settlement at *Idoba, Igbominaland*, is a direct reference to the bronze casting industry previously in the town. The authors report finding evidence of iron working in two-thirds of the settlements in *Igbominaland*, particularly in hill slope areas. Likewise, the name of the town *Okotóníyún* 'farm with beads' implies that both farming and the manufacturing of beads were the main economic activities of this settlement.

Toponyms provide us with valuable hints that aid the reconstruction of both past events and aspects of cultural history connected with the different stages of development of the landscapes. Yet, in order to accept these clues as indicating historical facts, we have to use complementary historical data from ethnographic and archaeological sources, such as oral traditions and excavations. The study by Aleru and Alabi (2010) is, indeed, also a useful example of how ethnographic methods are utilised in the study of landscape toponymy. Like many communities around the world, *Yorubaland* is a largely oral-word society. It is not surprising, therefore, that local oral traditions also feature strongly in the study of toponyms. In the absence of written records, it is by relying on oral traditions that scholars are often able to trace the naming processes. Aleru and Alabi (2010, p. 158) collected the oral accounts inherent in settlements in the *Badagry* area. What they were able to find was that early settlements in this territory were built by refugees fleeing the civil unrest due to the *Dahomey* Wars in the eighteenth and nineteenth centuries.[5] Thus, for instance, the *Igbogbélé* people were displaced by the wars and settled by the ocean in a place they named *Àfikú*, meaning 'only death could kill us here'. The name comes from their perception of safety from raids in their new location. From there, they later moved to their current territory, naming the place *Igbogbélé* 'bush of permanent settlement'. The glosses of these names imply first, in the name *Àfikú*, that these people were seeking refuge away from their original home, which they hoped to find in their new settlement. It appears that the *Igbogbélé* people would not want to leave their new home, and that only death could part them from *Àfikú*, as indicated by the meaning of the place name. In *Igbogbélé*, the same people believed that they had finally found a location where they were no longer victims of wars and, thus, a place of permanent residency, as indicated by the notion of 'permanent settlement'. This provides the researchers with a good case study, particularly from a non-Euro-American context, on how landscape archaeology, toponymy, and oral traditions intersect methodologically and enhance our understanding of the landscape, place names, and cultural history of people all over the world.

### 6.3.3    The Abui from *Alor Island*

How studies on the landscape can integrate both the physical/natural and social environments, and even the cultural and religious realms, can be tracked through an investigation of the relationship between the Abui landscape and toponyms. As mentioned in Chapters 1 and 4, the Abui are a Papuan aboriginal people living on *Alor Island* (*Alor-Pantar* archipelago, *Timor* area) in southeast *Indonesia*. They speak Abui, a Papuan language, which was undocumented and endangered until very recently. The Abui community of *Takalelàng* lives on the northern slopes of *Alor Island*, falling to the coast of the *Banda Sea* (see Figure 6.3). In the absence of detailed cartographic, topographic, and toponymic documentation, Kratochvíl, Delpada, and Perono Cacciafoco (2016) created a database of 288 Abui landscape terms. The lexemes were collected through extensive language documentation fieldwork and based on reconstructed oral traditions recorded in collaboration with local Abui consultants. After these terms were collected, they were stored in a database and annotated

---

[5] These wars were fought as the French wanted to colonise the Kingdom of Dahomey, a precolonial African kingdom located within present-day Benin.

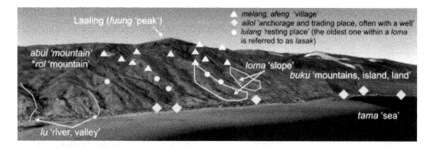

Figure 6.3  A view of the *Takalelàng* area from the northeast, generated using Google Earth. This picture illustrates the basic landscape categories in *Takalelàng*, such as villages located at the top of the mountains, trading places (*ailol*) along the coast, and resting places (*lulang*) (source: Kratochvíl et al., 2016, p. 85)

according to their possible etymology, the landscape features they describe, and, where possible, the oral-traditional narratives related to the mapped landscape lexemes.

Similar to the *alba*-type example in Chapter 4, where we explained how early European settlements were, generally, named after important features of the landscape (in the case of *Alba*, the water resource), the denominations of the Abui villages often derive from natural landscape features. These features include ravines (*bung*), hills (*miti*) and their peaks (*fuung*), plains (*fuui*), and streams (*lu*), among others. Table 6.1 lists examples of toponyms based on these landscape features.

As we can see, Abui toponyms markedly make reference to physical landscape features, as mentioned above, in association with the natural resources connected with each specific part of the landscape. Horticultural-based place names derived from tree names are common in the Abui landscape. Because (Due to the fact that) the Papuan people on *Alor Island* are organised as an agricultural society growing its own crops, this reliance on horticultural and agricultural sources is also reflected in their toponyms. Many Abui place names also derive from trees and crops that are commonly found in the natural landscape and are perceived as valuable, such as *mea* 'mango', *kalang* '*Cussambium*', *fiyaai* 'candlenut', and *kanaai* '*Canarium*', among others (see Table 6.2).

It is worth noting that, in toponyms such as *Meebung/Meabuung* 'mango ravine' and *Kalang Watika* '*Cussambium* on slope', we observe a compounding between the agricultural/horticultural resource + the physical landscape category in a single place name. As a testament to the saliency of agricultural or horticultural sources in the landscape, it is also possible to find place names that incorporate two crops, such as *Fiyaai Mea*, which translates into 'mango

Table 6.1 *Abui toponyms based on landscape features (Kratochvíl et al., 2016)*

| Toponym | English gloss | Type | Onomastic source |
|---|---|---|---|
| *Meebung/Meabuung* | mango ravine | village | natural resource (mango) + landscape feature (ravine) |
| *Fuung Afeng* | peak village | village | landscape feature (peak) + settlement type (village) |
| *Fe Fuui* | pig plain | village | natural resource (pig) + landscape feature (plain) |
| *Fuui Mia* | plain at | village | landscape feature (plain) |
| *Lu Meelang* (*Lu Melang*) | river village | village | landscape feature (river) + settlement type (village) |

Table 6.2 *Abui toponyms based on agricultural and horticultural sources*

| Toponym | English gloss | Type |
|---|---|---|
| *Meebung/Meabuung* | mango ravine | village |
| *Mea Meelang* (*Mea Melang*) | mango village | village |
| *Mea Kilikil* | idle mango | field |
| *Kalang Meelang* (*Kalang Melang*) | *Cussambium* village | village |
| *Kalang Maasang* | *Cussambium* sanctuary | village |
| *Kalang Watika* | *Cussambium* on slope | field |
| *Fiyaai Lelang* | lit. 'candlenut relatives' | village |
| *Fiyaai Mea* | lit. 'mango candlenut' | field |
| *Kanaai Loohu* | *Canarium* tall | garden |
| *Kanaai Peela* | *Canarium* near | village |
| *Kanaafeng* | *Canarium* village | village |
| *Kanaaisua* | three *Canarium* | valley |
| *Padak Kanai* | mud *Canarium* | field |
| *Karkanaai* | ten *Canarium* | valley |

candlenut', and *Keela Kanaai* 'bamboo *Canarium*' (see Table 6.4). This is probably due to the existence of multiple crops in the same place. In the Abui territory, many human settlements, villages, localities, and sanctuaries, and even ritual dance places (which are the only remainder of previous, older inhabited centres), are named after agricultural and horticultural crops, for example, *Mea Meelang* (*Mea Melang*) 'mango village'. The combination of numeral + commodity in names such as *Kanaaisua* 'three *Canarium*' and *Karkanaai* 'ten *Canarium*' suggests that quantity was also salient in the mental map of the local speakers and, potentially, even a single tree could have become a landmark. It is also worth mentioning that, because the Abui people share a close relationship with their landscape and the related crops, the qualities of these crops can in turn be embedded into the place names. These qualities describe aspects like height, spatial-distance awareness, and even negative traits, for example, *Kanaai Loohu* 'Canarium tall', *Kanaai Peela* 'Canarium near', and *Mea Kilikil* 'idle[6] mango'. Abui toponyms serve therefore as descriptors of the crops, and by implication they represent features of the physical and sociocultural landscapes where these crops are cultivated.

The findings by Lim and Perono Cacciafoco (2020b) also show that top-onyms on *Alor Island* are largely 'transparent' in their meanings. The authors collected over forty toponyms to determine the relationship(s) that link(s) plant species to Abui place names. The most common crops used in toponyms in that study are shown in Table 6.3.

Another source for place names is represented by the plants that are useful in everyday life, usually in building houses (Table 6.4). The most common are *Cussambium* (*kalang*), bamboo (*maai, tifool, keela*), ironwood (*laa, kawaaka*), blackboard tree (*mitaai*), and cactus (*kafiel*). *Kafiel* is, interestingly, used as a natural barrier to protect and fence off village walls. A number of toponyms connected with these plants contain two phytonyms in their names: a useful plant and an agricultural or horticultural crop (e.g., *Kalangfat[i]* 'Cussambium

Table 6.3 *A list of common crops used in the naming of places on* Alor Island

| Crop | English gloss and genus | Toponym count |
|---|---|---|
| *mea* | 'mango' (*Mangifera indica*) | 9 |
| *kanaai* | '*canarium*' (*Canarium indicum*) | 8 |
| *wata* | 'coconut' (*Cocos nucifera*) | 6 |
| *tamal* | 'tamarind' (*Tamarindus indica*) | 5 |
| *kalang* | '*cussambium* tree' (*Schleichera oleosa*) | 4 |
| *muur* | 'lemon' (*Citrus limon*) | 4 |
| *daa* | 'cassava' (*Manihot esculenta*) | 2 |
| *fiyaai* | 'candlenut' (*Aleurites moluccanus*) | 2 |
| *soong* | 'jackfruit' (*Artocarpus heterophyllus*) | 2 |
| *ayak* | 'rice' (*Oryza sativa*) | 1 |

[6] Interestingly, the 'idle' in this name does not actually derive from any feature of the mango in itself. The story goes that a particularly lazy man was famous in the local community for always resting under a mango tree, even when he was not tired. Therefore, this particular type of mango tree was given the name 'idle'. It was, indeed, the association of this man with a particular tree that became the motivation for the name.

Table 6.4 *Abui toponyms based on useful plants*

| Toponym | English gloss | Type |
|---|---|---|
| *Kalang Anu* | *Cussambium* market | trading place |
| *Kalangfat(i)* | *Cussambium* millet | coastal trading village |
| *Karetak Afeeng* | eucalyptus village | village |
| *Futing Maai* | yard bamboo | plant cluster |
| *Tifool ya* | bamboo water | spring |
| *Keela Kanaai* | bamboo *Canarium* | valley |
| *Kawaaka Loohu* | ironwood tall | garden |
| *Mitaai Uwo* | blackboard tree below | ridge garden |
| *Mitaai Pee* | blackboard tree near | ridge garden |
| *Kafiel Meelang* (*Kafiel Melang*) | cactus village | village |

millet' and *Keela Kanaai* 'bamboo *Canarium*'). Other names show the intersection of the physical environment and human settlements, and describe
anthropic facilities such as markets and villages (e.g., *Kalang Anu*
'*Cussambium* market', *Karetak Afeeng* 'eucalyptus village', *Kafiel Meelang*
'cactus village'). Some of these toponyms also indicate the distance and/or the
direction of a named place from and/or in relation to the connected useful plant,
as highlighted in *Mitaai Uwo* 'blackboard tree below' and *Mitaai Pee* 'blackboard tree near'. As such, not only do these plants serve useful purposes in the
daily lives of the Abui people, but they also function as landscape indicators
after which places are named.

The above place names effectively illustrate the fact that the naming of
localities depends on many aspects of the landscape or, more specifically, on
the types of crops which are grown or can be found naturally in a territory, and
on how an area in the wider landscape is good for human activities (and what
purposes it serves, e.g., settlements). That is what Levinson (2008, p. 277) calls
the 'landscape affordance'.

Many of the Abui toponyms shown in the tables above refer to human
settlements. In this case, we can see how representations of the natural landscape, be it via the hydro-geo-morphological features or agricultural and
horticultural resources, are compounded with the lexicon describing human
settlements, in a toponym. This highlights the interrelationship between nature
and man in the intrinsic essence of the related place names.

The *Takalelàng* area is a modern 'remnant' of the so-called *Meelang
Talaama* (*Melang Talama*) 'six villages' alliance, consisting of six small
settlements interconnected with each other and located on their respective
hilltops. The villages *Kaleen* (1), *Murafang* (2), *Mahafuui* (3), *Lilafang* (4),
*Fuungafeng* (5), and *Takalelàng* (6) are shown in Figure 6.4. This alliance was

Figure 6.4 The view of villages in the *Takalelàng* area, showing their location and the parallel coastal trading places. Legend: *Kaleen* (1), *Murafang* (2), *Mahafuui* (3), *Lilafang* (4), *Fuungafeng* (5), *Takalelàng* (6), *Ailol Kiding* (7), *Mas Beeka* (8), *Lu Meelang* (*Lu Melang*) (9), *Laakafeng* (10), *Leelawi* (11), *Kanaafeng* (12), *Fulful* (13), *Elahang* (14), *Al Meelang/Al Melang* (*Nurdin*) (15), *Kalangfati* (16) (source: Kratochvíl et al., 2016, p. 89)

part of a larger confederation of places known as *Lembur* that includes all the villages on the mountain top shown in Figure 6.4.

Abui villages and human settlements rely on a traditional system of governance according to which people are divided into societal groups, and every group has a specific political role. The Abui also have terms that refer to these groups. These terms specify where they live, as well as their roles (Table 6.5).

The terminology for this system of governance is a productive source for names of settlement parts and other toponyms. According to the Abui speakers, people belonging to certain groups, which have specific roles, as illustrated in Table 6.5, occupy a 'fixed space' in a village. This results in the addition of modifiers to the names of settlements that distinguish the different spaces (and, by implication, the people occupying them) in the same village. Examples of modifiers include *pee* 'neighbourhood' (from *pee/a* 'nearby'), *hapoong* 'entering hill ridge' (from the Abui term *hapong* 'forehead', or 'in front of'), and *taaha* 'upper hill ridge' (from *tāha* 'upper part'). These spatial and distal modifiers are, generally, added to the names of villages, and are a significant component of the naming process. For example, as seen in Chapter 5, *Afena Poming* means 'village above', or, more precisely, 'hamlet above'. Other instances we have analysed in Chapter 5 are *Afena Hapong* 'place located in front of the village', or 'village in front of', more precisely glossed as 'hamlet located in front of'; *Afena Hietang* 'place located below the village', or 'village below', or 'lower village', or, more precisely, 'hamlet located below'; *Lamang Tāha* 'village above'; and *Lamang Uwo* 'village below'.

Table 6.5 *Abui village governance terminology*

| Abui term | Location | Role in the village |
|---|---|---|
| *Poming* | lower part, below | guardians of the entrance, in charge of individual warfare and trade, lay people, care for the *maasang* 'sanctuary', or 'ritual dance place' altar |
| *Tamawaat* | central part, centre | mediation, judges, governance of the village, peace makers |
| *Hietang* | higher part, above | warfare and defence |

Table 6.6 *Abui terms that denote human settlements or their parts*

| Settlement | Definition |
|---|---|
| *afeeng (afeng)* | village (if *afena*, also 'hamlet') |
| *futing* | yard, or house yard |
| *kameeng* | three stones which are placed at the centre of a sanctuary or sacrifice place to symbolise three clans forming an alliance |
| *kota* | stone walls and terraces surrounding villages serving as fortifications or as a border of a house compound |
| *maasang* | sanctuary, or ritual dance place |
| *maayang* | the edge of a village, or ritual dance place where people gather |
| *meelang (melang)* | village |

It is now worth pointing out that a number of Abui terms and concepts refer to human settlements and their constituent parts, which are highlighted in Table 6.6. As we detailed in Chapter 5, the widespread form/forms which describes/describe a settlement, both at the level of common lexicon and in local toponymy, *afeng ~ afena (afeeng)*,[7] is/are derived from the Proto-Alor-Pantar proto-form *\*haban* 'village' (Holton et al., 2012, p. 96), and refers/refer to a 'standard' inhabited centre (while, when semantically specialised, in the form *afena*, they can indicate not only the notion of 'village', but the concept of 'hamlet', or a 'minor' locality dependent on another 'major' village). Generally, a larger village (which does not undergo the dichotomy 'major' vs. 'minor') is known as *melang (meelang)*[8].

[7] The form *afeeng* is equivalent to *afeng*, with an almost imperceptible quantitative vocalic variation in the Abui language which does not influence its meaning. It means, indeed, 'village' and possibly is a diachronically antecedent variant of *afeng*, the currently normalised/widespread form in Abui.

[8] The form *meelang* is equivalent to *melang*, with an imperceptible quantitative vocalic variation in the Abui language, which does not influence its meaning. It means, indeed, 'village' and possibly is a diachronically antecedent version of *melang*, the currently normalised/widespread form in Abui.

Table 6.7 *Abui toponyms derived from human activities*

| Toponym | English gloss | Type | Onomastic source |
|---|---|---|---|
| *Kameeng Taaha (Kaměng Tãha)* | sacrifice place above | village part | village features |
| *Kameeng Faking* | sacrifice place broken | field | village features |
| *Kota Pee* | wall near | garden | forward defence wall |
| *Kalang Maasang* | *Cussambium* sanctuary, or dance place | village | renewable resource + settlement type |

Traditionally, Abui inhabited centres are located on hilltops, resembling in a way 'little fortresses', with limited and protected means of access, blocked in the old days by stone walls, palisades, and bushes of thorny plants.

Human settlements are generally connected with many different activities, such as farming or religious practices. Toponyms reflect many of these endeavours and, therefore, a number of different Abui terms denote some of them. Several villages and gardens, especially in the past, were fortified with walls to avoid theft and to be protected in war times, and some of these walls are still recognisable in several currently inhabited Abui centres, and in villages by now in ruin or long abandoned. Some Abui place names that denote human activities are found in Table 6.7.

## 6.4    Toponymy and Abui Myths and Legends

The discussion above has shown how the Abui physical and spiritual landscape consists of a combination of the physical contours of the lands, and of socially and culturally produced dimensions. Abui myths and legends are the core of the Abui oral traditions, which are called *tira*. The storytelling inherent in place names is generally supported by references to the physical environment. Oral traditions often tell of prominent rock formations, caves, water bodies, as well as places and human movements among them. It is possible to highlight, therefore, a blending between the physical world and the human dimension, which adds to the authenticity of the myths. The landscape, then, is not only environmental, but also social, and an important marker and keeper of cultural identity. In Abui, a foundation myth is regarded as correct only if the ideal movement of the characters through the landscape is illustrated by a real and existing place name sequence. Genealogical stories usually conceptualise temporal progressions as movements through the landscape. Therefore, the names of places and pathways provide a narrative organisational frame. An example of this can be seen in the legend of *Mon Mot* presented below, which the Abui believe is one of the foundation myths (a genealogy) from which the

Abui communities descend. The story tells of a god-snake which attacked a number of Abui villages (among them *Karuwal, Mon Tooting, Kabilelang, Fuihieng, Lelawi, Roolmeelang, Bukulaka, Miitingfuui, Komea, Lelangtukoi, Tabenaafeng, Fenalelang, Forintal*, and *Kawaaka Loohu*) and killed everyone but one pregnant woman. This woman was able to escape and gave birth to twin sons who, in turn, killed the god-snake once they grew up. By killing the god-snake, they were able to bring back to life all the Abui people the primordial deity had killed. Thus, they became the new founders of the clans living in the Abui community today.

*Mon Mot* came down to *Lelawi* and killed everyone there. Just one pregnant woman was left and escaped into a cave. She stayed in a cave, or hole, with her dog. The dogs found water, and the woman followed. The woman gave birth to two twins and raised them in the cave, and taught them how to hunt, until they asked where their original village was. Both young men went to their original village, *Lelawi*, and rebuilt their house. Both young men built a treehouse on *Kawaaka Loohu*, where they stored various weapons and hid their mother. They went to *Mon Mot*'s village and challenged him to kill them. They first ran to *Roolmeelang*. Then, they ran down to *Mitiingfuui*. Then, they ran to *Kawaaka Loohu*. They climbed up to their tree house and found their mother scared. One of the twins, *Luutangfaan*, was more courageous. They killed the snake by throwing stones, axes, and pouring down [in its mouth] hot millet. They sliced the snake according to the instructions the snake gave them before dying. They made fire and dance, and their relatives returned. Their descendants live until the present in *Nurdin* and *Mitiingfui*. (Narrated by Anderias Padafani in 2003, adapted from Kratochvíl et al., 2016, pp. 100–1)

As mentioned, oral traditions continually make reference to landscape features like rocks, caves, and water bodies, among others. In the *Mon Mot* legend, the story involves a cave, called *Foring*. The name of a connected, neighbouring cave is *Anui Hieng*. The protagonist runs into the cave in order to escape the giant snake. which is devouring everything in its path. It is also in the cave that she teaches her twins how to hunt. The story also tells of the movement among places, for instance, when the twins return to their original village, *Lelawi*, and when they escape from the snake, going from *Roolmeelang* to *Mitiingfuui* and then to *Kawaaka Loohu*. These are all toponyms that are still in use among the Abui, who know these places very well. The landscape and its place names are configurable, therefore, in Abui culture, also as mnemonic tools that the storyteller uses to facilitate the memorisation and declamation of the oral-traditional stories and the narrative process in itself. This, in turn, allows the listeners to understand the narration better, as they are deeply immersed in the story because they know and recognise the places that the narrator is talking about. In sum, knowledge of the landscape, reflected in the use of real toponyms and in the movement schema, gives authenticity to the stories and credibility to the storyteller. In Abui culture, it is fundamental that the official narrator of an oral-traditional tale is universally considered and accepted by the community as the 'owner' of the story; other storytellers can provide people with a myth or legend, but only the official 'owner' of the story knows all its details and is authorised to share it in its entirety (Kratochvíl et al., 2016; Perono Cacciafoco & Cavallaro, 2017). These myths and legends establish and clarify the permanent bond between the landscape and its inhabitants, and are evidence of the fact that the landscape does not just consist of physical features, but has a deep human significance and a perennial anthropological value.

Place names can also be linked to local religions and the spiritual aspects of landscape. The story of *Lamòling* (Perono Cacciafoco & Cavallaro, 2017; 2018), mentioned in Chapters 1 and 5, is such an example for the Abui people. This Abui traditional religious myth is centred on how a local god, *Lamòling*, a deity (belonging to the polytheistic stage of the Abui religion) originally worshiped by the Abui people, was later replaced by the more powerful (and more recent) god *Lahatàla* (a sort of hypostasis of the Christian God). This replacement was due to the power shown to the Abui people by *Lahatàla*, and the consequent course of events, in which *Lamòling* was suddenly seen by the locals as a malevolent deity. In the story, *Lamòling*, as an act of retaliation for having been replaced with *Lahatàla* by the Abui people, killed an Abui child and offered the child's body parts as a meal to the Abui people. The story is a metaphorical representation of a dramatic change in Abui religion, with a passage from polytheistic practices to Christianity, which was introduced on *Alor Island* in the sixteenth century. With the spread of Christianity on the island, the old animistic and polytheistic beliefs were abandoned, and the story shows several diachronic layers and variants which reflect the representation of the passage to the new, monotheistic religion. *Lamòling*, in the oral story told by speakers, originally appears as an animistic god (at the same time belonging to a polytheistic *pantheon*), *in toto* equal to the more recent *Lahatàla*, both in power and status among the Abui. The servants of *Lamòling* are represented as minor deities who are worshipped by the local people as well. The key difference between *Lamòling* and *Lahatàla* is that *Lamòling* is a metaphorical figure of the more ancient and primordial gods in Abui religion, who are replaced, over time, by a new (and 'only') god, *Lahatàla*. Indeed, despite the power of *Lamòling* and his prestige as an ancestral deity, with the introduction of Christianity on *Alor Island*, the relationship between the two gods shifted. The Abui people note that the dichotomy between *Lamòling* and *Lahatàla* became, over time, synonymous with that of the Christian God and the devil. *Lamòling* became a sort of representation of the devil in Christian traditions, the fierce enemy of the Christian God, *Lahatàla*. With this, we also see the effort, produced over time by Abui storytellers and spiritual leaders, to merge the different religious aspects of their story, from an animistic/polytheistic layer, to the representation of the cohabitation of polytheistic and monotheistic elements, to the prevalence of the monotheistic Christian religion and its dogma. The story, therefore, unfolds through different narrative layers depicting animistic and polytheistic stages and then the passage to the monotheistic one. The myth merges the two different diachronic layers in a coherent plot, to keep the narrative consistent and to allow the legend to be configured as an effective explanation of the Abui cultural identity and tradition in relation to the religious context.

As we saw with the legend of *Mon Mot*, the story of *Lamòling* and *Lahatàla* is also linked to existing places. Some of the names of those places mirror, in their evocativeness[9] and in their spiritual connections with the Abui people, the religious changes from Abui traditional beliefs to Christianity. For instance, in the village of *Takpàla*, located on the hill above the village of *Takalelàng* (the two villages are interconnected, and their inhabitants claim to be the same people and, actually, belong to the same families), there are two ritual and ceremonial houses, called *Kolwàt* and *Kanurwàt* (see Figure 6.5). These houses are uninhabited, being sacred places, and are the expression of a type of 'architectural art' in Abui culture (Perono Cacciafoco & Cavallaro, 2017, p. 54). *Kanurwàt*, which means 'white, bright, luminous, shining' in Abui, is painted with a motif developed on a white background, while *Kolwàt* has a blackish geometrical pattern and means 'dark'. It is worth noting that both houses existed prior to the arrival of Christianity on *Alor*. In the *Lamòling* story, the area in front of the houses was the location of a ritual known in Abui as *karilìk hè hàk* (shortened to *karilìk*), meaning 'offer to the big old stones'.[10] These are three religious and apotropaic stones located on a central altar called *Karilìk* (the altar got its name from the ritual), which is still attested in its original position in the actual place. The houses and the altar were delimiting the religious area of the *Takpàla* village, and the Abui people, during their rituals, used to dance around them. The original significance of these houses is summarised by a metaphor: the 'dark' house represents the period in which the Abui people were following the 'dark' path of animism and polytheism. The 'white' house, conversely, symbolises the 'light' of the new religion (Christianity) and the 'liberation' of the Abui people from their 'obscure' religious past, represented by their friendship with the more ancient deity,

---

[9] For example, the place called *Lamòling Bèaka* (from the Lamòling myth) 'Lamòling the evil' (Perono Cacciafoco & Cavallaro, 2018), carries, in its denomination (therefore, in its morphology), the name of Lamòling. One inhabited centre located south of the settlements of *Takpàla* and *Takalelàng* mentioned in the *Mon Mot* story as one of the villages destroyed by the god-snake is called *Mon Tooting*, and it contains, in its morphology, *Mon Mot*'s name.

[10] The steps of the ritual are as follows. Three flat stones are placed upright on the altar in front of the two houses; before the ceremony, the Abui people bring cooked rice to the stones; the rice is placed on the altar and offered, symbolically, to the three stones and to the god, among which the first is *Lamòling*; people attending the ritual then eat the rice, as eating it, according to local beliefs, helps them draw closer to the gods.

Figure 6.5 The two Abui ritual and ceremonial houses, *Kolwàt* and *Kanurwàt* (source: Perono Cacciafoco and Cavallaro, 2017, p. 54)

*Lamòling*. Hence, the houses depict the passage from a 'dark' stage of religion, 'championed' by *Lamòling*, to the monotheistic spiritual stage portrayed by the metaphorical figure of *Lahatàla*, the Christian God.

Since being introduced to Christianity, the Abui now frame *Kolwàt* as the representation of the darkness derived from the absence of Christianity in their culture. Thus, in their opinion, the black house is a hypostasis of the lack of light coming from the right religious belief, which Christianity (now regarded as the 'true religion') provided to them. In contrast, the white house, *Kanurwàt*, is the architectural metaphor of the progresses in human history and the light brought to the Abui people by their new religion – Christianity. The names highlight the perception, by the Abui people, of the two houses as two different spiritual places, even though they are just a few metres apart, and signify the development and evolution of Abui history and cultural identity from a dark era to a brighter future.

One of the endings of the *Lamòling* and *Lahatàla* legend tells of how a weakened and defeated *Lamòling* leaves the Abui people and retreats to *Pakulàng Hièng*, a toponym which means 'bad place', in the neighbouring *Kabola* territory. The locality was named as such because it became the lair of the god, still threatening his old worshipers from a nearby territory, and the Abui people believe that *Lamòling* still 'lives' there. With Christianity gaining strength on *Alor*, the story behind *Pakulàng Hièng* was revised to give it a more 'Christian flavour'. According to a newer version, indeed, *Lamòling* did not go to *Pakulàng Hièng* of his own choice (as a sort of voluntary exile), but was hurled from the sky by *Lahatàla* (now regarded as the Christian God), who sunk *Lamòling* to the rocks there as a punishment, and trapped him there for eternity. The similarity of this version of the story with the Christian story of Lucifer is evident, who, as the most beautiful angel of Heaven, rebelled against God and was sunk to Hell as an eternal punishment. *Pakulàng Hièng* is a place characterised by darkish, stony slopes with hollow passages. When the winds blow through these passages, the sound produced is believed by local people to be the atavistic lament of the god. Since it is considered a 'bad place', and is named as such, *Pakulàng Hièng* remains uninhabited to this day, both by the *Kabola* and Abui people.

A few themes emerge from the legends we have just analysed. First, the stories are firmly linked to existing places, and these places are real places that belong to the Abui landscape and have names known to all of the Abui people. Second, and more importantly, not only do these places have sociocultural significance to the Abui people, in the sense that Abui people believe that they are a core component of their human and spiritual landscape and an important part of their meta-history (Perono Cacciafoco & Cavallaro, 2017, p. 54), but their names can also be infused with mythical and religious significance. The toponyms belonging to the *Lamòling* legend, such as *Kolwàt*, *Kanurwàt*, and *Pakulàng Hièng*, derive their names directly from the story itself, which emphasises the centrality of oral traditions in explaining Abui toponymy. Within the story we can also see the refashioning of the oral-traditional representation of a historical event due to the introduction of Christianity on *Alor Island*. Since then, these places are linked to the new (for the Abui people) monotheistic religion, and even serve as metaphors (in the case of *Kolwàt* and *Kanurwàt*) to illustrate how Christianity has 'enlightened' the local people. The newer spiritual meanings of specific place names, like *Pakulàng Hièng*, while still connected with the origins of the myth, have been further readapted to contain the Christian trope connected with the story of how God banished Lucifer to Hell, which is mirrored by *Lahatàla*'s action of exiling *Lamòling* to the rocks of *Pakulàng Hièng*.

## 6.5    Summary

While landscape is generally considered in association with the physical features of a territory, current approaches to its context, as we have shown in this chapter, take a holistic view of the landscape itself, to blend its physical, social, cultural, environmental, and even religious aspects, in order to enhance our understanding of its complex nature and systems. To this end, toponyms can also be useful tools which provide the researchers with insights into how people use or used the landscape. This is because toponyms reflect the physical environment and therefore unify the material, tangible world and the thoughts, perceptions, understandings, feelings, and values that people attach to their space. As Tilley aptly writes, 'in a fundamental way names create landscape' (Tilley, 1994, p. 19). Through naming, 'a space becomes place, and a territory becomes landscape' (Seidl, 2008, p. 35). Landscape, in the final analysis, is not just physical and environmental space, but also represents the sociocultural and religious ways (as in the Abui case studies we have described above) according to which people perceive and shape their physical environments, which often change over time.

In the next chapter, we will look at historical geography, which was briefly mentioned at the start of this chapter, and at how this discipline improves our understanding of toponymy and of recent and contemporary changes to the landscape.

# 7 Historical Toponomastics and Historical Geography

## 7.1 The Relationship between Historical Toponomastics and Historical Geography

Historical toponomastics, as explained in Chapter 3, focusses on reconstructing the original and remote etymology of place names in the context of well documented languages and language families, and in the presence of available historical documentation. Historical toponomastics aims to reconstruct the original and oldest possible etymology of a place name by going back in time till the remote developmental stages of place names. To do this, the historical toponymist often has to trace back the name of a place over millennia, possibly even to prehistoric times (see Chapter 4).

In many cases, historical toponomastics requires that the scholar not only look at historical sources that record aspects of the physical landscape and hydro-geo-morphological features of the places whose names are under examination, but also at sources that describe the anthropic presence and/or the human activities conducted, over time, in the same places. As we detailed in Chapter 3, examples of such historical resources include census data, land and title deeds, birth and death registry records, newspapers, diary entries and accounts written by people living in the places under scrutiny or by travellers who had visited those places, archaeological findings, paleo-anthropological evidence, and comprehensive analyses of the landscape (cf. Chapter 6).

This multidisciplinary approach enables the scholar to ascertain if the origin and meaning of a place name is concomitant with the natural and human landscapes surrounding the toponym and with historical events. To facilitate this endeavour, maps are frequently referenced. They are one of the central components in the study of toponymy and are closely connected with related disciplines, such as cartography, topography, and geography. Maps allow us to associate and identify toponyms as parts of a group. Furthermore, through the symbols and legends on a map, hydro-geo-morphological features, types of landscapes, buildings, historical events, and even people are represented cartographically. Maps can be deemed to have their own language written with abstract symbols (the connection between toponymy and cartography will be discussed in detail in Chapter 10). This is noted by Borchert, who equates maps to being a primary language in geography.

In short, maps and other graphics comprise one of three major modes of communication, together with words and numbers. Because of the distinctive subject matter of geography, the language of maps is the distinctive language of geography. (Borchert, 1987, p. 388)

One of the disciplines that has come to be associated with toponymy and historical toponomastics over time is historical geography. Historical geography is a subfield of human geography[1] and deals with past geographies, and 'the influence of the past in shaping the geographies of the present and the future' (Heffernan, 2009, p. 332). The first mention of historical geography was made by Carl Sauer in 1941, in his seminal work 'Foreword to historical geography'. He called for geographers to end what he described as the 'neglect of historical geography' (Sauer, 1941, p. 1). His work was based on the speech he gave at the *Association of American Geographers* a year before, and captured the *zeitgeist* of American geography at that time; American geographers, then, as Sauer noted, were disinterested in and even shunned the study of historical processes and sequences. Sauer called for human geography, an area that had received great scholarly attention in America, to include perspectives from historical geography. This is because every aspect of the human landscape (which, by implication, involves and constitutes human geography) is affected by the historical concept of change over time. Hence, Sauer believed that the study of historical processes should also be taken up by human geographers. Furthermore, an understanding of mankind and culture can only be possible when the geographer studies human activities and how people came to occupy their respective areas. These aspects imply a historical analysis indispensable to understanding how people became what they are in the present day. Sauer argues the following.

Every human landscape, every habitation, at any moment is an accumulation of practical experience and of what Pareto was pleased to call residues. The geographer cannot study houses and towns, fields and factories, as to their where and why without asking himself about their origins. He cannot treat the localisation of activities without knowing the functioning of the culture, the process of living together of the group, and he cannot do

---

[1] Human geography studies the ways in which 'place, space and environment are both the condition and in part the consequence of human activities' (Gregory, 2009, p. 350). It looks at how humans understand, use, and change the physical environments that they live in. Human geography, along with historical geography, is distinct from physical geography, which studies physical phenomena on, at, or near the Earth's surface, for example, geological, atmospheric, meteorological, and hydrological processes (Clifford, 2009, p. 531). Human geography deals, instead, with how space and place are used socially, economically, culturally, and politically by humans, and historical geography deals with these in a particular place and at a particular time in the past.

this except by historical reconstruction. If the object is to define and understand human associations as areal growths, we must find out how they and their distributions (settlements) and their activities (land use) came to be what they are [...] Such study of culture areas is historical geography. (Sauer, 1941, pp. 8–9)

Another simple but ideal definition of historical geography was given by Guelke (1982).

If all history is the history of thought, all historical geography is the history of thought with a bearing on human activity on the land [...] in historical geography the events of interest are those related to the human activity on the earth. This activity is dependent, in the first instance, on understanding the physical environment in terms of the human meaning it has. These meanings have changed as the human condition has changed and as knowledge of the environment has expanded. (p. 193)

Historical geography, therefore, combines an understanding of the physical landscape and, by extension, its physical geography, along with concepts belonging to the sphere of the human psyche and with an analysis of how humans organise knowledge and their activities, all of which change over time, with a specific focus on how these impact the human environment and, thus, the whole understanding of what is considered to be human geography.

Initially, historical geography focussed on regional (especially rural) settlements and landscapes (Golan, 2009; Heffernan, 2009), much like landscape archaeology. Subsequently, the 1950s and 1960s brought about a change in geography in general, and the discipline began to focus more on contemporary geographies, with an emphasis on urban areas (Golan, 2009). This shift was observed in historical geography too. Historical geography thus turned its attention to the relatively recent past and to urban settlements, partly due to the availability of empirical research materials (Jones, 2004). However, this modern-day disciplinary *locus*, as witnessed in historical geography, does not mean that the field cannot study older and more 'ancient' spaces, places, and time periods. Alan Baker, the former editor of the *Journal of Historical Geography*, noted that 'the study of no problem, period or place in the past was to be prohibited' in the application of approaches of historical geography (Baker, 1987, p. 1).

Hence, both historical toponomastics and historical geography deal, in their different settings, with the past. The two disciplines approach the place under study using available written records, for example, maps of the past, and other historical sources. In historical geography, the approach to the study of places from the past is usually informed by historical evidence obtained from archival sources, with the objective of investigating the settlements and land uses of a civilisation/society that occupies or previously occupied a specific area. As Sauer put it, 'the first step in reconstruction of past stages of a culture area is mastery of its written documents' (Sauer, 1941, p. 13). Some of these sources, which Sauer listed as constituting the 'archives' in historical geography (Sauer, 1941, p. 13), can be very useful to a historical toponymist. They include land grants, land titles, assessments, and records of the productions of goods (all of which provide insights on what the pioneer landscape looked like), diaries, reports made by visiting officials on the condition of a country (especially in colonial contexts), payments of taxes and tributes, data on mines, salt production, and the status of roads. These sources allow researchers to discover and assess details on the economic life of the settlements under examination. Human geography investigates how humans have shaped their physical environments, and Sauer urged the scholars to adopt a comparative approach that should involve both historical and modern sources, in order to understand the nature and direction of changes that have occurred in a place.

Take into the field, for instance, an account of an area written long ago and compare the places and their activities with the present, seeing where the habitations were and the lines of communication ran, where the forests and the fields stood, gradually getting a picture of the former cultural landscape concealed behind the present one. (Sauer, 1941, p. 14)

Naming the places where humans live reflects how people interact with, perceive, use, understand, and change their environment. This arguably makes the toponymist analyse a place name through the lens of human geography. The study of human settlements and of the anthropisation of a place based on historical and cartographical sources, as in the case of historical geography, can also provide valuable insights into the changes and developments in local toponymy, as mentioned in this introductory section. The examples in this chapter will show precisely how the application of historical geography criteria facilitates an understanding of not just historical toponomastics and the toponyms belonging to its context, but also of modern and contemporary place names, especially from urban areas.

## 7.2    The Case Study of *Bistagno*

*Bistagno* (*Bistàgn*, in the local Piedmontese dialect), a village located in *Piedmont*, northwest *Italy*, in the province of *Alessandria* (see Figure 7.1), is an example of how a toponym belonging to the context of the well documented Indo-European language family has been investigated using archival and historical sources by various scholars to explain its origins.

The village is located near the confluence of the two branches of the *Bormida River*, *La Bormida di Spigno* and *La Bormida di Millesimo*. *Spigno Monferrato* and *Millesimo* are two villages which give their names to the two segments of the watercourse. This position made it a very favourable place for human settlement already in remote times. The hydronym *Bormida* (derived from the root *\*borm-*,

Figure 7.1 Location of *Bistagno* (adapted from d-maps, 2021)

meaning 'warm', or 'hot', or 'hot water', or 'warm water') probably has Pre-Indo-European origins, and a number of places situated along the *Bormida River* are very ancient (prehistoric) settlements (cf. Chapter 4).

According to historical records, the village of *Bistagno*, in its current location, was founded only in 1253, during the Italian Middle Ages. It is said that, in the Middle Ages, possibly around the ninth or tenth century, the *Bistagno* (known as *Bestagno/Bestagnum* in Late Latin) predating the current inhabited centre (but way later than the possibly original prehistoric settlement situated on the *Bormida River*) was originally ubicated on a hill facing another village, *Melazzo* (known as *Melacio/Melacium* in Late Latin). Because the two villages were always at war with each other, the bishop of *Acqui Terme*, the neighbouring town with political and religious authority over these villages, sent his soldiers to stop the conflict. In 1253, after the attempts to stop the war failed, the bishop decided to forcibly remove the people of *Bistagno* to a new place further along the valley, on the *Bormida River*. This is how the current *Bistagno* was born. The bishop did not move the inhabitants of *Melazzo*, because *Melazzo* was the place where Saint Guido d'*Aquesana*, the first bishop of *Acqui Terme*, was born. A contemporary hamlet of the current *Bistagno*, called *Roncogennaro*, is still located on a steep hill in the area and possibly represents a fragment of the original settlement of *Bistagno*, or a place where some of the people who refused to be relocated to the new *Bistagno* founded a new village. Contextually, evidence to substantiate the existence of an older *Bistagno* village can be found in the subdivision of the present *Bistagno* called *Cartesio*, precisely in the so-called *Villa del Podestà*'s area. This is where, currently, there is a country house that in the Fascist era belonged to *Bistagno*'s *Podestà*, a mayor of a municipality during the Fascist era (1922–43) in Italy. On the hill where this villa is located, a number of prehistoric archaeological and paleo-anthropological findings have been unearthed, indicating that the place was possibly inhabited already in the Upper Palaeolithic and certainly in the Neolithic. This locality may be a possible candidate for the site of the medieval *Bistagno* before the deportation of its inhabitants along the course of the *Bormida River*. Another corroborating fact is that the hill of the *Villa del Podestà* is located almost in front of the hill where *Melazzo* is situated and geographically is more compatible with the dynamics of the rivalry between the two villages than *Roncogennaro*, located on another, relatively more distant, hill. As mentioned, indeed, *Roncogennaro* was possibly the result of a later migration of people from the 'deported' village on the river, or it may simply have been a more ancient settlement than the 'deported' village. Independently from the medieval origins of the inhabited centre, the *Villa del Podestà*'s site allows us to theorise the possibility that a prehistoric settlement of *Bistagno* was located on the *Bormida River*. It was placed there most likely to use the water of the river itself, and another possibly connected settlement was located on the hill of the current villa, which is a protected and less accessible place than the riverbank. It is possible that the prehistoric communities on the river and on the hill were not differentiated, but that they were the same community (sharing the same prehistoric culture), living on the river because of the need of water and, at times, living and/or retreating to the hill for defensive purposes.

Evidence from historical geography, landscape archaeology, and paleo-anthropology shows the presence of prehistoric (Neolithic and, in some cases, also dating back to the Upper Palaeolithic) settlements on the nearby hills (Colla, 1982). These settlements, dating back to the Stone Age, have been documented along the entire course of the *Bormida River* (Perono Cacciafoco, 2011) and in the area around *Bistagno*. Hence, an explanation of the place name *Bistagno* could have its basis in the fact that the village (or a related human settlement) plausibly already existed in the area during prehistoric times. A possible explanation, as suggested above, may be that the original *Bistagno* could have been located at a different place from the current village (but relatively close to it), corresponding to one of the prehistoric settlements on the watercourse, and that the village itself, because of anthropic dynamics, would have been 'moved' to its present location.

Possible interpretations and explanations of the place name are relatively numerous, and several other scholars have written about the origins and original meanings of *Bistagno* as a toponym (Perono Cacciafoco, 2016a; 2016b). According to Bosio (1972), the name derives from the confluence of the two branches of the *Bormida River*. The scholar proposed an interpretation of the toponym which implies the segmentation of the Italian version of the name into *bi-* and *-stagno* (*bi-* + *-stagno*), giving it the gloss of 'double pond' (*bi[s]* means 'double', and *stagno* is the Italian word for 'pond'). However, a closer look at the geographical morphology of the territory shows us that *La Bormida di Spigno* and *La Bormida di Millesimo*, the two branches of the *Bormida River*, join at about one kilometre from where *Bistagno* is presently ubicated. We can also see that the confluence of the two segments is not actually located in the administrative area of *Bistagno*'s municipality, but in the nearby territory of *Sessame*, precisely in a hamlet called *Gringàvoli*. Bosio (1972) used written records and contemporary maps to account for the name of *Bistagno*, and, in a way, it seemed plausible to link it to the convergence of the two branches of the *Bormida River* and, hence, to hypothesise the name of 'double pond'. Yet, this explanation is flawed, because it is based only on the Italian stage of the name of the village without taking into account the dia-chronic 'stratigraphy' of the name itself, through its possible Indo-European, Celtic, and Latin developmental stages. Moreover, this reconstruction does not consider the hydro-geo-morphological data, in particular the fact that the union of the two branches of the *Bormida River* does not actually occur in *Bistagno*'s area, but in the territory of the neighbouring village of *Sessame*.

According to Olivieri (1965), the name '*bistagno* was a common topographic term found in written records already in Antiquity'. He explained that *Bistagno* is a variant of the Italian word *stagno* ('pond'), with the addition of a *bis-* prefix. This prefix is not intended to carry the meaning of 'double', as Bosio (1972) proposed, or the Italian seme of 'again', as in, for example, *bisnonno* 'great-grandfather', but it functions as a pejorative or negative marker (Rohlfs, 1969). *Bis-*, combined with the word *stagno* 'pond', could have the composite meaning of a 'marshy land', with a negative semantic value. Olivieri's (1965) reconstruction of the toponym as 'swampy place' or 'marshy land' was achieved through an analysis of historical and physical-geographical data inherent in the area. His study of written records revealed that, in the past, the confluence of the two branches of the *Bormida River* did result in the development of marshy lands around *Bistagno*. This would, therefore, link the physical landscape consisting of swampy soils to the name, *Bistagno*, and would also explain the negative connotation associated with it, as swamps and mud-filled places would have represented very salient and dangerous areas to the ancient inhabitants of the territory.

Despite its plausibility, this explanation also has several flaws, both at the linguistic and historical-geographical level. Perono Cacciafoco (2016a; 2016b) noted that this account, like Bosio's reconstruction, is based on Italian terms and their meanings. Therefore, it does not take into account historical records and the archaeological and paleo-anthropological evidence that point to *Bistagno* as a place being inhabited from prehistoric times. Moreover, this proposal does not consider the possible different stages of *Bistagno*'s naming process, from Indo-European, to Celtic, to Latin, and ultimately to Italian. Indeed, it does not even account for the Latin and pre-Latin developmental stages of the toponym. In other words, the remote naming process of the place name is something that Olivieri, as well as a number of other scholars, did not explore, while it must always be necessarily the central aim of a historical-toponomastic study. The end result is that there is currently no unanimous etymological reconstruction of the toponym *Bistagno*.

There seems to be some agreement on the fact that this place name may be linked to the notion of 'water', with a possible pejorative connotation, compatible with the above-mentioned concept of 'swampy land'. The reconstruction of the place name *Bistagno*, therefore, could be connected with the Indo-European root \*ang-/\*-agn-, meaning 'water'. Olivieri (1965, p. 93), in his dictionary of Piedmontese toponyms, pointed out the relatively high frequency of place names similar to *Bistagno* in northwest *Italy*. Based on his studies of the related settlements and of the connected landscape features, these names appear especially linked to places characterised by marshy soils. Some of the toponyms cited by Olivieri are *Bestagnum*, on the *Orta Lake* (*Piedmont*, northwest *Italy*, in the province of *Novara*), *Bestagno*, a hamlet of the *Pontedassio* municipality

(*Liguria*, northwest *Italy*, in the province of *Imperia*), and *Bestagnu*, a hamlet of the *Pigna* municipality (*Liguria*, northwest *Italy*, in the province of *Imperia*). Another scholar, Pellegrini (1990), cited the similarly named *Bestagno*, in the *Sospel* municipality (southeast *France*, *Alpes-Maritimes*, near the French–Italian border). To this list, we can add another 'water name', morphologically very similar to *Bistagno*. That is, the hydronym *Bisagno* (in the local Ligurian dialect, *Besagno*), a stream from *Liguria*, northwest *Italy*, that flows through the city of *Genoa*, the administrative centre of the region. These toponyms are also interesting because they all include -*agn*- as part of their names. This could indicate the possible existence of a toponymic system characterised by a shared root (or prefix, *bis*- or *bes*-) merged with the stem *agn*-, producing a toponymic naming process connected with the notion of 'marshy soil'. At face value, the (Proto-)Indo-European root *agn*- is possibly shared by *Bistagno* and the other hydronyms and place names listed above.

All of these places are located in areas with evidence of being populated since the Upper Palaeolithic age. We can conclude, then, that *agn*- may have been an important stem in the prehistoric toponymic naming process of a (relatively large) territory. That is, the place names that share the root *agn*- could be part of a well-established prehistoric toponymic type that was developed at least during Indo-European times. This type is linked to the notion of 'water', in particular to the concept of the 'flowing water' of a watercourse. It is therefore possible to hypothesise that these place names christened the specific segments of the river where the original villages were situated (although why *Bistagno* was relocated along the *Bormida River* warrants further investigation) and then the toponyms became the names of the villages themselves. That is, the hydronimic denomination of a stretch of a river would have become the toponymic denomination of an inhabited centre located along that stretch of the watercourse. Therefore, it is possible that the original name of *Bistagno* was the prehistoric name of a specific segment of the *Bormida River*, along which the original (prehistoric) village was situated.

To corroborate the *agn*- hypothesis for the above-mentioned place names, it is useful to highlight the fact that a reconstruction connected with the root *agn*-/*ang*- 'water', or 'flowing water' can also be applied to the hydronym *Agno*, a mountain stream flowing in northeast *Italy*, in the *Vincenza* province. This hydronym represents a linguistic continuation of the use of the root *agn*- in Romance toponymy/hydronymy. The related Latin form *amnis* 'river' was not widely continued in Romance languages at the level of common lexicon, while the hydronym *Agno* clearly describes the notion of 'water' (the 'flowing water' of a stream) and we can consider it as part of the set of place names belonging to the toponymic type connected with the root *agn*.

Assuming the plausibility and presence, in this toponymic context, of the root *ang-/*-agn- 'water', the 'possible' segmentations are as outlined below.

1. Bistagno = *bi-s-t-agn-o

| bi- | -s- | -t- | -agn- | -o |
|---|---|---|---|---|
| 'double', or 'bad' | (possible) 'euphonic/ juxtaposed consonant' | (possible) euphonic/ juxtaposed consonant | the root *agn- (*ang-) 'water', or 'flowing water' | possible (originally) Celtic ending, nominative masculine singular, Latin -us (neuter -um), Italian -o |

2. Bistagno = *bis-t-agn-o

| bis- | -t- | -agn- | -o |
|---|---|---|---|
| 'double', or 'bad' | (possible) euphonic/ juxtaposed consonant | the root *agn- (*ang-) 'water', or 'flowing water' | possible (originally) Celtic ending, nominative masculine singular, Latin -us (neuter -um), Italian -o |

With solution 1, the challenge we face is how to explain the consonants 's' and 't'. A possible solution brings us back to the issue we described in trying to come up with a plausible etymology of *Squaneto* and *Spigno* in Chapter 3. The 'cutting' of a root consonant (or of a consonantal cluster in the stem), like in the examples of *s-ak^w a- and *s-p-agn- (Chapter 3), and here of *bi-s- or *bi-s-t-, together with the interpretation of the *s- as a '(possible) euphonic/juxtaposed consonant', do allow the postulation of plausible roots, such as *ak^w(a)- and *agn-/*ang-, respectively, which are consistent with the hydro-geo-morphology of the territories and with the 'nature' of the places. However, this is still an unproven and controversial etymology, highly experimental and in need of additional evidence and discussion. This does not mean that it is intrinsically 'wrong', and its postulation can help to shed light on the origins of the related place name(s). Solution 2 solves this problem somewhat better, also because *bis- 'double', or 'bad', as mentioned above, has consensus among scholars.

However, as a general and necessary rule, we should always try to provide a standard historical-phonetic reconstruction, like we did in *Squaneto*'s case (see especially footnotes 1 and 2 in Chapter 3), compare the two options (segmented vs. historical-phonetic), and 'decide' which one is more likely and acceptable, always in connection with the nature of the landscape of the places. In *Spigno*'s case (see the discussion in Chapter 3), a (simple) historical-phonetic reconstruction does not seem to provide convincing clues of its origin. In fact, it reinforces the widespread paretymology connecting the toponym with the Indo-European paretymological referents *spina* and *spineus*. As we said in Chapter 3, nonetheless, this reconstruction is another example of the challenges facing us when searching for the perfect etymological reconstruction. In particular, proposing the existence of 'juxtaposed (root) consonants' is still the subject of heated debate.

It is worth mentioning here that in prehistoric toponymy, more or less all the reconstructions (even if well documented and based on solid methods) belong to the context of what is hypothetical and, therefore, different methodologies (traditional and experimental) should never be seen as if they were in competition or developed against each other, but can sometimes, even when combined, allow the researchers to collect evidence of the development of very ancient naming processes, even if such kinds of postulations could never be confirmed or proven. After all, the duty of a historical linguist dealing with prehistoric etymologies is not to propose an absolutely true and irrefutable reconstruction (which is almost impossible for etymologies dating back to extremely remote times), but to provide all the possible and reasonable reconstructions for a lexeme in order to explore, assess, and document the full range of options and alternatives for a correct and comprehensive restitution of a form.

In order to explore a more standard approach to this toponymic reconstruction, it is worth mentioning another hypothesis here, on the etymological origins of *Bistagno* that Perono Cacciafoco (2016b, pp. 64–5) developed through the application of the comparative method and by reconstructing the historical phonetics and phonology of the place name according to a standard procedure. This complementary proposal is semantically unlinked to the 'water place' nature of the village, but could still be connected with the segment of the *Bormida River* where the village was located and, therefore, to the related inhabited centre.

The alternative hypothesis proposes that the toponym *Bistagno* could derive from an Indo-European (then Celtic) form *\*bĭst-ăgnŏ-s* (noun) 'little pheasant' (or 'little bird similar to a pheasant'), which would have generated, among others, the attested Old Irish word *ˈbesān* 'pheasant'. A related reconstructed adjective is *\*bĭst-ăgn-i̯ŏ-n* 'something linked to the pheasant(s)', or 'territory of the pheasant(s)'. In this case, the -*ăgnŏ(-)* component would not derive from or be connected with the Proto-Indo-European root *\*agn-*, but would be a (later) Celtic diminutive suffix. This alternative (proto-)Celtic etymological restitution seems to be a possible and plausible etymological alternative. Nonetheless, the 'water' component in toponyms like *Bistagno* appears to be very strong still and, while a historical-geographical analysis also has to consider the paleo-zoology (in this case the paleo-ornithology) of a territory, it is very difficult to reconstruct the elements of the ancient fauna of a prehistoric area and to gather enough evidence to link the existence of a particular animal, in this case a bird, to ancient lexemes. This alternative reconstruction in itself does not exclude the fact that if 'pheasants' were indeed the original motivation for the toponym, *Bistagno* could have been the name given to the segment of the *Bormida River* where this specific species of birds was possibly common at the time of the related naming process. In that case, *Bistagno* would not have meant 'water place', but something like 'village/place of the pheasant(s)'. This reconstruction is a tentative option, which can surely be object of a discussion. It could work, nevertheless, at the level of historical phonetics and historical morphology, and it would provide another possible explanation for the naming process of the toponym.

Naming a locality after the fauna that may have been predominant there, as may be the case with the 'pheasant' hypothesis for the toponym *Bistagno*, is not uncommon. Place names indicating common species, among others wolves and bears, are found in many areas of *Europe* and the *Northern Hemisphere* in general. For example, Pearce (1954, p. 203) reported that the word 'bear' (including the Spanish *oso* 'bear', and 'grizzly', referencing the grizzly bear) appears in about 500 place names in *California, USA*, for example, *Bearpaw, Bearskin*, and *Bear Pen Creek*. Pearce (1954, pp. 203–4) also found that the next most common animal that figures in Californian place names is the horse, with toponyms such as *Horse Creek, Horse Lake*, and *White Horse*. Aybes and Yalden (1995, p. 204) stated that about 230 'Place-names in England confirm both the widespread nature and, if numbers are to be believed, abundance of Wolves in former times. Most names derive from the Old English *wulf;* or from the Old Norse *ulfr*; Old English names date from AD450 onwards, the Old Norse names from around AD900 onwards.'

Two similar examples from places near *Bistagno* are represented by the names of two villages in northwest *Italy*, southern *Piedmont*, that is, *Orsara Bormida*, currently located in the province of *Alessandria*, and *Serole*, currently situated in the province of *Asti*. The territories of both places were characterised, at least until the Low Middle Ages, by the presence of bears, which were considered a dangerous threat to the inhabited centres and to the local populations. Bears were, therefore, hunted both as a defensive measure and for their fur. Nowadays, these animals are not attested in the territories anymore. Nonetheless, both place names tell us of these members of the local fauna in ancient times and of their existence in these areas until some centuries ago.

*Orsara Bormida* is located on a hill overlooking the course of the *Bormida River*. This gives rise to the specific component of its name, *Bormida*. The first attestation of the toponym, in the Medieval Latin form *Ursaria*, dates back to the year 1135 (Olivieri, 1965, p. 246). The place name is a derivative of the Latin word *ursus* (masculine singular) 'bear', with the common (masculine singular) suffix *-arius*, indicating a 'place' in general, and specifically the notion of 'belonging to a place' (Rohlfs, 1969, § 1072). It is necessary to note that the form of the place name is feminine both in Latin and in Italian, and is therefore connected with/derived from the Latin word (feminine singular) *ursa* ('she-bear'), with the common suffix *-arius*, in its feminine, singular form

-*aria*. Therefore, the possible translation of the denomination is 'territory of the bears' and the toponym is transparently connected with the presence of bears in the area up to the Middle Ages.

*Serole*, in turn, is located on a steep hill around 70 kilometres southeast of *Asti*. The first attestation of the place name, in the Medieval Latin form *Ursariola*, was in the year 991, from the *Charta di fondazione e donazione dell'Abbazia di San Quintino in Spigno* (the 'Founding and Donation *Charta* of the *Saint Quentin's Abbey* in *Spigno Monferrato*') (Bosio, 1972). *Orsairola* was attested in the year 1170 (Gasca Queirazza et al., 1999, s.v. Serole). The denomination (which both in Latin and in Italian is feminine singular), in all its variants, is equivalent to *Orsara* < *Ursaria*, with the implementation of the Latin diminutive suffix -*(i)olus* (masculine singular) (Rohlfs, 1969, § 1086), in this case in its feminine singular form -*(i)ola*. The standard Italian name shows apheresis and the reduction in /e/ of the diphthong /ai/, produced by prolepsis of /i/ (Gasca Queirazza et al., 1999, s.v. Serole). Like the case of *Orsara Bormida*, the place name means, basically, 'territory of the bears', with a diminutive morphological and semantic component, which would result in a more exact translation as 'little territory of the bears'.

Toponyms that indicate the presence in their territories of specific species of animals, like *Orsara Bormida* and *Serole*, are widespread in *Italy*. Many places, however, have seen these animals disappear over the centuries, although they still carry their names. Other Italian examples of place names indicating the presence of bears are, among others, another *Orsara*, currently located in the province of *Biella*, in northern *Piedmont*; *Orsiera*, in *Roreto Chisone*'s territory, currently in *Turin* province; *Piedmont*'s administrative centre *Montarsello*, belonging to the *Granozzo con Monticello* municipality, currently in the province of *Novara*, northern *Piedmont*; and *Orsara di Puglia*, currently located in the province of *Foggia*, *Puglia*, southeast *Italy*.

In the past, there were also toponyms connected with the presence of wolves in the Italian context. An instance is provided by the place name *Lupara*, belonging to a small municipality currently located in the province of *Campobasso*, *Molise*, southern *Italy*. The village is ubicated on a hill in the *Biferno Valley*. The first written attestation of the denomination comes from the *Catalogus Baronum* (1150–68) (Gasca Queirazza et al., 1999, s.v. Lupara), in the Medieval Latin form (accusative feminine singular) *Lupariam*. Exactly like the case of *Orsara* < *Ursaria* and *ursus/ursa*, the name is a derivative of the Latin word *lupus* (masculine singular) 'wolf', with the common (masculine singular) suffix -*arius*, indicating a 'place' in general, and specifically the notion of 'belonging to a place' (Rohlfs, 1969, § 1072). Moreover, like in the case of *Orsara* < *Ursaria* and *ursus/ursa*, the form of the toponym both in Latin and in Italian is feminine, and is therefore derived from the Latin word (feminine singular) *lupa* 'she-wolf', with the common suffix -*arius* in agreement (feminine singular), that is, *-aria*. The place name, therefore, would have originally meant 'place of the wolves', indicating the presence of those animals in the related territory. Giovanni Alessio proposed another explanation for the toponym, one that is also connected with the wolves (Gasca Queirazza et al., 1999, s.v. Lupara). According to the scholar, *Lupara* could derive from the expression *luparia (fossa)* 'trap (pit) to catch wolves', which in any case would be always etymologically linked to the notion of the animal the toponym refers to.

Another instance involving the ancient presence of wolves in a territory is represented by the place name *Cantalupa*, belonging to a small town located in northern *Italy*, *Piedmont*, in the province of *Turin* (the administrative centre of the region), in the valley of the *Noce* stream. The toponym is transparent in its meaning and belongs to a series of morphologically and semantically equivalent denominations characterising the territories located between *France* and *Italy*. Other Italian attestations of this toponymic type are, for example, *Cantalupo Ligure* (northwest *Italy*, southern *Piedmont*, in the province of *Alessandria*, documented from 1201 as *Cantalupus*), *Cantalupo nel Sannio* (southern *Italy*, *Molise*, in the province of *Isernia*, first attested between 1150 and 1168 in the *Catalogus Baronum*), and *Cantalupo*, a hamlet of the city of *Alessandria* (northwest *Italy*, southern *Piedmont*). French examples include, among others, *Chanteloup-les-Vignes* (*Yvelines Department, Île-de-France*, north-central *France*), *Chanteloup-en-Brie* (*Seine-et-Marne Department, Île-de-France*, north-central *France*), and *Chanteloup* (*Ille-et-Vilaine Department, Brittany*, northwest *France*).

*Cantalupa* is an imperative compound, used ironically to indicate a place where the wolves howl. Indeed, *canta*, in Italian, means 'sing' (imperative active present, second-person singular of the verb *cantare* 'to sing'), while *lupo* (masculine singular) is 'wolf' (Olivieri, 1965, p. 111). The toponym is 'ironic' because in local folklore the wolves 'sing' when they are hungry, but the people are well protected within their village and, therefore, the wolves cannot reach them. It is akin to saying: 'Sing, wolf, sing, but you cannot enter the village and eat us.' Furthermore, in this case, the form is in its feminine singular version, *lupa* 'she-wolf'. Hence, the morphology of the place name associates a verbal element with a noun, and is called 'imperative composition', frequent in local denominations in Romance contexts (Rohlfs, 1969, § 343).

There is a debate over 'place-name evidence for the former existence of extinct animals' (Aybes & Yalden, 1995, p. 202). Rackham (1986) pointed out how some place names that seem to derive from zoonyms in fact come from people's names (e.g., *Beowulf*) or groups of people being labelled as such. For example, the scholar stated that 'In Anglo-Saxon times, unpersons and men on the run were declared *wulvesheafod* (wolves-head) and if caught ended on a wolves-head tree' (1986, p. 34). Moreover, many places that apparently carry the names of animals actually do not refer to the presence of those animals at any time in the past in their territories (Gelling, 1987; Rackham, 1986). For example, the relatively widespread toponymic-type *montelupo* can have two derivations; *Montelupo Fiorentino*, the name of a town ubicated in *Florence* province, *Tuscany*, central *Italy*, and which dates back to the Italian Middle Ages, derives from the zoonym *lupus* (Latin)/*lupo* (Italian) 'wolf', being thus *monte* 'mountain' + *lupo* 'wolf', and belongs to the set that includes the above-mentioned *Lupara* and the numerous *Cantalupo*. *Montelupo Albese* (the name of a small town located in *Cuneo* province, northwest *Italy*, southern *Piedmont*), could also be analysed as *monte* 'mountain' + *lupo* 'wolf'. However, this etymology is wrong. In fact, the correct reconstruction segments the place name as *monte* 'mountain', plus the anthroponym *Lupo* (Italian), or *Lupus* (Medieval Latin) (Olivieri, 1965, p. 202). That is, the village, located on a mount, was named after a proper noun (*Lupo*), which, in Medieval Italian, was a common occurrence. Another interesting example is *Montelupone*, the denomination of a small town located in the province of *Macerata, Marche*, central *Italy*. This name could be analysed as *monte* 'mountain' + *lupo* 'wolf', in its augmentative variant *lupone* 'big wolf'. However, this etymology is also wrong. The place name was first attested in the years between 1290 and 1292 as *Monteluppone* and *Montelupone* (Gasca Queirazza et al., 1999, s.v. Montelupone). Both attestations are from the *Rationes Decimarum Italiae, Marchia* (Sella, 1950), which cites, '*a domno Iohanne de Monteluppone*' (n. 5794) 'by lord *Iohanne de Monteluppone*', and '*ecclesie S. Michaelis de Montelupone*' (n. 5879) 'the *St Michael Church of Montelupone*'. The place name *Montelupone*, like *Montelupo Albese*, derives from *monte* 'mountain' plus the above-mentioned proper noun *Lupo*. The ending in -*ne* is not to be identified as an augmentative suffix, but dates back to a Late Latin (and/or Vernacular Italian) version of the personal name *Lupo* (nominative singular masculine, not *Lupus*), *Luponis* (genitive singular masculine), assimilated to the Italian form *Lupone*, as a model of imparisyllabic inflection in -*o*/-*one* (therefore, *Lup-o*/*Lup-one*). This name was also widespread in the Italian Medieval anthroponymy.

All these examples tell us that place names can sometimes, when properly verified, be useful in providing scholars with information on the local fauna of a territory at a specific time. Aybes and Yalden (1995, p. 202) said that, in the British context, a place name most likely refers to an actual animal, if that toponym is 'traced back to an Anglo-Saxon or Old Norse form'. As an example, they show how *Owlands* (*North Yorkshire, United Kingdom* (*UK*)) seems to owe its name to the owls that may have once lived there. However, the authors proved that in historical documents the place was known as *Ulvelundes* (Old Norse *ulfr* 'wolf' and *lundr* 'grove'), referencing the presence of wolves and not owls. Another example is *Woodale* (*North Yorkshire, UK*), which used to be *wulf dael* 'wolf valley'.

The above discussion shows that, in a way, toponyms can have the function of supporting and/or replacing historical documents. Place names, therefore, are often able to provide us with important evidence on the local fauna of a territory at the diachronic level, unveiling the existence, in a specific area and at a specific time, of animal species which could have disappeared over centuries and millennia, or which are extinct due to a range of different reasons, for example, extensive hunting or the massive anthropisation of a territory. Nonetheless, those animals can survive in the names of the places, which tell us a story about when those creatures were emblematic and habitual presences (sometimes feared) of a territory.

To sum up, through this case study, we have been able to see how different scholars used historical records in their (sometimes not very effective or accurate) efforts to explain the place name *Bistagno*, albeit with varying successes. Among them, Bosio's (1972) reconstruction did not take into account the toponymic 'stratigraphy' and archaeological evidence and paleo-anthropological findings that attested the existence of prehistoric settlements along the *Bormida River* and around *Bistagno*'s territory. On the other hand, the analysis of available historical and physical-geographical records allowed us to propose and to postulate a plausible set of place names belonging to a toponymic type derived from a common root *agn-*, including settlements located in proximity of 'water' and 'water sources', like the *Bormida River*. As we have mentioned several times in this book, ancient settlements were often named after natural resources and primary goods for humans. If we accept the 'water' hypothesis, the naming of *Bistagno* would have followed this same rationale, as Stone Age settlers would most likely have linked their dwelling to a natural, primary resource, in this case water, or, if we accept the 'pheasant' option, to the name of a possibly valued species of (local) bird. Hence, an accurate and plausible linguistic reconstruction of a place name must always take into account all the available historical and hydro-geo-morphological data and look for the most ancient possible origins of a toponym.

## 7.3   Historical Geography and Contemporary Odonymy: The Case Study of *Bucharest*

As we have seen in the section above, methods in historical geography and the examination of historical documents can be used to study the names of ancient settlements like *Bistagno*. This notwithstanding, the same tools are also essential in the analysis of street names in contemporary and urban contexts, offering to the researcher a glimpse of how their inhabitants used and transformed their surroundings and the related toponyms. This is something we will take up in this section. With the word 'contemporary', we mean to indicate a period of time within the last 200 years, usually from the nineteenth century to the present day. The term 'contemporary', indeed, is semantically different in the historical context from 'modern', which usually refers to the era between the end of the fifteenth century and the early part of the nineteenth century, coming, therefore, just before the contemporary period. Therefore, settlements and cities developed in contemporary times are quite recent and connected with our everyday lives. They comprise streets, blocks, alleys, houses, parks, squares, and so on. The names of these places (or 'micro-places', or 'places within places') are part of an urbanonymic system[2] and are often considered micro-toponyms, as they are usually only known by the local people living in a specific area (Urazmetova & Shamsutdinova, 2017).

By consulting historical records, a common practice in historical geography, such as bills, laws, newspapers, maps, and town plans of a city across different time periods and under various political regimes, researchers can investigate the changes in the urbanonyms and the social, political, and ideological events that motivated naming and renaming processes. Changes can be due to both practical and symbolic purposes. For new political regimes, the urban and toponymic landscape of capital cities presents a perfect opportunity to demonstrate the values, ideologies, meanings, and aspirations that they hold dear. Thus, toponyms, and particularly odonyms, of capital cities often have a rich stratigraphy, as successive governments use street names symbolically as tools to propagate their sociopolitical agenda. Historical geography allows us to study the connections between toponyms and the historical and/or political events that happened in the places they define, which eventually influenced their naming.

It is with this background that now we turn our attention to *Bucharest*, the capital city of *Romania*. *Bucharest* has been the documentary source of and testbed for several historical geography studies focussing on changes in street names, especially from the late twentieth century (Light, 2004; Light, Nicolae, & Suditu, 2002; Light & Young, 2014; Niculescu-Mizil & A-M., 2014). These scholars focussed, generally, on the renaming of streets in the Communist (Light et al., 2002) and Post-Communist (Light, 2004; Light & Young, 2014) eras and showed, as aforementioned, how a historical-geographical analysis can help us understand the political and ideological shifts that resulted in the renaming of places.

In August 1944, the Soviet Army entered *Romania* and sought to bring the country, which at that point in time was ruled by Nazi *Germany*, into the Soviet orbit. The first Communist-dominated government was formed on 6 March 1945. On 30 December 1947, King Michael was forced to abdicate,

---

[2] The purpose of naming streets and other urbanonyms is to help people orientate around a city. This is because names serve to identify and differentiate particular urban 'micro-places' and contexts. A very practical example of this is the alphanumeric system used to name streets in megacities like *New York* (Azaryahu, 1996). This will be discussed in detail in Chapters 8 and 9.

and a Soviet-style *Romanian People's Republic* was formed. It was ruled by the Romanian Workers' Party (RWP), which from 1948 'rapidly set about remaking Romania in accordance with the model of Soviet communism' (Light et al., 2002, p. 136). *Romania* was now ruled by Gheorghe Gheorghiu-Dej, a committed Stalinist who pledged total loyalty to the *Soviet Union*. Just as how the *Soviet Union* and many of its satellite states mobilised a variety of symbols in the urban landscape (e.g., toponymic landmarks, memorial plaques, placards, signs, and banners) to legitimise the new rulers and their worldview, as well as to extol revolutionary Socialism, Romanian toponyms were politicised to 'declare the ideology and orientation of the People's Republic' (Light et al., 2002, p. 137).

Drawing from records of the *Monitorul Comunal* (*Community Monitor*), published by the *Bucharest Primărie* 'city hall' and *Scânteia*, the RWP's newspaper, Light et al. (2002) showed that over 150 toponyms were replaced in the first year that *Romania* turned Communist (see Table 7.1). This renaming process, therefore, has to be interpreted in the context of the ideology of the new Communist regime in the country. The motivations were mainly aimed at rewriting the nation's history. Previous non-Communist rulers were portrayed as repressive and illegitimate, and *Romania*'s history was spun around the theme of a longstanding class struggle. The subsequent declaration of the *People's Republic of Romania* thereby marked the victory of the Communists. The RWP was portrayed as being deeply embedded in *Romania*'s history

Table 7.1 *Renaming (in English translation) of major boulevards and squares in* Bucharest *by the ruling Communist Party in 1948 (adapted from Light* et al., *2002, p. 137)*

| Former name | New name allocated in 1948 |
|---|---|
| Carol I Boulevard | Boulevard of the Republic |
| Carol I Square | Republic Square |
| Queen Elisabeth Boulevard | 6 March Boulevard |
| Ferdinand I Boulevard | Georghi Dimitrov Boulevard |
| Ferdinand I Square | 23 August Square |
| Queen Maria Boulevard | Marshall Tito Boulevard |
| Queen Maria Square | Marshall Tito Square |
| Prince Mircea Boulevard | 1907 Boulevard |
| Constantin Brâncoveanu Boulevard | 1848 Boulevard |
| I. C. Brătianu Boulevard | Nicolae Bălcescu Boulevard |
| Tache Ionescu Boulevard | General Magheru Boulevard |
| Lascăr Catargiu Boulevard | Ana Ipătescu Boulevard |
| Jianu Square | General Stalin Square |
| Marshal Prezan Boulevard | A. A. Zdanov Boulevard |

(Shafir, 1985, cited in Light et al., 2002, p. 137). At the same time, being led by a Stalinist, the country had to show the supposedly lasting Russian and Slavic influences on the Romanian language and culture, while removing any connections with the West and western *Europe*.

In line with the rewriting of *Romania*'s history to downplay the roles of former leaders, while celebrating Communism and its rulers, the names of major boulevards and squares were renamed to reflect the new political realities. Boulevards that were named after *Romania*'s first king and queen (i.e., Carol I and Elisabeta) were renamed *Bulevardul Republicii* 'Boulevard of the Republic' and *Bulevardul 6 martie* '6 March Boulevard' after the date on which the first Communist government was formed in 1945. These were overtly ideological names which commemorated the establishment of a Communist government on a visible and public scale. Other boulevards were named after Communist leaders in neighbouring states, possibly to make reference to *Romania*'s position as a Soviet satellite state. For example, *Bulevardul Ferdinand I*, named after *Romania*'s second king, was renamed after the Bulgarian leader Georghi Dimitrov, while *Bulevardul Regina Maria*, named after Ferdinand's wife, was renamed after Tito, the leader of Yugoslavia. Light et al. (2002) also cited a 1948 *Scânteia* article that alluded to pre-Socialist politicians' references which were removed from *Bucharest*'s north–south boulevard. These changes were announced on 11 June 1948, the same day that a law aimed at nationalising the majority of Romanian industries was passed. The use of historical sources allowed the above-mentioned researchers to conclude that 'the replacement of the former order was marked in both concrete and symbolic ways' (Light et al., 2002, p. 137). The authors, from their analysis of historical documents, also argued that the renaming of streets was not the only symbolic aspect of the political (re)naming process that was produced in *Romania* under Communist rule. Records from the *Monitorul Comunal* and *Scânteia* published during that time showed that other public infrastructures were renamed. These included thirteen *Bucharest* hospitals, parks, markets, shops, factories, schools, cinemas, theatres, stadiums, university residences, and even bakeries. Indeed, the imposition of the Communist rule had changed the entire old urbanonymy in *Bucharest* into one that embodied the Communist worldview.

Light et al. (2002) also drew on secondary sources, like street guides written by people who lived in the 1950s, and tabulated the strategies used by the Communists to politicise toponyms in *Bucharest*. For instance, a particular name could be used multiple times in different parts of the city (see Table 7.2). The denominations that appeared most frequently centred around dates and people. Popular dates included 23 August, the day of the coup which overthrew the former Romanian government and paved the way for the pro-Soviet RWP leadership over *Romania*; 30 December, the date of the proclamation of the

Table 7.2 *Number of streets in* Bucharest *named after prominent dates and people according to the Communist national narrative in 1954 (adapted from Light* et al., *2002, p. 141)*

| Street name (in English) | Number of streets |
|---|---|
| *23 August* | 10 |
| *J. C. Frimu* | 10 |
| *Freedom* | 9 |
| *30 December* | 9 |
| *Vasile Roailă* | 9 |
| *Nicolae Bălcescu* | 9 |
| *Tudor Vladimirescu* | 9 |
| *Ilic Pintilic* | 9 |
| *Filimon Sîrbu* | 8 |
| *6 March* | 8 |
| *Peace* | 7 |
| *Constantin Dobrogeanu Gherea* | 7 |
| *1 May* | 7 |
| *Ana Ipătescu* | 7 |
| *Progress* | 6 |
| *Heroes* | 6 |
| *Olga Bancic* | 5 |
| *Elena Pavel* | 5 |
| *13 December* | 5 |
| *Work* | 4 |
| *Leontc Filipescu* | 4 |
| *Maxim Gorky* | 4 |

Republic in 1947; 6 March, the date on which the first Communist-dominated government was formed in 1945. Popular street names were renamed with reference to Socialist and Communist activists, like Vasile Roaită, and other revolutionary figures from Romanian history (such as Nicolae Bălcescu, Ana Ipătescu, and Tudor Vladimirescu). Verdery (1991) argued that the political aim of this process was to ingrain the populace with those ideals by saturating the consciousness of urban *Romania* with symbols of Communist presence and agenda, and over time to generate a new national narrative espoused by the Communists.

Through the use of historical records published by the *Bucharest* city hall and the RWP newsletter, along with secondary accounts by the residents of *Bucharest* in the 1940s and 1950s, Light et al. (2002) found that toponyms mirrored the 'changing constructions of history and identity in communist Romania' (p. 142), as the Communist regime sought to remove the pre-Communist rulers from the local collective memory and to introduce a new Communist-sanctioned account of history, while promoting its allegiance to the *Soviet Union* and its other satellite states. In the final analysis, Romanian odonyms from the period between 1948 and 1965 were examples of how street names, although often overlooked, are the micro- or local-scale manifestations of broader structures of power that shape a society.

The Romanian Revolution of 1989 saw the overthrowing of the Communist government of *Romania*. This uprising was widely seen as the starting point of a new *Romania* without the presence of the oppressive Communist/Socialist rulers. In the aftermath of the revolution, a new round of street renaming ensued. As Young and Light (2001) noted, the post-Socialist construction of national identities is often and expectedly marked by a rejection of the Socialist past. In this process, history was revised once again, as the national narrative that was imposed during the Socialist period was widely discarded. Instead, there was 'a "return" to an earlier historical trajectory, which was "interrupted" by the "aberration" of four or more decades of state socialism' (Young & Light, 2001, pp. 947–8). In the aftermath of the post-Socialist and post-Communist era, public spaces, which had hitherto propagated Socialist ideals and world-views as well as celebrating Socialist heroes, dates, and achievements, were being literally 'reconstructed'. At the level of street names, it is possible to witness what Azaryahu (1997, p. 482) called the process of 'de-commemoration and a new commemoration', where Socialism was de-commemorated and the old order and revolution that overthrew the Communist regime were celebrated.[3]

Light (2004) once again made use of historical records of the recent past to track the renaming of streets that occurred in the post-Socialist period. His key source was a document produced by the *Bucharest Primărie*, which listed street naming and renaming from 1990 to 1997. In total, he identified 288 streets in *Bucharest* that were renamed (along with their former and current names, and the dates when the renaming was approved). The researcher also utilised the *Bucharest Primărie* website and other newspapers to track street renaming in post-Socialist *Bucharest*. He found lists indicating former and current odonyms that had undergone renaming. These lists were published in newspapers in 1996, particularly in the *România Liberă*. In comparing these street names, Light also consulted a 1982 *Bucharest* street guide in order to obtain pre-1990 names of the streets. To confirm the names before adding them into his database, he also analysed various maps, and carried out fieldwork in the city. Light (2004) found that, in the target period, streets were renamed to commem-orate the 1989 revolution, to celebrate the period of the *Greater Romania*

---

[3] In some ways, the renaming process described above, that is, when the names of pre-Socialist rulers were removed, could also have been discussed in terms of de-commemoration (and a new, divergent commemoration) of the Socialist era in *Romania*.

(which was constructed as the golden era of *Romania*'s history between the First World War and 1940), and to restore pre-Socialist names, such as those of pre-Socialist-era politicians and the monarchy.

An interesting point brought up by Light (2004) is that most of the street renaming occurred in the city centre. In more peripheral parts of *Bucharest*, streets whose names referred to Socialism and its ideas generally remained untouched. These include odonyms with the words 'Proletarian', or 'Workers', or 'Cooperative' (all of which are undoubtedly Communist/Socialist concepts), important dates, and key figures in Socialist and Communist history. As Light (2004) concluded, the focus on renaming streets in the *Bucharest* city centre, to a large extent, could be due to the high cost of street renaming. The post-Socialist economic austerity meant that the *Bucharest Primărie* focussed the renaming operation in places in the city where the greatest number of people were concentrated (i.e., the city centre) and, hence, where the demonstrative effects had to be the highest. Therefore, changing the names of odonyms in the heart of the city was an emphatic sign to the people of *Bucharest* and the foreign visitors about the fact that *Romania* was no longer Communist, and a new government was in charge.

This section is an effective case study pointing out how human geographers can use historical records and the methodologies and sources of historical geography to investigate the diachronic concept of change in places and spaces. In this section, we highlighted the example of *Bucharest*, the capital city of *Romania*, which represents a relatively recent case study that documents the process of (re)naming streets over the last century. Odonyms, as symbolic elements belonging to the sphere of urbanonymy and to the urban landscape, are useful in analysing the values and ideologies of political regimes, a topic we will explore more in depth in Chapters 8 and 9. Thus, to understand some of the macro-political shifts happening over time in the world, human geographers have increasingly turned to studying micro-urbanonyms, prevalently odonyms, and other names of the urban landscape, which have been modified as a result of new political regimes coming to power. The changes to these names can then be studied using relatively recent historical sources, like newspapers, newsletters, municipal records, maps, and street guides, which were compiled by people living in the locality during the time period in question. Ultimately, such an approach would benefit from the integration of 'the historical geography of space and time within the frame of all our understandings of how human societies are constructed and change' (Harvey, 1990, p. 428). In this case study, the enmeshment of the historical geography of the street names in *Bucharest* over the last century contributes to our understanding of how political regimes seek to display their power via reshaping the urban landscape and, ultimately, of the sociopolitical changes in society that can be mapped within the context of urbanonymy. This also represents a shift from traditional approaches of historical geography, which were labelled as 'too closely tied to the apron strings of archival data sources and field observation, producing meticulous reconstructions of past patterns but without either investigating the processes behind the patterns or evaluating the data themselves in their cultural and political context' (Dennis, 1991, p. 266). Such a focus is, indeed, also indicative of current approaches in historical geography, which from the 1990s has undergone a shift 'from the study of residential patterns, interpreted according to the precepts of human ecology, towards more comprehensive analyses of urban structure, including industrial and commercial districts, and integrating social, economic, political, and architectural perspectives' (Dennis, 1991, p. 278).

## 7.4     Historical Toponomastics and Historical Geography in *Singapore* Toponymy

In the last section, we saw how a historical-toponomastic study can be developed by using sources and methods from historical geography, with the aim of reconstructing and determining changes to the physical and human landscapes and the related toponymy and, in so doing, understanding more about the culture of the humans occupying a territory. The same methods and approaches can be applied to a younger nation such as *Singapore*. Indeed, *Singapore* has a well-documented recent history since the arrival of the British in the early 1800s. However, researchers can also analyse a number of complementary sources from earlier periods to go into more depth in the diachronic investigations of *Singapore*, also known as the *Lion City*. These include ancient narrative poems, historical or pseudo-historical chronicles, travel diaries, logs, and letters. To provide an example, Hsü (1972) asserted that *P'u-lo chung* is 'the oldest name for Singapore' (p. 9). He found two references to this toponym in the travel tales written by Chu Ying (宣化從事朱應) and Kāng Tài (中郎康泰) in the third century (Cavallaro, Perono Cacciafoco, & Tan, 2019). Travel accounts have been utilised by several historians, such as the renowned Southeast Asian expert John Miksic, who made extensive use of archaeological data and examined travel accounts in his analysis of the region's history (Miksic, 2007; 2013).

A seminal article by Yeoh (1996) on street names in colonial *Singapore* is an application of historical geography to the Singaporean context. Through an investigation of colonial maps, like the Raffles Town Plan, also known as the Jackson Plan (Jackson, 1828), along with the Municipal Committee's documents and earlier records of Indigenous street names, such as an article by Firmstone (1905), Yeoh was able to delineate important remarks on the principle of parallel place names between the British and the locals in the island. Her study of Firmstone's document also enabled her to come up with a description of the naming strategies behind Chinese odonyms in *Singapore*. These included streets named after symbols and landmarks, economic and agricultural activities, directions, and commemorative elements. In recent years, a number of studies have also applied these principles to investigate the changes in *Singapore*'s odonyms (and other toponyms) over time, consulting, among others, precolonial and colonial maps and other secondary sources on Singaporean toponyms (see Cavallaro et al., 2019; Perono Cacciafoco & Shia, 2020; Yom & Cavallaro, 2020). In the sections below, we will highlight the changes in several of *Singapore*'s odonyms.

### 7.4.1   Bras Basah Road

In their investigation of the street name *Bras Basah Road*, Cavallaro et al. (2019) noted that the odonym first appeared on a map during George Coleman's survey in the form of *Bras Bassa Road* (Coleman & Tassin, 1836). This was the first attested topographical survey of *Singapore*, and was printed in 1836. In the 1828 Jackson Plan (Jackson, 1828) and prior to being named *Bras Basah Road*, the road was made up of two streets joined together, *Church Street* and *Selegy Street*. *Church Street* was named after the London Missionary Society Chapel, which was located in the street from 1819 to 1847 (Savage & Yeoh, 2003). Meanwhile, *Selegy Street* was named after *Bukit Selegie* (*Mount Sophia*), whose origins will be detailed below. In a newspaper advertisement, it was also referred to as *Raffles College Street*, due to the presence of the Raffles Institution (J. B. N., 1928, June 21).

   *Bras Basah Road* was built by convicts from *British India*. As mentioned above, this was the name given to the road by the British during Coleman's survey. The Chinese people referred to this place by many other denominations. One such name was the Hokkien *Lau Kha Ku Keng Khau* (老脚拘间口) 'mouth of the old jail', a reference to the jail where Indian convicts were held (Firmstone, 1905; Haughton, 1891). This prison was located between *Bras Basah Road* and the nearby *Stamford Road*. Thus, the Hokkien name alluded to the fact that this road was situated in close proximity to where the convicts were imprisoned. The street was also known as *Kau Ka-Ku Hau* (旧架古口) in Cantonese; the Hokkien *Kha Ku* and the Cantonese *Ka-Ku* both mean 'ankle chains'. These names were derived from the shackles on the ankles of the convicts and made reference to a salient trait shared by the people who built the street, that is, that they were convicts. This location gave rise to many other vernacular names that made reference to the Westerners living there. These included *He Lan Xi Li Bai Tang* (和兰西礼拜堂) 'beside the French church', which referred to a nearby French church, the Catholic Cathedral of the Good Shepherd; *Tek Kok Seng Nong* (德国神农) 'the German pharmacy', due to a German-owned pharmacy located nearby; *Hai Ki Ang-Neo Toa-Oh*

*Pi* (海墘红毛大学边) 'beside the seaside English big school' referred to the Raffles Institution (Firmstone, 1905; Haughton, 1891; Savage & Yeoh, 2003). Another name for the *Bras Basah Road* was *Thong Kwong Sen Kei* 'Thong Kwong Sen Street', a reference to the street where a tailor business owned by Hakka people was located. A close reading of the vernacular names of *Bras Basah Road* based on historical records thus indicates a preference by Chinese people to name places according to nearby human landmarks. In the case of *Bras Basah Road*, these features included a jail, places of worship, a pharmacy, a school, and a tailor shop.

### 7.4.2   Mount Sophia

Cavallaro et al. (2019) investigated the naming changes of an oronym, *Mount Sophia*, from the precolonial to the colonial period. The place name *Mount Sophia* has been attested since the 1800s. *Mount Sophia*, according to the authors, is both the name of the hill and of the road leading up to it, which today includes a relatively affluent neighbourhood. The researchers referred to a map from around the 1820s which was drawn by the Dutch and in which the hill is called *Bukit Silige* (Nationaal Archief Holland, 1820s). The first Resident of *Singapore*, William Farquhar, mentioned the hill in a letter to Raffles written on 23 December 1822.

> In reply, I beg to state that the first hill lying to the northward of the Government Hill is that of *Silligie*, which on clearing the country at the commencement of the establishment, was found to be occupied on the western side by a Chinese Planter, who had formed a Gambier Plantation there, the eastern half of the hill is at present occupied by Captain Flint & was a primitive forest which I caused to be partially cleared at the Government expense, to the extent of about 33 acres. (Farquhar, 1822)

The authors also studied a number of other maps from the period, all of which show variations of the specific element. In a survey map of 1822–3, the hill was known as *Bukit Selegie* (National Archives of Singapore, 1822–3). Another map labels the place as *Bukit Silegy* (Unknown, 1825). A crucial shift, as the researchers note, can be observed in Coleman's 1836 map, where the hill is marked as *Mount Sophia* and the neighbouring hillock is labelled *Bukit Seligie* (Coleman & Tassin, 1836). This was also the first instance in which *Bukit Selegie* was called *Mount Sophia*, providing an anglicised version of the hill's name. The origins of *Sophia*, just like *Selegie*,[4] in the denomination

---

[4] The etymology of *Selegie* is disputed. Savage and Yeoh (2003) propose several options for the denomination. The first states that *Selegie* could derive from the name of a famous Bugis pirate chief. The Bugis people who lived around the area were also named after him and known as the *orang selegie*. The second theory equates *Selegie* to a wooden spear, as the term *Selegie* is linked to the Malay word *seligi*, which is the Malay lexeme for 'wooden dart' (Haughton, 1891, p. 60). *Selegie* is also seen as a variant of *seligi*, which refers to the '*nibong* palm used in flooring and

remain disputed (Savage & Yeoh, 2003). People that may have possibly been commemorated by the name 'Sophia' include, among others, Sir Stamford Raffles' second wife, Sophia Raffles, and Mary Sophia Anne, the daughter of Captain William Flint,[5] who resided on the hill. Another plausible explanation was that the hill was named after the daughter of the merchant Charles Robert Prinsep. Prinsep also dedicated two adjacent hills to his daughters, Emily and Catherine, when he bought 217 acres of land in the *Selegie* area in 1831 (Savage & Yeoh, 2003). The case of *Mount Sophia* provides a glimpse into how scholars working in toponymy are able to use old maps from historical archives, written records, and even modern-day secondary sources to trace back the changes of an old place name and account for its etymology. In this context, an excellent example of modern-day resources is the online database developed by the National Archives of Singapore (www.nas.gov.sg). This will be discussed in more detail in the next section.

Cavallaro et al. (2019) relate their findings from the historical geography of *Singapore* toponymy to the nation's sociocultural landscape.

What the results of this work show us is that the influences of all the cultures which have 'sequentially' occupied Singapore from the past to the present can be seen in the history of its place names. Some places underwent numerous changes in their names before settling to what we see today. None of the pre-colonial toponyms were resilient to the socio-political forces at play and remained as originally named. (Cavallaro et al., 2019, pp. 14–15)

### 7.4.3  Sentosa

Another example of a study that utilised historical maps to try to explain the etymology behind place names on precolonial cartographic documents was carried out by Perono Cacciafoco and Shia (2020). One of the toponyms analysed by the authors was *Sentosa*, the denomination of an island located south of *Singapore*. The place was a military facility in the past, and is now a tourist attraction. The researchers reconstructed the development of the place name *Sentosa* by studying a number of maps from (pre-)colonial times and from the 1960s and 1970s. Through a close reading of these cartographic documents, they conducted a comparative assessment of the different versions

fishing stakes', in Malay (Savage & Yeoh, 2003, pp. 594, 758). The last reasoning, according to Cavallaro et al. (2019), may be the most plausible. A *Seligi* is usually made out of bamboo, *nibong* palm, or sago wood (Edwards & Blagden, 1931, p. 28). We know that bamboo was abundant on the hill because the Chinese called the area, in Hokkien, *Tek Kia Kha* 'the foot of the small bamboos' (Firmstone, 1905).

[5] As Captain Flint lived on the hill at the end of 1823, the hill is also referred to as *Flint's Hill* (SCCR, 1831).

of the toponym as it changed from the precolonial, to the colonial, and then to the independence periods.

Sentosa was renamed in 1972, and the toponym means 'peace and tranquil-lity' in Malay. The name actually derives from Sanskrit (Savage & Yeoh, 2003, p. 339), which was then readapted to an Austronesian context. In the *Map of Singapore Island, And Its Dependencies* (National Archive of Singapore (Cartographer), 1852), *Sentosa* was indicated as *Blakan Mati*, Malay for 'island of death behind'. The generic Malay word for 'island' is *pulau* and, indeed, other variants of the insulonym in colonial-era maps were *Pulau Blakang Mati* and *Blaken Mati*. As Perono Cacciafoco and Shia postulate, the 'minor spelling changes [are] most likely due to the incompetence of European cartographers in Malay language spelling' (Perono Cacciafoco & Shia, 2020, p. 101). Gibson-Hill (1954, p. 182) reports that other names that *Sentosa* went by include *Burne Beard Island* (in Wilde's 1780 map) and *Pulau Niry* by Hacke in 1690 and Eberard in 1700. An 1822 map by Farquhar shows that *Sentosa* was referred to as *Pulo Panjang* 'long island'. In another map, however, *Pulo Panjang* was used to label the main island of *Singapore*, a possible error which could have arisen due to a labelling mistake by the European cartographers.

The etymological explanations of the inauspicious name *Pulau Blakang Mati* are manyfold. It is possible that the island was, at a specific point in time, a place frequented by pirates. Morgan (1958) reported that piracy, in the Malayan waters where *Pulau Blakang Mati* was situated, was rampant in the nineteenth century. Pirates patrolled around the vicinity of *Pulau Blakang Mati*, and their victims were either murdered or taken into slavery, giving rise to the idea that death was lurking around and behind the island. Morgan even drew from oral history, where an interviewee commented, 'at this time, no mortal dared pass through the Straits of Singapore' (Morgan, 1958). Another possible explanation is that the islet *Pulau Brani*, which is located between *Sentosa* and the main island of *Singapore*, was a place where warriors were buried, and hence the name 'death behind' may be due to this island's proximity to *Sentosa* and its location in *Singapore*'s archipelago (Savage & Yeoh, 2013, p. 303). Through this example, we can see that even the names of islands, like the odonyms in *Singapore*, can have descriptive and directional values, and their denominations often take reference from nearby localities such as, in this case, other islands. Some locals connected the disturbing name with a malaria outbreak in the 1840s, which killed many of the original Bugis settlers on the island (Ng, 2017). However, as the name existed well before this particular epidemic, this explanation is demonstrably wrong, or at least inaccurate. However, the outbreak resulted in the belief that the island was cursed and, together with the killing of Chinese men in the Sook Ching Operation during the Japanese Occupation (Wynn, 2017, p. 35), gave rise to the notion of death and the negative connotation of this island.

It is worth noting that, in Godinho de Erédia's map from 1604, an islet referred to as *Blacan Mati* can be seen. The isle that represents *Blacan Mati*, according to Erédia's map, is nonetheless far away from the main island of *Singapore*. This significantly differs from where *Sentosa* is actually located geographically today, which is extremely near to *Singapore*. In fact, it is possible to walk from the southern sector of *Singapore* across a bridge to *Sentosa*. Hence, as Gibson-Hill (1954) believed, the *Blacan Mati* islet in Erédia's map was probably referring to two small islands currently known as *Sisters' Islands*, which are more compatible with his cartographic representation. It is therefore unclear whether the *Blacan Mati* on Erédia's map was an actual but misplaced reference to present-day *Sentosa*. While the location does not seem to match the island's actual position, this apparent 'misunderstanding' can be argued to be an earlier reference to the existence of the denomination *Blakang Mati*, proving that the toponym had existed in precolonial times (even if not linked directly to the actual *Sentosa*). The origins of *Blacan Mati* and *Blakang Mati* remain debatable because as, highlighted above, their naming processes can be traced back effectively (or comprehensively) only to the nineteenth and twentieth centuries. In the case of *Blacan Mati*, a possible semantic explanation of *mati* could be connected with the ideal representation of the terminal point of the *Straits of Singapore*. This is because the word *mati* does not just mean 'death', but can also mean 'end', as is evident, for example, in the Malay phrase *Jalan Mati* 'the end of a road'. Hence, *mati* in Erédia's map was probably referring to the 'end' of the *Straits of Singapore*. Although this is a possible explanation, this reasoning may not be, in any case, totally accurate.

In the context of toponymic renaming, the British periodically tried to rename the island and adopt a more English-sounding name. In 1827, Captain Edward Lake of the Madras Engineers, who was tasked to fortify *Singapore*, suggested that *Pulau Blakang Mati* be renamed as the *Island of St George* (Gibson-Hill, 1954). However, the renaming proposal was scrapped, as the authorities believed that the island was unsuitable for inhabitation. The toponym *Blakang Mati* survived for many years, up till the early 1970s. The diachronic continuity of this toponym, as postulated by Perono Cacciafoco and Shia, 'might be due to the consistent usage across the different local ethnicities, as well as the lack of other toponymic variations for the island' (Perono Cacciafoco & Shia, 2020, p. 102). In the late 1960s, the government introduced a naming competition in an effort to develop the island into a tourist destination. This was an exercise of toponymic rebranding, to rid the isle of its 'adverse' history and negative connotations, and to position it (also through its new name) into one that had 'a bearing on Singapore's culture and image as a tourist attraction' (*The Straits Times,* 1969). This ultimately gave rise to the name *Sentosa* (*The Straits Times,* 1970b).

In these examples, the use of historical maps and other written sources from precolonial and colonial *Singapore* has provided us with a window through which we are able to study the etymological origins and diachronic changes to toponyms from the *Lion City*.

## 7.5    Historical Geographic Information Systems

Gregory and Ell (2007, p. 1) pointed out that while geographic information systems (GIS) have been used in other disciplines, it was only very recently that they began to be adopted by historical geographers. Historical geographic information systems (HGIS) is thus a very new field of study. GIS is a framework which extracts and records spatial and geographic data, which can then be analysed and contextually mapped (see Chapter 10). GIS tools are computational applications which enable a generic user to perform active surveys, analyse, edit, and store spatial/non-spatial and geographic/non-geographic data. The analysis involves spatial information and the related output, and the results of the searches and analyses are visually shared in the format of digital maps. A HGIS, then, is a GIS that extracts, displays, records, and stores data of historical spaces and geographies from the past. This allows the user to keep a diachronic comparison of the changes that happened, over time, in those places and spaces. It is a new tool aimed at the historical analysis of environments and geographic areas and, as a discipline, is considered as a subfield of historical geography and GIS.

Bodenhamer is among the many who have pointed out the usefulness of this new field for many disciplines.

This capability has attracted considerable interest from historians, archaeologists, linguists, students of material culture, and others who are interested in place, dense coil of memory, artifact, and experience that exists in a particular space, as well as in the coincidence and movements of people, goods, and ideas that have occurred across time in spaces large and small. (Bodenhamer, 2013, p. 3)

The value of such systems in the study of toponyms is quite evident, as the availability of large amounts of searchable data provided from different disciplines and methodologies allows for very detailed and in-depth quantitative and qualitative studies (Fuchs, 2015).

In the last decade or so, many projects in the field of HGIS have been carried out. A fine example is the Digitally Encoded Census Information and Mapping Archive (DECIMA), an adaptable and multipurpose platform that utilises a wide variety of data supplied by historians from different subfields. This HGIS project focusses on the city of *Florence, Italy*, and DECIMA was developed to be an instrument to enable collaboration among scholars and to 'encourage historians working from various methodologies and in various subfields to begin thinking and practicing spatial history' (Rose, 2016, p. 15).

Another example of HGIS is the Archives Hub (https://archiveshub .jisc.ac.uk), which manages the physical and digital collections of over 350 institution in the *UK*. One such collection is the Great Britain Historical GIS Project (https://archiveshub.jisc.ac.uk/search/locations/b029e58b-84f2-31c0-a9dc-46760f2e3e71). This database holds data from between 1801 and 2000, obtained from a variety of sources including statistics from general elections, census reports, historical maps, and travel writings from the *UK*. Its main collections are Old Maps Online and A Vision of Britain Through Time.

Several studies using HGIS and GIS to study place names and the ethnic and cultural aspects of the populations occupying their territories have been conducted in *China* (see, for instance, Qian, Kang, & Weng, 2016; Wang et al., 2006; Wang et al., 2012; Zhao et al., 2020; Zhu et al., 2018), showing how scientific and objective approaches, when combined with the analysis of historical data and sources, can aid the study of historical geography and our understanding of toponymy in general.

The China Historical Geographic Information System (CHGIS) is a recent example of HGIS that blends several scientific disciplines with physical geography and historical geography.[6] The aim of this project was to create a common GIS platform for Chinese history from 222 BCE to 1911 CE (i.e., the period from the first symbolically unified *Chinese Empire* to the end of the *Qing* Dynasty). In this sense, the CHGIS is somewhat like an electronic and historical atlas of *China* that allows users to track all known boundary and settlement changes over time. The CHGIS functions, indeed, as a 'historical gazetteer' (Bol & Ge, 2005, p. 151). Researchers can use its data to find information about any place name that was handed down through historical records, which Bol and Ge attribute to 'the government's long tradition of conducting land surveys and household registration, holding censuses, and compiling national administrative geographies' (2005, p. 150). Wang et al. (2014) described their efforts to develop a database of toponyms in *Yunnan*, southwest *China*, using an established toponymic dictionary, and to identify their ethnic roots. The authors classified place names in *Yunnan* according to three administrative subdivisions commonly adopted in *China*: prefecture, county, and township (in descending order of importance). They also classified the toponyms as either Han, Zang-Mian,[7] or Zhuang-Dong,[8] based on their linguistic origins. Using spatial analysis and statistical methods, the researchers

---

[6] It is worth noting that an early advocate of the use of historical quantitative spatial analysis was the geographer William Norton, who defined historical geography as the historical evolution of 'spatial form' (Norton, 1984). Norton's tools of investigation included computer simulation models and counterfactual analysis.

[7] In this study, Zang-Mian toponyms include place names from the Yi, Naxi, Bai, Lisu, Nu, Hani, Lahu, Jinuo, Zang, and Jingpuo ethnic groups.

[8] In this study, Zhuang-Dong toponyms include place names from the Zhuang, Dai, and Buyi ethnic groups.

also sought to identify possible clusters of ethnic toponyms and correlated these ethnic place names to the physical landscape features of their territories, like elevation (height above sea level), slope (measurement in degrees of the change of elevation), and aspect (denoting the compass direction faced by the slope of a mountain). Lending a historical perspective to their study, the authors examined the diachronic evolution of toponyms in *Yunnan*, with a particular attention to the 'Sinification of Chinese toponyms', an issue that we will discuss in Chapter 8.

Chloupek (2018) provided us with a fascinating read in which he uses HGIS to analyse toponyms as an element of *Nebraska*'s cultural landscape. He collected information on the origins of nearly all of *Nebraska*'s toponyms (including those which have ceased to exist), from toponymic dictionaries compiled by scholars Lilian Fitzpatrick and Elton Perkey. Chloupek also created a taxonomy to classify these toponyms, so that most of them can be coded into one specific category, by using the ArcGIS 10.1 software. This allows for different categories to be 'visualised discretely' (Chloupek, 2018, p. 27). Chloupek's study utilised geographical and cartographic modes of analysis to identify the political actors and sociopolitical naming processes behind many Nebraskan toponyms in the last decades of the nineteenth century. Additionally, he also coded the founding dates of these toponyms to identify time-specific patterns in these chronological periods. He found the following.

Because a limited number of actors brought about the majority of Nebraska place names, the variation of place name origins is largely limited and repetitive, indicative of influential naming entities like the railroads, the United States Postal Service, and groups of settlers from the eastern United States or Europe. (Chloupek, 2018, p. 27)

The links between Chloupek's findings and critical toponymies (see Chapter 8) are also evident, particularly the assertion of power onto the landscape via the naming process by a few prominent actors.

The use of HGIS approaches in themselves enables a new epistemological approach to, and substantially helps the study of, place names.

## 7.6    Summary

This chapter looked at how toponymists and linguists utilise diachronic evidence from the landscape and hydro-geo-morphology of territories, available written records, and historical maps in their bid to reconstruct the etymology of the names of places. This is where the fields of historical toponomastics and historical geography intersect with great success. This was shown in the example of *Bistagno*, for which several scholars, who did not apply proper historical-toponomastic and historical-geographical methods, came up with several interpretations with different degrees of success. The study of relatively recent historical documents (like newspapers, newsletters, and city hall records) and spatial representations (in maps and street guides) of *Bucharest* and *Singapore* over the years has allowed the analysis of the overtly political, social, and ideological considerations behind street renaming and, consequently, of how political shifts can impact an urban landscape. Moreover, we have also seen how various disciplines, like landscape sciences, computer engineering, computing, statistics, (historical) geography, toponymy, and linguistics, can converge in the implementation of HGIS to map toponyms and to describe their characteristics (be they physical, topographic, linguistic, demographic, or even depicting possible migration patterns) – a testament to the truly interdisciplinary nature of the study of toponymy.

In the following chapter, we will explore some of the above-mentioned thematic areas, such as street renaming and its politics, in greater detail, while looking at toponymy from a synchronic perspective.

# 8    Synchronic Toponymy

## 8.1    Contemporary Naming Processes

We have, thus far, covered the methods and approaches to diachronic toponymy and historical toponomastics. We have also seen that languages change over time, but ancient toponyms are often linguistic fossils whose roots remain generally stable in the midst of changing population and settlement dynamics. Toponyms also display the effects of these historical changes in their linguistic features. We have discussed how place names are closely tied to the landscape, and how historical documents such as written records and maps (more on maps in Chapter 10) may allow us to explain the origins and original meanings of place names and account for the sociopolitical shifts that mark toponyms in the urban landscape. In the example of *Bucharest* in Chapter 7, we explored how place names were used as political tools to consolidate the power of the government of the day and how successive governments, through the toponymic renaming process, promoted their narrative of the country's history and who/what should be celebrated. The focus of this chapter will be on the more contemporary naming concerns and the sociopolitical factors that affect the naming processes.

As argued in Chapter 1, names are a way of referring to things, people, and places. Place names, unlike most proper nouns, are not simply referring expressions of a physical location. Instead, they are '"brimful" of connotative meaning' and have social and cultural significance (Basso, 1990, p. 143; Helleland, 2012, p. 99). More than a means of attaching meaning to one's surroundings, place names also 'act as sources of information, facilitate communication, help us to know and serve as repositories of values' (Cohen & Kliot, 1992, p. 655). Basso (1990) even goes as far as suggesting that they are 'among the most highly charged and richly evocative' of linguistic symbols, as they elicit an 'enormous range of mental and emotional associations' (p. 144), including that related to history and social activities. Saparov (2003) stated that when defining any ethnic community, whether a tribe or nation, it is necessary to 'mention the common living space of that ethnic group. Within that territory a national toponymy has been formed – a system of geographic names in the native language of the indigenous population' (p. 179). Eriksen (2012, p. 72) stated that when new place names are needed, for example, in the ever-increasing urban sprawls, '[...] careful deliberation is often needed to capture the *genius loci* in ways presumed to be acceptable for the public in the years to come'.

Everett-Heath (2000) tells us that places can acquire names in many different ways. He gives the example of *Pakistan*, which was named from the initials of *Punjab*, *Afghanistan*, and *Kashmir*, and with the addition of the Persian word *stan* 'land' (p. ix). Places may be named after their discoverer, for example, *Cook Islands*, named after Captain James Cook, or *Bolivia*, named after the statesman and politician Simón Bolívar. Commemorative naming, or the naming of a place to honour someone, is very common. There are many examples of this, such as *Melbourne*, named after British Prime Minister Lord Melbourne, or the many *Washington*s in the *USA*, named after the first US President George Washington. Countries can be named after people (cf. *Bolivia* above) or their inhabitants. An example of this is *France*, named after the Franks (an Indo-European Germanic people), who, incidentally, were not the original inhabitants of present-day *France*. Previously, the country was called *Gaul*, and was inhabited by the Gauls, an Indo-European Celtic people. Finally, saints feature as the names of many towns and cities, such as *San Francisco* or *St Petersburg*.

More akin to the naming practices in very ancient times, as illustrated in this volume so far, are the names given to places due to an important natural resource. The town of *Apatity*, in *Murmansk Oblast, Russia*, was named after *apatite*, a raw mineral essential for producing fertilisers (Took, 2004). An example of lesser-known place names named after such resources is the Italian town of *Zafferana Etnea* (*Catania, Sicily*), which was named after the abundant herb saffron (or *zafferano* in Italian) found in the region, and the fact that it is located on the slope of the volcano *Etna* (Boccardo, 1875–1888). Natural features, such as nearby rivers or natural formations, have also inspired the naming of places. This has spawned a significant number of names containing the terms 'hill' (e.g., *Broken Hill* and *Adelaide Hills*, in *Australia*), 'valley' (e.g., *Barossa Valley* and *Clare Valley*, in south *Australia*), or 'river' (e.g., *Blackburn*, from Old English *burna*, meaning 'stream') (Gelling & Cole, 2000; Jones, 2015). As pointed out in Chapter 1, many of these namings have given rise to humorous tautologies. The *River Avon*, in the *UK*, is an example of this. The name *Avon* derives from the Welsh word *afon*, which means 'river'. The hydronym *River Avon* etymologically means 'River River'. *Bergeberget*, the name of a hill in *Norway*, can be translated as 'Hill Hill'. *Fjällfjällen*, in *Sweden*, is translated as 'Mountain Mountains'. For the *Gezira Island*, meanwhile, located along the course of the *Nile River*, in *Cairo, Egypt*, *gezira* الجزيرة in Arabic means 'island'. Therefore, the name is made up of the Arabic word for 'island' and the English word 'island', so we end up with 'Island Island'.

Place names can also be purely descriptive. For example, the name *Nippon/ Nihon* (*Japan*) means the 'land of the rising sun'. Modern denominations might also have very transparent meanings. This can be seen in the many places around the world called 'New Town'. For example, *Nové Město* (translated as 'New Town') is a district of *Prague, Czechia*. *Novgorod, Russia* is the Russian word for 'New Town'. This naming practice can also be seen in older examples. The name of the Italian city of *Napoli* (*Naples*) derives from Ancient Greek *Neapolis* (Νεάπολις), which means 'New City'.

Earlier in this volume, we have explained how places were named in very ancient times. However, what we see in this brief introduction is that, to research more contemporary naming issues, we need different approaches from the historical-toponymic tools and methods discussed so far. In the rest of this chapter, we will introduce and detail these approaches.

## 8.2    What Is Synchronic Toponymy?

Synchronic toponymy deals with place names in a particular moment in time in a specific area. The synchronic toponymist collects these toponyms, categorises them, and searches for common naming patterns. This approach to toponymy is an extensive/quantitative one (Tent, 2015a), in which the scholar looks at datasets of place names, gazetteers, maps, atlases, and the like to identify patterns in both the naming of places of a particular region, as well as the distribution of certain types of toponyms, features, or settlement patterns (Tent, 2015a, p. 72), and 'the condition of their use and their structure and lexical status as well as the psychological, sociological, and political implications of their use and function in discourse' (Löfström & Schnabel-Le Corre, 2015, p. 11). This is in contrast to the intensive/qualitative method of reconstructing the origins of individual place names that we have covered thus far.

Given the focus on identifying sociopolitical patterns, when studying toponymic *corpora* and evaluating the ramifications of the use of related place names, as detailed by Schnabel-Le Corre and Löfström, it is no surprise, then, that synchronic toponymy deals with the function of place names in society and the perception of these names by the members of a society (Karpenko, 1964, cited in Belen'kaya, 1975, p. 315). Thus, the discipline lends an undoubtedly 'human' touch to the study of place names. As Belen'kaya notes, a synchronic approach to toponyms:

[...] not only points up the relationship between place names in the overall system of toponymics, but suggests the linkage between place names and objective reality, i.e., the way in which the population perceives the name and understands its content, regardless of whether this understanding corresponds to the original meaning of the word. (Belen'kaya, 1975, p. 320)

Synchronic toponymy relies on methods and data from a number of associated fields, for example, human geography, political sciences, and cultural studies. One other field that is deeply intertwined with synchronic toponymy is sociolinguistics. Sociolinguistics is the study of language and the social factors that influence how we speak and interact with others. The discipline studies how language is used to convey social meaning. It is, by nature, multidisciplinary, with connections to dialect geography, anthropology, sociology, philosophy, and pragmatics.

We saw with the example of *Bucharest*, in Chapter 7, how sociopolitical factors were key to (re)conceptualising or changing the names of places that inhabitants encounter daily. These social and political forces are also the focus of sociolinguistic studies. In relation to toponyms, sociolinguists study the language policies governing the naming processes and the shifts in the languages that are spoken in a society. The intersections between language, people, societies, and power structures are often seen in place names and the place naming processes, as is inherent in sociolinguistics. Because of this, we argue that contemporary toponymy is inherently sociolinguistic in nature. Indeed, socio-onomastics, as a discipline focussing on the analysis of names and naming practices, has been gathering more and more attention over time. Ainiala and Östman (2017) note the following in the introduction to their edited book *Socio-Onomastics: The Pragmatics of Names*.

Although socio-onomastics acknowledges the historical dimension of names and naming, the role of names in the construction of (social) identities is in focus in recent developments in the field. Socio-onomastics stresses the importance of looking at the use of names in every-day interaction: variation in name usage, why some names are avoided, why some names are coupled with particular pejorative attitudes, and how name users themselves perceive the very names they use. (p. 3)

The sociolinguistic study of synchronic toponymy also involves a historical component, taking into account past language policies and comparing them with policies of the present, along with the changes in the languages spoken in an area by studying the language shifts over time. It is normal, therefore, that both 'diachronic' and 'synchronic' aspects may converge when studying the local toponymy. Moreover, insights from human geography, political sciences, and cultural studies are also relevant when the synchronic toponymist studies local perceptions of place names and the political matters that affect naming processes.

It is important to note that the toponyms themselves are not synchronic, as they often have ancient or even prehistoric origins, which may or may not be observable in the current time period. Toponyms are, generally and prevalently, creations of the past, and often preserve certain features from past environments, historical events, or anthroponyms belonging to bygone individuals. We call a place name 'synchronic' because that toponym exists now and can be understood only in relation to human society and its history (Poenaru-Girigan, 2013). However, any study looking into the actual names will need to include diachronic approaches to find the etymology, that is, the historical origins and meanings and the related naming processes of the toponyms themselves.

## 8.3    Methodologies in Synchronic Toponymy

Synchronic toponymy focusses on the function of toponyms in society (an area that will also be explored in Chapter 9) and on the perception of names by various social groups. Unlike the historical approaches that we have examined in this book, which study the etymology of a place name, synchronic toponymy examines the actual semantics and semantic structure of a toponym, people's perception of it, and the sociopolitical values in a particular time period associated with the place naming process, be it the present context or in an era that is not too far back in time.

Studies in synchronic toponymy have been carried out on different chronological timeframes, from the colonial period (Bigon, 2008; Wanjiru-Mwita & Giraut, 2020; Yeoh, 1992; Yom & Cavallaro, 2020) to postcolonial times (Casagranda, 2013; Nyambi, Mangena, & Pfukwa, 2016; Wanjiru & Matsubara, 2017; Yeoh, 1996), and even to the present-day context (Mamvura, 2020; Perono Cacciafoco & Tuang, 2018; Wideman & Masuda, 2018; see also Chapter 7). The common theme among them is that the method is not based on etymological and/or historical-linguistic reconstructions. Instead of looking at the morphology of a place name, the toponymist zooms out and looks at the context of the denomination, considering the events that have resulted in the conception (or change) of the place name itself. Synchronic toponymy can therefore be characterised, in Tent's words, as 'extensive toponymy' (Tent, 2015a, p. 70), where place names 'function as independent variables which can be tested against dependent variables such as region, toponym type, or feature type' (Tent, 2015a, p. 71).

The starting point of synchronic toponymy research involves the collection of a dataset, or *corpus*, of toponyms, from (usually) written and drawn documents like maps, atlases, surveyor journals, government records, and the like. The scholar may then interpret the semantics and semantic structure of the place names according to the social and political realities of the time period under examination, or chart the place naming practices of a specific locality under a specific chronological frame. For example, Bigon (2008) examines the French colonial policy on street names in *Dakar, Senegal* (which was part of the colonised *French West Africa*). She drew from the first master plan of the city (1862), compiled by Jean-Marie Émile Pinet-Laprade, then head of the local Corps of Engineers, and a figure who was instrumental in imposing French colonisation in *Dakar*, and a toponymic list by Claude Faure, published in 1863, which listed all the street names suggested by Pinet-Laprade for the city. These sources showed how the French colonisers created an informal residential segregation between the expatriates and the locals. The places where expatriates resided in *Dakar*, like other French colonies in *West Africa*, were known as *Plateaux*.[1] The name itself was representative of French elitism and ideals of French colonisation in *West Africa*, where Indigenous lifestyles, knowledge, and place names were regarded as inferior, and the European equivalents were extolled. In French colonial urban terminology, a *Plateau* was regarded as a *ville européenne* 'European city', or *ville blanche* 'white city/town'. The African living part of town was documented as *ville africaine* 'African city', *village indigène* 'Indigenous village', or *quartier indigène* 'Indigenous quarter' – distinctions that were clearly stated in *Dakar*'s colonial maps, and they show how the Indigenous and African living quarters were embedded in language. In other French colonies in *North Africa*, the *Plateau* was sometimes called *zone urbaine* 'urban zone', while the African living quarters were called *zone semi-urbaine* 'semi-urban zone'. The European quarters were *beaux quartiers* 'beautiful suburbs', in contrast with the Africans' *bidonvilles* 'slums' (the French *bidon* means 'garbage can' and describes dirty houses occupied by poor people). In *Dakar*, the Indigenous quarter northwest of the older sections of *Dakar-ville* was first derogatorily referred to as *le village* 'the village', *le village ségrégation* 'the segregated village', and *le nouveau village indigène* 'the new Indigenous village'. This was before the French borrowed the name *Médina* (from Arabic *Al-Madinah* اَلْمَدِينَة 'The city'), as a word (*medina*) meaning 'the non-European part of a Northern African city', from their North African colonies in 1914, due in part to the large number of Muslims inhabiting them. The semantics of all of these names reveals a binary relationship between a modern, cosmopolitan, beautiful, and liveable expatriate living quarter as opposed to a dull, old, inward-looking, shabby, and backward Indigenous shanty town. Bigon noted the following.

What was common to all these terms was the notion that the African population, including its norms and forms of residence, was not a substantial part of the colonial urban landscape. By regarding the indigenous residential areas, or the 'actual' city, as an only partly urbanised, or even a rural sphere in relation to the white area, implied a conceptual exclusion of the first from the latter. It also promoted the narrative of the colonisers and their values as being the ultimate and absolute ones. (Bigon, 2008, p. 491)

---

[1] The *Plateau* did not necessarily need to be located on high ground. Sometimes, all that was needed was the presence of European buildings (or features with European designs) and the stationing of French soldiers or servicemen before the place was known as such.

Unsurprisingly, few precolonial names were preserved during French colonisation. When the French introduced the concept of 'streets' into *Dakar*, locals would refer to these places by a landmark rather than by the colonial name, as 'streets' were a colonial modification of the Indigenous landscape. In some ways, this mirrors colonial settlements elsewhere, particularly the situation of a parallel set of street names in colonial *Singapore* (cf. Chapter 7). More importantly, this shows that locals in colonised societies have some agency (i.e., the involvement, action, or intervention by the local inhabitants) in circumventing the official, colonial toponyms. This was expressed by using the local language(s) and Indigenous knowledge, rather than the colonial and official place manes, to describe their organisation of the cultural space and environment they lived in, one that was independent from the colonisers' (see the example of *Singapore* in the next section).

A study that investigates the place naming patterns and practices of colonial toponyms can be found in Tent and Slayter (2009). The authors examined the different place naming practices of the Dutch, English, and French explorers as they gave names to places along the Australian coastline before European settlement on the continent in 1788. The authors grouped the naming practices according to the first seven toponymic types outlined in Table 1.4 in Chapter 1. What they found was that the motivations for naming were quite different across the groups. The results are displayed in Table 8.1.

The results show that all three groups favoured the 'eponymous' category. Within this category, though, the French preferred it the most and the English

Table 8.1 *Results of a study on the naming practices in* Australia *by the Dutch, English, and French, 1603–1803 (Tent and Slayter, 2009, p. 27)*

|  | Number of toponyms (%) | | |
| --- | --- | --- | --- |
| Toponymic types (cf. Table 1.4) | Dutch | English | French |
| Descriptive (indicating an inherent characteristic of the feature) | 14.4 | 20.2 | 9.3 |
| Associative (indicating something that is associated with the feature or its physical location) | 12.2 | 14.9 | 6.3 |
| Occurrent (indicating an event, incident, occasion, date, or action associated with the feature) | 3.6 | 11.3 | 1.9 |
| Evaluative (reflecting a strong emotion evoked when the namer named the place, or a strong connotation associated with the feature) | 5.0 | 3.6 | 1.2 |
| Shift (use of a toponym from another location or feature) | 4.3 | 6.0 | 0.6 |
| Indigenous (importing an Indigenous toponym or word) | 0.7 | 0.4 | 0 |
| Eponymous (commemorating a person or other named entity) | 59.7 | 43.5 | 80.6 |

used it the least, with the English having a greater preference for 'descriptive' toponyms than the others.

In the postcolonial context, Perono Cacciafoco and Tuang (2018) studied the place naming patterns of street names in modern *Singapore*. The authors collected 150 street names from the *Mighty Minds Street Directory* (which in itself can be considered a toponymic *corpus* of place names in *Singapore*). The meanings of these toponyms in Singaporean society were verified through a number of sources, such as maps from the National Archives of Singapore, newspapers and online documents published by the National Heritage Board and the National Library of Singapore, and books on Singaporean toponyms. These sources, when collectively used, shed light not only on the possible meanings of the place names, but also reflect how perceptions of these odonyms are embedded into both written and drawn sources. The authors then deduced possible trends in naming practices within each language. Their findings are detailed later in this chapter.

Nash and Low (2015) proposed 'toponymic ethnography' as a handy methodology in studying the relationship of people with their environment, and indeed ethnographic tools, such as interviews and group discussions, have been used in toponymic studies over the years (Crețan & Matthews, 2016; Light & Young, 2014). An ethnographic and fieldwork approach locates the toponym 'within the series of contemporary and historical social relationships and activities that enliven it as a place' (Nash & Low, 2015, p. 401). Nash (2015b, p. 234) advises studying toponyms in terms of their 'active and actual use' and to explore 'how' toponyms are utilised 'as cultural deictics, as toponymic knowledge connected to land and mores, and as mappable linguistic history' (Nash, 2015b, p. 235). As Nash concluded through his toponymic ethnographic fieldwork in *Norfolk Island*, the local islanders see themselves as different from non-islanders because of the toponymic identity[2] they have developed over generations and also because of their insider knowledge of places and their names on the island. As Nash and Low (2015, p. 403) observed of the inhabitants of *Norfolk Island*, 'these informants as possessing great (unconscious) wisdom connected intrinsically to *Norfolk*'s topographical and identity-based social landscape'. This cultural identity and self-perception of differences 'is expressed in how they judge their onomastic relationships to the place they inhabit' (Nash, 2015a, p. 155). Accordingly, place names can also be markers of spatial identity and can be used to assert differences. Ultimately, interdisciplinary approaches can be utilised in synchronic toponymy. This

---

[2] Toponymic identity refers to the bonds that people establish with their surroundings. This is related to the concept of 'toponymic attachment', which Kostanski (2009) developed based on the principle of 'place attachment'. 'Toponymic attachment' is defined as the relationship that people develop with the toponyms they come into contact with in their everyday lives (Kostanski, 2016).

facilitates the study of 'phenomena between, within, and across toponymic contexts, but also consider what these contexts actually mean' (Nash, 2015b, p. 234).

The fields of political toponymy (Rose-Redwood, 2011) and critical topo-nymies (i.e., how political and, increasingly over time, economic contexts shape place naming practices and patterns) can be studied using synchronic toponymy methodologies, such as ethnographic interviews, which can be carried out with locals to investigate their responses towards phenomena like street (re)naming. This advances the inquiry of 'bottom-up responses to top-down changes' (Creţan & Matthews, 2016, p. 93). In other words, these methods shift the emphasis from the macro-context (political factors and governmental considerations that motivate street renaming) to the micro-context (local responses) and accord agency to the locals. This is something that Light and Young (2014) say critical toponymy needs to do more, especially by investigating how changes in place names are received by locals.

In the next section, we will first look at odonymy in a young country, *Singapore*, and through this case study we will explore the naming practices and sociopolitical circumstances that have shaped place naming processes in the *Lion City*. This case study also allows us to explore some of the themes presented in Chapter 1, such as the toponymic classification systems.

## 8.4     Odonymy in a Young Country: The Case of *Singapore*

*Singapore* (also known as the *Lion City*) is a country (city-state) located in *Southeast Asia*, positioned between *Malaysia* to the north and *Indonesia* to the south (see Figure 8.1). The size of the island is, currently, 710.3 km$^2$.

*Singapore* is an ethnically, culturally, and linguistically diverse nation, and its resident population of 4.04 million inhabitants is made up of 74.3 per cent Chinese, 13.5 per cent Malays, and 9.0 per cent Indians. The remaining 3.2 per cent of the resident population is classified as Others, people who are usually of Eurasian or European (Department of Statistics, 2020) extraction. The *Lion City* is also home to over 1.5 million transitory workers. *Singapore*'s ethnic and linguistic diversity is reflected in its place names and naming practices. In this section, we detail some of the toponymic processes prevalent in Singaporean toponyms since the 1800s. In particular, we detail the policies from three time periods, colonial *Singapore* (1819 to 1950s), the aftermath of *Singapore*'s independence (right after 1965), and modern-day *Singapore*.

### 8.4.1     *Colonial* Singapore

Most people regard 1819 as the year that modern-day *Singapore* was founded. This was the year in which Sir Stamford Raffles first landed on the island.

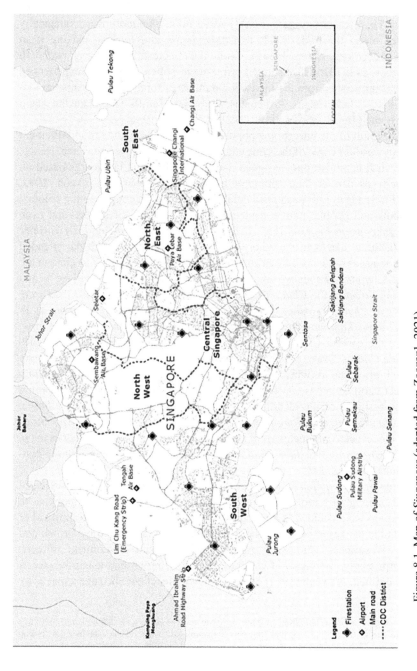

Figure 8.1 Map of *Singapore* (adapted from Zoozaz1, 2021)

*Singapore* was from then established as a trading post in the region, to serve as a bulwark against Dutch influence (the Dutch colonised the nearby *Dutch East Indies*, i.e., present-day *Indonesia*). Furthermore, *Singapore* was strategically located along the trade routes to *China*, *India*, and *Europe*, making it an attractive colony to the British. From the nineteenth and early twentieth centuries, as the British instituted a free-trade policy, *Singapore* experienced cultural influences from the increasing number of foreign immigrants, including Chinese, Indonesians, Armenians, Arabs, and Tamils, who made the island their home (Tan, 1986; Turnbull, 1989, p. 14; Yan, 1986, pp. 1–9).

As a result of the burgeoning population in *Singapore*, the initial settlement pattern was for people of the same ethnic group to live in the same area. Hence, the British administrators assigned names to streets and landmarks based on ethnicity as part of their 'principle of residential separation' (Yeoh, 1992, p. 316). Roads in European residential areas received names denoting colonial symbols and people, names depicting British imagery of streets, and even namesakes from *England* (e.g., *Crawford Street*, *Orchard Road*, *Devonshire Road*). Street names in the other divisions were identified with the intended inhabitants, as evidenced by *Arab Street*, *Bussorah Street* and *Haji Lane* in the *Arab Kampung* (*kampung/kampong* is the Malay word for 'village'), and *Chuliah Street* in the *Chuliah Kampung* (Indians across *Southeast Asia* were known as *Chuliahs*, named after the *Chola Kingdom* in *Tamil Nadu, India*). In the Chinese *Kampung*, street names made references to provinces in *China*, where the earliest Chinese settlers in *Singapore* had come from. Examples include *Canton Street*, *Macao Street*, and *Nankin Street* (these odonyms were named after the provinces of *Guangdong/Canton*, *Macau*, and *Nanjing*, respectively). Likewise, in the various *kampungs*, the colonial street naming policy assigned ethnic identities to specific places. Names like *Amoy Street*, *Tew Chew Street*, and *Hong Kong Street* could be found in *Chinatown*, coined after the respective hometowns of the early Chinese settlers. Street names in the *Bugis*[3] *Kampung*, like *Java Road* and *Palembang Road*, emphasised the connections with *Indonesia*, where the Bugis originated from (Yeoh, 1992).

In colonial *Singapore*, we begin to see elements of how the British used street naming as a tool to assert their power over the colony. Toponyms in *Singapore* were decided at municipal meetings and subject to the approval of the municipal commissioner. These meetings were dominated by British and other Westerners, who were usually municipal and government officers. Unsurprisingly, the views of common people living on and using the streets were omitted. As Yeoh (1992) noted, 'street nomenclature became a means by

---

[3] The Bugis originally came from *Celebes* (now known as *Sulawesi*), an Indonesian island. They were one of the first groups that sailed to *Singapore* when the British established a trading settlement. The Singaporean odonym *Bugis Street* is named after this ethnic group.

which the authorities were able to project onto the urban landscape their perceptions of what different areas in the city represented' (p. 313). Moreover, street names were also a celebration of colonisers and their world-view, specifically those who contributed to the Empire, like colonial adminis-trators and the British royalty. Even in the realm of language, one can witness the early primacy of English, the language of the colonial masters, over that of local languages in *Singapore*. Indigenous toponyms that were derived from the Malay language were often changed, over time, to take on a more Anglo-sounding version. An example of this is the place name *T'mpenis*, coined after the Malay term for the *Riau* ironwood tree, which became *Tempenis* and, finally, *Tampines*, in its present form, denoting a large suburb in east *Singapore*.

This did not mean, however, that the locals always accepted the British-given name of streets. Apart from the official, municipal-approved names, *Singapore*'s Asian inhabitants often gave informal names to places according to their community-based norms. Hence, there were two (parallel) sets of names used to denominate the streets in colonial *Singapore*: one for the British/Westerners, and another for the Indigenous/non-European settlers. This is an example of how locals in colonised societies express agency in circumventing the official toponyms imposed on them by the colonial author-ities, which we discussed in the previous section. Yeoh effectively outlined the differences between the official British and non-official Asian place names.

Whereas street names primarily sought to identify the urban landscape notions of appropriateness and ordering, Chinese nomenclature was anchored to local features, symbols, and activities that formed a role in daily experience. Whereas Chinese names tended to match of streets to which they were attached, municipal street names level of signification that conveyed meaning over and above the material functions of the streets. (Yeoh, 1992, p. 319)

These alternative names were based on: the socioeconomic activities con-ducted at the places, for example, *Albert Street*, named after Queen Victoria's consort, was known as *Bo Moan Koi* to the Chinese, meaning 'street where sesame oil is pressed'; religious places, for example, the same *Albert Street* was also known to some Chinese as *Mang Ku Lu Seng Ong* '*Bencoolen Street* district joss-house (temple)'; the names of gangs, for example, *Carpenter Street* was referred to by some Chinese as *Ghi Hok Koi*, the name of a former secret society based there. Through a study of street names in colonial *Singapore*, a story begins to emerge; the British did not enjoy total toponymic supremacy, as the locals developed from the bottom-up another competing set of landscape terms and place names which reflected the Asian perceptions and use of the landscape. It was even possible to have multiple informal names for the same place, owing to the different Chinese vernaculars spoken. This was in opposition to the single, unitary, top-down, and British-approved street names from the Municipal Committee that lacked Asian representation. As Yeoh concludes, the 'failure to impose and to enforce adoption of one uniform system of place-names partly reflected the absolute power for the government and its acceptance of multicultural terns of behaviour' (Yeoh, 1992, p. 322).

### 8.4.2    *Post-Independence* Singapore

The period between the 1950s and 1960s was one of great political uncertainty, leading to self-government in 1959. *Singapore* then entered a short-lived merger with the *Federation of Malaya* in 1963. In 1965, *Singapore* declared its independence. In this period and the subsequent years, the *Lion City* underwent a number of sociopolitical changes, and it is unsurprising that the toponymic landscape mirrored some of these shifts. One important moment was when, in the late 1950s, *Singapore* adopted English, Malay, Mandarin, and Tamil as official languages, and the toponyms coined during this period mirrored this multilingualism.

In post-independence *Singapore*, place names became tools that the state used to inscribe a sense of nationhood and national identity among Singaporeans. Yeoh (1996) identified three aspects of the toponymic inscriptions of nationhood and how toponyms in post-independence *Singapore* are shaped by broader sociopolitical elements. These are 'Malayanising' the colonial landscape, 'multi-ethnicising' the landscape, and the standardisation of odonyms.

The nation-state, in the immediate period after 1965, sought to emphasise a local Malayan identity instead of a colonial one. This led to an increase in local names, especially in the Malay language, which was a sign of allegiance to the Malay world rather than the British colonial masters. *Singapore* saw a proliferation of Malayanised names, such as *Jalan Tembusu* and *Angsana Avenue* (these places were named after local trees). However, the local Malay vocabulary was soon exhausted, while at the same time this naming practice had many opponents among the Chinese population, who claimed to find the names difficult to pronounce or remember. Yeoh (1996, p. 302) stated that, 'ironically, people preferred road signage and residential addresses in English, the language of the colonial masters, which they perceived as neutral if not superior'. This strategy was also considered as favouring one ethnic group, the Malays, over the other layers of the population. A 'Malayanised' naming strategy did not mean that colonial toponyms were totally removed. Founding Prime Minister Lee Kuan Yew resisted calls to modify colonial road names, saying that *Singapore*'s legacy as a Crown Colony was 'nothing to be ashamed of' (Ho, 2017). Hence, even as *Singapore* wanted to align itself with a Malayan identity, this did not mean the total removal of its colonial history.

Another important development in the post-independence period was the standardisation of street names in the *Lion City*. In 1967, the Committee on the Standardisation of Street Names in Chinese was formed. This committee was tasked with simplifying and systematising 'existing renderings of street names in Chinese so as to avoid confusions and unhappy transliterations' and creating transliterations that will 'not only be a faithful rendering by sound but should also be elegant and meaningful' (*The Straits Times*, 1970a). Such a development has to be read in context; while the state sought to reflect the multilingual landscape, only the Romanised script was used in street names and in street directories. This proved to be somewhat problematic initially, as most of the population was illiterate in English and, thus, the Romanised street names were incomprehensible to them. Furthermore, because Chinese Singaporeans spoke a number of Chinese vernaculars, there were also a number of vernacular names for the same street, leading to confusion. Therefore, this committee's work, besides standardising street names, was to create accurate, simple, but yet plausible transliterations.

In the 1980s, the state sought to apply the *Hanyu Pinyin* system (a system of Romanising Chinese characters based on the Mandarin pronunciation) as a way of standardising Chinese and Chinese-sounding street names and place names in *Singapore*. This essentially meant changing the spelling of the place names that were originally written and pronounced in Chinese vernaculars, to reflect the Mandarin pronunciation (Ng, 2017, p. 45). One prominent example is *Nee Soon*, which was named after the famous Teochew pineapple planter Lim Nee Soon. It was later *pinyinised* to *Yishun* (Ng, 2017, p. 43; Savage & Yeoh, 2013, p. 407; Yeh, 2013, p. 146). The *pinyinisation* of Singaporean place names, however, gave rise to heated debates, with many Singaporeans calling for the retention of old vernacular names due to the inconvenience of the new pronunciation, along with the belittling of the historical meanings and values of the original names.

The Chinese vernacular Hokkien was, until recently, the *lingua franca* of local Chinese people. It is therefore not surprising that a significant number of Singaporean place names were coined in Hokkien or derived from Hokkien terms. For example, the suburb of *Tiong Bahru* is made up of the Hokkien word *tiong*, meaning 'cemetery/burial ground', and the Malay word *bahru*, meaning 'new'; the street *Lorong Lew Lian* is made up of the Malay *lorong*, meaning 'alley', and the Hokkien term for durian (a tropical fruit). Another instance is represented by the name of *Tekka Centre*, a shopping complex in *Little India*. Originally, it was known by the Malay name *Kandang Kerbau* 'buffalo pens'. It was also referred to by the Hokkien term *Tek Kia Kha*, which means 'foot of the small bamboos', a reference to the bamboos that used to grow in that area. It later became the *Tekka Pasar* (*pasar* is the Malay word for 'market'). In the late 1980s, it was *pinyinised* to *Zhujiao*. This received very strong reactions from locals who claimed that the new name did not sound anything like the original Hokkien name, and that it ignored the market's rich history. The building was renamed *Tekka Centre* in 2000.

In sum, the naming of streets in *Singapore*, in general, is intertwined with various social and political considerations. While the British sought to portray order and their worldview through 'ethnicising' the urban landscape and commemorating colonial figures and their royalty in colonial street names, the post-independence government had a slightly different approach. Names were initially Malayanised, and a preference was given to local and Malay names, ostensibly to project a new postcolonial identity rooted in *Southeast Asia*. Yet, this did not mean that colonial names were totally expunged. In later years, the Malayanisation of the landscape and the use of Malay to name toponyms was seen to be at odds with *Singapore*'s multiculturalism and multilingualism. In the early years of post-independence *Singapore*, streets reflected *Singapore*'s nation-building aspirations for economic survival and progress, as well as a multiethnic landscape. Hence, the focus shifted from an ethnic landscape in the colonial era to a multiethnic one. Multiculturalism, as espoused in Singaporean toponyms and the national discourse, meant the elimination of multiethnic heterogeneities, such as that of the different Chinese vernacular groups, and instead the construction of a Singaporean identity based on the main ethnic groups and on the state's language policies.

### 8.4.3    *Toponymic Classification Systems in* Singapore

In colonial *Singapore*, a number of articles detailing the names of *Singapore*'s streets were published (see, for instance, Firmstone, 1905; Haughton, 1889; 1891). These works explore the origins and meanings of local toponyms. In one of the first known lists detailing the names of places in *Singapore*, Haughton (1889) explained the etymologies and meanings of over seventy Malay toponyms and three Chinese place names. Likewise, Haughton (1889) continued this approach with more than 100 Chinese toponyms and 35 Indian place names. It is worth noting that these early records of Singaporean toponyms sought to document places in *Singapore* rather than developing and/or using a multifaceted tool to group toponyms according to their naming strategies. In some ways, this process is reminiscent of the extensive approach to toponymy described by Tent (2015a) in terms of coming up with datasets of place names and studying existing documents and the landscape. Yet, it falls short of the aim of extensive toponymy in itself, that is, to reveal place naming patterns and strategies through a study of the toponyms.

Coming up with taxonomies to classify place names has been the focus of toponymy in twenty-first-century *Singapore*. One of the first classification schemes for *Singapore* toponymy emerged in *Toponymics: A Study of*

*Singapore Street Names*, published in 2003 by geographers Victor Savage and Brenda Yeoh. In the book, Savage and Yeoh show that *Singapore*'s toponyms are organised according to at least seven categories:

- colonial names derived from important places and people in the *British Empire*
- Malayanised names after places, flora, and fauna
- names associated with different ethnic groups
- names commemorating famous Asian leaders, wealthy landowners, and other people
- descriptive names which either denote topographical features, the presence of landmarks, or indicate former or current land uses, trades, and activities
- numerical names as found in the majority of Housing and Development Board (HDB) 'New Towns'
- 'themed' names associated with opera, colours, or local bird species

In *What's in the Name? How the Streets and Villages in Singapore Got Their Names*, Ng (2017) claims that his book is the first of its kind, in that it analyses naming trends of *Singapore*'s streets and villages. Ng (2017) provided a comprehensive list of the possible contents in Singaporean place names:

- roads named after foreign places
- anthroponyms named after non-residents (i.e., people who did not live in *Singapore*) and residents (i.e., people who lived in *Singapore*)
- places named after the main economic activity conducted there, such as entrepot trade and agriculture
- places named due to activities of war
- places named after the political system
- places named after historical sites
- places associated with religion
- place names linked to families (be they British royalty or Chinese families or others)
- place names related to education
- place names named after women
- housing estates with a 'theme', including trees, flowers, operas

In the two above-mentioned books, the authors identified the distributions of certain types of toponyms (e.g., numerical names of places in 'New Towns', or 'themed' toponyms and housing estates in particular areas of *Singapore*). However, their analyses stopped short of determining the naming patterns of those place names. An unanswered question is, for instance, 'what is the percentage of toponyms in each category?'.

Perono Cacciafoco and Tuang's (2018) study aimed at developing a typology to classify Singaporean odonyms. Their classification borrowed some of the internationally oriented works listed in Chapter 1, as well as from past research on *Singapore* toponymy, such as, among others, the work by Savage and Yeoh (2013) cited above and Ng (2017). The authors came up with six categories of street names:

- commemorative toponyms, with streets named after prominent figures or significant events
- borrowed toponyms, with streets named after foreign places/languages, or borrowed from the names of local ethnic groups
- thematic toponyms connected with specific areas
- descriptive toponyms, with streets referring to either landscape features, such as the morphology of roads or anthropic facilities that exist(ed) in the places, or to the description of the economic and agricultural activities that had flourished in their corresponding areas
- place names derived from trees', plants', or flowers' names (phytonyms)
- other toponyms, which do not fall into the naming practices listed above, or whose etymologies and origins are unknown

The authors also went a step further and, rather than merely developing this toponymic classification system, also analysed the naming practices applied to Singaporean odonyms according to three of the four official languages of the *Lion City*: English, Malay, and Chinese. They collected 50 odonyms in each of these official languages as a sample for analysis. The authors also counter-checked the origins of the 150 odonyms using a variety of historical-geographical resources.

The findings of this study show a local inclination towards commemorative naming, especially in Chinese and English street names. Commemorative naming is observed most frequently in Chinese street names. They commemorate influential Chinese figures in the community and their families. Additionally, odonyms which have English as their source language tend to have been borrowed more frequently in comparison to street names in Malay or Chinese. That is, English names were 'borrowed' from places in Britain and other Western countries with similar or the same names, for example, both *Oxford Road* and *Devonshire Road* were borrowed from the *UK*. Malay place names depict a relatively more balanced frequency of usage across thematic names, descriptive names, names derived from trees/plants/flowers, and names which are considered to belong to the category 'others'. However, as mentioned, many of the Malay toponyms categorised under this group also show descriptive functions. An example of this is, according to the authors, *Kasai Road*. *Kasai* means 'cosmetic powder' in Malay (Ng, 2017, p. 266). The place could have been named descriptively after a cosmetic item or a product that was once popular in that area, although the lack of historical records makes the origins and meaning of the name difficult to verify and, hence, the denomination is placed under the category 'others'. Thus, a preference towards a descriptive naming strategy could also be postulated in Malay street names. The authors concluded that, while commemorative street names and odonyms coined after the names of trees/plants/flowers may be linked to specific languages (i.e., Chinese, English, and Malay, respectively), it appears that descriptive names are common across toponyms in these three languages.

### 8.4.4  *Toponymic Structures in* Singapore

Most Singaporean toponyms show a combination of specific elements indicating their location, such as *Jurong, Serangoon, Bedok,* and so on, and generic elements, like *Road, Street,* or their equivalents in local languages, such as *Jalan, Bukit* (these are the Malay words for 'road' and 'hill', respectively) (Ng, 2017, p. 7). The most basic toponymic structure observed involves the combination of a specific and generic element, giving rise to double or duplex names, such as *Pekin Street, Serangoon Road,* and *Jalan Kayu.* The sequence of combination for such double names depends largely on the structure of their source languages. A common combination is represented by a *generic* element + a specific element (as in <u>*Jalan*</u> *Kayu,* which follows the structure of its source language, Malay). Likewise, some toponyms might show another order, that is, a specific element + a *generic* element (as in *Pekin* <u>*Street*</u> or *Serangoon* <u>*Road*</u>, which follow the English structure) (Ng, 2017, p. 8). In addition to double names, many complex toponyms consist of more than two elements, as in *Ang Mo Kio Industrial Park 1*; this is known as the 'derivative method', according to which the street has one specific element (*Ang Mo Kio*) and more than one generic element (*Industrial Park + 1*) (Ng, 2017, pp. 7–10; Perono Cacciafoco & Tuang, 2018, p. 17). Given the multiethnic context of *Singapore,* it is also unsurprising to witness combinations of languages within a single street name, such as *Bukit Mugliston* (Malay + English) and *Jalan Lam Sam* (Malay + Chinese), where different languages are deployed for the specific and generic element of the street name.

Ng (2017, p. 7) lists numerous ways of labelling *Singapore*'s place names. He states that place names in the *Lion City* follow three main categories.

1. Simplex name. This is made up of a single word (but which can have multiple elements, e.g., *Queensway*). Ng states that these are rare now, but can still be seen in the denominations of suburbs or towns such as *Queenstown, Bishan,* and *Jurong.* One other example is the street near the *Seletar Airport* simply named *Piccadilly,* with no generic element.
2. Duplex name. This is made up of a specific element + a generic element. This accounts for the majority of place names in *Singapore.* Examples of this type include *Orchard Road, Changi Airport,* and *Jalan Hajijah.*
3. Complex name. This is made up of one or more specific element(s) + one or more generic element(s). Examples include *Choa Chu Kang Avenue 1, Sin Ming Industrial Estate Sector A,* and *Toa Payoh West.*

This classification can be criticised as Ng tried to apply this categorisation to place names that do not fall into any of his categories, such as, among others, *Kallang Tengah*, which has the element *Kallang* and is the name of the district. This name, however, has no generic element as *Tengah* is simply Malay for 'middle'.

In this section, we have seen how some themes that we have listed previously, such as the morphosyntactic structure of place names, toponymic classification systems that categorise toponyms, the use of historical geography in studying place names, and even how places and streets are influenced by issues of governmentality and politics, can be applied to a local context. As seen throughout the case study of *Singapore*, place names have been utilised by various governments (the British colonial rulers and, later, the People's Action Party (PAP) in independent *Singapore*) to achieve their various sociopolitical goals, such as asserting colonial order over the colony or shaping the landscape according to a multicultural and multilingual ideology. Place names are, thus, not as neutral or 'innocent' as they are sometimes believed, but in fact are rich social, cultural, and political tools that demonstrate the power of one group over another. This is an area which is explored by the theories of critical toponymies, a field that has enjoyed increased visibility in the context of synchronic toponymy (and, more generally, toponymy and toponymic studies) in the last few decades.

## 8.5    Critical Toponymies

In this volume, we have seen that toponymy is mainly concerned with deciphering the origins and original meanings of place names and with the organisation of toponymic data into coherent categories. These traditional approaches in studying toponyms have given rise to criticisms, as pointed out by a pioneer in the study of critical toponymies, Maoz Azaryahu.

Place name studies has long focused on the description and classification of toponyms and treated 'place' as an unproblematic geographical concept. However, recent critical toponymic research has shifted the focus away from the name itself and towards a political analysis of naming practices and the cultural production of 'place'. (Azaryahu, 2011b, p. 32)

The shortcomings in the traditional study of toponymy and toponomastics lie in the fact that the sociocultural and political aspects of the naming process have been under-researched, and scholars working through traditional approaches have often treated toponyms in an atheoretical and apolitical manner (Vuolteenaho & Berg, 2009, p. 1). That this is the case is not surprising, as toponymy for a very long time has been the discipline of historians, historical linguists, cartographers, and etymologists. In response to this, the last decade or so has seen a growth in critical toponymies approaches. Vuolteenaho and Berg (2009) summarised the approach as follows.

Given that naming a place is always a socially embedded act, one that involves power relations, the 'pure' linguistic standpoint remains inadequate for the critical study of toponymy. Accordingly, whilst we agree with the need to be specific about what type of 'naming' we are talking, we advocate an understanding of place names as 'social facts' embedded in intricate cultural interrelations and tension-filled conceptions of space. As such, the practices of place naming are also caught up, in any given society, in the power and possibilities of 'making places'. (p. 9)

Through the studies conducted in the field of critical toponymies, it is possible to see how toponymy is becoming increasingly influential in urban geography, human geography, and urban studies (Light & Young, 2015; see also Rose-Redwood, Alderman, & Azaryahu, 2010). Light and Young (2015) stated that the critical approach to the study of place names has made the discipline consider the connections between urban space, power, and identity.

Critical toponymies has a number of approaches and focuses. One of these situates the role of naming urban places within the practices of modern governmentality (Light & Young, 2015, p. 436). As argued elsewhere (Rose-Redwood, 2006; 2008; 2009), naming practices are forms of governmentality that function as technologies of classification, command, and control, ultimately allowing the state 'to consolidate and exercise power through the identification of populations and the implementation of infrastructure, taxation systems, and policing strategies' (Wideman & Masuda, 2018, p. 495). For example, Yeoh (1992) pointed out how the British's street nomenclature reflected their bid to impose order and ethnic differentiation in colonial *Singapore*.

Another approach 'examines the role of attributing commemorative names (in remembrance of key individuals or historical events) in the construction of collective memories' (Light & Young, 2015, p. 436). In this context, naming is a strategy that the ruling elites use to give meaning to and to legitimise their version of history (i.e., who and what is worth remembering), which is then projected onto the landscape. This is something that was poignant in the *Bucharest* example from the previous chapter, and is also noted in the place names of both Communist and post-Communist contexts like *East Berlin, Germany* (Azaryahu, 1997; 2011a), *Budapest, Hungary* (Palonen, 2008; 2015), and *Košice, Slovakia* (Chloupek, 2019). As pointed out by Azaryahu (1996), the introduction of names into the most banal everyday settings, like roads, streets, boulevards, and avenues, is a way of inserting the hegemonic discourse into social reality.

[C]ommemorative street names not only evince and substantiate a particular version of history, but are also instrumental in introducing it into spheres of social communication that seem to be outside of the realm of political control and manipulation. (Azaryahu, 1996, p. 328)

A prominent focus of critical toponomies is inherent in toponymic renaming during times of profound political changes. This ensures that the urban landscape is aligned with the political ideals and worldview of the reigning political regime, something that was explored in Chapter 7. Recently, a number of studies have explored this issue, focussing, for example, on the toponymic renaming in post-independence *Zimbabwe* (Mamvura, Muwati, & Mutasa, 2018), post-Communist *Romania* (Rusu, 2020), post-Nazi *Germany* (Vuolteenaho & Puzey, 2018), post-apartheid *South Africa* (Adebanwi, 2017), and post-revolutionary *Ukraine* (Gnatiuk, 2018). Extreme cases of toponymic renaming are referred to as 'toponymic cleansing' (Rose-Redwood et al., 2010, p. 460). This term is used in nationalistic contexts to 'weld the national language to the national territory by excluding "foreign" place names' (Rose-Redwood et al., 2010, p. 460). Street names and other urbanonyms, which are seen as incongruent with the political goals and ideology of an incoming regime, are expunged and excluded from a city as the regime seeks to symbolically mould the urban landscape in its image. Light and Young (2018) posited that the renaming of streets is a feature of what Czepczyński (2008, p. 109) calls 'landscape cleansing', or 'landscape revolution'. As Czepczyński stated, 'Landscape then becomes a battlefield, where buildings and arrangements representing opposing ideas become enemies and rivals, as well as victims and winners' (p. 109).

The field of critical toponymies is still developing. In the past, the call was to shift how we perceived toponyms from being atheoretical and apolitical to see them as tools that are full of social, political, and cultural meaning and significance. Toponyms, as mentioned, are not neutral or 'innocent', but are subjected to a number of factors. In recent times, scholars have begun to see how toponyms, particularly denominations of public places, such as stadia and arenas, can be commodified, thereby adding an economic dimension to the study of toponymy. A useful read summarising the shortcomings of current research and future directions in critical toponymies is Bigon (2020), which identifies two *lacunae* in critical toponymy literature. One is related to the overwhelming geopolitical coverage of how the place naming process is a tool of governmentality and nationalistic biases. Bigon points out that topics like wars, political revolutions, governmental and doctrinal changes, and historiographical debates tend to dominate the present literature. Research work is also overconcerned with the *Northern Hemisphere*, represented by *Europe* and *North America*. Very little attention is paid to *South America*, *Africa*, and *Asia*. The second *lacuna* is inherent in the methodological obsession with the notion of 'index', which, in the context of toponymy, refers to concrete urban inscriptions of toponyms and odonyms. These include street signages, gazet-teers, map legends, archives of name committees, and so on. According to Bigon (2020), this essentialises the role and existence of a 'text' (in the form of city-texts, street names, and other toponymic inscriptions) in the study of toponymy. Nonetheless, the reasoning as a whole is problematic, given that these 'indexes' and 'texts' reflect Western logics of governmentality, calcula-tive space, and urban planning, as well as the habit of top-down naming, with the aim of projecting it onto the rest of the world. Hence, 'indexes' and 'texts' cannot be applied as blanket terms in Southern contexts. Bigon argued the following.

> Because toponymic inscriptions are not always inscribed into the linguistic landscapes of Southern cities, the urban spatial terminologies in this context need to be decoded as text, without the obligatory presence of, or in addition to, the official conventional 'index' of a written text (street signs, accurate city maps, detailed digital maps). Such an approach promotes seeing the landscape as text rather than looking for texts inscribed in the landscape, for 'nondescript spatial structures' characterise many cities in Africa and generally in the global South. Streets are nameless, have multiple names or have names that are not signposted, and buildings are not necessarily numbered. (Bigon, 2020, p. 5)

To this end, Bigon calls for creative and interdisciplinary methods that investigate places beyond their traditional 'indexes'. These include examining the relations between orality and writing and orality–literacy dynamics and the use of methodologies from anthropology, folklore studies, postcolonial studies, and subaltern studies. A key shift should also occur away from the 'index', which Bigon labels as 'redundant', 'unidimensional', and 'relativist' – one that is 'biased towards the exploration of micro-toponymies of placemaking and place attachment of the urban majority' (Bigon, 2020, p. 6). The exploration of micro-toponymies and the concomitant discourses of bottom-up place making is important in creating toponymic research that is global and relevant and, at the same time, in understanding the geographic and perceptual differences between the *West* and the rest of the world.

We will, now, turn our attention to what is referred to as the phenomenon of 'commodification of place names', something which is under the 'economic dimensions of naming practices' (Light & Young, 2015, p. 436).

## 8.6    The Commodification of Place Names

Duncan Light, in his 2014 paper 'Tourism and Toponymy: Commodifying and Consuming Place Names', noted that a recent development in critical topony-mies is the focus on the economic, rather than the political, roles of place names (Light, 2014). There is a growing interest in 'toponymy as commodity', when the making and naming of places produces urban worlds: a process known as 'worlding' (Rose-Redwood, Sotoudehnia, & Tretter, 2019). Indeed, the concept of 'toponymic commodification' was raised as early as 2011, when Rose-Redwood wrote that 'one of the major transformations that will likely reshape the toponymic landscape of the next century is the commercialisation of public space-naming systems' (Rose-Redwood, 2011, p. 34). At the time that article was published, however, the corporate branding and commercialisation of public infrastructure through the purchase of naming rights was a field that had received scant attention. Rose-Redwood detailed the early example of the *Dubai* Metro and the decision by the Metro and the Roads and Transport Authority (RTA) of the Government of *Dubai* to sell the naming rights of twenty-three of the forty-seven Metro stations to corporate buyers in 2006. This was followed by a public relations campaign targeting potential buyers with the motto 'Turn your brand into a destination' (Rose-Redwood, 2011, p. 34). The RTA also marketed this as an opportunity for corporate sponsors to interact with commuters at various Metro stations, providing an 'immersive marketing opportunity' (RTA, cited in Rose-Redwood, 2011, p. 35), which Rose-Redwood notes is 'a significant extension of the "immersive" powers of corporate marketing in reshaping the publicly-sanctioned, official toponymic landscape' (Rose-Redwood, 2011, pp. 35–6). This is an example of how public–private partnerships, through the naming of urbanonyms after corporate sponsors, may turn place names into branded destinations associated with top business names and, therefore, can attach 'symbolic capital' to places. 'Symbolic capital', in turn, is defined by Bourdieu as the power accumulated by prestige and honour (Bourdieu, 1991) . Ultimately, toponyms become valued because they are associated with the prestige and the perception of excellence conferred by an established brand.

A toponym named after a person (or corporation) has social distinction, and the related individual or entity can accrue 'symbolic capital' by the decision to name a public space after them. Bourdieu (1986) also suggested that 'symbolic capital' can be converted into economic capital (and vice versa). Economic capital, in the monetary form, can also be garnered through the commodification of place names, as aforementioned. Likewise, the symbolic value of an urban place name is monetised and treated like a commodity. According to Rose-Redwood et al. (2019), when a corporate sponsor signs a naming rights agreement to lease the right to name a place, this 'symbolic capital' becomes an economic transaction. The authors go on to say the following.

Through naming rights agreements, corporations and wealthy individual sponsors are granted the power to take ownership over, even if just in name, parts of the cityscape by branding them with their names or logos. Transforming public place names into potential rent-generating assets, city politicians and administrators are directly trading on a place's potential symbolic value, particularly as a site of public visibility, by transforming the symbolic capital of place naming – i.e. the prestige, distinction, and legitimacy associated with public commemoration and honouring – into a form of economic capital (i.e. a financial asset with an ongoing stream of revenue). (Rose-Redwood et al., 2019, p. 849)

However, the business of buying and selling naming rights, especially by big corporations, is a story on how 'monetising symbolic capital associated with urban place naming reconfigures the symbolic value of public recognition into a more explicitly economic affair' (Rose-Redwood et al., 2019, p. 865). Furthermore, toponymic commodification also reduces naming rights to 'dollars and cents', which devalues non-economic aspects of place names, such as the use of toponyms to challenge existing sociocultural hierarchies or to create a more socially inclusive urban landscape that recognises minority groups.

A number of scholars have worked on the commodification of stadia names in Western contexts. Medway et al. (2019) focussed on the scalar tensions occurring when stadium toponyms are named after international brands, given the strong connections of football clubs to urban locales and their populations. The imposition of international brands on stadia names and on their locally embedded fan communities has led to resistance among fans to corporate stadium toponyms, best witnessed in the case of *Oldham Athletic*, whose 'fans articulated a "ferocious" protection and preservation of the original Boundary Park toponym in the face of its corporate replacement' (Medway et al., 2019, p. 794). To manage these tensions, Medway et al. (2019) recommended that the corporate management of football clubs integrate these brands into community life, with the stadium name becoming one of the many ways through which the brand is interspersed within the toponymic district. Former stadia names could also be commemorated, as the memories and nostalgia evoked can 'quell the spatially disruptive and locally de-embedding forces of stadium relocations and associated name changes to internationally positioned brands' (Medway et al., 2019, p. 798). These scalar tensions are intertwined with socioeconomic and political considerations, along with temporal and locational factors (e.g., how long the stadium has been at a location, how long the former toponym was previously associated with the football club, whether the stadium has moved before, etc.). Perhaps most importantly, the scalar tensions encapsulate the uneasy relationships between the global and the local. For instance, *Etihad Stadium* (the stadium of Manchester City Football Club) is the most prominent brand in terms of international outreach and worth. The authors contended that the stadium name is reflective of the promotion of the club through *Etihad*'s brand on a global stage, showing that, once again, corporate names can function as significant 'symbolic capital'. Yet, Medway et al. (2019) question whether the club can maintain its local embeddedness, as it emphasises a global perspective (where there is a sensitivity to local fandom, while having an eye on the globe), or if it is the case where the global focus of the *Etihad* brand is imposed at the club, and the club thus has a 'grobal' outlook (a combination of the words 'growth' and 'global', where these two aspects take greater precedence over the local).

In their study of fan discourses on the corporate renaming of football stadia in *Manchester*, Gillooly et al. (2021) noted that the agency among football fans is very important. Fans can reluctantly accept, actively resist, or passively ignore corporate stadium names. This is reminiscent of how people, even in colonies of the past, could also resist or ignore names given by the colonial powers. The links between urban geography, toponymy, discourse analysis, and even performativity appear in this survey, as fans, through their stylised, repeated, and repetitive speech acts, subvert corporate renaming of stadiums, as we can see from the two examples below (Gillooly et al., 2021).

A million pounds is not a little amount of money [. . .] We accept it to a degree, but we're still never going to change that name. To us it's still Boundary Park and will always be Boundary Park (*Oldham* fan c)

They can call it what they want. Nobody here acknowledges the [SportsDirect.com Park] name. (*Oldham* fan f)

In the final analysis, the study highlighted that:

[. . .] toponymic geographies can be subtler than the imposition of top-down regimes of performative spatial inscription, and a subsequent acquiescence or counter-performative resistance to these. Consequently, the corporate appropriation of football space(s) occurs more on fans' terms than might initially be realised. Certainly, our analysis suggests that any overtures of corporate involvement in football via toponymic inscription are potentially undermined by fans' unconscious, routinised and everyday acts of speech. (Gillooly et al., 2021, p. 15)

The names of sports stadia can be full of 'symbolic capital' for fans. At the same time, they can have great standing, value, and loyalty among the same fans because of feelings that come from strong local traditions and shared experiences and emotions. To sell the naming rights of a new stadium is one thing, but to rename an existing arena can be a rather touchy and controversial affair. Light and Young (2015) provided the example of *St James' Park*, the stadium of Newcastle United Football Club, an English Premier League (EPL) club. In 2011, a sport clothing company bought the naming rights, and the stadium was renamed *Sports Direct Arena*. Another example comes from the stadium of Southampton Football Club, another EPL club, founded by members of a church called *St Mary's*. When Southampton Football Club moved from its old stadium, *The Dell*, to a new one in 2001, the denomination of the new ground became *The Friends Provident St Mary's Stadium*. The Friends Provident was the name of an insurance company that sponsored the club at that time. However, fans pressured the club into including the name *St Mary's* as a link to their historical origins. When the naming rights went back to the club, the name *St Mary's* became the official one for the new stadium.

An interesting quantitative study on the toponymic commodification of the names of European sport complexes comes from Vuolteenaho, Wolny, and Puzey (2019). The authors surveyed 193 stadium grounds and 115 indoor arenas to chart how sporting and entertainment brands have been infused in these stages and grounds across six European countries, *England, Finland, Germany, Italy, Norway,* and *Scotland.* The authors noted that sporting facilities 'have been in the vanguard of implementing naming rights deals since the early-1990s, and particularly in the first decade of the new millennium' (Vuolteenaho et al., 2019, p. 779). They also noted the following.

Across Europe, too, an increasing number of sporting and entertainment facilities (and, more recently, other types of principally 'public' urban infrastructures) have become stages for this 'innovative' revenue-generating strategy. Naming rights have been sold for many hundreds of European venues, whether by local councils with shrinking finances, or by private teams and corporations attempting to stay competitive. (Vuolteenaho et al., 2019, p. 762)

The general trend is that the younger the venue is, the more the sponsorship money (from the sale of naming rights and name sponsorship deals) will tend to benefit the seller. In less historic venues, the engagement by corporate entities is also seen as less problematic by locals and, hence, it is easier to implement naming rights deals. Beyond that, as previous commentators have noted, there are local peculiarities that have to be accounted for as well. These forces can explain the (non-)diffusion of venue naming rights. An example is *Norway,* where public finances are healthy and, hence, there is less financial pressure to sell naming rights. In contrast, in some other countries, the occurrences of unruly supporters, hooliganism, and the mismanagement of football clubs and their financial problems, among other reasons, have discouraged sponsors who value a family-friendly and polished brand image. This results in what the authors call a 'locally path-dependent dimensions of neoliberal urbanism' (Vuolteenaho et al., 2019, p. 779).

## 8.7    Toponymic Commodification, Identity, and Tourism

Toponymic commodification can imply the creation of new place identities. Medway and Warnaby put it succinctly that 'toponyms represent an attempt to create places from placelessness' (Medway & Warnaby, 2014, p. 161). This is seen in *Dubai*'s place names, like *Media City, Internet City,* and *Knowledge Village,* where business zones are created in a desert city. This can also be observed in *Singapore,* with names like *Biopolis* and *Fusionpolis,* given with the aim of creating international research hubs where there were none before. Moreover,

Light and Young (2015) noted that the symbolic capital of places can be harnessed in the realm of place branding and promotional strategies in order to create distinct place identities. To this end, authorities have appropriated the historical and cultural associations of a place to create a 'coherent themed landscape' (Light, 2014, p. 143). Often, this involves the creation of new names, particularly those that are coined through literary, heritage, and cultural associations that showcase to people (especially tourists) the type of experiences they can find in a locality. Examples of this are *Brontë Country* (literary association), *Robin Hood Country* (heritage association), and *Last of the Summer Wine Country* (associated with television and popular culture), all in the *UK* (Light, 2014, p. 143).

A related theme is the intersection of tourism studies and toponymy. Light notes the following.

Initially, it might appear ridiculous that something as seemingly insubstantial as a 'mere' name could be of any interest to tourists. However, it is clear that, in certain circumstances, names are the object of the tourist gaze. (Light, 2014, p. 141)

He goes on to add the following.

The simplest form of marker is a name. Thus allocating a name (or appropriating an existing toponym) is the first stage of sight sacralisation,[4] and in this formulation place names can function as on-sight markers of the attraction. (Light, 2014, p. 142)

The significance of place names in tourist sites is something that has been documented in past academic literature, long before the advent of critical toponymies. MacCannell (1999) argued that (place) names can become more important than the actual places they indicate. Morgan (2006) stated that the first thing people usually get about a place is its name. Indeed, because of the initial impressions upon seeing or hearing a toponym, place names can function as tourist attractions in and of themselves. In Light's words, place names can be consumed as tourist sites (Light, 2014, p. 144). Light gives the example of some of the longest place names in the world, which by virtue of their exceptional length are sufficient to pique tourists' interests and attract them to visit the places. Examples include *Taumatawhakatangihangakoauauotamateaturipukakapikimaungahoronukupoka-iwhenuakitanatahu*, in *New Zealand* (Figure 8.2), and *Llanfairpwllgwyn-gyllgogerychwyrndrobwllllllantysiliogogogoch*, in north *Wales*, the *UK*. The former is reported (Toitū Te Whenua LINZ, 2022) as the official name for a hill

---

[4] MacCannell (1999) defines sight sacralisation as the process whereby objects, places, and landscapes are constructed and differentiated as exceptional sights of interest to the tourist. This process involves markers, which (place) names are, and therefore the place names can function as markers of attraction by differentiating a place from others. Toponyms can be sacralised through popular culture. Examples include place names featured in movies, such as *Sunset Boulevard* and *Mulholland Drive* (both in *Los Angeles*), *Miracle on 34th Street* (*New York*) (Light, 2014), and *84 Charing Cross Road* (*London*).

Figure 8.2 The longest place name in the world, *New Zealand* (adapted from Schwede66, 2015)

located about 500 kilometres southeast of the capital, *Auckland*. It is in the Maori language and has eighty-five letters, making it the longest single-word toponym in the world. The Maori translation reads: 'The summit where Tamatea, the man with the big knees, the climber of mountains, the land-swallower who travelled about, played his nose flute to his loved one.' The latter, on the other hand, is a longer, non-official version of the Welsh name for the town of *Llanfairpwllgwyngyll*. The longer variant can be translated as '*St Mary's Church* in the hollow of the white hazel near a rapid whirlpool and the *Church of Saint Tysilio* of the red cave.' Both are clearly marked as tourist sites. Light writes that the Maori place name 'is inscribed on a large sign at the side of the road for visitors to stop and observe, while advance signs inform visitors that the name is ahead' (Light, 2014, p. 144) and, as for the Welsh toponym, the name is emblazoned on the various buildings in the village, as well as the platform of the railway station for tourists to view in full. Other toponymic tourist attractions are constituted by surprising or unusual names, generally decontextualised from their respective languages, such as *Hell* (in *Norway* and in several American states), *Condom* (*France*), and *Fucking* (pronounced *Foo-king*, in *Austria*).

Alderman, Benjamin, and Scheider (2012) made reference to significant studies that have researched the relationship between geography and mass media. They also point out that many people worldwide travel to places made famous because of movies and TV shows. They stated that 'film-induced tourism is increasingly promoted in the United States and globally as a marketing and economic development tool' (Alderman et al., 2012, p. 213). Film-induced tourism can involve fans visiting places where their favourite films or television series were shot. For example, *New Zealand* is a destination for *The Lord of the Rings* fans (Alderman et al., 2012). *South Korea*, especially the islands of *Nami* and *Jeju*, is a destination for fans of South Korean dramas (Korean Culture and Information Service, 2011). This phenomenon can involve visiting places represented in the plot or storyline of productions, even though the films or series may never actually have been shot in those locations. Alderman et al. (2012, p. 213) provide the example of *Forks*, a town in *Washington*, which never saw any filming but was the setting for the *Twilight* movie series. We can also include the real-world location of fictitious place names. One such example is the town of *Vigata* in the novels by the Italian writer Andrea Camilleri. *Vigata* is the town where the lead character, Inspector Montalbano, lives, and while the name is fictitious the writer admitted that the town is based on his home town of *Porto Empedocle*, near *Agrigento*, *Sicily*. In fact, in 2003, the town officially changed its name to *Porto Empedocle Vigata* (Marshall, 2013). One other form of film-induced tourism involves places that 'simulate or mimic film and television representations and allow tourists to reexperience those images vicariously' (Alderman et al., 2012, p. 213). These include places like *Universal Studios* and *Disneyland*.

This notwithstanding, seemingly ordinary toponyms can also draw tourists due to the cultural associations of the places they name, which makes the places attractions themselves. Light provides the example of *Penny Lane*, in *Liverpool*. This is a common name of British streets, but that specific one attracts many visitors due to its association with a legendary band, The Beatles ('Penny Lane' is the title of a hit by the group in the 1960s). Hence, this place invites fans of The Beatles on a 'secular pilgrimage' (Light, 2014, p. 146). It is even a part of the *Liverpool Beatles Trail*, regularly visited by tour buses of The Beatles fans. Another example of a street associated with The Beatles is *Abbey Road*, in *London*. *Abbey Road* was the title of the band's last album, and the road graced the album cover. Today, *Abbey Road* still receives numerous visitors, especially the pedestrian crossing featured on the album cover. These odonyms might sound undistinguished, uninspiring, and unexceptional – and, as Light noted, both streets are 'suburban, residential thoroughfares' (Light, 2014, p. 146). Yet, they are important destinations for fans of The Beatles.

Ordinary toponyms can serve as tourist destinations, since the tourists look to the names (i.e., the markers of a street) which are loaded with intangible heritage because of the important people or events that they are associated with. The examples of *Penny Lane* and *Abbey Road* show how toponyms and odonyms have been 'sacralised' through popular culture – they are celebrated and regarded

Figure 8.3 *Penny Lane, Liverpool*, with Paul McCartney's signature (in the white oval) (adapted from Roblespepe, 2018)

as revered because of their association with 'The Fab Four'. At the same time, place names can also be consumed as souvenirs (Light, 2014, p. 150). Toponyms might be so famous that their inscriptions and markers are highly valued, to the point that they are even stolen. In the case of *Penny Lane* in *Liverpool*, the sign was stolen so often that local authorities painted a replica of the street name on a wall to avoid theft (see Figure 8.3). A place name, as an object, may be considered as the representation of a prized possession and proof that the tourist did visit a place. Street signs are often produced in single or small quantities and, hence, they are not entirely a souvenir created for mass tourist consumption. Yet, the act of stealing place name signs provides the 'owner' with a type of symbolic and cultural capital, while attesting to his/her fandom (i.e., the person was prepared to go great lengths to get this original object).

## 8.8 Summary

In this chapter, we have described how the synchronic toponymist collects toponyms, categorises them, and searches for common naming patterns. We have also detailed how synchronic toponymy works and presented how it can be applied to the study of modern and contemporary places names. Synchronic toponymy can give a snapshot of the languages and cultures of a given area that motivate the naming processes and practices. This endeavour can be strengthened by the adoption of some of the methods of historical toponomastics (e.g., investigating changes in toponyms over time, using sources from historical geography, etc.), showing that it is indeed possible for diachronic and synchronic approaches to coexist harmoniously. The *Singapore* case study highlighted a number of ways in which toponymic research is conducted in a relatively young (historically and politically speaking) country. The study revealed the many ways colonial authorities and then the people that followed them into power used place naming as a political and a nation-building tool. This led to the discussion of the burgeoning discipline of critical toponymies, which aims to link place names to the socioeconomic and political factors that play a role in their formation, and of the concept of 'toponymic commodification'. In the latter, place names have increasingly been acquiring symbolic and economic capital.

In the next chapter, we will build on the issues explored in the above sections by looking in more detail at the relationship between toponymy and society.

# 9    Place Names and Society

## 9.1    Toponyms as a Social Construct

As 'abstractions of the place they refer to' (Helleland, 2012, p. 109), place names connote a mental cluster of intimate knowledge, expressions, and impressions. For an individual, place names function as social signals of belonging to a group. They are markers of solidarity because they denote shared memories and experiences among members of the group and, as such, the more names shared between individuals, the stronger the bond between them (Helleland, 2012, p. 96). Huldén (1994) put it very nicely.

Namn och plats hör ihop, oberoende av hur namnen etymologiskt sett är bildade. Namnet är en nyckel till minnen och upplevda intryck. Att känna samma namn är detsamma som att veta lite om varandra. Namnen är en social signal för samhörighet. Ju fler namn man delar med någon, dess större är samhörigheten. (p. 33)

[Name and place belong together, regardless of how the name is formed etymologically. The name is a key to memories and experiences. To be familiar with the same name is to know a little about each other. Names are social signals of solidarity. The more names one shares with others, the stronger the solidarity with them is]. (Translation in Helleland, 2012, p. 96)

Naturally, there are individual variations in the meanings attached to a place. However, as Basso (1990, p. 140) noted, 'the meanings of landscapes and acts of speech are personalised manifestations of a shared perspective on the human condition'. Despite the variations in mental representations, place names are ultimately grounded in the same shared underlying events and experiences, and the nature of the meanings remains consistent across individuals within a group (Basso, 1990, p. 140). The importance of place names to individuals and groups is best exemplified by the toponymic knowledge of the Sami, who are Indigenous people of northern *Fennoscandia* (the *Scandinavian Peninsula* including *Finland, Norway, Sweden, Karelia,* the *Kola Peninsula, Murmansk Oblast,* and parts of northern *Leningrad Oblast,* in *Russia*). Cogos, Roué, and Roturier (2017) documented how the cultural landscapes of the Sami reindeer herding communities of *Sireges,* in *Jokkmok,* northern *Sweden,* are transmitted and passed down through their oral traditions. The Sami have never used maps to facilitate their orientation in their environment. Instead, they have developed and relied on their own way of mapping, based on oral narratives and discourses built around place names. For the Sami, toponyms 'constitute "mental maps", drawing a landscape by telling a story within the series they form together' (Cogos et al., 2017, p. 45). A native inhabitant compared the Sami mapping system to having 'a GPS in there [his head]' (Cogos et al., 2017, p. 46).

Toponyms are also 'mirrors reflecting various scenarios and activities of the past' and serve as a connection to the past itself (Helleland, 2012, p. 102). They form an essential part of a group's cultural heritage, in that they tie the past – with its historical events and personalities – to the present. In many cases, such as that of the Sami, place names are orally transmitted, passed down from one generation to the next. For example, most of the Sami people learn them as children, when they accompany their older relatives during reindeer migrations. While many place names are related to physical features of the landscape, some toponyms are associated with myths or stories of the Indigenous culture (Cogos et al., 2017, p. 46), illustrating how place names are culturally rich and closely tied to the narratives of the past. For the same reason, there is a growing concern among the Sami that, with the increasing use of maps and technologies (see more on mapping technologies in Chapter 10), traditional toponymic knowledge will disappear, along with the narratives and stories that accompany them (Cogos et al., 2017).

In a way, place names also serve as social consensus across generations. This can be seen in the issue of standardised versus colloquial/dialectal toponymic forms. In *Norway*, when local people talk about places, they use the dialectal forms and not the standardised ones (Helleland, 2012, p. 103). As a result, the standardised written forms (on road signs or maps) of place names in *Norway* face a negative reception as they are seen as a departure from the 'correct' (dialectal) names (Helleland, 2012, p. 103). 'Correctness', here, is not determined by the standard decided by the government, but by the generations that came before. At the same time, this conflict highlights the importance of ensuring that the historical value of toponyms is not lost in the standardisation of place names.

Additionally, toponyms shed light on the changes in the cultural and historical landscape of a place. Saparov (2003, p. 179) claimed that place names are 'some of the most durable of national symbols', as they can 'outlive' changes in the cultural landscape. This was reflected in an analysis of the diachronic and synchronic development of *Singapore* urbanonymy, which revealed that 'the influences of all the cultures which have "sequentially" occupied *Singapore* from the past to the present can be seen in the history of its place names' (Cavallaro, Perono Cacciafoco, & Tan, 2019, p. 16).

For example, the etymology of *Fort Canning Hill*, a small hill located in southeast *Singapore*, reflects its origins as a Malay settlement, before it became a colonial outpost during British rule and, eventually, a landmark in the modern *Lion City*. Indeed, its earliest recorded name, in 1330, was (probably) *Ban Zu*, attested by the Chinese traveller Wang Dayuan (Wheatley, 1961). *Ban Zu* is thought to be a transliteration of the Malay word *pancur*, meaning 'spring', or 'stream' (Miksic, 2013, p. 177). Before the arrival of the British on the island, the place was known to the Malays as *Bukit Larangan* 'Forbidden Hill'. During the colonial rule, a residence was built on the hill for Sir Stamford Raffles (the British statesman credited for the founding of *Singapore*), and the place came to be known as the *Singapore Hill*. After a series of name changes, the hill's denomination was finally fixed as *Fort Canning Hill*, as a military fort was built on the hill in a bid to strengthen harbour defences (Cavallaro et al., 2019). What we see here are the historical and cultural changes in *Singapore* reflected in the naming process of this hill. This is a further confirmation of the fact that place names are a reflection of the historical events and changing landscape that occur at a specific location across time.

## 9.2    Toponymy and Indigeneity

The connection between place names and social groups is keenly felt among Indigenous communities. An 'Indigenous' person is, generally, defined as:

anyone who is born in a place; thus anyone who has not migrated to that place may be regarded as indigenous. Yet, within the political context of ongoing neo-colonial relations in places like North America, Australia, and New Zealand, indigeneity has a specific meaning intended to distinguish between colonized groups and colonizers or settlers. Thus, in this context, indigenous specifically means peoples with ancestral and spiritual ties to particular territories, whose ancestors lived in relation to that land prior to colonization and settlement by others. (Hunt, 2017, p. 1)

The relationship that Indigenous people have with their territories has sparked the interest of many scholars on 'indigeneity'. Hunt (2017, p. 2) stated that, while there are different definitions of indigeneity, all Indigenous peoples share a number of 'cultural markers'. That is, 'indigeneity' is generally rooted in living in a reciprocal relationship with the places that comprise Indigenous peoples' territories. Trigger and Martin (2016, p. 826) also reinforced this attachment to the land by saying that 'an autochthonous connectedness to place remains central to conceptualizations of indigeneity'. This is further supported by Heikkilä (2018, p. 1), because 'tension, naming and re-naming the landscape are deeply intertwined with the politics of identity and belonging'. This relationship has been recognised by many 'settler nations' who have granted civil and land rights to Indigenous minorities. This has usually gone together with the recognition of the past injustices against Indigenous people and efforts to revive or revitalise the languages and cultures of Indigenous groups. The relevance of this to toponymic studies is illustrated by Heikkilä (2018, p. 1), who noted that 'One aspect of indigenous cultural revival, particularly in the North American, Australasian and northern European contexts, is the documentation of indigenous ancestral place-names.'

This topic will be taken up in our discussion of colonialism and of the practices of renaming and decolonising toponyms later in this chapter.

### 9.3    Toponyms, Ideology, and Power Relationships

Place names are a means for groups to assert ownership, legitimise conquest, and flaunt control (Monmonier, 2007, p. 121). The more powerful claim the toponymy, while 'the losing side can make its own maps, designed to refresh memory, sustain dreams and reinforce resentment' (Monmonier, 2007, p. 121). After all, place names have symbolic, cultural, and historical significance to both individuals and groups.

At this point, it is important to note that toponyms are part of a much broader 'linguistic landscape' (hereafter LL). Ben-Rafael et al. (2016, p. 7) described this as the 'symbolic construction of public space'. More importantly, though, there is a distinction between top-down and bottom-up discourse. Top-down LL elements are 'used and exhibited by institutional agencies which in one way or another act under the control of local or central policies' (Ben-Rafael et al., 2016, p. 10). On the other hand, bottom-up LL elements are produced more autonomously by individual social actors (Ben-Rafael et al., 2016). As such, official place names, along with other official semiotic features, are part of the top-down discourse that reveals much about the power relations that exist among people in a community.

Place names are used as means to reinforce political ideologies as well, as we outlined in Chapters 7 and 8 (Rose-Redwood, 2016; Saparov, 2003). They have a symbolic role in representing abstract or concrete national, as well as local, sentiments and goals (Cohen & Kliot, 1992, p. 653). Saparov (2003) argued that place naming, as a top-down discourse, is an important vehicle for a state or nation's ideological system.

The conscious use of place-names by a state can be seen as an instrument to preserve the unity and uniqueness of the nation; to enforce in the national consciousness its moral right to inhabit a particular territory; to protect its land from the territorial claims of its neighbours; or to justify its own territorial claims. A recreated or artificially created place-name landscape is a symbolic part of national identity. (p. 180)

Other place naming practices that reflect the political ideologies and beliefs of a particular period of time can be seen in the naming patterns in *Israel*.

According to Cohen and Kliot (1992), Zionist symbolism featured prominently in place names in the contemporary country's pre-state period (i.e., before 1948). This was done through the use of ancient biblical or talmudic names and those of Zionist leaders or philanthropists when developing new toponyms. After 1948, ancient and new names played an important role in transforming the landscape of the new country. The recreation of an ancient Zionist home-land with biblical roots meant that there was very little transposing of names from places or cultures outside of *Israel*. Instead, ancient names and those of military heroes became toponymically widespread. After the Six-Day War of 1967, ancient biblical themes were the most used in place names (Cohen & Kliot, 1992, p. 668). Cohen and Kliot (1992) attributed this to the political goal to avoid antagonising the country's Arab neighbours, as affected settlements were densely populated by Palestinians. Interestingly, Monmonier (2007, p. 114) highlighted how this period coincided with a rise of abstract names that 'signify change and optimism'. For example, *Urim* ('lights') and *Alumim* ('youth') are *kibbutzim* 'collective communities' that have names associated with ideas of 'joy, stability, or confidence'.

Benvenisti (2000) pointed out that, due to the limited number of Hebrew names in ancient sources and the limited number of actual biblical places within *Israel*, there have been some creative naming practices. For example, he tells us (2000, p. 20) that the name of the *Kibbutz Grofit* came from the Arabic *Umm Jurfinat*, that the place name *Be'er Ada* was originally the Arabic *Bir Abu 'Auda*, and that the name of *Yerukham*, a town located near *Beer Sheva*, shows remnants of the Arabic name it replaced, *Rakhma*. He also reported some controversial naming of 'uncertain locations' (see also Monmonier, 2007, p. 115). For example, *Mount Hor*, the burial place of Aaron the High Priest (Moses' brother), is recognised to be near *Petra*, in *Edom*, which is now in *Jordan*. However, mapmakers placed it in *Israel*, in the middle of *Negev*. Nearly twenty years later, 'it became clear that it was impossible to persist in identifying this mountain as Mt. Hor (which had been a dubious exercise from the start), and it was re-named Mt. Zin. But in order to maintain the honor of the committee, the name Mount Hor was left in parentheses' (Benvenisti, 2000, p. 21).

In her study of the Moso (Na) people who live on the border between *Tibet*, *Yunnan*, and *Sichuan*, in *China*, Xu (2017) analysed several place names that refer, in pairs or triplets, to the same localities. The names were originally coined in Moso (Na) and Tibetan, and have been transliterated and reformu-lated, over time, in Mandarin Chinese, in order to transcribe them into the standard language of the country, and to make them official toponyms. This double-/triple-naming for the same villages is still attested and these inhabited centres are still called and/or indicated in official documents and landmarks by two or more different denominations.

One example of this is the village of *Wujiao* 屋脚, the headquarters of *Wujiao* Township. The name was transliterated, sometime between the *Ming* and *Qing* Dynasties, into *Renjiang* 仁江, from Tibetan. It was then converted again into *Wujiao*. Nowadays, both names, *Wujiao* and *Renjiang*, are attested in local signs and in plaques on public buildings and temples. They both share the same origin, being connected with the same place, but they naturally have different morphologies. The local Na people pronounce *Wujiao* as [ʁɯˈdzo˥]. A visual representation of the naming process is as follows.

| Original name | Currently used Chinese name | | Currently used Moso (Na) name |
|---|---|---|---|
| /ʁiˈdzo˥/ (IPA transcription of the old Tibetan language name) | → | *Renjiang* (Old Mandarin transliteration) ↓ *Wujiao* (current Mandarin transliteration) | → /ʁɯˈdzo˥/ (IPA transcription of the current Na name) |

Some Moso (Na) place names, already transliterated into Chinese (for the reasons explained above), have been wholly renamed in order to better match with the geopolitical setting of the mainland and now have an official Chinese name, an 'older' Mandarin Chinese transliteration, and their original Moso (Na) name, all attested at the same time.

One such example, among others, is *Qiansuo* 前所 *Village*. *Qiansuo* is a name connected with the denomination of a Chinese Army base during the *Ming* Dynasty (Zhang, 1999 (1773)). It was redesignated as *Lugu Lake Township* in 2020. The current Na endonym is [naˈ˥]. It also retains its original Moso (Na) name, /ʁwaˈʐu˥/, meaning 'village-warm', which is still attested, albeit only orally. This local name is based on a hydro-geo-morphological feature of the landscape of the village, that is, the presence of a natural hot spring in its territory. The names currently in use are listed below.

Current Mandarin transliteration        *Qiansuo*
Current Na endonym                      [naˈ˥]
Original Moso (Na) name of the village  /ʁwaˈʐu˥/

Another example of how the differences in power relations in a community affect toponyms can be seen in the case of the Tai people in southern *China*. The Tai people originated from the border areas between southern *China* and northern *Vietnam*. They speak a language known as Tai, which is characterised by basic agrarian vocabulary and naming traditions. Over the course of Chinese

history, successive waves of Han Chinese migration into Tai-speaking areas
have led to the Sinification of these territories, and this process has affected Tai
place names. Wang et al. (2006) reported that the Tai people often named their
villages based on landscape features like rice fields, rivers and their basins,
mountains, and so on. However, with the influx of Chinese speakers into these
areas, the Chinese-speaking officials have renamed many Tai toponyms by
transliterating them, in order to make them sound 'more Chinese', disregarding
the actual meaning of the names themselves. For example, in *Yunnan*, the
prefecture of *Sipsongpanna*, a toponym which means 'Twelve Thousand Rice
Fields' in Tai, was transliterated into Chinese as *Xishuangbanna* (a name
without any semantic content),[1] ignoring the original meaning in Tai and its
historical importance to the related minority group (Wang et al., 2006). The
original name was altered to better fit with the language spoken of the new more
powerful populace, even though the new name has no real meaning.

In this section, we have seen how in some cases power dynamics involved in
naming processes imply that a new and more powerful linguistic group asserts
its influence linguistically and subdues minority groups and their languages.


## 9.4    Colonialism

The fact that place names 'possess a symbolic power that can inflame as well as
claim' (Monmonier, 2007, p. 121) is also apparent in the context of colonialism. Naming becomes a main part of the colonisation process, because it
'appropriates, defines, captures the place in language' (Ashcroft, Griffiths, &
Tiffin, 2003, p. 392). The contested naming of *Mount Douglas*, a mountain
located in *Saanich, British Columbia, Canada*, provides us with an insight into
the complex and delicate issues of colonial renaming.

Since the colonisation of *Vancouver Island*, the mountain has been known as
*Mount Douglas* to the settler society. The Indigenous peoples of *W̱SÁNEĆ* and
*Lekwungen Territories*, however, knew it as *PKOLS*. In May 2013, members of
the Indigenous nations and their supporters gathered on the very mountain in
a bid to reclaim the name – *PKOLS*.

The mountain had been renamed *Mount Douglas* in the mid-nineteenth
century after James Douglas, who, as the governor for colonial settlements in
*Vancouver Island* and *British Columbia*, was responsible for the signing of the
Douglas Treaty. The treaty resulted in the expropriation of the lands from the
Indigenous population to the colonising people. Therefore, its existing name
was very much a constant reminder that 'the material and symbolic violence of
colonial dispossession continues to shape Indigenous-Settler relations in the

---

[1] This is also a good example of what has commonly happened in the Europeanisation of native
names around the world.

neocolonial present' (Rose-Redwood, 2016, p. 189). Yet, the ceremonial reclamation of *PKOLS* was not simply a response to past injustice. Instead, it rekindled Indigenous connections with the land and served as 'a declaration of cultural resurgence, and an assertion of the right to authorize the decolonization of "place" without seeking prior permission from the settler-colonial state' (Rose-Redwood, 2016, p. 191).

Often, place names are used to assert the asymmetrical power relations between colonisers and colonised. This was evident in early *Singapore*, where street names, like *Arab Street* in the *Arab Kampung*, were used by colonial administrators as markers, seeking to order and divide the colonised groups into 'recognisable containers', in order to prevent a united resistance against them (Yeoh, 1996, p. 300; cf. Chapter 8). British place names in early *Singapore* were starkly disconnected from their locality, suggesting that the settlers were seeking to 'escape the impress of the tropics and native culture and symbolically exist in British settings' (Yeoh, 1992, p. 316). For example, names such as *Devonshire Road* and *Chatsworth Road* were highly detached from their local environment, and instead 'conjured the idyllic imagery of the English countryside' (Yeoh, 1992, p. 315). The fact that these place names reflected the cultural assumption of the settler only highlights this aspect of imperialism that accompanies colonisation, one that reinforced the superior status of the colonisers.

Given the historical and cultural value of place names, the assertion of dominance by colonisers demonstrated their disregard of the history, or 'storyscapes' (Elsey, 2013), of the Indigenous populations (Rose-Redwood, 2016). According to Ndletyana (2012), the replacement of aboriginal toponyms by settlers is part of their 'civilising mission', in which colonisers sought to '[convert] natives into the image of settlers' (p. 90). The collective Indigenous history, culture, and identity denoted in place names were lost with the use of colonial toponyms. Thus, it is not surprising to see the Indigenous population's strong emotional response to being cast into insignificance, as in the renaming of *PKOLS* outlined above.

## 9.5    Renaming and Decolonising Toponyms

Toponymic inscriptions serve as means of public commemoration, and this gives rise to the question of who has official power to determine what should be remembered and forgotten (Rose-Redwood, Alderman, & Azaryahu, 2010, p. 463). Thus, the renaming and decolonising of place names is, ultimately, part of a much larger picture – the cultural politics of naming, which looks at 'how people seek to control, negotiate, and contest the naming process as they engage in wider struggles for legitimacy and visibility' (Rose-Redwood et al., 2010, p. 457).

In reclaiming the original name, for example, *PKOLS*, Indigenous peoples seek to reclaim part of their history, culture, and identity that vanished with the renaming process operated by the settlers. As such, place names also serve as a form of cultural recognition – or lack thereof – in the public sphere for social groups (Rose-Redwood, 2016). For minorities or the socially marginalised, toponyms offer the opportunity to challenge the existing political situation. The reinstallation of the *PKOLS* sign, initially installed during the ceremonial reclamation of the mountain and then temporarily removed over safety concerns by the *Saanich* government, signalled the latter's implicit recognition of the name (Rose-Redwood, 2016, p. 192). However, *Mount Douglas* remains the official denomination, while *PKOLS* is listed as the traditional name on the British Columbia Geographical Names website (Rose-Redwood, 2016, p. 192). Rose-Redwood (2016) sees this as having the opposite effect to an official acknowledgement. As such, the move by the government can be viewed as 'recognising the PKOLS yet relegating it to the realm of history' (p. 191).

The reclaiming of *PKOLS* is just one of many examples of 'toponymic resistance'. While, in this case, the Indigenous population had taken matters into their own hands, there are other instances in which marginalised groups have (successfully) utilised formal, political means to challenge existing names. Ethnic minorities in the *United States*, such as African Americans, have been actively adopting place naming as a 'political strategy for addressing their exclusion and misrepresentation within traditional, white-dominated constructions of heritage' (Rose-Redwood et al., 2010, pp. 463–4). One such example was the attempt in *Texas* to rename the ethnically offensive *Negrohead Lake* to *Lake Henry Doyle*. The original name of the body of water used to be *Nigger Lake*, but this was changed in 1962. Naming decisions in the *United States* are made by the US Board on Geographic Names, which recently rejected the new name *Lake Henry Doyle* because, in the opinion of the board members, there was not enough community or local involvement in the renaming process. Henry Doyle was the first African American to apply to the temporary Law School for Blacks established by the Texas State University for Negroes, which is now known as Texas Southern University. This happened at a time when he was not allowed to enter the classroom with his White peers. Another example was the push by the Native Americans in *Phoenix, Arizona*, for the renaming of *Squaw Peak*, which was deemed as obscene, as well as ethnically derogatory (Monmonier, 2007, p. 2). The place was eventually renamed *Piestewa Peak*, in honour of the first Native American female soldier to die in combat during the *Iraq* War in 2003 (Monmonier, 2007, p. 4). To the Native Americans, it was a move that recognised their link to the land and their historical importance.

This is also an example of how nations around the world have been addressing place names that contain ethnically offensive terms. For example, the Australian state of *Queensland*, in 2017, deleted ten ethnically loaded names from its register. The toponyms included *Niggers Bounce, Mount Nigger, Nigger Head*, and seven places named *Nigger Creek* (RTÉ, 2021).

Toponyms that commemorate individuals with an unsavoury past have also come under close scrutiny. In 2020, a mountain range in *Western Australia, The King Leopold Ranges*, was renamed *The Wunaamin Miliwundi Ranges*. The new name featured the traditional ethnonyms of the *Ngarinyin* (*Wunaamin*) and *Bunuba* (*Miliwundi*) aboriginal peoples. The landmark had originally been named, in 1879, after the Belgian King Leopold II, who was responsible for the death of millions of people in what is now the *Democratic Republic of the Congo*. The minister for aboriginal affairs in *Western Australia*, Ben Wyatt, said at the time, 'The traditional owners of the region have always known the ranges by their own name, so it's momentous to finally remove reference to King Leopold II and formalise the name' (Australian Associated Press, 2020).

That being said, not every Indigenous community shares the same desire to restore Indigenous memory through renaming. Ndletyana (2012) explained that this is largely influenced by how an Indigenous population relates to colonial memory, which in the example he provided accounts for the unevenness in the renaming process across the nine provinces of post-apartheid *South Africa*. For most natives, colonial toponyms were an unavoidable reminder of subjugation and the times they had lived through. However, the extent to which they 'remained a permanent object of local enmity' was dependent on the nature of colonial policy towards the natives – whether they adopted an assimilationist approach or reinforced settler-native separation and hostility (Rose-Redwood, 2016, p. 98).

The former led to some extent of acculturation and identification, with natives eventually '[embracing] the culture and the authority it symbolises' (Ndletyana, 2012, p. 99). This was the case in *Eastern Cape*, where the British were able to justify their conquest as part of their civilising mission. As a result, even though the province had numerous Eurocentric town names, such as *Queenstown, King Williams Town*, and *Port Elizabeth*, none of them were renamed (Ndletyana, 2012, p. 93). Instead, the province concentrated its resources on orthographic corrections, such as *Bisho* to *Bhisho* and *Umtata* to *Umthatha* (Ndletyana, 2012, p. 93).

While the assimilationist approach adopted in British colonial states ultimately 'softened the alien, invasive symbolism' of colonial toponymy, the settler-native relationship in *Boer Republics* in the northern provinces was characterised by hostility (Ndletyana, 2012, p. 98). This only 'accentuated the strangeness and invasiveness of colonial memory', motivating a stronger desire and urgency to replace colonial toponyms (Ndletyana, 2012, p. 99). For example, *Mpumalanga*, a province in eastern *South Africa*, renamed ten major towns at once, which included renaming *Ellisrus* to *Lephalale* and *Warmbaths* to *Bela-bela* (Ndletyana, 2012, pp. 92, 101).

In provinces such as *Western Cape*, the absence of local agency led to indifference towards the renaming of local toponyms with colonial names. This was because the surviving Khoe-San community was not only small, but also somewhat detached from the unpleasant experiences of their ancestors (Ndletyana, 2012). Therefore, what Ndletyana (2012, p. 96) summarised as the 'effect of colonial symbolism on the collective psyche of the indigenous populace' plays a significant role in local agency and attitudes towards renaming.

The position taken by the *Saanich* government in the naming of *PKOLS* is only reflective of a much broader message – that the power to name, ultimately, is concentrated in the hands of the settler-colonial state, thereby reaffirming its influence in neocolonial societies. This ideology is also reinforced by the ubiquitous presence of colonial odonyms in the spaces of everyday life, as is the case of the *Greater Victoria Region* of *British Columbia* (Rose-Redwood, 2016, p. 194). The result is the '[normalisation] of colonial imaginary as the taken-for-granted order of the discursive universe through which neocolonial modes of being-in-the-world are experienced' (Rose-Redwood, 2016, p. 194).

Needless to say, the postcolonial process of renaming is largely influenced by political forces. It appears that the motivation to replace colonial toponyms is very much dependent on a government's political stance, which, by extension, determines the pace and extent of the renaming. This was a major factor in accounting for the unevenness in the renaming process in *South Africa* (Ndletyana, 2012).

Indeed, most provinces in *South Africa* had initially mirrored, to varying degrees, the cautious approach adopted by Nelson Mandela's inaugural post-apartheid administration in toponymic renaming. This was because Mandela was wary that replacing apartheid toponyms associated with names of personalities involved in the liberation struggle would undermine reconciliatory efforts (Ndletyana, 2012, p. 92). On the other hand, the extent and pace of renaming picked up once Thabo Mbeki took office in the early 2000s. Unlike Mandela, Mbeki pressed for changes in colonial place names. Not only did he express 'bewilderment at the persistence of colonial toponymy', but he was also '[disgusted] at the continuing celebration of colonial personalities that wrought agony on the indigenous population', while those who fought for liberation were not recognised (Ndletyana, 2012, p. 93).

While it appears that colonial toponyms ought to be renamed, whether as part of conciliatory efforts or as means to re-establish previously disregarded 'storyscapes', there are those that argue against renaming. Opponents see renaming as historical erasure, equating the removal of place names honouring historical events or personages of settler colonialism to denying their very place in history, and that regardless of the injustice towards the Indigenous people, their history, culture, and identity should be recognised and celebrated (Rose-Redwood, 2016).

## 9.6    The Cultural Politics of Naming

The cultural politics of naming remain a contested social phenomenon, which Newton (2016) argues requires a closer look at the 'intersection between corporate profit, government policy and meaning-based issues of belonging' (p. 114). The rejection of the aboriginal name *Mullawallah* for a suburb located in west *Ballarat, Victoria, Australia*, in December 2014 sheds light on the influence of such contextual conditions on place naming (or renaming).

In a time where 'belonging and national [had] been sought through acknowledging, and reaching out towards, Indigenous people and culture', the proposed name *Mullawallah* could have been viewed as an official reconciliation effort to recognise the Indigenous *Wadawurrung* people that had become 'invisible' as a result of historical silences and effacements (Newton, 2016, pp. 119–22). However, the perceptions at the time were that the Indigenous population had disappeared and that there were no legally recognised *Wadawurrung* descendants. These perceptions, along with a limited knowledge of the name *Mullawallah*, 'contributed to wiping Indigeneity from the landscape and cultural worldview' (Newton, 2016, p. 127). Therefore, it was easy for a few individuals who strongly opposed the renaming to galvanise support with inaccurate reasons, such as *Mullawallah*'s difficult pronunciation and spelling, as well as how it would be easily confused by emergency services – all of which are untrue (Newton, 2016, p. 127). Furthermore, the democratisation of place naming procedures meant that the minority *Wadawurrung* had little real power in reclaiming what had once belonged to them.

This Australian example comes while the country as a whole has been embracing the use and promotion of Indigenous place names. Indeed, since the 1990s, there has been a practice of promoting and reinstating Indigenous place names in *Australia*. In fact, it is now very common to pay respect to the Aboriginal and Torres Strait Islander people and cultures by recognising the Traditional Owners of the land, and there are two ways to formally recognise the Traditional Owners (NIAA, n.d.).

(1) A 'Welcome to Country'. This welcome can only be given by the Traditional Owners of the land where the ceremony takes place. The format of this welcome depends on who is giving it.

(2) An 'Acknowledgement of Country'. This 'acknowledgement' can be done by anyone. It does not have to be by an Indigenous person. This is usually chosen when there are no Indigenous people present at the event. In turn, there are two types of acknowledgements (NIAA, n.d.).

   i General: 'I begin today by acknowledging the Traditional Custodians of the land on which we <gather/meet> today, and pay my respects to their Elders past and present. I extend that respect to Aboriginal and Torres Strait Islander peoples here today'.

ii Specific: 'I begin today by acknowledging the <insert name of people here (e.g., *Ngunnawal*)> people, Traditional Custodians of the land on which we <gather/meet> today, and pay my respects to their Elders past and present. I extend that respect to Aboriginal and Torres Strait Islander peoples here today'.

In the case of *Melbourne, Australia*, which is recognised as belonging to the *Kulin Nation*, the Acknowledgement of Country would be: 'I begin today by acknowledging the *Kulin Nations* people, Traditional Custodians of the land on which we gather today, and pay my respects to their Elders past and present. I extend that respect to Aboriginal and Torres Strait Islander peoples here today'.

In fact, Australians now have the option of including the 'Traditional place name (if known)' when they mail a parcel. Australia Post stated that 'To mark NAIDOC [National Aborigines and Islanders Day Observance Committee] Week in November 2020, Australia Post updated the addressing guidelines to include Traditional Place names. Australia Post is also updating 22 of its satchels' labels to include Acknowledgement of Country and a dedicated Traditional Place name field in the address panel' (Australia Post, 2021).

As Tent (2019) stated, 'Reinstating an Indigenous placename amounts to reinstating a way of looking at the land, together with a set of associated responsibilities, and is may only be really possible in regions where Aboriginal people hold title or have a strong presence' (p. 10). He also pointed out that assigning names to places that are yet unnamed is neither difficult nor controversial. The same can be said about giving new names or reinstating Indigenous names in remote areas. However, in territories that have been settled by Europeans for a long time, 'the reinstatement of an Indigenous name can be highly contentious' (Tent, 2019, p. 10).

The strategy adopted in *Australia* for reinstating Indigenous toponyms has been to use dual designations for such places. This calls for the reinstating of an Indigenous denomination alongside an 'introduced' (Tent, 2019, p. 10) one. When the local appellation is first restored, the two toponyms are gazetted, with the introduced name first, followed by the Indigenous name. After some time, the order of the names is switched. A very famous example of this is the toponym *Ayers Rock* that was renamed *Uluru* in 1993. In that year, the two denominations were gazetted as *Ayers Rock/Uluru*. In 2002, the doublet was gazetted as *Uluru/Ayers Rock*. This also gave the opportunity for the introduced name to be dropped altogether. Another example is represented by *Mount Olga*, which, in the same year *Uluru* was reinstated, had its Indigenous name, *Kata Tjuta*, announced. The place was then known as *Mount Olga/Kata Tjuta*. Later, in 2002, the place was gazetted as *Kata Tjuta/Mount Olga*. Generally, though, only one name is used in non-official circumstances, for example, after nearly thirty years, most people refer to the above-mentioned places as *Uluru* and *Kata Tjuta*, respectively (Tent, 2019, p. 10).

The reinstating of Indigenous toponyms is not always simple. Tent (2019) recounted how, in 2008, the government of *Victoria, Australia*, renamed *Mount Niggerhead*, a mountain in the *Alpine National Park*, as *The Jaithmathangs*. The renaming was aimed at deleting a derogatory name and at promoting Indigenous heritage and culture. The chosen denomination is the ethnonym of an Indigenous group, purportedly from the area. Unfortunately, another aboriginal group, the *Dhudhuroa* people, claim that the mountain is not in the territory of the *Jaithmathangs*, but in their own country. For the *Dhudhuroa*, the new name is as distasteful as *Mount Niggerhead*. As Gary Murray, co-chair of the Dhudhuroa Native Title Group, put it bluntly, 'It's a bit like re-naming *Australia* as *England*. The name is linguistically and culturally inappropriate' (Reuters, 2008).

The rejection of the above-mentioned *Mullawallah* was also fuelled by the 'contemporary corporate culture of commercial naming' (Newton, 2016, p. 122). In proposing the concept of 'toponymic dependence', Kostanski (2011) pointed out that 'place branding is depended on for its ability to portray the unique characteristics of a place' (p. 18), which would ultimately aid in promoting tourism and supporting the economy. In some instances, Indigenous toponyms are thought to help in branding an area as a unique travel experience (Kostanski, 2011, p. 18). Scholars (see Hercus & Simpson, 2002) agree on the fact that when Indigenous names are brought into the public domain, this will give 'public recognition of the names, and thus of prior occupation of the country by Aboriginal and *Torres Strait* Islander peoples. But once the names are in this public domain, they become a commodity. They can be used, say, in business names, without permission being granted by the Indigenous owners of the placenames' (Tent, 2019, p. 10).

In the case of *Mullawallah*, however, it was suggested that the use of the aboriginal name would decrease property values, and that the name did not suit the environment and failed to match with surrounding street names (Newton, 2016, p. 125). This fits into the discussion on the commodification of place names in Chapter 8. Commercial developers have often opted for marketable 'high status' English names that allude to an English landscape, giving, for example, new retirement villages names such as *Riverside Gardens* and *Windsor Country Village* (Newton, 2016, p. 122). As such, the democratisation of place naming and the influence of commercial developers have played a major role in the rejection of *Mullawallah*. The suburb in question was eventually named *Winter Valley*. The name *Mullawallah* was subsequently given to a wetland reserve outside of *Ballarat*.

## 9.7    Other Toponymic Changes

Sweeping changes in place names reflect 'ideological upheavals and are often expressions of revolutionary values' (Cohen & Kliot, 1992, p. 653). Following major power shifts, toponymic purges are a strategy adopted by new regimes to alter once official narratives and remove traces of past governments. In post-revolutionary administrations, the purpose of creating new state symbols is to 'at once remove evidence of the deposed regime and to establish an identity for the usurper' (Lewis, 1982, p. 99).

A discussion inherent in this topic was presented in Chapter 7, where we analysed the contemporary odonymy of *Bucharest*. Ideological renaming was also evident in the toponymic changes undertaken by the *Union of Soviet Socialist Republics* (*USSR*), which Saparov (2003) summarised as 'directly related to the ideological, political and national policy of the authorities' (p. 181). In his study of Soviet Armenian toponymy, Saparov (2003, p. 186) revealed that place naming in the *Armenian Soviet Socialist Republic* reflected the internal political processes of the *USSR*. Place names that were either religious in nature or associated with feudal landowners were deemed unacceptable and formed a large part of early renamings (Saparov, 2003). Christian and Muslim place names, like *Kilisakend* (Turkish for 'church') and *Hojakend* (which is associated with a pilgrimage to *Mecca*), were replaced with *Srashen* and *Kuzikend* respectively, while toponyms that reflected feudal relationships, such as *Hussein Kuli Agalu* and *Siltan Ali Kishlag*, were renamed as *Narimanlu* and *Janahmed*, respectively (Saparov, 2003, p. 186).

A number of toponyms fell under what Saparov (2003) categorised as 'socialist place names', which were, by the Soviet ideological formula, 'national by form, socialist by content' (Saparov, 2003, p. 195). These consisted of toponyms that were names of local communists, as well as other terms important to the communist regime (Saparov, 2003). For instance, a village in *Azerbaijan* was named *Bir May* '1 May', commemorating the Soviet Labour Day (Saparov, 2003, p. 196). Therefore, place naming was used as a tool to create a national cultural landscape that aligned with the totalitarian Communist regime. It is interesting to note that the village *Bir May* was renamed *Bahrāmtepe* in 1992, after the dissolution of the *USSR*. *Bahrāmtepe* is a relatively transparent place name, meaning 'Bahrām's Hill'. *Tepe* comes from Ottoman Turkish *tepe*, تپه, 'crown of the head', 'peak', 'highest point', 'hill', from Proto-Turkic *\*tepü*, *\*töpü*, 'hill', 'top'. *Bahrām* is the name of a god of war (or of military victory), Armenian *Vahagn*, Proto-Ind-Iranian *Wr̥tragʰnás*, from *\*wr̥trás*, 'shield', but also 'obstacle', *\*gʰan-*, 'to slay', *\*-ás* (< Proto-Indo-European *\*wer-*), 'to cover', and *\*gʷʰen-*, 'to strike', 'to slay'. The proper noun is generally translated as 'The Destroyer of Obstacles'. *Bahrām* is among the main gods in the Zoroastrian pantheon of *yazatas* ('entities which are worthy of worship') (Justi, 1895).

Renaming can be a way of making new claims over a territory, as in the case of the island of *Cyprus*. Greek and Turkish Cypriots were ethnic rivals that occupied opposite sides of the *Green Line*, a demilitarised buffer zone patrolled by the United Nations. The de facto partition occurred after the ceasefire between Greek and Turkish forces in 1974, with Greek Cypriots moving south of the *Green Line* and Turkish Cypriots moving north. In a bid to claim *Northern Cyprus* as the (self-declared) *Turkish Republic of Northern Cyprus*, Turkish Cypriots begun what politicians in the south called 'cultural genocide' (Monmonier, 2007, p. 108). This involved a series of 'cultural assaults' that sought to remove Greek elements of the pre-1974 cultural landscape, which included replacing all Greek place names with Turkish ones (Monmonier, 2007). Ladbury and King (1988, p. 364) gave a detailed account of the renaming process. They stated that the names fall into three categories. First, those toponyms that were already 'Turkish-rooted names' were not changed but, in some cases, the Turkish spelling was adopted (e.g., *Geunyeli* became *Gönyely*). Second, in villages that traditionally had two names, a Greek and a Turkish one, the Turkish denomination was kept or the Greek name was changed so that it sounded Turkish, for example, the Greek name *Lapithos* became *Lapta*. Third, the villages that used to have only Greek denominations received brand-new Turkish names. For example, the town that went by the Greek name of *Morphou* was known to the Turkish Cypriots as *Omorfo* before 1974. After 1974, however, it was renamed to *Güzelyürt*, meaning 'beautiful home'. The village of *Bellapais*, whose name came from the Italian *Belpaese* (i.e., *bel paese* 'beautiful village', or 'beautiful country'), was 'phonetically rendered into the nearest meaningful Turkish word that meant something', *Beylerbeye*, meaning 'lord of men' (Ladbury & King, 1988, p. 364). The Turkish Cypriots were responsible for what Kadmon (2004) deemed as the 'most extreme form of verbal toponymic warfare' (p. 85).

*Berlin*'s streets, along with its parks and squares, from the early nineteenth century have been peppered with commemorative names (Azaryahu, 2011). Odonyms which were named from 1813 to 1920 mainly commemorated *Prussia*'s military achievements and members of the House of *Hohenzollern*. Among them are the *Belle-Alliance-Platz* in *Kreuzberg*, which commemorated the Prussian victories in the battle of *Waterloo, Yorkstraße, Gneisenaustraße, Blücherstraße*, and also in *Kreuzberg*. There were also names remembering the Prussian heroes of the War of Liberation (1813). Additionally, there were many streets named *Kaiser-Wilhelm-Straße* and *Auguste-Viktoria-Straße* that honoured the king and queen of *Prussia*. Shortly after the end of the German Empire in 1918, and the creation of the *Weimar* Republic, many streets and squares named after monarchical figures were changed to names that represented the republic, for example, *Königsplatz* 'King's Square' was renamed *Platz der Republik*, and *Budapesterstraße* (a name referring to the times of the Austro-Hungarian Empire) was replaced by *Frieddrich-Ebert-Straße* (now *Ebertstraße*) after the name of the republic's first president. Following the republic, in 1933 *Germany* was ruled by the Nazis, who proceeded to remove all names representing republican values and replaced them with names of important figures of the Third Reich. *Reichskanzlerplatz* became *Adolf-Hitler-Platz*, *Friedrich-Ebert-Straße* made way to *Hermann-Göring-Straße*, and *Bülowplatz* was renamed after the Nazi Horst Wessel, becoming *Horst-Wessel-Platz*. Post-1945 *Berlin* saw a two-year-long, large-scale toponymic renaming (both officially by the competent *Magistrat*, and unofficially by the local boroughs) of not only Nazi street names, but also of those that represented the 'dynastic' *Germany*. Although the initial proposal officially presented a list of over 1,000 streets to be renamed, in 1947 only 151 streets received new designations, due to the high cost involved in replacing street signs.

Over time, the streets of *Paris* also saw numerous renamings, many of them going back and forth between the old and new names, in line with the changes of governments and their ideology (Ferguson, 1988). *Place de la Concorde* was, originally, *Place Louis XV* in 1755, *Place de la Revolution* during the Revolution, *Place de la Concorde* in 1795, and then again *Place Louis XV* in 1814, then *Place Louis XVI*, until finally reverting to *Place de la Concorde* in 1830. The same goes for streets commemorating events. Odonyms bearing references to victories in the Napoleonic Wars were replaced after the Napoleonic era. For example, *Austerlitz* became *Hôpital* in 1815, after the fall of Napoleon, but later was reinstated during the July Monarchy (i.e., under the 1830–48 reign of Louis-Philippe, brought about by a revolution that started in July 1830). During the Second Empire (1852–70), names bearing references to Napoleonic victories were present in the public sphere again. By the time the Third Republic (1870–1940) had completed a renaming of the street names, *Napoléon* made way for *Opéra*, and *Prince-Eugène* for *Voltaire*. Haussmann's renovation of *Paris* during the Second Empire also changed significantly the odonymic landscape at the time. His project involved the demolition of medieval neighbourhoods and the annexation of the immediate suburbs, the removal of old and narrow streets, and the making of around 450 new, wider streets, in addition to numerous newly constructed parks and squares. Along with this restructuring of the city, medieval streets with names such as *Rue l'Arche-Marion*, *Rue de Chevalier-le-Guet*, *Rue des Mauvaises-Paroles*, and *Rue Tirechamp* disappeared (Maneglier, 1990, p. 28), making way for newer, wider streets named after writers, artists, scholars, and doctors who, as Ferguson (1988) puts it, 'bourgeoisify' the urban space (p. 387).

## 9.8    Toponymic Nicknames

So far in this volume, we have discussed how places have acquired their names and how these names are formalised by acts of government or by being transcribed on a map (see Chapter 10). However, as Cassidy, (1977, p. 19) asked: 'What about the hundreds of others [place names] which live unrecorded – the very local labels that people apply half humorously but nevertheless function as names?' In Chapters 7 and 8, we saw how during the colonial period in *Singapore* locals used their own vernacular names for places and streets rather than referring to them by their official denominations. What this shows is that the connection between place names and society is very clear in how places are referred to informally by speakers, as opposed to using their official names. Duckert (1973, p. 153) accurately stated that nicknames are essentially a social construct and that 'Nicknames are neither coined nor used by the indifferent; whether they are affectionate or derogatory or merely convenient, their making and application speak involvement.' This means that place nicknames can offer us a better 'insight into the humour, spirit, lifestyle, temper, and attitudes of a locality' than any survey ever could (Duckert, 1973, p. 153).

Nicknames for places can be classified into two main categories. One is represented by the names given by institutions or organisations. These can include tourist offices or advertising companies. These bodies create very artificial or, as Duckert (1973, p. 154) put it, 'synthetic or store bought' denominations. Examples of this type can be seen on the number plates of cars, such as, from *Australia, Canberra – The Heart of the Nation*, or *Victoria – The Education State*, and, from the *USA, Nevada – the Silver State*, or *Minnesota – Land of 10,000 Lakes*. These nicknames are often only used in their written forms on brochures or other promotional materials and are not popular with the locals. Many of these nicknames change as the advertising campaigns are reviewed. The second category includes those nicknames that were created 'spontaneously' (Duckert, 1973, p. 155) and express the feelings that the locals have for the places. These feelings could be, among others, affection, humour, anger, disgust, and frustration.

A number of researchers have identified various patterns in place nicknaming. The *Australian National Dictionary* (https://australiannationaldictionary .com.au/) identified the following patterns of the process of toponymic nicknaming.

1. Abbreviation. This is what Duckert (1973) calls 'shortening'. For example, *Frisco* for *San Francisco*, *Melbs* for *Melbourne*, and *The Alice* for *Alice Springs*. In *Australia*, abbreviations are commonly seen alongside the insertion of the ending *-y* or *-ie*, as in *Brissy/Brissie/Brizzy*, for *Brisbane*.
2. Tongue-in-cheek. Duckert calls this 'affectionate deprecation'. This usually involves a play in the pronunciation of a name or a play of words from the name itself: *Charlie's Trousers* from *Charters Towers* and *Swinging Pig* from *Rockingham*.
3. Other patterns. This is a general category, very similar to what Duckert calls 'Puns to Pollution'. The *Australian National Dictionary* reports the addition of 'town' in nicknames, as in *A-town* for *Adelaide* or *P-town* for *Perth*, as well as the addition of *-ers*, as in *Sydders* for *Sydney*, and the use of *-bong*

instead of *-ong*, as in *Dandebong* for *Dandenong* (*Melbourne*) and *Getabong* for *Ettalong*.

Duckert's (1973) list also includes the following.

4. *Shibboleths.*[2] These are certain names of places that are only known to locals or to those people that have been accepted in a particular community. Just like a linguistic *shibboleth*, the knowledge of these names and the correct pronunciation distinguish members of the local community from outsiders.

5. Determined deprecation. These nicknames are usually created by outsiders or by people who do not feel or want to be part of a community. For example, *Grahamstown*, in *South Africa*, is called *Grimtown* by the boarding school residents.

6. Promotional coinages and occupation names. These include the 'artificial' nicknames mentioned above.

7. Points of the compass. The four points of the compass are common references around the world. Worldwide, we see that people either come from the *East*, which includes most of *Asia*, or the *West*. Within countries, the *North–South* divide is also very commonplace, usually with different connotations, such as the 'poor *South*' and the 'rich *North*' in *Italy*. We see these equivalences played out in cities as well, where the *North Side* can be the expensive part of a town (e.g., in *Chicago* and *Sydney*).

8. Ethnic and economic names. Ethic nicknames are often due to the concentration of a particular population group in an area. Famous examples of these are the many instances of *Little Italy* around the world. The contrast here is with *Chinatown*, which is normally reflected in the official maps, while *Little Italy* usually is not, unless it is recorded in a tourist brochure. For many years, a part of *Richmond, Melbourne*, was referred to by locals as *Little Saigon*. Nicknames like *The Wrong Side of the River* or *Shanty Town* refer to the poorer side of a city.

9. *Ruralia*. Rural areas are often named after the main crop that is grown there. Hence, for example, we have a number of places around the world known as *Wheat Belt*.

Cassidy (1977, p. 20) collected a large number of place nicknames from the *USA*. He found that the addition of *-town* or *-ville* was the most common feature of the nicknames he collected. These two elements were added to denominations referring to people's names, both given names (*Jimtown*) and surnames (*Brownstown, Holtville*). This notwithstanding, he found that *-ville* was more commonly added to surnames and not to given names, and coined after the type

---

[2] A *shibboleth* (from the Hebrew word *shibbólet*, שִׁבֹּלֶת, indicating the part of a plant containing grain, generally the head of a stalk of wheat or rye) is a custom, tradition, habit, or belief that distinguishes a particular class or group of people from others. This can also be the way locals speak, exemplified by their unique pronunciation.

Table 9.1 *Examples of nicknames of cities*

| Chicago, USA | **Windy City** |
|---|---|
| Rome, Italy | The Eternal City, City of the Seven Hills |
| Paris, France | The City of Light, The City of Love |
| Lima, Peru | The City of Kings |
| Beijing, China | The Forbidden City |
| London, UK | The Big Smoke (no longer current) |
| Cape Town, South Africa | The Mother City |
| Jerusalem, Israel | The Holy City |
| Vienna, Austria | The Imperial City, The City of Dreams, The City of Music |
| Singapore | The Lion City |
| Kolkata, India | The City of Palaces, The City of Love, The City of Joy |
| Edinburgh, UK | Auld Reekie 'Old Smoky' |

of people who lived in a specific place and their occupations (*Cheesemakers Town, Dutchtown, Indianville*). These toponyms also referred to animals (*Dogtown, Turkeyville*), plants (*Potato Town, Pickleville*), and physical-geographical features (*Stony Town, Windyville*). Moreover, Cassidy (1977, p. 20) came up with a large set that he categorised as 'others', for example, *Stump Town, Bone Town, Gun Town, Muttonville*. Cassidy stressed on the fact that, in most cases, the nicknames in this category were derogatory.

While place nicknames are coined by local people, some apply to large areas, such as cities, states, or even countries, and many become well known around the world. For instance, *The Big Apple* is easily recognisable as referring to *New York*. Many have more than one nickname. Some examples are outlined in Tables 9.1–9.3.

Indeed, toponymic nicknames have many different forms, and there are many different reasons for their creation. What they all share is a strong social and emotional connection with the places, and they reflect the feelings of those that conceived them.

## 9.9     Summary

In this chapter, we have shown how place names are, by nature, social constructs. Toponyms show the attachment that people have with the land they live in. From prehistoric times, people needed to name places in order to survive and to orientate around them, be it to avoid dangerous territories or to know where drinking water and edible plants could be found. This intrinsic link to the land can still be seen among Indigenous populations around the world and, in postcolonial times, this has sparked an interest in indigeneity, particularly in the so-called 'settler countries'. Colonialists used the renaming of places as a way

Table 9.2 *Examples of nicknames of states*

| | |
|---|---|
| *Alaska, USA* | *The Last Frontier* |
| *Arizona, USA* | *The Grand Canyon State* |
| *Florida, USA* | *The Sunshine State* |
| *Texas, USA* | *The Lone Star State* |
| *Georgia, USA* | *The Peach State* |
| *Hawaii, USA* | *The Aloha State* |
| *Queensland, Australia* | *The Sunshine State, The Smart State* |
| *New South Wales, Australia* | *The Premier State, The First State* |
| *Western Australia, Australia* | *The Golden State, The Real Thing, The State of Excitement, The Wildflower State* |
| *Tasmania, Australia* | *The Apple Isle, The Holiday Isle, The Natural State* |
| *Himachal Pradesh, India* | *The State of All Seasons, The Fruit Bowl of India, The Apple State, The Mountain State* |
| *Kerala, India* | *The Spice Garden of India, God's Own Country* |

Table 9.3 *Examples of nicknames of countries*

| | |
|---|---|
| *Iceland* | *The Land of Fire and Ice* |
| *Ireland* | *The Emerald Isle, The Green Island* |
| *Italy* | *The Boot* |
| *USA* | *Uncle Sam* |
| *Paraguay* | *The Island Surrounded by Land* |
| *Bhutan* | *Land of the Thunder Dragon* |
| *Philippines* | *The Pearl of the Orient Seas* |
| *Australia* | *Land Down Under, Oz* |
| *Madagascar* | *The Red Island* |
| *North Korea* | *The Hermit Kingdom* |

of taking possession of the newly colonised lands and, in many cases, we have seen efforts to reclaim these names by Indigenous groups. The naming and renaming practices are also 'windows' on the relationships between groups, where those with more power are able to claim more places as their own. Within these sociopolitical imbalances, people demonstrate creative ways of subverting those in authority by ignoring the official toponyms and using unofficial and vernacular names for places or by creating nicknames for them.

# 10    Toponymy and Cartography

## 10.1    What Is Cartography?

As we are writing this chapter, we are thinking of the recent football news that caught our attention. The news reported *Russia*'s uproar over *Ukraine*'s football jersey, which was emblazoned with a map of *Ukraine*. What was significant about this map was that it included the Russian-annexed *Crimea*. *Russia* controversially took *Crimea* from *Ukraine* in 2014 and currently considers it part of its territory. This is something that *Ukraine* and the rest of the world reject. According to one Russian MP, the Ukrainian move amounted to a 'political provocation'. Another MP called the shirt 'totally inappropriate' and asked the Union of European Football Associations (UEFA) to stop *Ukraine* from using it (BBC, 2021).

Beyond the umbrage taken by *Moscow*, this episode demonstrates the power of maps not only to identify and locate places, but also how maps and their content can be used as tools by political and administrative entities to stake their claims over a particular piece of land (see also Chapters 7, 8, and 10). *Ukraine*'s act of outlining a map that included a contested territory, before labelling the entire borders as belonging to *Ukraine*, was an effort to assert its control (albeit a symbolic one) over the *Crimean Peninsula* occupied by the Russians. Therefore, as mentioned, this episode is emblematic in illustrating how maps can be made and used politically, and therefore provides a glimpse into one of the most controversial aspects of the world of cartography.

The International Cartographic Association (ICA), the most authoritative organisation in the discipline, defines cartography as 'the discipline dealing with the art, science, and technology of making and using maps'. The body also defines a map as 'a symbolised representation of geographical reality, representing selected features or characteristics, resulting from the creative effort of its author's execution of choices, and is designed for use when spatial relationships are of primary relevance' (ICA, 2021).

It is worth noting that the ICA's definitions of the cartographic discipline and maps in general have shifted over time. In 1995, the ICA defined a map as a 'symbolised image of geographical reality' (ICA, 2021). According to Kainz

(2020, p. 56), the newer definition includes the art of making and using maps, which he notes accounts for a growing tendency to consider the 'artistic aspect in maps and map making'. Moreover, while both definitions of a map describe a model of geographical reality, the newer definition uses the word 'representation' whereas the older one uses the word 'image' to describe this model of reality (Kainz, 2020, p. 56). The use of the term 'image' seems to indicate, semantically, an exact and 'neutral', and therefore unbiased, reproduction of the 'cartographic item(s)', while 'representation' could imply a sort of 'interpretation', which may also be 'non-neutral', and therefore potentially biased.

Beyond the making and using of maps, the perennial question over the definition of cartography has been explored by many scholars. Research has focussed on the definitions of cartography (Goodrick, 1982), past and present definitions of maps and cartography as provided by the ICA (Kraak & Fabrikant, 2017), and on creating working definitions of the discipline, even as the field has undergone significant changes over time (Morrison, 1978; Olson, 2004; Taylor, 1994). Other scholars have reflected on the art/science dichotomy in the discipline. Some have approached cartography according to artistic (Cartwright, Gartner, & Lehn, 2009) or scientific perspectives (Buchroithner & Fernández, 2011; Morrison, 1978), while other researchers have called for a greater convergence of both art and science (Krygier, 1995). The aim of this discussion is not to provide an exhaustive summary of the field. This chapter instead focusses on an area that has so far received little attention: the links between toponymy and cartography.

Consequently, this chapter aims at briefly introducing the relationship between toponymy and cartography through case studies from different historical periods. It begins by giving an overview on how place names might be made or used in maps. We will then see how toponyms are reflected in ancient and contemporary maps and what a study of these names tell us. The chapter also aims to unveil how toponyms and maps might go hand-in-hand in two situations: to possess and control (especially during colonial times) territories, and the generation of imaginary place names and their representations on the map.

## 10.2    The Functions of Place Names on the Map

Mark Monmonier, in his celebrated book *How to Lie with Maps* (2018), noted that there are three main elements of a cartographic document: map scales, map projections, and map symbols. He writes that 'most maps are smaller than the reality they represent, and map scales tell us how much smaller' (Monmonier, 2018, p. 5). Scales can assume the form of a ratio or fraction (e.g., 1:10,000 or 1/10,000, where a distance of one unit on the map represents a distance of 10,000 units on the ground), a short sentence (e.g., one centimetre represents

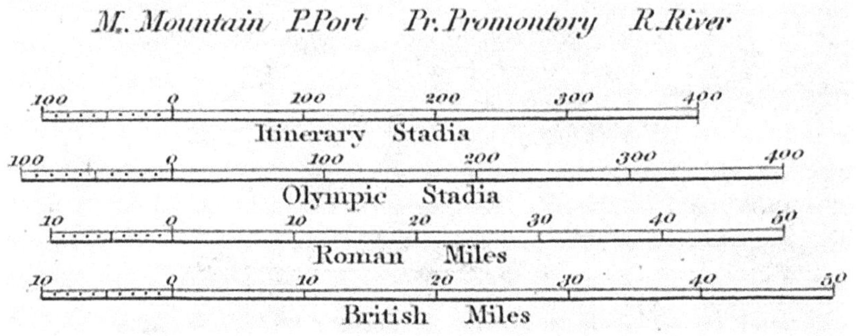

*M. Mountain    P.Port    Pr. Promontory    R.River*

Figure 10.1  Scale and symbols on an old map (adapted from Megistias, 2010)

one kilometre), or a graph (see Figure 10.1). Map projection transforms the curved, three-dimensional surface of the earth to the flat, two-dimensional layout that we see on maps. This normally occurs in a two-stage process. First, the earth is shrunk to a globe, for which the ratio holds true everywhere and in all directions. Then, the symbols from the globe are projected onto a surface that can be flattened (e.g., a plane, a cone, or a cylinder). Finally, map symbols make the features, places, and other locational information on the map visible. Road maps and most generic maps use a combination of three types of symbols: point symbols, to mark where landmarks and villages are; line symbols, to indicate the length and layout of rivers and roads; and area symbols, to show the shape and size of major cities and state parks.

Beyond point, line, and areal symbols, which are essential visual elements of the map, Fairbairn (1993, p. 104) stated that 'text is one of the four main components contributing to the visual appearance of a map', with the other three being the aforementioned map symbols. Fairbairn (1993, p. 104) also underscored the importance of the textual aspect on maps, noting that:

[t]ext on a map is indispensable. Many would argue that a map without text is impossible, such a product being merely an image or a graphic. At its most fundamental level, text is necessary to identify the location being mapped, the symbolisation employed, the scale of the representation and any reference system used.

The focus of this chapter is not on how these three symbols (and even how map scales and map projections) are used in cartography; rather, we will focus on how toponyms, as 'map symbols', came to be used and represented on maps. Atchison (1982) noted that toponyms are generally taken for granted on maps. Place names, he said, 'seem so minor an aspect of map production that the cartographer can ignore them, surely, to concentrate on what is, after all, the massive task of mastering the ever-technological requirements of his trade' (p. 111). It is worth noting that most of the textual components on maps are toponymic in nature, that is, appearing to indicate the names of objects which are located by point, line, and areal symbols. However, text can be used for other purposes. Among some of these functions are describing additional properties of the object portrayed by map symbols (e.g., the use of the expression 'conspic.' to indicate the visibility of the object), 'warnings' to caution against the dangerous nature of the feature (e.g., through the expression 'danger area'), and terms used to indicate the legal, administrative, or political bodies which own or govern the territory.

Jordan (2009) provides an excellent read on the practical functions of place names on maps. He divides their uses into two: for map users who are not acquainted with the place name (and/or place) on the map and, conversely, for people who are acquainted with the place name (and/or place). For the former group, place names, as text on the map, help the user to identify and search for places. As Jordan (2009, p. 1) stated:

[...] the place name has in the first line the function of facilitating map use. Identification of a place indicated by a cartographic symbol becomes much easier, when it is in addition explained by a place name [...] place names enable search for places. Place names indices or name search functions with interactive electronic maps enable the reader to search for a place on the map via the place name. Without place names this would not be possible.

Place names make maps easier to use; they attach a word to the cartographic symbol, thereby complementing these symbols and providing geographical and topographic meaning to them. In doing so, toponyms facilitate map use as they are signifiers of places in the representation of the geographical reality. At the same time, toponyms help users to search for places on maps. Indeed, the place name is the first thing we type when we do an Internet search for a place or location.

For those acquainted with the place name (and/or the place), the act of seeing and reading place names on the map evokes an emotional function that (re)connects the person with the place, and is reminiscent of the identity building and emotive functions of place names, as highlighted in Chapter 9. Jordan (2009) sums it up as follows.

Users acquainted not only with the place name, but also with the place, especially persons with emotional ties to a certain place, feel a certain emotion, when they read the name on the map. Reading the name consciously makes them not only recalling their factual concept of the place (as with the function before), not only recalling their memories of the place as it looks like, but also memories of persons and events they are associating with it. Reading the name activates their emotional ties, their 'feel of a place'. (p. 2)

Beyond the geo-locational and emotional functions of toponyms on carto-graphic documents, maps are also ideological weapons (Harley, 1988). They appear to be innocently factual, representing the geographical and topographic reality as it is. However, they are cloaked in an 'elaborate rhetoric of power' that determines the map symbols, destines the inclusion and exclusion of territories, and decides the intrinsic 'discourse' of toponyms (Jacob, 1996, p. 194). The sociopolitical and ideological functions of maps and representa-tions of place names is a theme that we will explore later in this chapter.

## 10.3     Place Names and Cartography across Time

While toponymy and cartography might have played an integral role in the age of colonialism, some of the earliest maps also recorded place names of ancient settlements. Maps are a very ancient invention, although the modern historical phenomenon of colonialism led to the contemporary cartographic development of map making techniques and the use of maps as tools to subjugate Indigenous peoples. Cartography has undergone a series of phases, across its history. In this section, we will give a brief outline of how these phases transitioned from Ptolemaic cartography to modern and contemporary cartography.

The Ptolemaic conception of the universe is that of a geocentric world, where the *Earth* is at the centre of the universe itself, surrounded by the 'spheres' of the planets which are, in turn, surrounded by the fixed stars and the band of the Zodiac. Till the sixteenth century, this conception was dominant. In medieval maps, the world is often drawn as a trilobate figure, with three areas, *Africa*, *Europe*, and *Asia*. These areas are completely surrounded by the *Ocean*. In other medieval maps, the *Ocean* surrounds the *Earth* and is configured as a swirling river. In some other maps from the Middle Ages, conversely, the *Mediterranean Sea* becomes an internal 'cavity', with *Europe* located in the north, *Asia* in the east, and *Africa* in the west. In many maps from this period, the *Finis Terrae* 'the end of the *Earth*' is the westernmost point of the world, represented by *Spain*. The system of the world which would replace the Ptolemaic conception is the heliocentric setting proposed by Copernicus, with the *Earth* in motion around the sun and with new astronomical dynamics generated by this change.

At the cartographic level, the Ptolemaic contribution to the history of cartog-raphy was significant because it strove for an accurate cartographic representa-tion of the '*Ecumene*', that is, the inhabited and known world. Indeed, this aspect of cartography was absent from maps produced in the Middle Ages. Only in the fifteenth century, with the rediscovery of the Ptolemaic cartography tradition from several maps recovered in the *East*, did the *Earth* regain its real 'shape', that is, a sphere which has to be represented on a geometrical plane in order to keep the proportion consistent. This is something that could be achieved through the Ptolemaic projection techniques, as they allowed cartographers to represent the planet and the morphology of the territories in an impressively exact way.

After this rediscovery, modern cartography generated a better understanding of the world by cartographers and geographers due, mainly, to the more detailed observations made by explorers and the development of new surveying techniques. These techniques were helped by the invention of surveying tools that made observations and measurements much more accurate, such as the magnetic compass, the telescope, and the sextant. Cartographers, therefore, aimed for perfection both at the level of the drawing of maps and at the level of the accuracy of measurements.

Contemporary cartography has been influenced by many advancements in technology. Aerial photography, satellite imagery, remote sensing, and, more recently, global positioning systems (GPS) and geographic information systems (GIS) have provided efficient and very precise means for mapping physical features. This has allowed the enhancement of cartographic techniques and of the quality and accuracy of maps in general. The impressive progress of the cartographic models and procedures across centuries, however, has been achieved without distorting their essential principles of accuracy originated from the Ptolemaic cartography.

The passage between Ptolemaic cartography and modern cartography, as mentioned, can be attributed to several historical events, such as the discovery of *America* (1492) and the subsequent transfer of economic trades to the *Atlantic*, the loss of the *Middle East*'s privileged position in Western commercial routes that followed the circumnavigation of *Africa*, the rise of modern states and the centralisation of power in *Europe*, and what was perceived by the *West* as an increasingly aggressive attitude on behalf of Islam against Christianity (evidenced by the fall of *Constantinople* to the Ottoman Empire in 1453). These events meant that map making, in the context of modern cartography, became less the product of exploration and increasingly subservient to the 'needs of knowledge and territorial control of the modern state' (Siniscalchi & Palagiano, 2018, p. 207).

Kainz (2020) listed some of the earliest maps. He noted that the oldest map, dating back to around 25,000 BCE, was found near *Pavlov, Czechia*, and was carved on a mammoth tusk (see Figure 10.2).

In Ancient *Mesopotamia*, the Sumerians, Akkadians, and Babylonians developed a remarkable system of land measurement and allocation, and examples of early cartographic attempts were the *Gasur* Map and the City Map of *Nippur*, engraved on clay tablets and dating back to 2350 BCE and 1500 BCE, respectively. The Romans developed a road map of the Roman Empire. The only copy remaining is a medieval copy from the twelfth/thirteenth century known as the Tabula Peutingeriana. The map is made up of eleven sheets, each thirty-four centimetres wide. When placed alongside each other, the sheets form

Figure 10.2  Carving on a mammoth tusk found near *Pavlov, Czech Republic* (Zde, 2007)

a 6.82-metre-long map. Due to the odd size, the territories outlined on the cartographic document are drawn out almost beyond recognition. An excerpt can be seen in Figure 10.3.

The markings on these maps reveal to us important information about the landscape as well as the symbolic nature of place names. For example, Svoboda (2017) notes that the linear symbols on the *Pavlov* tusk, shown in Figure 10.2, could have represented landmarks (like rivers and slopes) and their qualities (such as accessibility to animals and humans or natural barriers). The markings found on the tusk could have been used by prehistoric people to locate and direct animal herds, and to develop their hunting strategy. The Tabula Peutingeriana is, in itself, a significant treasure trove of information, containing around 2,700 place names, as well as relatively detailed depictions of ancient cities like *Rome, Antioch*, and *Constantinople*. It also shows the main roads of the Roman Empire and landscape features like rivers, mountains, and islands (Fodorean, 2013), making it possible to study place names and the landscape of territories during the Roman Empire, as some scholars have done using this map (see, for instance, Finkelstein, 1979; Pazarli, 2009; Pazarli, Livieratos, & Boutoura, 2007; Tappy, 2012).

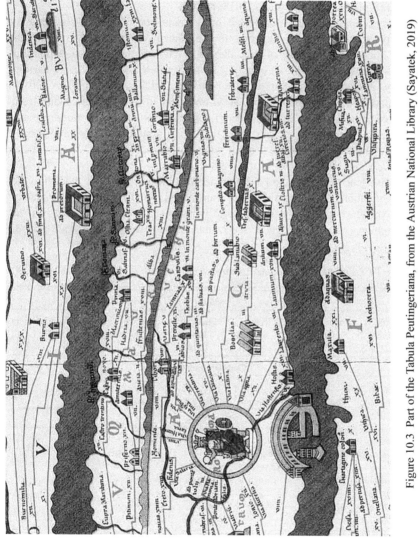

Figure 10.3 Part of the Tabula Peutingeriana, from the Austrian National Library (Sayatek, 2019)

Silvano's map (1511) represented a modified version of Ptolemaic cartography's models. It integrated classic Ptolemaic geography with the knowledge coming from more contemporary nautical charts. Silvano mapped the world's regions in a more realistic manner that is similar to the modern depiction of the globe. His world map (Figure 10.4) was designed in a heart-shaped form, which projected the world very differently from the way Ptolemy did (Conti, 2009). Silvano's map is thus a fine example of the Ptolemaic cartographic tradition that integrated modern techniques, thereby improving on Ptolemy's original maps (Siniscalchi & Palagiano, 2018, p. 209).

Very old maps, like the Tabula Peutingeriana, record ancient place names and provide us with an insight into the ancient cultures and civilisations they document. Because of this, they allow us to study ancient toponyms and landscapes, as well as enabling us to develop a study of early cartography. A good example of this is how Siniscalchi and Palagiano (2018) compared the representation of *Syria* and *Iraq* in five Western maps from between the sixteenth end eighteenth centuries, as well as in modern maps (see Table 10.1). In the process, they highlighted some of the abovementioned cultural changes in the relationship between the *West* and the *Middle East*.

Siniscalchi and Palagiano (2018) argued that these changes are evident in the transformation of place names as they transitioned from the Ptolemaic geography context, which depicted a single large world and the *Mediterranean Sea* 'as a common connotative sign of the countries that overlook it' (Siniscalchi &

Table 10.1 *List of place names examined by Siniscalchi and Palagiano (2018)*

| Maps | | | | |
|---|---|---|---|---|
| Bernardo Silvano (1511) | Abraham Ortelius (1594) | Pierre Mortier (1695) | Emanuel Bowen (1744) | Current place names or area where the place is located |
| **Country names** | | | | |
| Babylonia | | | | Iraq |
| Mesopotamia | Diarbech | Diarbek | Diarbekr | Iraq, Syria |
| **Place names** | | | | |
| Chalybon | Aleppo | Alep | Aleppo | Aleppo |
| Nicephorium | Racha | Raqqa | | Al-Raqqah |
| Bibla | Bagdet | Baghdad | Baghdad | Baghdad |
| Damascus | Damascus | Damas | Damascus | Damascus |
| Hierapolis | | | | Manbij |
| | Mosul | Musol | Mosul | Mossul |
| Palmyra | | | Palmyra | Palmyra |

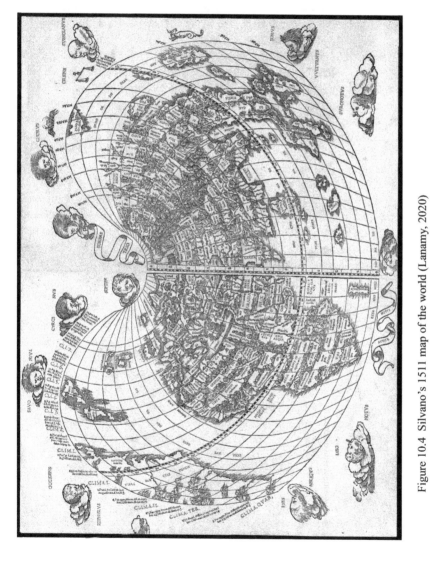

Figure 10.4 Silvano's 1511 map of the world (Lanamy, 2020)

Palagiano, 2018, p. 206), to what we call modern cartography. What the authors found was that historical denominations of countries and territories, such as *Babylonia* and *Mesopotamia*, and the names of cities like *Chalybon*, *Nicephorium*, *Bibla*, and *Hierapolis* were replaced by other names, in a process that the authors argue is indicative of the gradual disappearance of the 'vision of the classical world' as reflected by Ptolemaic cartography (Siniscalchi & Palagiano, 2018, p. 209).

These toponymic changes were not immediate and all-encompassing. The use of Latin for many former Roman place names, for instance, demonstrates that this transition did not happen instantaneously and that there are still remnants of the Latin Western culture in Middle Eastern place names. Furthermore, some place names, like *Damascus* and *Palmyra*, survived these cultural and ideological changes. These are ancient cities which have been attested in both ancient and modern cartography with the same name, and they are naturally linked to the Semitic civilisations of *Mesopotamia* and their subsequent, Semitic and non-Semitic, cultures and civilisations (e.g., Phoenicians, Greeks, and Romans).

As an example of how maps are used for political purposes rather than having a geographical-cultural slant from Ptolemaic cartography, Siniscalchi and Palagiano (2018) noted that *The New & Accurate Map of Turkey in Asia, Arabia & c.*, by Emanuel Bowen (1744) (reproduced in Siniscalchi & Palagiano, 2018, p. 212), displayed the Ottoman Empire in all its complexity. Its Asian part is divided into states and governates, much like how modern maps are, and there is evidence of how place names do not follow those of the Ptolemaic tradition, that is, they have been updated to better represent geographical and political contexts of that time.

## 10.4    Colonialism and the Age of Discoveries

There is abundant scientific literature on colonialism and cartography, particularly on how the colonial powers utilised maps and the making of colonial boundaries to extend their powers over colonised groups (Brealey, 1995; Collier, 2006; Fedman, 2012; Kalpagam, 1995; Kaufman, 2015; Rivard, 2008). Indeed, as Mishuana Goeman suggested, 'maps, in their most traditional sense as a representation of authority, have incredible power and have been essential to colonial and imperial projects' (Goeman, 2013, p. 16). As we have seen while discussing the definition of maps, they are representations of geographical reality. In the colonial context, these topographic[1] depictions, as well as the toponymic inclusions and exclusions we can find in them, are

---

[1] Colonial maps are often 'topographic' because they have a military focus component. This means that they aim to depict very accurately, indeed topographically, mountains, villages, rivers, roads, and landscape features. Colonial cartography, therefore, was often topographic. Paradoxically, in most of these maps, the least attention was given to place names, because the

neither 'arbitrary' nor 'apolitical' (Hunt & Stevenson, 2017, p. 375). Rather, they are part of the geographical understandings (Harvey, 2001, p. 213) that serve to 'entrench and justify European colonialist and nationalist narratives' (Oliver, 2011, p. 67).

In this section, however, our discussion moves away from the framing of maps solely as a power exercise and a form of governmentality by the colonisers. While considering the overtly political and ideological slants of map making and map usage, something that maps share with toponyms, we hope to delve deeper into the intersection of and the relationships between toponymy and cartography during the age of colonialism. Through the study of map making and map usage during colonial times, scholars can extract and use toponyms as primary data, which in turn yield important information on the sociopolitical and ideological motivations and attitudes of the colonisers.

The analysis of maps drawn up by colonial powers and the toponyms they display highlight the political objective of the colonisers to show that they are firmly in charge. This was evident, for example, in what is now *Zimbabwe*, formerly *Rhodesia*, where the toponymic process was:

a political monologue – a one-sided conversation from which the settlers meant to inform the locals about the new political order and thus the country and local places had acquired foreign names as an indication that they were now under foreign rule, and was no longer under the control of the original inhabitants. (Snodia, Muguti, & Mutami, 2010, p. 23)

Colonial maps of *Salisbury*, the capital of *Rhodesia* (named after the British Prime Minister Lord Salisbury), show that in urban areas where the Europeans resided, toponyms in European languages sought to immortalise the colonisers' presence in the landscape. Many place names honoured the British royal family and paid homage to personalities and politicians who made *Rhodesia* a colonial state, including Cecil Rhodes himself, whom the colony was named after. These European toponyms 'naturalised the relationship between Europeans and places that had European identities' (Mamvura, Mutasa, & Pfukwa, 2017, p. 45). Meanwhile, the British, as the colonial masters in *Rhodesia*, ensured that all local politically loaded toponyms were removed. Although many of the local urban areas in *Salisbury* were named in native languages, the colonial naming authorities banned local inhabitants from immortalising and memorialising those who fought against colonisation. As argued by other scholars, 'this was a clear message that as a defeated people, the locals had lost all freedoms, including the freedom to an identity that the local names represented' (Snodia et al., 2010).

maps themselves have the ultimate aim of helping the movement of troops and do not care too much about toponymic exactness.

Unsurprisingly, the desire to impose political control has resulted in the erasure of Indigenous knowledge and ways of life. Mapping and toponymy were tools used by the colonial authorities to disconnect Indigenous peoples 'from their histories, their landscapes, their languages, their social relations and their own ways of thinking, feeling, and interacting with the world' (Smith, n.d., cited in Goeman, 2013, p. 3). Place names in the Indigenous landscape that are attested on Western maps are 'most often reinterpreted, decontextualized, and deprived of their true cultural meanings and histories' (Aporta et al., 2014, p. 230).

Indigenous toponyms were heavily regulated or ignored in colonial times, as seen in the *Rhodesia* example. In other instances, they were adapted to the colonial place naming strategy, particularly the 'one name for one place' method. This is exemplified by *Peel River* in western *Canada*, named in commemoration of British Prime Minister Robert Peel. The same area and watercourse are known to the Gwich'in people living in the *Northwest Territories (NWT)* of *Canada* as *Teetl'it Gwinjik* 'at the head of the waters river'. Indeed, many islands, riverbanks, canyons, hills, and camps along the river have traditional Gwich'in names, which do not show up on official colonial maps. This reveals that the Gwich'in people have an intensive use of and intimate relationship with the landscape and highlight the multiple connections that the Indigenous people share with the landscape, as opposed to the singular connection indicated by the official label of *Peel River* (Aporta et al., 2014). The erasure of Indigenous peoples' knowledge from the geographical representation of their toponyms is representative of how people in power – in the past and present – use the mapping of place names as a form of governmentality, to control the territories they rule. It is, therefore, little wonder that Vuolteenaho and Berg (2009, p. 4) argue that '[...] the mapping of toponyms has formed an ancillary form of knowledge production in the service of a wider scientific-geopolitical project of knowing the world as accurately as possible as part of the process of controlling its spaces'.

The playbook of erasure is utilised in modern settler colonies as well. A case in point would be present-day *Palestine*. As we briefly discussed in Chapter 9, after the reorganisation of *Palestine* in 1948 and the creation of *Israel*, the newly formed state superimposed biblical and talmudic toponyms to erase the Indigenous Palestinian and Arab-Islamic heritage of the land. This renaming project demonstrates the indelible impact of colonial methods in exercising power and control over the modern toponymic and cartographic process. The Israeli Governmental Names Committee of the 1950s sought to impose a 'New Hebrew' identity on the landscape. To this end, new Hebrew place names appeared, and Israeli maps slowly removed Palestinian-Arabic toponyms. Palestinian historian Ilan Pappe drew on the concept of cultural memoricide as he highlighted how the Israeli state de-Arabised the

Palestinian landscape of its names for religious sites, villages, towns, and cityscapes (Pappe, 2006). Some examples are the Hebrew versus Arabic names of *Jerusalem – Al-Quds, Akko (Acre) – Akka, Yafo (Jaffa) – Yafa, Tzora – Sora'a, Ayelet Hashaḥar – Najmat al-Subh, Agur – Ajur,* and *Ein Limor – Eyn Al'amor.* This systematic deletion of the Palestinian past had the aim of not only strengthening the newly created state, but also to allude to a continued passage from biblical Israel to the modern Israeli state (Masalha, 2015, p. 31). Thus, Masalha (2015, p. 30) argued that the Palestinians share similarities with Indigenous groups who were colonised elsewhere; their self-determination and narratives were discredited, their culture was devastated, and their histories were distorted.

As we have mentioned in this book, place names can have an ideological function; toponyms are an 'instrument of an ideological imposition, because there is a direct connection between the name and the ideology that binds it' (Carvalhinhos, Lima-Hernandes, & Lima, 2018, p. 96). Herling (2020) ana-lysed colonial maps of coastal areas in present-day *USA* from the sixteenth to eighteenth centuries. She notes that these maps provide a 'detailed insight' into the toponymy (Herling, 2020, p. 28) and inscribe the 'moment of naming' as geographical reality (Herling, 2020, p. 29). This offers crucial information on colonial naming practices. She found that commemorative toponyms are com-mon in Spanish and French linguistic contexts. Spanish and French place names contain, among others, references to kings and notable people, or allude to dynasties (e.g., *Louisiane, Charlesfort, Punta de los Reyes* 'Headland of the Kings'), politicians (e.g., *Rivière Colbert* 'Colbert River'), explorers (e.g., *Val Laudonnière* 'Valley Laudonnière', *Bahía de Juan Ponce* 'Bay of Juan Ponce'), or Saints (e.g., *Isle Saint Michel* 'Saint Michael Island', *Río de San Antonio* 'River of Saint Anthony'). Herling noted that 89.5 per cent of the Spanish toponyms examined, as well as 77.5 per cent of the French toponyms, are exonymous (i.e., they originate from the language of the colonial power, not from local languages). A number of these toponyms also contain geo-classifiers (e.g., *Punta* 'Headland' (Spanish), *Rivière* 'River' (French), *Val* 'Valley' (French), *Bahía/Baia* 'Bay' (Spanish)). These classifiers, coined in the lan-guage of the colonisers, reflect how the European powers organised their landscapes. In choosing to name places in the colonies in their language(s), with references to important European figures and geography, the rulers were developing a colonial strategy to install their languages, histories, social rela-tionships, landscapes, and worldviews on their newly conquered territories – all of which have an overtly ideological function of demonstrating the supremacy of the Western worldview.

Similar practices can be observed in colonial toponyms in *Africa*. Batoma (2006, p. 3) noted that 'some of the names bestowed by European or Arab colonialists on African people and places tell more about the colonial mind of the namers and of their intentions than about the named African reality'. As argued elsewhere in this volume, a study of colonial maps and toponyms can reveal the projection of idyllic colonial imagery into Western-dominated areas in the urban landscape (see Chapters 8 and 9), or the portrayal of Indigenous residential areas as 'rural', as opposed to the 'urban' places where the Europeans lived, thereby promoting the colonial 'civilising mission', extolling the colonial narrative and values (see Chapter 8), and ultimately allowing for European colonialist and nationalist values to take root and be magnified in the colonial landscape.

Yet, it is worth noting that colonialism was not simply a process of 'coming and conquering'. Far from seeing voyages as the foreshadow of colonisation, where great (and White) men discovered new places, named them, and ignored or demonised Indigenous presence, there was Indigenous presence, action, and agency during these encounters. Douglas (2014) cautions against viewing the cartographic construction of the world as a 'confident, cumulative, linear process of imperial "discovery," knowing, and naming' (p. 24). Douglas (2014) proposes the notion of 'countersigns', which are lexical, grammatical, and syntactical items, or visual analogues. These 'countersigns' were created in the uncertainties and whirlwind of emotions, and express distrust, dissatisfaction, and despair during human encounters between the colonisers and the Indigenous people. Most recognisable in their choice of words, names, and motifs, the 'countersigns' become embedded in the narrative, cartographic, and toponymic processes.

Douglas (2014) based his argument on his analysis of the travel journals of two Dutch explorers who were searching for the *Terra Australis*, in modern-day *Oceania*. He found that, rather than proving colonial beliefs 'of the natural domination of Christian Europeans over Wilden (savages)' (Douglas, 2014, p. 17), his analysis strongly suggests 'that Dutch recourse to violence was usually preemptive or defensive, signalling their own anxieties and tenuous control of encounters' (Douglas, 2014, p. 17). A notable example is the Dutch renaming of the island of *Niuatoputapu* (located in *Tonga*) as *Verraders Eylandt* 'Traitors Island'. The journals of two leading Dutch explorers, Willem Schouten and Jacob Le Maire, reported that after an initial peaceful and fruitful encounter and trade, their ship, the *Eendracht*, was surrounded by close to 1,000 people on canoes. The chief or king of the island signalled for an attempt to capture the ship, which the locals bombarded with stones. However, the Dutch were able to repel the attack. Douglas argues that the name *Verraders* is a 'double-countersign'; it encodes Indigenous agency and the rarely acknowledged weakness of these explorers, who rely on the cooperation and goodwill of the Indigenous people for important supplies. As Douglas (2014, p. 19) noted, the name 'is thus a metonym for a whole narrative of foreign arrival, indigenous action, and

European response'. This toponym and its multilingual variants (*Verraders Eiland*, *Ile des Traîtres*, or *Traitor's Island*) were recorded in some of the most widespread maps well into the nineteenth century.

Cartographic agency can be exercised by various parties involved in contested places. Maps can be depicted in unconventional ways, as we saw with the Ukrainian football jersey at the beginning of the chapter. A 1992 Argentinian postage stamp shows a map with the Argentinian province of *Tierra del Fuego*, parts of *Antarctica*, and the *South Islands*. The map includes the *Falkland Islands* (*Islas Malvinas*) as part of the Argentinian *Tierra del Fuego* province. The *Falkland Islands* (or *Falklands*) are a British overseas territory located near *Argentina*. However, *Argentina* lays territorial claims to these islands, calling them the *Islas Malvinas*. An armed conflict erupted between *Argentina* and the *UK* over the sovereignty of the islands in June 1982, when the Argentinian army invaded them. After seventy-four days of fighting, the occupying forces were defeated, and the islands were returned to the British.

The inclusion of the disputed islands on the postage stamp was an effective act of cartographic propaganda over *Argentina*'s claim on the *Falklands* (Klinefelter, 1992). In response, the Falkland Islands Philatelic Bureau published its own stamps portraying a narrative of continuous British control over the islands since the eighteenth century. Beyond demonstrating the agency of the local Falklanders and their allegiance to the British, this episode also highlights how maps can name a place, claim a stake over it, and inflame great passions among those with opposing claims.

Another example is the long-disputed name of the stretch of water between *Japan* and the *Korean Peninsula*. In the 1920s, without any Korean representation, the International Hydrographic Bureau accepted the Japanese recommendation to name it the *Sea of Japan*. This has been disputed by both *North* and *South Korea*. The arguments for and against this toponym by the Japanese and Koreans have been largely based on the names reported on historical maps. *Japan* has been arguing that the name did not come about due to its annexing of the *Korean Peninsula* in the late 1800s and early 1900s, but it has a much longer history, dating back to the early 1600s, and hence it has priority. Korean scholars have argued that there were other historical maps from the same period that do not refer to that body of water by that name. Monmonier (2007), however, argued that 'old maps seem neither relevant nor definitive, while current usage, clearly on the side of the Japanese, ignores the historical reality that toponyms, like boundaries, are political constructions, subject to change' (p. 94). The reality now is that most maps still label this sea as the *Sea of Japan*, and others have the alternative name the *East Sea* in parenthesis alongside the *Sea of Japan* or below it.

## 10.5     Cartography Today

Cartography has evolved over time with the development of navigational instruments, like the sextant, and with the invention of other technological innovations, such as the printing press. These technological advancements have allowed for more accuracy in drawing maps and for their quick and mass printing and dissemination. Nonetheless, with the digital innovations of our times, the technological processes in cartography have been tremendously accelerated. Two complementary aspects have developed over the last thirty to forty years: satellite remote-sensing (and image processing techniques), and geographic information systems (GIS), including computer-aided cartography and database management systems (Denegre, 1992). These have been aided by advancements in computer-aided drawing of maps. The increasing shift to GIS has led scholars to ponder on how GIS has influenced the discipline of cartography and how cartographers should use digital tools to ensure that 'the heterogeneous datasets in databases will be made comparable, both from a geometrical, semantical, updatedness and completeness point of view' (Grelot, 1994, p. 56). In essence, technology has revolutionised the way maps are made and used, and it is the reason why the ICA includes 'technology of map making and map using' in its definition of the field.

GIS and other 'modern spatio-statistical methods and cartographic techniques' can 'provide new perspectives for toponymic research by evoking and directing interpretive discussions' (Fuchs, 2015, p. 331). To this end, toponymic mapping, that is, the combination of spatial analysis and cartographic methods to map the complex rules and characteristics in a particular locality, has been gaining traction as a research methodology (Slingsby, Wood, & Dykes, 2010). As covered in Chapter 7, in recent years, there has been an upsurge in research that utilises toponymic mapping and other GIS tools to present the geophysical, environmental, cultural, historical (see the discussion on historical GIS in Chapter 7), and linguistic characteristics of toponyms in maps.

Ultimately, GIS allows for 'patterns to be discovered within immense historical datasets'. These findings help geographers, historians, and of course toponymists and linguists with new and previously undiscovered research foci, 'which can then be regarded with the nuanced interpretation of qualitative, critical historical research methods' (Chloupek, 2018).

Modern technologies like GIS and GPS are steadily diminishing the importance of hand-drawn, pen-and-paper maps. Yet, traditional maps still offer an insight into the intersections between language, feelings, geographical and Indigenous knowledge, history, and collective imaginary. Nash (2018) experienced this in his 'linguistic pilgrimage' in *Norfolk Island*, which describes essentially a personal relationship between the human and the observed environment (see also Chapters 2 and 8 for more information on Nash's research in *Norfolk Island*). The 'linguistic pilgrim' reflects as they see language in the landscape, signs, and how language is used within sociocultural contexts. Nash recounted how a Norfolk Islander, Bev McCoy, drew a map of *Shallow Water* for him, an offshore fishing ground. This drawing is a 'drawn linguistic artefact, a map, language as spatial representation, and an aesthetic marker of cultural selfhood impounded within the Norfolk Islander community' (Nash, 2018, p. 139). The drawing also contained other place names, such as *No Trouble Reef, Mount Pitt, Alligator's Eye, Duncombe Bay,* and *Captain Cook Monument*, which Nash described as being part of the 'linguistic and non-linguistic appeal of *Shallow Water*' (Nash, 2018, p. 145). In this sense, the map drawn indicates other connected place names and their significance in the toponymic landscape, which may not always appear on the official map. Bev also recounted the landscape, locality, and naming process of *Shallow Water* to Nash. A digital map of the offshore islands of *Norfolk Island* compiled by Nash then showed *Shallow Water*, and is evidence of how the drawn has become 'computerised'. Nash poignantly notes that there is a movement within the name-event, where cultural and Indigenous knowledge is transferred:

from Bev to me, Norfolk Islander to blowin-cum-Westerner-cum-non-indigenous writer, local to linguist, mind maps to linguistics manifested in the world. I move through spaces and words inside the triangulation points and marks of the maritime and wet geography used in connection to the terrestrial topography in names like *Shallow Water*. (Nash, 2018, p. 141)

Ultimately, Nash blends the analogue (Bev's drawing) with the digital (digitised mapping), demonstrating the interface between the old and new, traditional and modern. And, despite modern technologies like GPS making Bev's drawings or even these offshore fishing ground names potentially worth-less, Nash's quote, penned in a beautiful, emotive language, highlights that map drawing (and the connected toponyms drawn on the map) still has a place within the larger toponymic ecosystem and epistemology, and is an art in itself.

However, what I learned through the abject drawn, through interaction with person, language, space, emotion, and place, and through the recording of drawing is far from fruitless. An artistic arena was established on paper, a name-place worthy of pilgrimage in the world, a locale I met and with which I interacted. Through the interaction of self (ego)–artefact (drawing)–arena (placename), a nucleus involving language–pilgrimage, artist–documenter, insider–outsider, and mover–shaker has been realised. The produc-tion of placenames and linguistic data is art, is artistic. (Nash, 2018, p. 145)

## 10.6  Phantom Place Names on the Map

We have seen, thus far, that maps have been made and used to represent geographical realities in the ancient and colonial world. Of particular salience is how maps are intertwined with the sociopolitical and ideological attitudes and motivations of the rulers of the day, an argument which can be also proven by analysing place names on early cartographic endeavours. See, for example, the above-mentioned Tabula Peutingeriana, a map of the Roman Empire with 'Romanised' place names; the various cartographic documents that represented the world from a 'Christianised' perspective, such as the Χριστιανικὴ Τοπογραφία 'Christian Topography' by Cosmas Indicopleustes (sixth century CE); the *T and O Map* (*Isidoran Map*), another 'Christianised' map of the world from the seventh century CE representing the *Earth* as described by Isidore of *Seville* in his *De Natura Rerum* and in his *Etymologiae*, with the representation of the 'location' of the 'Paradise'. The question we hope to explore in this section is inherent in the opposite: can maps illustrate places (believed to exist) that may not exist? 'Phantom places' are defined as places that, although believed to be real and despite having been officially charted on maps, turned out to be non-existent. Phantom places form part of a broader umbrella of fascinating legendary places that include lands that really existed but are shrouded in mystery, lands that are thought to have enjoyed a purely 'spiritual' existence and others that existed only in religion, lands that clearly do not exist today but that may have existed once, and destinations borne out of false documentation (Eco, 2015, pp. 8–9). These places, which often are islands (Nah & Perono Cacciafoco, 2018), can be labelled on historical maps with the words 'E.D.', which represent 'existence doubtful'. The phenomenon of phantom islands is instructive in demonstrating that maps can indeed demarcate geographical fiction. In the *North Pacific* alone, the British Royal Navy cleared at least 123 such falsely recorded islands in 1875 (Brooke-Hitching, 2016). There are two broad reasons explaining why phantom islands were mapped: error and human imagination (Tallack, 2016, p. 5). As a result of human error, sailors and seafarers mistake mirages, low clouds, rock formations, and other misleading geographical phenomena for land. Imprecise navigational equipment can also deceive explorers, ultimately leading to phantom islands being drawn on maps (Brooke-Hitching, 2016, pp. 9–10). On other occasions, phantom islands can also emerge due to the human imagination, most noticeable in creative writers whose tales of adventure claim to have discovered new lands (Brooke-Hitching, 2016, p. 11).

Modernisation has resulted in technological advancements and improvements in navigation and mapping. This has led to the debunking of these phantom places and islands. Modern technology diminishes the need for explorers to solve geographical mysteries in the form of searching and uncovering new places. Today, we have comprehensive navigational databases, free and accessible maps on our computers and phones, and satellites telling us where we are and what is around us (Tallack, 2016). This has led to a feeling of our world being 'flatter'. Places feel extremely familiar, and people may think that the world is not as extraordinary or exciting as it was in the age of discoveries. To put it simply, it feels that our world is becoming 'all-discovered' (Elborough, 2016, p. 8). Yet, there will always be something else to discover or, in some cases, something else to be un-discovered – some phantom 'hiding in plain sight [...] masquerading as fact, enjoying its quiet nonexistence, just waiting to be undiscovered' (Brooke-Hitching, 2016, p. 11).

Nah and Perono Cacciafoco (2018) presented the histories (and stories) of three such phantom place names. One of them constitutes the recent example of *Sandy Island*, supposedly located between *Australia* and *New Caledonia*, in the *South Pacific*. The island was first reported by a whaling ship called *Velocity* in 1876 and its first cartographic appearance was in 1908 (see Figure 10.5) in a British admiralty chart (Seton et al., 2013). This phantom island could also be the *Sandy I(sland)* that Captain James Cook charted off of the cost of northeast *Australia* and published in *The Chart of Discoveries in the South Pacific Ocean* (1776). Not much is known about how *Sandy Island* got its name, although one self-evident and possible reason is that the place was christened after its sandy appearance (Nah & Perono Cacciafoco, 2018).

*Sandy Island* remained in roughly the same shape, size, and location for around 100 years in various maps (Tallack, 2016). The insulonym continued to appear in maps even in the twenty-first century. One such example was the World Vector Shoreline Database (WVS), a free and readily accessible data source used by a large proportion of the international scientific community. Its 'un-discovery' happened only in 2012, when Australian oceanographers surveying the floor of the *Coral Sea* and plate tectonics in the area where *Sandy Island* was believed to be located found no trace of the island itself (Dossey, 2015). The 'removal' of *Sandy Island* from the maps was rapid. *Google* deleted it from the Google Earth database and *National Geographic* removed the island from its maps by the end of November 2012 (Tallack, 2016).

How did the island possibly end up on maps and what did the whaling ship *Velocity* see? Scholars believe that it was a case of human error handed down through the years, because the island was attested on admiralty maps, and this meant that the error continued during the conversion from hard-copy maps to digitised map forms like the WVS and Google Earth (Seton et al., 2013). It is widely accepted that what the crew members on *Velocity* saw could have been a large pumice sea raft. Pumice rafts refer to lava that has been ejected into the sea from an underwater volcano and that has cooled rapidly. These rafts are light enough to float on water and can travel for long distances (Dossey, 2015). Considering that *Sandy Island* was reported to be twenty-five kilometres long and five kilometres wide, it is possible the island spotted in 1876 was not an island that was sandy, but a large raft made of cooled, solidified floating lava (Seton et al., 2013). The case of *Sandy Island* is, thus, a good example of a 'phantom island'. It was believed to be real and featured on maps for centuries, although no such place existed, and was arguably a result of both

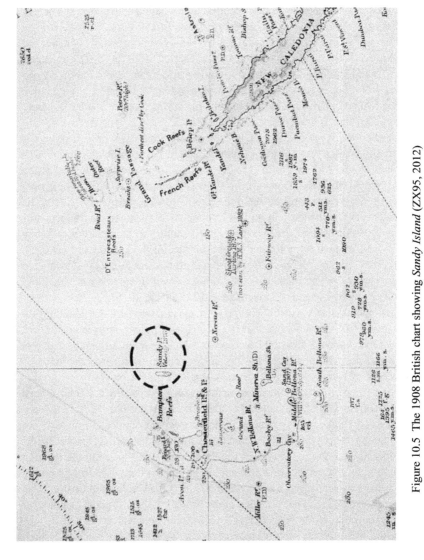

Figure 10.5  The 1908 British chart showing *Sandy Island* (ZX95, 2012)

human error in mapping and mistaking the possible pumice sea raft for a whole island.

Another source of phantom place names comes from and is witnessed in literary works which are often guided by ideologies of adventure, wonder, and utopia. Phantom and imaginary places have been attested since antiquity. The Greek explorer Pytheas allegedly sailed northward from *Marseilles* (*Massalia* [*Μασσαλία*], or *Masalia* [*Μασαλία*] in Ancient Greek, having been founded by Greek settlers from *Phocaea* around 600 BCE), *France*, around 330 BCE. Six days later, he reached the land he called *Thule*. The exact location of *Thule* was hotly debated, as Pytheas' accounts were lost and later were dismissed by scholars as fabrication (Stefansson, 2019). *Iceland*, the *Shetland Islands*, the *Faroe Islands*, *Norway*, and *Finland* have been cited as possible options of the legendary place (Simpson-Housley, 1996). The phrase '*Ultima Thule*', meaning '*Furthest Thule*', became widespread and appeared in poems and tales, symbolising a distant northern place which was geographically undefined and cloaked in mystery (Gilberg, 1976). Many fables about Thulean discoveries abound, and each story tells of *Thule* 'as a place of mysteries and wonders, a distillation of northern myths and fantasies, but also, at the same time, a reminder of their imaginative limits' (Huggan, 2015, p. 331).

Since the Middle Ages, *Cockaigne*, an imaginary place filled with natural beauties and earthly pleasures, has also consistently appeared in utopian literary works across time and space, be they poems (*The Big Rock Candy Mountain* in Medieval *England*, for example), or a folksong that was popular in the *USA* during the Great Depression (Elliott, 2013), or the *Cuccagna* in the well-known book *Le avventure di Pinocchio: Storia di un Burattino* (*Pinocchio's Adventures: Story of a Puppet*), published in 1881–3 by Carlo Collodi.

In more recent times, Italo Calvino's *Invisible Cities* (1972) portrayed fifty-five literary 'fantastical constructions' in which cities, fashioned from an imaginary dialogue between Marco Polo and Kublai Khan, were described in detail. Kublai Khan asks Marco Polo to describe to him the cities he has visited across the Chinese Empire he rules, but the latter talks about fabulous cities, which are a product of his imagination, for example, reflected in lakes or located under the surface of the earth (Psarra, 2018, p. 143). These cities are 'invisible' because they do not exist and are fantastic variations on the theme of Marco Polo's hometown, *Venice*. Each city has the name of a woman. The *Invisible Cities* has become somewhat of a manifesto for the notion of 'imaginary places' and 'imaginary place names'.

Literature, toponymy, and cartography all have one element in common. They are, essentially, and for different reasons, narratives at work. 'Narratives', in this context, refers to what we can call the *what* and the *how*. That is, the stories that are told constitute the '*what* is told' and, as defined by Prince (1987), the presentation of the stories in particular ways, gives us the '*how* it is told'.

(Literary) place names presented in this section, like *Ultima Thule*, *Cockaigne*, and those in *Invisible Cities*, evoke the 'feeling of place', which constructs the narrative world that is the heart of literature. The sense and 'feeling of place' evoked by place names in literary texts relate to their associative meanings, defined by the information, images, and, importantly, the associations surrounding toponyms (Ameel & Ainiala, 2018). In turn, these meanings help the audience to make sense of the story's narrative both rationally, by placing the location within a network of complex relationships, and 'corporeally', by triggering sensory experiences, especially if there are counterparts in the real world (Ameel & Ainiala, 2018). Moreover, toponyms build up, by themselves, a narrative strategy that identify meta-poetical relations within the text or place a character within a social or moral epistemology. In some cases, the act of narration in folklores and ballads, which can naturally be considered literary genres, precedes the act of naming a place. This is where place names crystallise the narrative and act as a 'shorthand' of the story. A narrative of truth becomes synonymous with the toponym. As Nicolaisen (1984, pp. 266–7) noted:

[...] by situating this story on the map among other names it has given it a topographic identity that amounts to veracity [...] Since the name is attached to such and such a place, the past must have been the way the story tells it. The name, in addition to other narrative functions in this context, takes on the role of verification, of precisely locating the truth.

The narrative potential of literary toponyms is concomitant with how toponyms, as demonstrated throughout this book, tell stories about cultures and civilisations and, particularly for Indigenous communities, are part of the everyday narrative and discourse that are passed from generation to generation, forming a mental map of the characteristics of the landscape and facilitating communication about the place names and the 'hidden landscape' attached to the places they name (Cogos et al., 2017, p. 46). Likewise, maps tell stories. A particularly useful quote on the narratives and stories that map tell comes from Kenneth Field, who writes the following.

Whether we're looking at the topography of a reference sheet and exploring the detailed story of the landscape; imagining the people wandering across the children's atlas; or interpreting what a statistical map means for people in different areas we're doing one thing – following the narrative of the map to better understand the story it is telling. Story telling is the very essence of good map-making and good cartographers have forever been successfully telling stories. In fact, good story-tellers have made very good use of maps as vehicles for their work. (Field, 2014, p. 99)

The storytelling potential of maps can be harnessed to tell and support narratives, particularly in novels and films, in what are known as 'internal maps', where, among other functions, they base the story at a specific site (Ryan, 2003). Maps can also support the narrative process. It is well known that James Joyce wrote *Ulysses* with *Dublin*'s map in front of him (Budgen, 1934). Increasingly, over time, a focus has developed on linking maps with the map making process from which they emerge. This narrative of mapping, particularly in an era where maps are believed to be an 'unfinished business', 'is essential to documenting the mapping genealogy and to tell the story of the map's life' (Caquard & Cartwright, 2014, p. 105). The process of mapping place names, then, builds on the narrative structures that not only tell what a place is, but, through encoding affective, sociopolitical, cultural, historical, and ideological stories, tell of the prevailing (and competing) discourses that come to characterise these places.

## 10.7    Summary

This chapter explores the relationship between cartography and toponymy. Toponyms on the map not only have a locational function, whereby they give geographical and topographic meaning to map symbols and help the user to better navigate the environment using a map, but they also have an affective role and bring about certain emotions when people familiar with specific places look at the map that records them. More importantly, place names allow us to study the sociopolitical, cultural, and ideological functions of maps – both in ancient times and in more recent years, and even now that mapping technologies have undergone significant changes in the GIS age. For example, an analysis of place names and their representations on the maps show the cultural division that existed between the *West* and the *Middle East* during the sixteenth and eighteenth centuries. On the sociopolitical and ideological front, the survey of historical literature and documents reveals that ruling bodies (particularly colonisers) use maps to impose political control and enforce the superiority of their worldviews, often at the expense of Indigenous cultures, languages, knowledge, and toponyms. Maps confirm this power differential and portray the historical events through their representations of places and place naming. Furthermore, literary place names, like *Ultima Thule* and *Cockaigne*, mapped and at the same time unmapped, also reveal certain traits of human nature, such as the propensity for travel and exploration and the desire for beauty and earthly pleasures. While most people think that the map is innocent and neutral, especially the study of the toponyms on the map, which is just one of the many ways of approaching cartographic documents, the reality is that maps, like toponyms, are 'political' and ultimately 'human products', and hence they are 'an abstraction of reality' according to the mapper and reflect their political and ideological goals, but they are 'not reality itself' (Taylor, 1991, p. 2).

# Glossary

**Alor-Pantar languages**: A family of related Papuan languages spoken on the islands of the *Alor-Pantar* archipelago. The language family is divided into two branches, the Alor branch and the Pantar branch, spoken on the islands of *Alor* and *Pantar*, respectively.

**anthroponym**: A proper (or personal) name of a person – a proper noun.

**anthroponymy and anthroponomastics**: A branch of onomastics that focusses on the study of personal names.

**associative meaning (of place names)**: The information, images, and other associations surrounding a toponym that give the place name the sense and 'feeling of place'.

**associative name**: A name that, according to Stewart's toponymic categories, evokes associations with different objects. It also indicates a place name that is associated with a feature or its physical context or location.

***bona fide* paretymology**: See paretymology.

**bottom-up linguistic landscape**: The situation where language use is produced freely by individual actors (e.g., people), rather than a central organisation, for example, in naming shops or marking private business signs.

**cartography**: The discipline concerned with the art, science, and technology of map making and map usage.

**cognate**: A word that descends from a (proto-)word common to other lexemes belonging to the same lexical family and to languages from the same language family.

**commemorative name**: A name that commemorates a person, place, or event. One of Stewart's ten toponymic categories.

**commendatory name**: A name given by some attractive peculiarities of a geographical object. One of Stewart's ten toponymic categories.

**comparative method**: A method of comparing cognates from two or more languages that derive from a common or shared ancestor language (a proto-language) and belong to the same language family. It is based on the principle of regular sound change, which holds that any change in the sounds of a language that happens over time occurs in a prevalently regular way according to patterns (sound laws), with no exceptions.

**contact etymology**: A three-step framework proposed by Robert Mailhammer for dealing with words derived from language contact.

**contemporary**: In the context of this book, contemporary refers to a period of time within the last 200 years, usually from the nineteenth century to the present day.

**critical toponymies (or critical toponymy theory)**: The study of how political – and, increasingly over time, economic – contexts shape place naming practices and patterns, for example, the treating of place names as commodities (toponymic commodification).

**demonym**: A name that refers to groups of people connected with a particular place. It is derived from Ancient Greek *dêmos* (δῆμος) 'people', and *ónoma* (ὄνομα) 'name'.

**dendronym**: A name of a plant. It is derived from Ancient Greek *déndron* (δένδρον) 'tree, plant', and *ónoma* (ὄνομα) 'name'.

**descriptive name**: A name that describes and characterises the qualities of a place. One of Stewart's ten toponymic categories.

**diachronic toponymy**: The study of the possible origins of a place name (a) in the context of undocumented and endangered languages, and (b) in the absence of historical records.

**diachronic**: The term 'diachronic' means, literally, 'throughout time'. It is derived from Ancient Greek *diá* (διά) 'through', and *chrónos* (χρόνος) 'time'

**dryonyms**: A name that refers to forests. It is derived from Ancient Greek *drýs* (δρῦς) 'tree', and *ónoma* (ὄνομα) 'name'.

**endonym**: A name of a place in one of the languages spoken in a specific area. For example, the pinyin place name *Beijing* is an endonym, while its (Western) equivalent *Peking* is an exonym.

**ethnonym**: A name that refers to nationalities or ethnic groups.

**etymology**: The study of the origins of words and their original meanings.

**exonym**: A name of a place in a language that is not spoken in a specific area and where a specific language does not have 'official' status. The name is also different from the related toponym in the official language(s) spoken in that area (see endonym).

**extensive approach to toponymy**: A quantitative model that looks for toponymic patterns in a collection of place names, unearthing observations such as naming practices and distribution of geographical features when studying toponymy.

**false/folk etymology**: See paretymology. One of Stewart's ten toponymic categories.

**foundation myth**: A founding (or creation) myth is a story that explains the origins of the world or the creation of humans. It is a story handed down through oral traditions and explains the origins of a ritual or the founding of a group. It is presented as a genealogy from which the community descended and accounts for the spiritual origins of a belief or philosophy, and the connection between god(s) and humans. The members of the community believe that this is core to their identity, and a foundation myth can only be correct if the ideal movement of the characters through the landscape is illustrated by a real and existing place name sequence.

**generic element**: A geographic term that classifies the type of geographical territory of a place. For example, 'Road' in *Orchard Road*, or 'Lane' in *Penny Lane*.

**geographic information system (GIS)**: A framework which extracts and records spatial and geographic data. It then analyses and maps this data.

**glottonym**: The name of a language.

**historical geographic information systems (HGIS)**: A GIS that extracts, displays, records, and stores data of historical spaces and geographies from the past.

**historical geography**: A subfield of human geography which deals with how space and place were used socially, economically, culturally, and politically by humans in a particular place and at a particular time in the past.

**historical linguistics**: The study of the development and history of languages, such as how languages relate to one another, for example, whether they are derived from a common origin or how language contact has affected them.

**historical phonetics**: The diachronic development of sounds in a language and the relation of one sound to another in the same language.

**historical semantics**: The study of the changes in the meaning (semantic shift) of words or expressions over a period of time.

**historical toponomastics**: The study of how to reconstruct the remote etymology of place names (a) in the context of well-known languages and language families, and (b) in the presence of available physical historical records and sources.

**human geography**: The discipline that deals with how space and place are used socially, economically, culturally, and politically by humans.

**hydronym**: A name that refers to all water bodies, including rivers, streams, brooks, lakes, and seas. It is derived from Ancient Greek *hýdōr* (ὕδωρ) 'water', and *ónoma* (ὄνομα) 'name'.

**hydronymy**: The discipline studying hydronyms. It can also indicate the set of specific hydronyms belonging to a specific area.

**Ice Age**: The Late Cenozoic Ice Age began around 34 million years ago. The Quaternary glaciation, its last stage, is currently in progress, and started 2.58 million years ago.

**incident name**: A name that associates a place with an incident at a particular time. One of Stewart's ten toponymic categories.

**insulonym**: A name that refers to islands (see also *nesonym*). It is derived from Latin *insula* 'island' and Ancient Greek *ónoma* (ὄνομα) 'name'.

**intensive approach to toponymy**: A qualitative approach used in the study of toponymy by answering questions on the etymology and meaning of particular toponyms at the micro-level.

**landscape archaeology**: The study of the past use of the landscape, determined by archaeological findings.

**landscape**: The natural features of an area such as mountains, trees, rocks, lakes, rivers, sand, grass, and so on. Over time, the definition of 'landscape' has become more encompassing, including social, cultural, environmental, and even religious aspects connected with the land.

**language change**: The phenomenon where features of a language (e.g., phonology, morphology, lexicon, syntax, and semantics) change over time.

**language variation**: A subfield of language change which deals with how languages vary across different regions and across social groupings such as age, gender, class, religion, ethnicity, occupation, and so on.

**limnonym**:  A name that refers to lakes. It is derived from Ancient Greek *límnē* (*λίμνη*) 'lake' and *ónoma* (*ὄνομα*) 'name'.

**Linear A**:  An undeciphered Aegean writing system used in the Bronze Age (ca. 3300 BCE to 1200 BCE) in *Crete* by the Minoan civilisation.

**Linear B**:  A syllabic writing system transcribing Mycenaean Greek, an archaic form of Ancient Greek.

**linguistic fossil**:  A term that describes an intrinsic feature of a toponym, as place names are generally stable over time. They can be preserved over a very long time and contain valuable information which may have been lost elsewhere when local languages were forgotten or replaced.

**linguistic landscape**:  The visibility and use of languages to construct public space in a particular area.

**linguistic pilgrimage**:  The personal relationship between the human and the observed environment. The linguistic pilgrim reflects as he/she sees language in the landscape, signs, and how language is used within sociocultural contexts.

**linguistic substrate**:  An Indigenous or local language that provides features (lexical, phonetic, syntactic, etc.) to the language of the people who invade and impose their language on the local population.

**macro-toponym**:  A name of a larger/major geographical site, including denominations of countries, capitals, regions, and even major streets.

**manufactured name**:  A name which is manufactured or coined from sounds, letters, or fragments of other words. One of Stewart's ten toponymic categories.

**micro-hydronym**:  A name given to smaller and more localised bodies of water, for example, brooks, springs, and wells.

**micro-toponym**:  A name of smaller places known to a smaller set of people (usually locals). These include wells, gates, local streets, and brooks.

**Middle Ages**:  The time period lasting approximately from the fifth century to the late fifteenth century (476 CE, the collapse of the Western *Roman Empire*, to 1492 CE, the 'discovery' of *America* by Cristoforo Colombo).

**mistake name**:  A name which appeared from a mistake made in the transmission from one language to another. One of Stewart's ten toponymic categories.

**Modern Ages**:  The time period from the end of the Middle Ages to the middle of the twentieth century (1492 CE, the 'discovery' of *America* by Cristoforo Colombo, to 1815 CE, the end of the Congress of *Vienna*).

**Neolithic**: The time period in prehistory when the practice of agriculture began and when polished stone tools and weapons were used. This time period is also known as the New Stone Age.

**nesonym**: A name that refers to islands (see also *insulonyms*). It is derived from Ancient Greek *nēsos* (νῆσος) 'island' and *ónoma* (ὄνομα) 'name'.

**oceanonym**: A name that refers to oceans. It is derived from Ancient Greek *Ōkeanós* (Ὠκεανός) *Oceanus* (a water deity) 'ocean' and *ónoma* (ὄνομα) 'name'.

**odonym**: A name that refers to streets, avenues, boulevards, drives, lanes, and other denominations relating to inhabited areas. It is derived from Ancient Greek *hodós* (ὁδός) 'a way, path, track, road', and *ónoma* (ὄνομα) 'name'.

**odonymy**: The discipline studying odonyms. It can also indicate a set of specific odonyms of a specific area.

**onomasiological**: The assigning of a name to a place: 'how do we, or should we, express terminologically the elements in system Y (and the relations among them)?'

**onomastics**: The scientific study of all kinds of names. It is derived from Ancient Greek *ónoma* (ὄνομα) 'name'.

**oral/mental map**: The oral/mental systematic organisation of a geographical landscape in order to aid people in orientating in the space in the absence of drawing tools and writing systems.

**ornithonym**: The name that refers to a bird. It is derived from Ancient Greek *órnis* (ὄρνις) 'bird' and *ónoma* (ὄνομα) 'name'.

**oronym**: A name that refers to mountains, hills, and hillocks. It is derived from Ancient Greek *óros* (ὄρος) 'mountain' and *ónoma* (ὄνομα) 'name'.

**oronymy**: The discipline studying oronyms. It can also indicate a set of specific oronyms of a specific area.

**Palaeolithic**: The time period in prehistory when primitive men used unpolished tools and weapons made of stone.

**Papuan languages**: Non-Austronesian and non-Australian languages commonly spoken on the Pacific island of *New Guinea* and neighbouring islands. An example of a Papuan language is Abui, which is spoken on *Alor Island* in southeast *Indonesia* (*Alor-Pantar* archipelago, *Timor* area).

**paretymology** (also known as folk etymology): The linguistic misinterpretation of words/lexemes which occurs when speakers look for analogical forms in their common and contemporary lexicon, or use local oral-traditional stories, to explain their origins, whose original morphology and/or meaning has been lost.

**pelagonym**:  A name given to seas. It is derived from Ancient Greek *pélagos* (πέλᾶγος) 'sea' and *ónoma* (ὄνομα) 'name'.

**personal name**:  The name of a person, an anthroponym.

**phantom places**:  Places that, although believed to be real and despite having been officially charted on maps, turned out over time to be non-existent.

**physical geography**:  The discipline that studies physical phenomena on, at, or near the *Earth*'s surface.

**phytonym**:  A name given to trees, plants, or flowers. It is derived from Ancient Greek *phytón* (φυτόν) 'plant' and *ónoma* (ὄνομα) 'name'.

**possessive name**:  A name that denotes some ideas of ownership or the notion according to which a place is associated with something or someone. One of Stewart's ten toponymic categories.

**potamonym**:  A name given to rivers. It is derived from Ancient Greek *potamós* (ποταμός) 'river' and *ónoma* (ὄνομα) 'name'.

**Pre-Indo-European**:  A non-Indo-European language (or set of languages) which predated (Proto-)Indo-European.

**pre-language**:  A language spoken in a specific territory before a proto-language. It is unrelated to the proto-language which follows it, and can only be hypothesised. Unlike a proto-language, it cannot be reconstructed.

**Pre-Proto-Indo-European**:  A stage of Indo-European before the possible language contact with other prehistoric (proto-)languages and/or language families.

**prehistory**:  The period of time before written records and documentations existed.

**proper noun**:  Linguistic signs that can denote a range of entities (e.g., person, a group of persons, plants, animals, living things, landmarks, etc.).

**Proto-Alor Pantar**:  The common ancestor from which Alor-Pantar languages derive.

**proto-form/root**:  The basic, most remote, and abstract components of a proto-language. While the proto-form is a proto-word in itself, the root is a stem or matrix of a family of words deriving from it. A root can also be defined as the smallest part of a word that carries meaning.

**Proto-Indo-European (or Indo-European or Common Indo-European)**: The proto-language at the origins of the so-called Indo-European languages.

**proto-language**: An unattested, remote, abstract, reconstructed, and theoretical language spoken in the distant past and in the absence of writing or of any other form of historical documentation by prehistoric individuals belonging to the genus *Homo*. It is reconstructed using the comparative method on the basis of attested (both living and dead) languages which derive from it. From this language, a group of specific known, historical, and attested/documented languages are believed to have descended.

**refunctionalisation**: The process according to which a linguistic form that is borrowed/imported from a language is incorporated into the linguistic system of another, possibly unrelated, language.

**scholarly paretymology**: A toponymic paretymology produced by scholars, who may not account for all the historical evidence, or lack of, or may have an ulterior motive in doing so, for example, to 'ennoble' a place or to 'belittle' it, to provide false evidence for a genealogy, to tendentiously prove linguistic or academic theories, or to flatter powerful people.

**semasiological**: The understanding of a place name from a historical and linguistic perspective: 'why and how did X come to be called X?'

**settlement dynamics**: The movement of population(s) into an area, for instance, due to immigration or invasion.

**shift name**: A name which has been moved from one location to another. One of Stewart's ten toponymic categories.

**socio-onomastics**: The discipline focussing on the analysis of names and naming practices.

**sociolinguistics**: The study of language and the social factors that influence how we speak and interact with others.

**specific element**: The actual name and/or name component of a place. For example, *Mexico* in *Mexico City*, or British in British Museum.

**speleonym**: A name that refers to caves, chasms, grottoes, mines, and entire underground systems. It is derived from Ancient Greek *spélaion* (σπήλαιον) 'cave' and *ónoma* (ὄνομα) 'name'.

**synchronic toponymy**: The branch of toponymy that deals with the function of names in society and with the perception of names by members of society. It uses a non-etymological approach in the context of a specific time frame.

**synchronic**: A term that refers to events that occur during a particular time frame, usually without taking into consideration historical antecedents.

*tira*: A word in the Abui language referring specifically to Abui myths and legends (the narrative genre of the Abui).

**top-down linguistic landscape**: The situation where language use is determined by institutional agencies and imposed by specific policies, for example, the language used for public signs and street names.

**toponym**: A name that refers to a place. It is derived from Ancient Greek τόπος (*tópos*) 'place' and ὄνομα (*ónoma*) 'name'.

**toponymic paretymology**: The linguistic misinterpretation of place names (see paretymology).

**toponymic system**: A set of place names (toponyms, hydronyms, oronyms, and odonyms) that belong to a specific area and share the same etymological stem (and related meaning) and/or the same naming process and, therefore, the same origins.

**toponymy and toponomastics**: A branch of onomastics that focusses on the study of place names, or toponyms.

**urbanonym**: A name that refers to urban elements, such as streets, blocks, parks, avenues, drives, churches, buildings, and so on. It is derived from Latin *urbs* 'city' and Ancient Greek *ónoma* (ὄνομα) 'name'.

**urbanonymy**: The discipline studying urbanonyms. It can also indicate a set of specific urbanonyms of a specific area.

**zoonym**: The name for a species of animal or for an animal in itself. It is derived from Ancient Greek ζῷον (*zô[i]on*) 'animal' and ὄνομα (*ónoma*) 'name'.

# References

Adebanwi, W. (2017). Colouring 'Rainbow' Streets: The Struggle for Toponymic Multiracialism in Urban Post-Apartheid South Africa. In R. S. Rose-Redwood, D. H. Alderman, & M. Azaryahu (Eds.), *The Political Life of Urban Streetscapes: Naming, Politics, and Place* (pp. 218–39). New York: Routledge.

Ainiala, T. & Östman, J.-O. (2017). Introduction: Socio-Onomastics and Pragmatics. In T. Ainiala & J.-O. Östman (Eds.), *Socio-Onomastics: The Pragmatics of Names* (pp. 2–18). Amsterdam: John Benjamins.

Alderman, D. H., Benjamin S. K., & Scheider P. P. (2012). Transforming Mount Airy into Mayberry: Film-Induced Tourism as Place-Making. *Southeastern Geographer*, 52(2), 212–39.

Aleru, J. O. & Alabi, R. A. (2010). Towards a Reconstruction of Yoruba Culture History: A Toponymic Perspective. *African Study Monographs*, 31(4), 149–62.

Algeo, J. & Algeo, K. (2000). Onomastics as an Interdisciplinary Study. *Names: A Journal of Onomastics*, 48(3/4), 265–74.

Alinei, M. (1996). *Origine delle lingue d'Europa. I. La Teoria della Continuità.* Bologna: Il Mulino.

Alinei, M. (2000). *Origini delle lingue d'Europa. II. Continuità dal Mesolitico al Ferro nelle principali aree europee (Origins of European Languages. II. Continuity from Mesolithic to the Irong Age in the Main European Areas)*. Bologna: Il Mulino.

Ameel, L. & Ainiala, T. (2018). Toponyms as Prompts for Presencing Place-Making Oneself at Home in Kjell Westö's Helsinki. *Scandinavian Studies*, 90, 195–210.

Anthony, D. W. (1995). Horse, Wagon & Chariot: Indo-European Languages and Archaeology. *Antiquity*, 69, 554–65.

Antrop, M. (2013). A Brief History of Landscape Research. In P. Howard, I. Thompson, & E. Waterton (Eds.), *The Routledge Companion to Landscape Studies* (pp. 12–22). London: Routledge.

Aporta, C., Kritsch, I., Andre, A., et al. (2014). The Gwich'in Atlas: Place Names, Maps, and Narratives. In D. R. F. Taylor & T. Lauriahault (Eds.), *Developments in the Theory and Practice of Cybercartography: Applications and Indigenous Mapping* (pp. 229–44). Amsterdam: Elsevier.

Ashcroft, B., Griffiths, G., & Tiffin, H. (2003). Introduction to Part XII: Place. In B. Ashcroft, G. Grffths, & H. Tiffin (Eds.), *The Post-Colonial Studies Reader* (pp. 391–4). London: Routledge.

Aston, M. & Rowley, T. (1974). *Landscape Archaeology: An Introduction to Fieldwork Techniques on Post-Roman Landscapes*. Newton Abbot: David and Charles.

Atchison, J. F. (1982). Australian Place-Names and Cartographers. *Cartography*, 12(3), 151–5.

Australian Associated Press. (2020). Western Australia's King Leopold Ranges Renamed Wunaamin Miliwundi Ranges. *Guardian*, 3 July. www.theguardian.com/australia-news/2020/jul/03/western-australias-king-leopold-ranges-renamed-to-honour-aboriginal-heritage.

Aybes, C. & Yalden, D. (1995). Place-Name Evidence for the Former Distribution and Status of Wolves and Beavers in Britain. *Mammal Review*, 25, 201–26.

Azaryahu, M. (1996). The Power of Commemorative Street Names. *Environment and Planning D: Society and Space*, 14, 311–30.

Azaryahu, M. (1997). German Reunification and the Politics of Street Names: The Case of East Berlin. *Political Geography*, 16(6), 479–93.

Azaryahu, M. (2011a). The Politics of Commemorative Street Renaming: Berlin 1945–1948. *Journal of Historical Geography*, 37, 483–92.

Azaryahu, M. (2011b). The Critical Turn and Beyond: The Case of Commemorative Street Naming. *ACME: An International E-Journal for Critical Geographies*, 10(1), 28–33.

Baker, A. (1987). Editorial: The Practice of Historical Geography. *Journal of Historical Geography*, 13(1), 1–2.

Ballester, X. & Benozzo, F. (2018). The Paleolithic Continuity Paradigm for the Origins of Indo-European Languages. www.continuitas.org/index.html.

Basso, K. H. (1988). 'Speaking with Names': Language and Landscape among the Western Apache. *Cultural Anthropology*, 3(2), 99–130.

Basso, K. H. (1990). *Western Apache Language and Culture: Essays in Linguistic Anthropology*. Tuscon: The University of Arizona Press.

Basso, K. H. (1996). *Wisdom Sits in Places: Landscape and Language among the Western Apache*. Albuquerque: University of New Mexico Press.

Batoma, A. (2006). African Ethnonyms and Toponyms: An Annotated Bibliography. *Electronic Journal of Africana Bibliography*, 10(1), 1–40.

BBC. (2021). Ukraine's Euro 2020 Football Kit Provokes Outrage in Russia. June 7. www.bbc.com/news/world-europe-57379875.

Beekes, R. S. P. (2010). *Etymological Dictionary of Greek. With the Assistance of Lucien van Beek*. Leiden and Boston, MA: Brill.

Belen'kaya, V. D. (1975). Current Tendencies in the Naming of Places: On the Synchronic Approach to Place Names. *Soviet Geography*, 16(5), 315–20.

Ben-Rafael, E., Shohamy, E., Amara, M., & Trumper-Hecht, N. (2016). Linguistic Landscape as Symbolic Construction of the Public Space: The Case of Israel. *International Journal of Multilingualism*, 3(1), 7–30.

Bentley, A. R., Chikhi, L., & Price, D. T. (2003). The Neolithic Transition in Europe: Comparing Broad Scale Genetic and Local Isotopic Evidence. *Antiquity*, 77, 63–6.

Benveniste, É. (2001). *Il vocabolario delle istituzioni indoeuropee. Volume II. Potere, diritto, religione [The Dictionary of Indo-European Institutions. Volume II. Power, Law, Religion]*. Turin: Einaudi.

Benvenisti, M. (2000). *The Buried History of the Holy Land since 1948*. Los Angeles: University of California Press.

Beretta, C. (2003). *I nomi dei fiumi, dei monti, dei siti. Strutture linguistiche preistoriche [The Names of Rivers, Mounts, Sites. Prehistoric Linguistic Structures (Bilingual Edition)]*. Milan: Centro camuno di studi preistorici/Ulrico Hoepli Editore.

Biagi, P. (1980). Some Aspects of the Prehistory of Northern Italy from the Final Palaeolithic to the Middle Neolithic: A Reconsideration on the Evidence Available to Date. *Proceedings of the Prehistoric Society*, 46, 9–18.

Bichlmeier, H. (2012). Anmerkungen zum terminologischen Problem der 'alteuropäischen Hydronymie' samt indogermanistischen Ergänzungen zum Namen der Elbe [Notes on the Terminological Problem of the 'Old European Hydronymy' with Indo-European Additions to the Name of the Elbe]. *Beiträge zur Namenforschung*, 47(4), 365–95.

Bigon, L. (2008). Names, Norms and Forms: French and Indigenous Toponyms in Early Colonial Dakar, Senegal. *Planning Perspectives*, 23(4), 479–501.

Bigon, L. (2020). Towards Creating a Global Urban Toponymy: A Comment. *Urban Science*, 4(4), 75.

Blair, D. (2015). From the Editor. *Placenames Australia: Newsletter of the Australian National Placename Survey*, March 2.

Blair, D. & Tent, J. (2020). *Toponym Types: A Revised Typology of Place-Naming. Australian National Placenames Survey Technical Papers, Vol. 5.* South Turramurra: Placenames Australia.

Blair, D. & Tent, J. (2021). A Revised Typology of Place-Naming. *Names: A Journal of Onomastics*, 69(4), 31–47.

Blust, R. (1984–5). The Austronesian Homeland: A Linguistic Perspective. *Asian Perspectives*, 26(1), 45–67.

Boccardo, G. (1875–8). *Nuova enciclopedia italiana ovvero, Dizionario generale di scienze, lettere, industrie, ecc.* Turin: Unione tipografico-editrice torinese.

Bodenhamer, D. J. (2013). Beyond GIS: Geospatial Technologies and the Future of History. In A. v. Lünen & C. Travis (Eds.), *History and GIS: Epistemologies, Considerations and Reflections* (pp. 1–14). New York and London: Springer.

Bol, P. & Ge, J. (2005). China Historical GIS. *Historical Geography*, 33, 150–2.

Bolelli, T. (1995). *Dizionario etimologico della lingua italiana [Etymological Dictionary of the Italian Language]*. Milan/Turin: TEA/UTET.

Borchert, J. R. (1987). Maps, Geography, and Geographers. *The Professional Geographer*, 39(4), 387–9.

Bosio, B. (1972). *La Charta di fondazione e donazione dell'Abbazia di San Quintino in Spigno. 4 Maggio 991 [The Founding and Donation Charta of the Saint Quentin's Abbey in Spigno Monferrato. May the 4th, 991]*. Alba/Visone: Tipografie Domenicane.

Bourdieu, P. (1986). The Forms of Capital. In J. Richardson (Ed.), *Handbook of Theory and Research for the Sociology of Education* (pp. 241–58). New York: Greenwood Press.

Bourdieu, P. (1991). *Language and Symbolic Power* (G. Raymond & M. Adamson, Trans. J. B. Thompson, Ed.). Cambridge: Polity Press.

Branton, N. (2009). Landscape Approaches in Historical Archaeology: The Archaeology of Places. In D. Gaimster & T. Majewski (Eds.), *International Handbook of Historical Archaeology* (pp. 51–65). New York: Springer.

Brealey, K. G. (1995). Mapping Them 'Out': Euro-Canadian Cartography and the Appropriation of the Nuxalk and Ts'ilhqot'in First Nations' Territories, 1793–1916. *The Canadian Geographer [Le Géographe Canadien]*, 39(2), 140–56.

Bright, W. (2003). What IS a Name? Reflections on Onomastics. *Language and Linguistics*, 4(4), 669–81.

Brooke-Hitching, E. (2016). *The Phantom Atlas: The Greatest Myths, Lies, and Blunders on Maps*. New York: Simon & Schuster.

Buchroithner, M. F. & Fernández, P. A. (2011). Cartography in the Context of Sciences: Theoretical and Technological Considerations. *The Cartographic Journal*, 48(1), 4–10.

Budgen, F. (1934). *James Joyce and the Making of 'Ulysses'*. Bloomington: Indiana University Press.

Burridge, K. & Bergs, A. (2016). *Understanding Language Change*. New York: Routledge.

Calvino, I. (1972). *Le città invisibili* [*Invisible Cities*]. Turin: Giulio Einaudi.

Cambi, F. (2011). *Manuale di archeologia dei paesaggi: Metodologie, fonti, contesti* [*Handbook of Landscapes' Archaeology: Methodologies, Sources, Contexts*]. Rome: Carocci.

Campbell, L. (2004). *Historical Linguistics: An Introduction*. Cambridge, MA: The MIT Press.

Campbell, L. (2013). *Historical Linguistics: An Introduction* (3rd ed.). Edinburgh: Edinburgh University Press.

Campbell, L. & Mixco, M. J. (2007). *A Glossary of Historical Linguistics*. Edinburgh: Edinburgh University Press.

Cantù, C. (1858). *Grande illustrazione del Lombardo-Veneto, ossia Storia delle città, dei borghi, comuni, castelli, ecc. fino ai tempi moderni* [*Great Description of the Lombardo-Veneto, i.e., History of the Cities, Villages, Towns, Castles, etc., Until Modern Times*]. Milan: Corona e Caimi Editori.

Caquard, S. & Cartwright, W. (2014). Narrative Cartography: From Mapping Stories to the Narrative of Maps and Mapping. *The Cartographic Journal*, 51(2), 101–6.

Cartwright, W., Gartner, G., & Lehn, A. (Eds.) (2009). *Cartography and Art: Lecture Notes in Geoinformation and Cartography*. New York: Springer.

Carvalhinhos, P., Lima-Hernandes, M. C., & Lima, A. (2018). The Ideological Function in Names of Public Spaces in the City of São Paulo, Brazil. *Onomastica Uralica*, 14, 93–110.

Casagranda, M. (2013). *From Empire Avenue to Hiawatha Road: (Post)colonial Naming Practices in the Toronto Street Index*. Paper presented at the International Conference on Onomastics 'Name and Naming', 2.

Casalis, G. (1833–56). Dizionario geografico-storico-statistico-commerciale degli Stati di S. M. il Re di Sardegna [Geographical, Historical, Statistical, Commercial Dictionary of the Countries Belonging to His Majesty the King of Sardinia]. In *Dizionario geografico-storico-statistico-commerciale degli Stati di S. M. il Re di Sardegna* [*Geographical, Historical, Statistical, Commercial Dictionary of the Countries Belonging to His Majesty the King of Sardinia*]. Turin: G. Maspero librajo e Cassone, Marzorati, Vercellotti tipografi.

Cassidy, F. G. (1977). Notes on Nicknames for Places in the United States. *American Speech*, 52(1/2), 19–28.

Cassiodorus, M. A. S. V. C. (1583). *Variarum libri XII & Chronicon* [*The XII Books of Variae and the Chronicles*]. Paris: Sebastianus Nivellius.

Cavallaro, F., Perono Cacciafoco, F., & Tan, Z. X. (2019). Sequent Occupance and Toponymy in Singapore: The Diachronic and Synchronic Development of Urban Place Names. *Urban Science, Special Issue on Urban Place Names: Political, Economic, and Cultural Dimensions*, 3(3), 98.

Cavalli-Sforza, L. L. (2001). *Genes, Peoples, and Languages*. Berkeley, CA: University of California Press.

Cavalli-Sforza, L. L., Menozzi, P., & Piazza, A. (1994). *The History and Geography of Human Genes*. Princeton, NJ: Princeton University Press.

Ceragioli, F. (2014). File:Bormidanames location map.jpg. Retrieved from https://commons.wikimedia.org/wiki/File:Bormida_names_location_map.jpg.

Chadwick, J. (1958). *The Decipherment of Linear B*. New York: Vintage Books.

Chambers, J. K., Trudgill, P., & Schilling, N. (Eds.). (2008). *The Handbook of Language Change and Variation*. Hoboken, NJ: John Wiley & Sons.

Chen, Y. (1516). Jinling Gujin Tu Kao [A Research on Jinling Ancient Maps]. Nanjing.

Chloupek, B. R. (2018). A GIS Approach to Cultural and Historical Toponymic Research in Nebraska. *Journal of Cultural Geography*, 35(1), 23–43.

Chloupek, B. R. (2019). Public Memory and Political Street Names in Košice: Slovakia's Multiethnic Second City. *Journal of Historical Geography*, 64, 25–35.

Clark, I. (2009). Reconstruction of Aboriginal Microtoponymy in Western and Central Victoria: Case Studies from Tower Hill, the Hopkins River, and Lake Boga. In L. Hercus & H. Koch (Eds.), *Aboriginal Placenames: Naming and Re-Naming the Australian Landscape* (pp. 207–21). Canberra: The Australian National University Press.

Clifford, N. (2009). Physical Geography. In D. Gregory, R. Johnston, G. Pratt, M. J. Watts, & S. Whatmore (Eds.), *The Dictionary of Human Geography* (pp. 531–7). Chichester: Wiley-Blackwell.

Coates, R. (2013). Onomastics. In C. A. Chapelle (Ed.), *The Encyclopedia of Applied Linguistics* (pp. 4315–20). Oxford: Blackwell Publishing Ltd.

Coates, R. (2020). The Island Name Krk, Croatia, in Its Mediterranean and European Context. *Вопросы ономастики*, 17(3), 186–208.

Cocchetti, C. (1859). *Brescia e sua Provincia descritte da Carlo Cocchetti* [*Brescia and Its Province Described by Carlo Cocchetti*]. Milan: Corona e Caimi Editori.

Cogos, S., Roué, M., & Roturier, S. (2017). Sami Place Names and Maps: Transmitting Knowledge of a Cultural Landscape in Contemporary Contexts. *Arctic, Antarctic, and Alpine Research*, 49(1), 43–51.

Cohen, S. B. & Kliot, N. (1992). Place-Names in Isarael's Ideological Struggle over the Administered Territories. *Annals of the Association of American Geographers*, 82(4), 653–80.

Coleman, G. D. & Tassin, J. B. (1836). Map of The Town and Environs of Singapore. National Archives of Singapore. Retrieved from www.nas.gov.sg/archivesonline/maps_building_plans/record-details/f98c5272-115c-11e3-83d5-0050568939ad.

Colla, E. (1982). *Castrum Bestagni: Bistagno nella Storia* [*Castrum Bestagni: Bistagno in History*]. Bistagno: Municipality of Bistagno.

Collier, P. (2006). *The Colonial Survey Committee and the Mapping of Africa*. Paper presented at the International Symposium on 'Old Worlds-New Worlds': The History of Colonial Cartography 1750–1950, 21–23 August 2006, Utrecht, the Netherlands.

Comune di Pareto (2017). Comune di Pareto [Municipality of Pareto]. Retrieved from https://comune.pareto.al.it/comune-di-pareto/.

Comune di Spigno (2004). Le frazioni di Spigno [Hamlets of Spigno]. Retrieved from http://web.mclink.it/MH0688/Spigno/Frazioni.html.

Conti, S. (2009). Bernardo Silvano y sy obra cartogràfica [Bernardo Silvano and His Cartographic Work]. *Revista de estudios colombinos*, 65(6), 63–74.

Council of Europe (2000). *European Landscape Convention*. European Treaty Series No. 176. Florence.

Cremaschi, M. (Ed.) (2008). *Manuale di Geoarcheologia [Handbook of Geo-Archaeology]* (6th ed.). Rome/Bari: Laterza.

Crețan, R. & Matthews, P. W. (2016). Popular Responses to City-Text Changes: Street Naming and the Politics of Practicality in a Post-Socialist Martyr City. *Area*, 48(1), 92–102.

Cruikshank, J. (1981). Legend and Landscape: Convergence of Oral and Scientific Traditions in the Yukon Territory. *Arctic Anthropology*, 18(2), 67–93.

Crystal, D. (Ed.) (1990). *The Cambridge Encyclopedia of Language*. Cambridge: Cambridge University Press.

Czepczyński, M. (2008). *Cultural Landscapes of Post-Socialist Cities: Representations of Powers and Needs*. Aldershot: Ashgate.

d-maps (2021). North Italy. Retrieved from https://d-maps.com/carte.php?num_car=5890&lang=en.

David, B. & Thomas, J. (2008). Landscape Archaeology: Introduction. In B. David & J. Thomas (Eds.), *Handbook of Landscape Archaeology* (pp. 27–43). Walnut Creek. CA: Left Coast Press.

Dejeant-Pons, M. (2006). The European Landscape Convention. *Landscape Research*, 31(4), 363–84.

Denegre, J. (1992). De Christophe Colomb à la geographie d'aujourd'hui [From Christopher Columbus to Today's Geography]. *Bulletin du Comite Français de Cartographie*, 134, 5–8.

Dennis, R. (1991). History, Geography, and Historical Geography. *Social Science History*, 15(2), 265–88.

Department of Statistics (2020). *Population Trends 2020*. Singapore: Ministry of Trade & Industry.

Devoto, G. (1962). *Origini Indoeuropee*. Florence: Sansoni.

Devoto, G. & Oli, G. C. (1975). *Vocabolario illustrato della lingua italiana: Volume I: A-L*. Firenze: Le Monnier.

Dossey, L. (2015). The Sandy Island Syndromes: On Seeing What Is Not There and Not Seeing What Is There. *EXPLORE: The Journal of Science and Healing*, 11(4), 239–48.

Douglas, B. (2014). Naming Places: Voyagers, Toponyms, and Local Presence in the Fifth Part of the World, 1500–1700. *Journal of Historical Geography*, 45, 12–24.

Duckert, A. R. (1973). Place Nicknames. *Names*, 21(3), 153–60.

Eco, U. (2015). *The Book of Legendary Lands*. London: Quercus Publishing.

Edwards, E. D. & Blagden, C. O. (1931). A Chinese Vocabulary of Malacca Malay Words and Phrases Collected between A.D. 1403 and 1511. *Bulletin of the School of Oriental and African Studies*, 6, 715–49.

Elborough, T. (2016). *Atlas of Improbable Places: A Journey to the World's Most Unusual Corners*. London: Aurum Press.

Elliott, R. C. (2013). The Shape of Utopia: Studies in a Literary Genre. In P. E. Wegner (Ed.), *Ralahine Utopian Studies* (Vol. 10). Berlin: Peter Lang.

Elsey, C. (2013). *The Poetics of Land and Identity among British Columbia Indigenous Peoples*. Halifax: Fernwood.

Eriksen, T. H. (2012). Place Names in Multicultural Societies. In B. Helleland & C.-E. Ore (Eds.), *Names and Identities*. (pp. 72–81). Oslo: University of Oslo.

Everett-Heath, J. (2000). *Place Names of the World – Europe: Historical Context, Meanings and Changes*. London/Oxford: Macmillan.

Facchini, F., Beltrán, A., & Broglio, A. (Eds.) (1993). *Paleoantropologia e Preistoria. Origini, Paleolitico, Mesolitico*. Milan: Jaca Book.

Fairbairn, D. J. (1993). On the Nature of Cartographic Text. *The Cartographic Journal*, 30(2), 104–11.

Farquhar, W. (1822). No. 34 To Lieut. L.N. Hull. In. Singapore. 1822. Retrieved from www.nas.gov.sg/archivesonline/private_records/Flipviewer/prism_publish/d/da493 b96-029f-11e9-bebd-001a4a5ba61b-L11__Letters_to_and_from_Raffles%20%281 %29/web/html5/index.html?launchlogo=tablet/PrivateRecords_brandingLogo_.png &pn=167.

Fedman, D. A. (2012). Japanese Colonial Cartography: Maps, Mapmaking, and the Land Survey in Colonial Korea. *The Asia-Pacific Journal | Japan Focus*, 10(52), 4.

Ferguson, P. P. (1988). Reading City Streets. *The French Review*, 61(3), 386–97.

Field, K. (2014). The Stories Maps Tell. *The Cartographic Journal*, 51(2), 99–100.

Finkelstein, I. (1979). The Holy Land in the Tabula Peutingeriana: A Historical-Geographical Approach. *Palestine Exploration Quarterly*, 111(1), 27–34.

Firmstone, H. W. (1905). Chinese Names of Streets and Places in Singapore and the Malay Peninsula. *Journal of the Straits Branch of the Royal Asiatic Society*, 42(February 1905), 53–208.

Fodorean, F.-G. (2013). Tabula Peutingeriana. In R. S. Bagnall, K. Brodersen, C. B. Champion, A. Erskine, & S. R. Huebner (Eds.), *The Encyclopedia of Ancient History*. Hoboken, NJ: Wiley-Blackwell.

Fuchs, S. (2015). An Integrated Approach to Germanic Place Names in the American Midwest. *Professional Geographer*, 67(3), 330–41.

Gasca Queirazza, G., Marcato, C., Pellegrini, G. B., Petracco Sicardi, G., Rossebastiano, A., & with collaboration of Papa, E. (1999). *Dizionario di Toponomastica. Storia e significato dei nomi geografici italiani* [*Toponomastics Dictionary: History and Meaning of the Italian Geographical Names*]. Turin: UTET.

Gelling, M. (1987). Anglo-Saxon Eagles. *Leeds Studies in English*, 18, 173–81.

Gelling, M. & Cole, A. (2000). *The Landscape of Place-Names*. Donington: Shaun Tyas.

Gibson-Hill, C. A. (1954). Singapore: Notes on the History of the Old Strait, 1580–1850. *Journal of the Malayan Branch of the Royal Asiatic Society*, 27(1)(165), 163–214.

Gilberg, R. (1976). Thule. *Arctic*, 29(2), 83–6.

Gillooly, L., Medway, D., Warnaby, G., & Roper, S. (2021). 'To Us It's Still Boundary Park': Fan Discourses on the Corporate (Re)Naming of Football Stadia. *Social & Cultural Geography*. doi:10.1080/14649365.2021.1910990.

Gimbutas, M. (1974). *The Goddesses and Gods of Old Europe: Myths and Cult Images (6500–3500B.C.)*. London: Thames & Hudson.

Gimbutas, M. (1989). *The Language of the Goddess: Unearthing the Hidden Symbols of Western Civilization*. San Francisco, CA: Harper & Row.

Gimbutas, M. (1991). *The Civilization of the Goddess: The World of Old Europe*. San Francisco, CA: Harper & Row.

Gimbutas, M. (1999). *The Living Goddesses*. Berkeley, CA: University of California Press.

Gnatiuk, O. (2018). The Renaming of Streets in Post-Revolutionary Ukraine: Regional Strategies to Construct a New National Identity. *AUC Geographica*, 53(2), 119–36.

Goeman, M. (2013). *Mark My Words: Native Women Mapping Our Nations*. Minneapolis: University of Minnesota Press.

Golan, A. (2009). Historical Geographies, Urban. In R. Kitchin & N. Thrift (Eds.), *International Encyclopedia of Human Geography* (Vol. 1, pp. 146–51). Oxford: Elsevier.

Goodrick, B. E. (1982). What Is Cartography? *Cartography*, 12(3), 146–50.

Gregory, D. (2009). Human Geography. In D. Gregory, R. Johnston, G. Pratt, M. J. Watts, & S. Whatmore (Eds.), *The Dictionary of Human Geography* (5th ed., pp. 350–4). Chichester: Wiley-Blackwell.

Gregory, I. N. & Ell, P. S. (2007). *Historical GIS: Technologies, Methodologies, and Scholarship*. Cambridge: Cambridge University Press.

Grelot, J.-P. (1994). Cartography in the GIS Age. *The Cartographic Journal*, 31(1), 56–60.

Guelke, L. (1982). Historical Geography and Collingwood's Theory of Historical Knowing. In A. R. H. Baker & M. Billinge (Eds.), *Period and Place: Research Methods in Historical Geography* (pp. 189–97). Cambridge: Cambridge University Press.

Guerrini, P. (1969). *Pagine sparse IX: Note varie sui paesi della provincia di Brescia*. Brescia: Edizioni del Moretto.

Guerrini, P. (1986). *Pagine sparse VII: Note varie sui paesi della provincia di Brescia*. Brescia: Edizioni del Moretto.

Guidi, A. & Piperno, M (Eds.) (2005). *Italia Preistorica* (*Prehistoric Italy*). Bari: Laterza.

Haak, W., Forster, P., Bramanti, B., Matsumua, S., Brandt, G., Tänzer, M., Villems, R., Renfrew, C., Gronenborn, D., Alt, K. W., & Burger, J. (2005). Ancient DNA from the First European Farmers in 7500-Year-Old Neolithic Sites. *Science*, 310, 1016–18.

Harley, J. B. (1988). Maps, Knowledge, and Power. In D. Cosgrove & S. Daniels (Eds.), *The Iconography of Landscape: Essays on the Symbolic Representation, Design, and Use of Past Environments* (pp. 277–312). Cambridge: Cambridge University Press.

Harvey, D. (1990). Between Space and Time: Reflections on the Geographical Imagination. *Annals of the Association of American Geographers*, 80(3), 418–34.

Harvey, D. (2001). *Spaces of Capital: Towards a Critical Geography*. Edinburgh: Edinburgh University Press.

Haughton, H. T. (1889). Notes on Names of Places in the Island of Singapore and Its Vicinity. *Journal of the Straits Branch of the Royal Asiatic Society*, 20, 75–82.

Haughton, H. T. (1891). Native Names of Streets in Singapore. *Journal of the Malayan Branch of the Royal Asiatic Society*, 6, 49–65.

Hedquist, S. L., Koyiyumptewa, S. B., Whiteley, P. M., Kuwanwisiwma, L. J., Hill, K. C., & Ferguson, T. J. (2014). Recording Toponyms to Document the Endangered Hopi Language. *American Anthropologist*, 116(2), 324–31.

Heffernan, M. (2009). Historical Geography. In D. Gregory, R. Johnston, G. Pratt, M. J. Watts, & S. Whatmore (Eds.), *The Dictionary of Human Geography* (pp. 332–5). Chichester: Wiley-Blackwell.

Heikkilä, K. A. (2018). Understanding Ancestral Land as a Definer of Indigeneity: The Evidence of Toponyms from the Semai and Tl'azt'en Cultural Contexts (unpublished Ph.D. dissertation, University of Helsinki).

Helleland, B. (2012). Place Names and Identities. *Oslo Studies in Language*, 4(2), 95–116.

Hendriks, K. & Stobbelaar, D. J. (2003). Landbouw in een leesbaar landschap : hoe gangbare en biologische landbouwbedrijven bijdragen aan landschapskwaliteit [Agriculture in a Legible landscape: Landscape Quality of Conventional and Organic Farms] (unpublished Ph.D. dissertation, Wageningen University).

Hercus, L. & Simpson, J. (2002). Indigenous Placenames: An Introduction. In L. Hercus, F. Hodges, & J. Simpson (Eds.), *The Land Is a Map: Placenames of Indigenous Origin in Australia*. Canberra: The Australian National University Press.

Herling, S. (2020). Spanish and French Colonial Toponyms in the Territory of Present-Day USA (16th to 18th Century). In N. Levkovych (Ed.), *Advances in Comparative Colonial Toponomastics* (pp. 25–50). Berlin: De Gruyter.

Ho, A. L. (2017). Behind Every Road Name Is a Story of Singapore. *The Straits Times*, 26 May. Retrieved from www.straitstimes.com/singapore/behind-every-road-name-is-a-story-of-spore.

Hodder, I. (1978). *The Spatial Organisation of Culture*. London: Duckworth.

Holton, G. (2009). File:Alor-pantar map color.png. Retrieved from https://commons .wikimedia.org/wiki/File:Alor-pantar_map_color.png.

Holton, G., Klamer, M., Kratochvíl, F., Robinson, L. C., & Schapper, A. (2012). The Historical Relations of the Papuan Languages of Alor and Pantar. *Oceanic Linguistics*, 51(1), 86–122.

Hsü, Y.- t. i. (1972). Singapore in the Remote Past. *Journal of the Malayan Branch of the Royal Asiatic Society*, 45(1), 1–9.

Huggan, G. (2015). Ultima Thule/The North. In C. Thompson (Ed.), *The Routledge Companion to Travel Writing* (pp. 331–40). London: Routledge.

Huldén, L. (1994). Ortnamnens upplevelsevärde [The Value of Experiencing Place Names]. In Ulfsparre, G. (Ed.), *Ortnamn värda att vårda. Föredrag från Riksantikvarieämbetets symposium Ortnamnskultur. Stockholm, 5–7 May 1993* (pp. 32–7). Stockholm: Riksantikvarieämbetet.

Hunt, S. (2017). Indigeneity. In D. Richardson, N. Castree, M. F. Goodchild, A. Kobayashi, W. Liu, & R. A. Marston (Eds.), *International Encyclopedia of Geography* (pp. 1–9). Chichester: Wiley.

Hunt, D. & Stevenson, S. A. (2017). Decolonizing Geographies of Power: Indigenous Digital Counter-Mapping Practices on Turtle Island. *Settler Colonial Studies*, 7(3), 372–92.

ICA (2021). International Cartographic Association, Mission. Retrieved from https:// icaci.org/mission/.

Ilves, K. (2006). Place Names about Life by the Sea: An Archaeological Perspective on the Estonian Swedish Landscape. *Folklore*, 34, 87–102.

J. B. N. (1928). Raffles College – Old and New! *The Singapore Free Press and Mercantile Advertiser*, 21 June. Retrieved from http://cresources.nlb.gov.sg/news papers/Digitised/Article/singfreepressb19280621-1.2.3.

Jackson, P. (1828). Plan of the Town of Singapore.

Jacob, C. (1996). Toward a Cultural History of Cartography. *Imago Mundi*, 48, 191–8.

Jones, R. (2004). What Time Human Geography? *Progress in Human Geography*, 28(3), 287–304.

Jones, R. (2015). Place-Names in Landscape Archaeology, 'Detecting and Understanding Historical Landscapes'. In A. C. Arnau & A. Reynolds (Eds.), *Detecting and Understanding Historic Landscapes* (pp. 209–24). Mantova: SAP Societa Archeologica.

Jordan, P. (2009). Some Considerations on the Function of Place Names on Maps. Paper Presented at the 24th International Cartographic Conference (ICC 2009), Santiago, 15–21 November.

Joseph, B. D. & Janda, R. D. (Eds.) (2003). *The Handbook of Historical Linguistics*. Oxford: Blackwell.

Justi, F. (1895). *Iranisches Namenbuch* [*Iranian Name Book*]. Marburg: N.G. Elwert Verlagsbuchhandlung.

Kadmon, N. (2004). Toponymy and Geopolitics: The Political Use – and Misuse – of Geographical Name. *The Cartographic Journal, Special Issue, International Geographical Congress Glasgow, UK, 2004*, 41(2), 85–7.

Kadmon, N. (Ed.) (2007). *Glossary of Terms for the Standardization of Geographical Names*. New York: United Nations Publications.

Kainz, W. (2020). Cartography and the Others: Aspects of a Complicated Relationship. *Geo-Spatial Information Science*, 23(1), 52–60.

Kalpagam, U. (1995). Cartography in Colonial India. *Economic and Political Weekly*, 30(30), PE87–PE98.

Kaufman, A. (2015). Colonial Cartography and the Making of Palestine, Lebanon, and Syria. In C. Schayegh & A. Arsan (Eds.), *The Routledge Handbook of the History of the Middle East Mandates* (pp. 225–43). London: Routledge.

Keith, D. & Scottie, J. (1997). *Harvaqtuuq 1997: Place Names and Oral Traditions of the Lower Kazan River*. Hull: National Historic Sites Directorate, Parks Canada.

Kiparsky, P. (2014). New Perspectives in Historical Linguistics. In C. Bowern & B. Evans (Eds.), *The Routledge Handbook of Historical Linguistics* (pp. 64–102). New York: Routledge.

Kitson, P. (1996). British and European River Names. *Transactions of the Philological Society*, 94(2), 73–118.

Klinefelter, W. (1992). Falkland Islands. *The Carto-Philatelist*, 37, 7–8.

Koopman, A. (2016). Ethnonyms. In C. Hough (Ed.), *The Oxford Handbook of Names and Naming* (pp. 1–13). Oxford: Oxford University Press.

Korean Culture and Information Service (2011). *K-Drama: A New TV Genre with Global Appeal*. Republic of Korea: Ministry of Culture, Sports and Tourism.

Kostanski, L. (2009). 'What's in a Name?': Place and Toponymic Attachment, Identity and Dependence. A Case Study of the Grampians (Gariwerd) National Park Name Restoration Process (unpublished Ph.D. dissertation, University of Ballarat).

Kostanski, L. (2011). Toponymic Dependence Research and Its Possible Contribution to the Field of Place Branding. *Place Branding and Public Diplomacy*, 7(1), 9–22.

Kostanski, L. (2016). Toponymic Attachment. In C. Hough (Ed.), *The Oxford Handbook of Names and Naming* (pp. 412–26). Oxford: Oxford University Press.

Kraak, M.-J. & Fabrikant, S. I. (2017). Of Maps, Cartography, and the Geography of the International Cartographic Association. *International Journal of Cartography*, 3(Sup. 1), 9–31.

Krahe, H. (1962). *Die Struktur der alteuropäischen Hydronymie [Die Struktur der alteuropäischen Hydronymie]*. Wiesbaden: Steiner.

Krahe, H. (1964). *Unsere ältesten Flussnamen [Our Oldest River Names]*. Wiesbaden: Harrassowitz.

Kratochvíl, F., Delpada, B., & Perono Cacciafoco, F. (2016). Abui Landscape Names: Origin and Functions. *Onoma, Journal of the International Council of Onomastic Sciences*, 51, 69–102.

Krygier, J. B. (1995). Cartography as an Art and a Science? *The Cartographic Journal*, 32(1), 3–10.

Ladbury, S. & King, R. (1988). Settlement Renaming in Turkish Cyprus. *Geography*, 73(4), 363–7.

Lanamy (2020). File:Sylvanus map 1511.jpg. Retrieved from https://commons .wikimedia.org/wiki/File:Sylvanus_map_1511.jpg.

Laurence, K. M. (1975). Continuity and Change in Trinidadian Toponyms. *Nieuwe West-Indische Gids (New West Indian Guide)*, 50(2–3), 123–42.

Levinson, S. C. (2008). Landscape, Seascape and the Ontology of Places on Rossel Island, Papua New Guinea. *Language Sciences*, 30(2–3), 256–90.

Lewis, P. (1982). The Politics of Iranian Place-Names. *Geographical Review*, 72(1), 99–102.

Li, P. (1928). *The Works of Li Po, translated by Shigeyoshi Obata*. Boston, MA: E.P. Dutton & Company.

Light, D. (2004). Street Names in Bucharest, 1990–1997: Exploring the Modern Historical Geographies of Post-Socialist Change. *Journal of Historical Geography*, 30, 154–72.

Light, D. (2014). Tourism and Toponymy: Commodifying and Consuming Place Names. *Tourism Geographies*, 16(1), 141–56.

Light, D., Nicolae, I., & Suditu, B. (2002). Toponymy and the Communist City: Street Names in Bucharest, 1948–1965. *GeoJournal*, 56(2), 135–44.

Light, D. & Young, C. (2014). Habit, Memory, and the Persistence of Socialist-Era Street Names in Postsocialist Bucharest, Romania. *Annals of the Association of American Geographers*, 104(3), 668–685.

Light, D. & Young, C. (2015). Toponymy as Commodity: Exploring the Economic Dimensions of Urban Place Names. *International Journal of Urban and Regional Research*, 39(3), 435–50.

Light, D. & Young, C. (2018). The Politics of Toponymic Continuity: The Limits of Change and the Ongoing Lives of Street Names. In R. Rose-Redwood, D. Alderman, & M. Azaryahu (Eds.), *The Political Life of Urban Streetscapes: Naming, Politics and Place* (pp. 185–201). New York: Routledge.

Lilomaiava-Doktor, S. i. (2020). Oral Traditions, Cultural Significance of Storytelling, and Samoan Understandings of Place or Fanua. *Native American and Indigenous Studies*, 7(1), 121–51.

Lim, S. T. G. & Perono Cacciafoco, F. (2020a). Then and Now: A Comparative Historical Toponomastics Analysis of Station Names in 2 of Singapore's Mass Rapid Transit (MRT) Lines. *Urban Science*, 4(3), 37.

Lim, S. T. G. & Perono Cacciafoco, F. (2020b). Plants and Place Names: A Case Study of Abui Toponymy. *Review of Historical Geography and Toponomastics*, 15(29–30), 121–42.

Löfström, J. & Schnabel-Le Corre, B. (2015). Introduction. In J. Löfström & B. Schnabel-Le Corre (Eds.), *Challenges in Synchronic Toponymy: Challenges in Synchronic Toponymy: Structure, Context and Use* (pp. 11–20). Tübingen: Narr Francke Attempto Verlag GmbH + Co.KG.

MacCannell, D. (1999). *The Tourist: A New Theory of the Leisure Class* (2nd ed.). Berkeley: University of California Press.

Macfarlane, R. (2016). *Landmarks*. New York: Penguin.

Mailhammer, R. (2013). Towards a Framework of Contact Etymology. In R. Mailhammer (Ed.), *Lexical and Structural Etymology: Beyond Word Histories* (pp. 9–32). Berlin/New York: de Gruyter Mouton.

Mailhammer, R. (2015). Diveristy vs. Uniformity: Europe before the Arrival of the Indo-European Languages – A Comparison with Prehistoric Australia. In R. Mailhammer, T. Vennemann, & B. A. Olsen (Eds.), *The Linguistic Roots of Europe: Origin and Development of European Languages* (pp. 29–75). Copenhagen: Museum Tusculanum Press.

Mailhammer, R. (2016). Place Names as Clues to Lost Languages? A Comparison between Europe and Australia. In P. K. Austin, H. Koch, & J. Simpson (Eds.), *Language, Land & Song: Studies in Honour of Luise Hercus* (pp. 318–29). London: EL Publishing.

Mamvura, Z. (2020). Reconstituting the Cultural Geography in Zimbabwe: Place Renaming in Zimbabwe's 'New Dispensation'. *Geopolitics*. doi:10.1080/14650045 .2020.1850443.

Mamvura, Z., Mutasa, D. E., & Pfukwa, C. (2017). Place Naming and the Discursive Construction of Imagined Boundaries in Colonial Zimbabwe (1890–1979): The Case of Salisbury. *Nomina Africana*, 3(1), 39–49.

Mamvura, Z., Muwati, I., & Mutasa, D. E. (2018). 'Toponymic Commemoration Is Not for One Sex': The Gender Politics of Place Renaming in Harare. *African Identities*, 16 (4), 429–43.

Maneglier, H. (1990). *Paris impérial: La vie quotidienne sous le Second Empire*. Paris: Armand Colin.

Maria, S. S. (2021). Rachael McPhail: Making Traditional Place Names Part of Mailing Addresses. *Australia Post*, 16 December. Retrieved from https://auspost.com.au/ about-us/supporting-communities/rachael-mcphail-making-traditional-place-names-part-of-mailing-addresses.

Marshall, L. (2013). Sicily: Montalbano's Island. *The Telegraph*.

Marsyas (2005). Mycenaean Tablet (MY Oe 106). Retrieved from https://commons .wikimedia.org/wiki/File:Linear_B_(Mycenaean_Greek)_NAMA_Tablette_7671.jpg.

Martina, G. (1951). *Cortemilia e le sue Langhe* [*Cortemilia and Its 'Langhe'*]. Cuneo: Edizioni Ghibaudo.

Masalha, N. (2015). Settler-Colonialism, Memoricide, and Indigenous Toponymic Memory: The Appropriation of Palestinian Place Names by the Israeli State. *Journal of Holy Land and Palestine Studies*, 14(1), 3–57.

Maschner, H. D. G. & Marler, B. C. (2008). Evolutionary Psychology and Archaeological Landscapes. In B. David & J. Thomas (Eds.), *Handbook of Landscape Archaeology* (pp. 109–20). Walnut Creek, CA: Left Coast Press.

Medway, D. & Warnaby, G. (2014). What's in a Name? Place Branding and Toponymic Commodification. *Environment and Planning A*, 46(1), 153–67.

Medway, D., Warnaby, G., Gillooly, L., & Millington, S. (2019). Scalar Tensions in Urban Toponymic Inscription: The Corporate (Re)Naming of Football Stadia. *Urban Geography*, 40(6), 784–804.

Megistias (2010). File:Ancient Greece Northern Part Map.jpg. Retrieved from https://commons.wikimedia.org/wiki/File:Ancient_Greece_Northern_Part_Map.jpg.

Miccoli, P. (2019). Colonial Place-Names in Italian East Africa (AOI) (with additional data from Tripoli). In B. Weber (Ed.), *The Linguistic Heritage of Colonial Practice* (pp. 75–92). Berlin: Walter de Gruyter GmbH.

Miksic, J. N. (2007). *Historical Dictionary of Ancient Southeast Asia*. Lanham, MD: Scarecrow Press.

Miksic, J. N. (2013). *Singapore & The Silk Road of the Sea: 1300–1800*. Singapore: National University of Singapore Press.

Möller, L. A. (2019). Multilingual Place Names in Southern Africa. *Names: A Journal of Onomastics*, 67(1), 5–15.

Monmonier, M. (2007). *From Squaw Tit to Whorehouse Meadow: How Maps Name, Claim, and Inflame*. Chicago, IL/London: The University of Chicago Press.

Monmonier, M. (2018). *How to Lie With Maps* (3rd ed.). Chicago, IL: University of Chicago Press.

Moore, N. & Whelan, Y. (2016). *Heritage, Memory and the Politics of Identity: New Perspectives on the Cultural Landscape*. London: Routledge.

Morgan, L. (1958). Century of Piracy in Malayan Waters. *The Straits Times*, 13 September, p. 9.

Morgan, M. (2006). State Park Names: Implications for Tourism Marketing. *Tourism Analysis*, 11(1), 71–4.

Morrison, J. L. (1978). Towards a Functional Definition of the Science of Cartography with Emphasis on Map Reading. *The American Cartographer*, 5(2), 97–110.

Nah, V. E. M. Y. & Perono Cacciafoco, F. (2018). Ex-Isles: Islands That Disappeared. *Review of Historical Geography and Toponomastics*, 13(25–6), 31–58.

Nash, J. (2009). Toponymy on Norfolk Island, South Pacific: The Microcosm of Nepean Island. In W. Ahrens, S. Embleton, & A. Lapierre (Eds.), *Proceedings of the 23rd International Congress of Onomastic Sciences*. York: York University.

Nash, J. (2015a). Island Placenaming and Insular Toponymies. *Names*, 63(3), 146–57.

Nash, J. (2015b). The How of Toponymy: A Comment on Tent's 'Approaches to Research in Toponymy'. *Names*, 63(4), 233–6.

Nash, J. (2018). Drawing, Toponymy, and Linguistic Pilgrimage. *Journal of Cultural Geography*, 35(1), 133–48.

Nash, J. & Low, M. (2015). Language and Place-Knowledge on Norfolk Island. *Ethnos*, 80(3), 385–408.

Nash, D. & Simpson, J. (2012). Toponymy: Recording and Analysing Placenames in a Language Area. In N. Thieberger (Ed.), *The Oxford Handbook of Linguistic Fieldwork* (pp. 392–404). Oxford: Oxford University Press.

National Archives of Singapore (Cartographer) (1852). *Map Of Singapore Island, And Its Dependencies, 1852*. Retrieved from www.nas.gov.sg/archivesonline/maps_building_plans/record-details/fb830a64-115c-11e3-83d5-0050568939ad.

Nationaal Archief Holland (1820s). Map of Singapore and Environment (draft). Retrieved from www.nas.gov.sg/archivesonline/maps_building_plans/record-details/faea412e-115c-11e3-83d5-0050568939ad.

National Archives of Singapore (1822–3). Singapore 1822–3. Retrieved from www.nas.gov.sg/archivesonline/maps_building_plans/record-details/fa3d03c7-115c-11e3-83d5-0050568939ad.

Ndletyana, M. (2012). Changing Place Names in Post-Apartheid South Africa: Accounting for the Unevenness. *Social Dynamics*, 18(1), 87–103.

Newton, J. (2016). Rural Autochthony? The Rejection of Aboriginal Placename in Ballarat, Victoria, Australia. *Cultural Studies Review*, 22(2), 114–31.

Ng, Y. P. (2017). *What's in the Name? How the Streets and Villages in Singapore Got Their Names*. Singapore: World Scientific Publishing.

NIAA (n.d.). Welcome to Country or Acknowledgement of Country. Retrieved from www.indigenous.gov.au/contact-us/welcome_acknowledgement-country.

Nichols, J. (1998). The Eurasian Spread Zone and the Indo-European Dispersal. In R. B. M. Spriggs (Ed.), *Archaeological Data and Linguistic Hypotheses* (pp. 220–66). London: Routledge.

Nicolaisen, W. F. H. (1984). Names and Narratives. *The Journal of American Folklore*, 97(385), 259–72.

Nicolaisen, W. F. H. (1993). Scottish Place Names as Evidence for Language Change. *Names*, 40(1), 306–13.

Niculescu-Mizil, & A-M. (2014). (Re)Naming Streets in Contemporary Bucharest: From Power Distribution to Subjective Biography. *Analize: Journal of Gender and Feminist Studies*, 3(17), 69–94.

Norton, W. (1984). *Historical Analysis in Geography*. London: Longman.

Nyambi, O., Mangena, T., & Pfukwa, C. (Eds.) (2016). *The Postcolonial Condition of Names and Naming Practices in Southern Africa*. Newcastle upon Tyne: Cambridge Scholars Publishing.

Obata, S. (1928). *The Works of Li Po*. Boston, MA: E. P. Dutton & Company.

Odorici, F. (1856). *Storie Bresciane dai primi tempi sino all'età nostra [Brescia's Histories from the Origins to the Present Time]* (Vol. 6). Brescia: Gilberti.

Oliver, J. (2011). On Mapping and Its Afterlife: Unfolding Landscapes in Northwestern North America. *World Archaeology*, 43(1), 66–85.

Olivier, J.-P. (1986). Cretan Writing in the Second Millennium B.C. *World Archaeology*, 17(3), 377–89.

Olivieri, D. (1965). *Dizionario di toponomastica piemontese [Piedmontese Toponomastics' Dictionary]*. Brescia: Paideia.

Olson, J. M. (2004). Cartography 2003. *Cartographic Perspectives*, 47, 4–12.

Owens, G. A. (1994). Was SE-TO-I-JA at Archanes? *Kadmos*, 33(1), 22–8.

Pain, M. (Ed.) (1989). *Transmigration and Spontaneous Migrations in Indonesia: Propinsi Lampung*. Jakarta: ORSTOM – Department Transmigrasi.

Palonen, E. (2008). The City-Text in Post-Communist Budapest: Street Names, Memorials, and the Politics of Commemoration. *GeoJournal*, 73, 219–30.

Palonen, E. (2015). The Politics of Street Names: Local, National, Transnational Budapest. In M. Beyen & B. Deseure (Eds.), *Local Memories in a Nationalising and Globalising World* (pp. 51–71). London: Palgrave Macmillan.

Pappe, I. (2006). *The Ethnic Cleansing of Palestine*. London: Oneworld Publications.

Pato, E. (2018). Indefinite Article + Possessive + Noun in Spanish: A Case of Refunctionalization? *Languages*, 3(4), 44.

Pavord, A. (2016). *Landskipping: Painters, Ploughmen, and Places*. London: Bloomsbury.

Pazarli, M. (2009). Mediterranean Islands in Tabula Peutingeriana. *e-Perimetron*, 4(2), 101–16.

Pazarli, M., Livieratos, E., & Boutoura, C. (2007). Road Network of Crete in Tabula Peutingeriana. *e-Perimetron*, 2(4), 245–60.

Pearce, T. (1954). Animal Place Names in the West. *Western Folklore*, 13(3), 203–5.

Pellegrini, G. B. (1981). Toponomastica celtica nell'Italia settentrionale [Celtic Toponymy in Northern Italy]. In E. Campanile (Ed.), *I Celti d'Italia* [*The Celts in Italy*] (pp. 35–68). Pisa: Giardini.

Pellegrini, G. B. (1990). *Toponomastica italiana: 10.000 nomi di città, paesi, frazioni, regioni, contrade, monti spiegati nella loro origine e storia* [*Italian Toponomastics: 10,000 Names of Cities, Villages, Hamlets, Regions, Districts, Mounts Explained in Their Origin and History*]. Milan: Ulrico Hoepli Editore.

Pellegrini, G. B. (2008). *Toponomastica italiana. 10.000 nomi di città, paesi, frazioni, regioni, contrade, monti spiegati nella loro origine e storia*. Milan: Ulrico Hoepli Editore.

Perono Cacciafoco, F. (2011). Tracce di pietra. Cenni inerenti all'Acquese tra il Paleolitico e l'età del Bronzo [Stony Traces: The Acquese Territory between Paleolithic and Bronze Age]. *Iter. Ricerche fonti e immagini per un territorio*, 25, 3–20.

Perono Cacciafoco, F. (2013). Water Origins: The *alb- Root in the Pre-Latin Toponymy of Ancient Liguria. *Acta Linguistica: Journal for Theoretical Linguistics*, 7(1), 70–86.

Perono Cacciafoco, F. (2014). Beyond Etymology: Historical Reconstruction and Diachronic Toponomastics through the Lens of a New Convergence Theory. *Acta Linguistica, Journal for Theoretical Linguistics*, 8(3), 79–98.

Perono Cacciafoco, F. (2015a). Toponymic Persistence: The Proto-Indo-European *kar- Root in the Pre-Latin Ligurian Context. *Acta Linguistica: Journal for Theoretical Linguistics*, 9(1), 35–50.

Perono Cacciafoco, F. (2015b). Pre-Indo-European Relics: The *borm- Root in the European Pre-Latin Context. *Acta Linguistica, Journal for Theoretical Linguistics*, 9 (2), 57–69.

Perono Cacciafoco, F. (2016a). Where the River Converges: Toponymic Stratigraphy of Bistagno and Sessame. *Annals of the University of Craiova: Series Philology – Linguistics*, 38(1–2), 69–81.

Perono Cacciafoco, F. (2016b). The Origins of Naming Process: Toponymic Archaeology of Two Indo-European Place Names. *Review of Historical Geography and Toponomastics*, 11(21–22), 57–67.

Perono Cacciafoco, F. (2017). Linear A and Minoan: Some New Old Questions. *Analele Universității Din Craiova: Seria Științe Filologice, Linguistică* [*Annals of the University of Craiova: Series Philology, Linguistics*], 39(1–2), 154–70.

Perono Cacciafoco, F., Binte Adzman, N., & Binte Sharin, N. S. (2017). Mythical Place Names: Naming Process and Oral Tradition in Indonesian Toponymy. *Review of Historical Geography and Toponomastics*, 12(23–24), 25–35.

Perono Cacciafoco, F. & Cavallaro, F. (2017). The Legend of Lamòling: Unwritten Memories and Diachronic Toponymy through the Lens of an Abui Myth. *Lingua*, 193, 51–61.

Perono Cacciafoco, F. & Cavallaro, F. (2018). Lamòling Bèaka: Immanence, Rituals, and Sacred Objects in an Unwritten Legend in Alor. *Religions*, 9(7), 211.

Perono Cacciafoco, F., Cavallaro, F., & Kratochvíl, F. (2015). Diachronic Toponomastics and Language Reconstruction in South-East Asia According to an Experimental Convergent Methodology: Abui as a Case-Study. *Review of Historical Geography and Toponomastics*, 10(19–20), 29–47.

Perono Cacciafoco, F. & Shia, D. Z. Z. (2020). Singapore Pre-Colonial Place Names: A Philological Reconstruction Developed through the Analysis of Historical Maps. *Review of Historical Geography and Toponomastics*, 15(29–30), 79–120.

Perono Cacciafoco, F. & Tuang, S. Q. (2018). Voices from the Streets: Trends in Naming Practices of Singapore Odonymy. *Review of Historical Geography and Toponomastics*, XIII(25–26), 9–30.

Petracco Sicardi, G. (1962). *Toponomastica di Pigna* [*The Toponymy of Pigna*]. Bordighera: Istituto Internazionale di Studi Liguri.

Podolskaya, N. V. (1988). *Slovar' russkoy onomasticheskoy terminologii* [*Dictionary of Russian Onomastic Terminology*] (2nd ed.). Moscow: Nauka.

Poenaru-Girigan, O.-M. (2013). The Relationship between Toponymy and Linguistics. *Anadiss*, 15(1), 154–66.

Pokorny, J. (1969). *Indogermanisches etymologisches Wörterbuch* [*Indo-European Etymological Dictionary*]. Bern/Munich: Francke.

Prince, G. (1987). *A Dictionary of Narratology*. Lincoln, NE: University of Nebraska Press.

Psarra, S. (2018). *The Venice Variations: Tracing the Architectural Imagination*. London: UCL Press.

Qian, S., Kang, M., & Weng, M. (2016). Toponym Mapping: A Case for Distribution of Ethnic Groups and Landscape Features in Guangdong, China. *Journal of Maps*, 12(S1), 546–50.

Racheli, A. (1894). *Francia-corta: Memorie storiche di Rovato* (*Francia-Corta: Historical Memories from Rovato*). Bologna: Atesa Editrice.

Rackham, O. (1986). *The History of the Countryside*. London: J.M. Dent.

Rampoldi, G. B. (1833). *Corogradia dell'Italia*. Milan: Antonio Fontana.

Raper, P. E., Möller, L. A., & Du Plessis, L. T. (2014). *Dictionary of Southern African Place Names* (4th ed.). Johannesburg/Cape Town: Jonathan Ball Publishers.

Ras67 (2017a). File: Old European hydronymic map for the root *Sal-, *Salm-.jpg. Retrieved from https://commons.wikimedia.org/wiki/File:Old_European_hydronymic_map_for_the_root_*Sal-,_*Salm-.jpg.

Ras67 (2017b). File: Old European hydronymic map for the root *al-, *alm- Krahe.jp. Retrieved from https://commons.wikimedia.org/wiki/File:Old_European_hydronymic_map_for_the_root_*al-,_*alm-_Krahe.jpg.

Ravera P., Tasca G., & V., R. (Eds.) (1997). *I Vescovi della chiesa di Acqui. Dalle origini al XX secolo* [*The Bishops of the Church of Acqui. From the Origins to the XX Century*]. Acqui Terme: Editrice Impressioni Grafiche.

Redmonds, G. (2007). *Names and History: People, Places and Things*. London: A&C Black.

Reed, M. (1990). *The Landscape of Britain: From the Beginnings to 1914*. London: Routledge.

Rennick, R. (2005). How to Study Placenames. *Names*, 53, 291–308.

Reszegi, K. (2010). Possibilities of Onomatosystematical Comparative Research in Uralian Languages (On the Examples of Early Hungarian Oronyms). *Folia Uralica Debreceniensia*, 17, 95–110.

Reuters (2008, 17 November 2008). Aborigines oppose name change of Mt Niggerhead. Thomson Reuters, 17 November. Retrieved from www.reuters.com/article/idINIndia-36534020081117.

Rivard, É. (2008). Colonial Cartography of Canadian Margins: Cultural Encounters and the Idea of Métissage. *Cartographica*, 43(1), 45–66.

Robinson, A. (2009). Decoding Antiquity: Eight Scripts that Still Can't Be Read. *New Scientist* (2710), 24–30.

Roblespepe (2018). File:Penny Lane - McCartney signature.jpg. Retrieved from https://commons.wikimedia.org/wiki/File:Penny_Lane_-_McCartney_signature.jpg.

Rohlfs, G. (1969). *Grammatica storica della lingua italiana e dei suoi dialetti (volume I, Fonetica; volume II, Morfologia; volume III, Sintassi e formazione delle parole)* [*Historical Grammar of the Italian Language and Its Dialect (Vol. I, Phonetics: Vol. II, Morphology; Vol. III, Syntax and Word Formation)*]. Turin: Einaudi.

Rose, C. (2016). Thinking and Using DECIMA: Neighbourhoods and Occupations in Renaissance Florence. In N. Terpstra & C. Rose (Eds.), *Mapping Space, Sense, and Movement in Florence: Historical GIS and the Early Modern City*. London/New York: Routledge.

Rose-Redwood, R. S. (2006). Governmentality, Geography, and the Geo-Coded World. *Progress in Human Geography*, 30(4), 469–86.

Rose-Redwood, R. S. (2008). Indexing the Great Ledger of the Community: Urban House Numbering, City Directories, and the Production of Spatial Legibility. *Journal of Historical Geography*, 34(2), 286–310.

Rose-Redwood, R. S. (2009). Indexing the Great Ledger of the Community: Urban House Numbering, City Directories, and the Production of Spatial Legibility. In L. Berg & J. Vuolteenaho (Eds.), *Critical Toponymies: The Contested Politics of Place Naming* (pp. 199–223). Farnham: Ashgate.

Rose-Redwood, R. S. (2011). Rethinking the Agenda of Political Toponymy. *ACME: An International E-Journal for Critical Geographies*, 10(1), 34–41.

Rose-Redwood, R. S. (2016). 'Reclaim, Rename, Reoccupy': Decolonising Place and the Reclaiming of PKOLS. *ACME: An International Journal for Critical Geographies*, 15(1), 187–206.

Rose-Redwood, R. S., Alderman, D. H., & Azaryahu, M. (2010). Geographies of Toponymic Inscription: New Directions in Critical Place-Name Studies. *Progress in Human Geography*, 34(4), 453–70.

Rose-Redwood, R. S., Sotoudehnia M., & Tretter, E. (2019). 'Turn Your Brand into a Destination': Toponymic Commodification and the Branding of Place in Dubai and Winnipeg. *Urban Geography*, 40(6), 846–69.

Rosemeyer, M. (2018). Refunctionalization and Usage Frequency: An Exploratory Questionnaire Study. *Languages*, 3(4), 39.

RTÉ (2021). Australia to Give Ten Offensive Place Names the Bounce. Raidió Teilifís Éireann, 29 August. Retrieved from www.rte.ie/news/2017/0829/900697-australia-placenames/.

Rusu, M. S. (2020). Political Patterning of Urban Namescapes and Post-Socialist Toponymic Change: A Quantitative Analysis of Three Romanian Cities. *Cities*, 103, 102773.

Ryan, M.-L. (2003). Cognitive Maps and the Construction of Narrative Space. In D. Herman (Ed.), *Narrative Theory and the Cognitive Sciences* (pp. 214–42). Stanford, CA: Centre for the Study of Language and Information, Stanford University.

Sabatti, A. (1807). *Quadro statistico del Dipartimento del Mella*. Brescia: per Nicolo Bettoni.

Sacchi, G. (1852). *Annali universali di statistica, economia pubblica, geografia, storia, viaggi e commercio* (*Universal Annals of Statistics, Public Economy, Geography, History, Travels, and Trade*). Milan: *Società degli Editori degli Annali Universali delle scienze e dell'industria* (Society of the Editors of the Universal Annals of Sciences and Industry).

Saparov, A. (2003). The Alteration of Place Names and Construction of National Identity in Soviet Armenia. *Cahiers du Monde russe*, 44(1), 179–98.

Sauer, C. O. (1941). Foreword to Historical Geography. *Annals of the Association of American Geographers*, 31(1), 1–24.

Savage, V. R. & Yeoh, B. S. A. (2003). *Toponymics: A Study of Singapore Street Names*. Singapore: Eastern Universities Press.

Savage, V. R. & Yeoh, B. S. A. (2013). *Singapore Street Names: A Study of Toponymics*. Singapore: Marshall Cavendish Editions.

Sayatek (2019). File:Tabula peutingeriana lazio abruzzo.png. Retrieved from https://commons.wikimedia.org/wiki/File:Tabula_peutingeriana_lazio_abruzzo.png.

*Singapore Chronicle and Commercial Register* (1831). *Singapore Chronicle and Commercial Register*, Thursday, 26 May 1831. NewspaperSG. Retrieved from https://eresources.nlb.gov.sg/newspapers/Digitised/Article/singchronicle18310526-1.2.9.

Schlerath, B. (1973). *Die Indogermanen: Das Problem der Expansion eines Volkes im Lichte seiner sozialen Struktur*. Innsbruck: Instiut für vergleichende.

Schlerath, B. (1981). Ist ein Raum/Zeit-Modell für eine rekonstruierte Sprache möglich? *Historische Sprachforschung*, 95(2), 175–202.

Schrijver, P. (2001). Lost Languages in Northern Europe. In C. Carpelan, A. Parpola, & P. Koskikallio (Eds.), *Early Contacts between Uralic and Indo-European: Linguistic and Archaeological Considerations* (pp. 417–25). Helsinki: Soumalais-Ugrilainen Seura.

Schwede66 (2015). File:Thelongest place name in the world.jpg. Retrieved from https://commons.wikimedia.org/wiki/File:The_longest_place_name_in_the_world.jpg.

Seidl, N. P. (2008). Significance of Toponyms, with Emphasis on Field Names, for Studying Cultural Landscape. *Acta Geographica Slovenia*, 48(1), 33–56.

Sella, P. (1950). *Rationes decimarum Italiae nei secoli XIIIe XIV: Marchia*. Vatican City: Biblioteca apostolica vaticana.

Seton, M., Williams, S., Zahirovic, S., & Micklethwaite, S. (2013). Obituary: Sandy Island (1876–2012). *Eos: Transactions of the American Geophysical Union*, 94(15), 141–2.

Simpson-Housley, P. (1996). *The Arctic: Enigmas and Myths*. Toronto: Dundurn Press.

Siniscalchi, S. & Palagiano, C. (2018). The Place Names of the Middle East Before and After Ptolemaic Cartography: An Emblematic Selection from Ancient Maps. *The Cartographic Journal*, 55(3), 205–16.

Slingsby, A., Wood, J., & Dykes, J. (2010). Treemap Cartography for Showing Spatial and Temporal Traffic Patterns. *Journal of Maps*, 6(1), 135–46.

Snodia, M., Muguti, T., & Mutami, N. (2010). Political Dialoguing through the Naming Process: The Case of Colonial Zimbabwe (1890–1980). *The Journal of Pan African Studies*, 3(10), 16–30.

Stefansson, V. (2019). *Ultima Thule: Further Mysteries of the Arctic.* Stockholm: Librorium Editions.

Stewart, G. R. (1945). *Names on the Land: A Historical Account of Place-Naming in the United States.* Boston, MA: Houghton Mifflin.

Stewart, G. R. (1954). A Classification of Place Names. *Names*, 2, 1–13.

Stewart, G. R. (1975). *Names on the Globe.* Oxford: Oxford University Press.

Svoboda, J. (2017). On Landscapes, Maps, and Upper Paleolithic Lifestyles in the Central European Corridor: The Images of Pavlov and Předmostí. *Veleia*, 34(1), 67–74.

Tallack, M. (2016). *The Un-Discovered Islands: An Archipelago of Myths and Mysteries, Phantoms, and Fakes.* London: Picador.

Tan, T. T. W. (1986). *Your Chinese Roots: The Overseas Chinese Story.* Singapore: Times Books International.

Tappy, R. E. (2012). The Tabula Peutingeriana: Its Roadmap to Borderland Settlements in Iudaea-Palestina, with Special Reference to Tel Zayit in the late Roman Period. *Near Eastern Archaeology*, 75(1), 36–55.

Taylor, D. R. F. (1991). Geographic Information Systems: The Microcomputer and Modern Cartography. In D. R. F. Taylor (Ed.), *Geographic Information Systems: A Guide to the Technology* (pp. 1–20). Oxford: Pergamon Press.

Taylor, D. R. F. (1994). Cartography for Knowledge, Action, and Development: Retrospective and Prospective. *The Cartographic Journal*, 31(1), 52–5.

Taylor, K. (2012). Landscape and Meaning: Context for a Global Discourse on Cultural Landscape Values. In K. Taylor and J. L. Lennon (Eds.), *Managing Cultural Landscapes* (pp. 21–44). London: Routledge.

Tent, J. (2015a). Approaches to Research in Toponymy. *Names: A Journal of Onomastics*, 63(2), 65–74.

Tent, J. (2015b). Microtoponymy 2. *Placenames Australia: Newsletter of the Australian National Placename Survey* (March 2015), 8–9.

Tent, J. (2019). Indigenous Toponymy (3). *Placenames Australia: Newsletter of the Australian National Placenames Survey* (March 2019), 10–12.

Tent, J. (2020). Simplex Generic Toponyms in Four English-Speaking Jurisdictions. *Names: A Journal of Onomastics*, 68(1), 17–31.

Tent, J. & Blair, D. (2009). *Motivations for Naming: A Toponymic Typology. Australian National Placenames Survey Technical Papers, Vol. 2.* South Turramurra: Placenames Australia.

Tent, J. & Blair, D. (2011). Motivations for Naming: The Development of a Toponymic Typology for Australian Placenames. *Names: A Journal of Onomastics*, 59(2), 67–89.

Tent, J. & Slayter, H. (2009). Naming Places on the 'Southland': European Placenaming Practices from 1606 to 1803. *Australian Historical Studies*, 40(1), 5–31.

Tilley, C. (1994). *A Phenomenology of Landscape.* Oxford and Providence, RI: Berg Publishers.

Tilley, C. (2006). Introduction: Identity, Place, Landscape and Heritage. *Journal of Material Culture*, 11 (1–2) 7–32.

Toitū Te Whenua LINZ (2022). New Zealand Gazetteer. Retrieved from https://gazetteer.linz.govt.nz/place/5847.

Took, R. (2004). *Running with Reindeer: Encounters in Russian Lapland*. Boulder, CO: Westview Press.

Torrence, R. (2002). Cultural Landscapes on Garua Island, Papua New Guinea. *Antiquity*, 76(293), 766–76.

Tovar, A. (1977). *Krahes alteuropäische Hydronymie und die westindogermanischen Sprachen* [*Krahe's Old European Hydronymy and the Western Indo-European Languages*]. Heidelberg: Winter.

Tovar, A. (1982). *Die Indoeuropäisierung Westeuropas* [*The Indo-Europeianization of Western Europe*]. Innsbruck: Institut für Sprachwissenschaft der Universität Innsbruck.

Trask, R. L. (1997). *The History of Basque*. London: Routledge.

Trigger, D. & Martin, R. (2016). Place, Indigeneity, and Identity in Australia's Gulf Country. *American Anthropologist*, 118(4), 824–37.

*The Straits Times* (1969). A Contest to Re-Name Pulau Blakang Mati. *The Straits Times*, 25 November, p. 12. NewspaperSG. Retrieved from http://eresources.nlb.gov.sg/newspapers/Digitised/Article/straitstimes19691125-1.2.97

*The Straits Times* (1970a). When Mental Hospital Was 'House of Devils'. *The Straits Times*, 13 June, p. 2, NewspaperSG. Retrieved from http://eresources.nlb.gov.sg/newspapers/Digitised/Article/straitstimes19700613-1.2.19.

*The Straits Times* (1970b). The New Name Is Sentosa. *The Straits Times*, 11 September, p. 11. NewspaperSG. Retrieved from http://eresources.nlb.gov.sg/newspapers/Digitised/Article/straitstimes19700923-1.2.48.

Tucker, B. & Rose-Redwood, R. S. (2015). Decolonizing the Map? Toponymic Politics and the Rescaling of the Salish Sea. *The Canadian Geographer/Le Géographe canadien*, 59(2), 194–206.

Turnbull, C. M. (1989). *A History of Singapore*. Singapore: Oxford University Press.

Ucko, P. J. & Layton, R. (Eds.) (2005). *The Archaeology and Anthropology of Landscape: Shaping Your Landscape*. New York: Routledge.

Unknown (1825). Part of Singapore Island. Retrieved from www.nas.gov.sg/archiveson line/maps_building_plans/record-details/fb6eb3fd-115c-11e3-83d5-0050568939ad.

Untermann, J. (2009). Zur Problematik der alteuropäischen Hydronymie: Hispanien und Italien [On the Problem of the 'Old European Hydronymy': Spain and Italy]. *Beiträge zur Namenforschung*, 44(1), 1–34.

Urazmetova, A. V. & Shamsutdinova, J. K. (2017). Principles of Place Names Classifications. *XLinguae*, 10(4), 26–33.

Vale93b (2019). File:Borgomale Stemma.png [Borgomale's Coat of Arms]. Retrieved from https://commons.wikimedia.org/wiki/File:Borgomale_Stemma.png.

Valentini, A. (Ed.) (1898). *Gli statuti di Brescia dei secoli XII àl XV illustrati e documenti inediti* [*Brescia Statutes from the Twelfth to the Fifteenth Century, Illustrated and Unpublished*]. Venice: Fratelli Visentini.

Vennemann, T. (1994). Linguistic Reconstruction in the Context of European Prehistory. *Transactions of the Philological Society*, 92(2), 215–84.

Vennemann, T. (2003). *Europa Vasconica: Europa Semitica* (P. A. H. Noel Ed.). Berlin: De Gruyter.

Verdery, K. (1991). *National Ideology under Socialism: Identity and Cultural Politics in Ceaușescu's Romania*. Berkeley, CA: University of California Press.

Villar, F. (1996). *Los Indoeuropeos y los orígenes de Europa. Lenguaje e historia. Segunda edición corregida y muy aumentada*. Madrid: Editorial Gredos.

Villar, F. (1997). *Gli Indoeuropei e le origini dell'Europa. Lingua e storia* [*Indo-Europeans and the Origins of Europe. Language and History*] (2nd ed.). Bologna: Il Mulino.

Vuolteenaho, J. & Berg., L. D. (2009). Towards Critical Toponymies. In L. D. Berg & J. Vuolteenaho (Eds.), *Critical Toponymies: The Contested Politics of Place Naming* (pp. 1–18). Ashgate: Aldershot.

Vuolteenaho, J. & Puzey, G. (2018). 'Armed with an Encyclopedia and an Axe': The Socialist and Post-Socialist Street Toponymy of East Berlin Revisited through Gramsci. In R. S. Rose-Redwood, D. H. Alderman, & M. Azaryahu (Eds.), *The Political Life of Urban Streetscapes: Naming, Politics, and Place*. Abingdon/New York; Routledge.

Vuolteenaho, J., Wolny, M., & Puzey, G. (2019). 'This Venue Is Brought to You By...': The Diffusion of Sports and Entertainment Facility Name Sponsorship in Urban Europe. *Urban Geography*, 40(6), 762–83.

VV.AA. (1899–). *Biblioteca della Società Storica Subalpina* [*Library of the Sub-Alpine Historical Society*]. Pinerolo/Torino: BSSSS.

Wainwright, F. T. (1962). *Archaeology and Place-Names and History: An Essay on Problems of Coordination*. London: Routledge.

Walman, C. & Mason, C. (2006). *Encyclopedia of European Peoples: Facts on File*. New York: Infobase Publishing.

Wang, F., Hartmann, J., Luo, W., & Huang, P. (2006). GIS-Based Spatial Analysis of Tai Place Names in Southern China: An Exploratory Study of Methodology. *Geographic Information Sciences*, 12(1), 1–9.

Wang, F., Wang, G., Hartmann, J., & Luo, W. (2012). Sinification of Zhuang Place Names in Guangxi, China: A GIS-based Spatial Analysis Approach. *Transactions of the Institute of British Geographers*, 37, 317–33.

Wang, F., Zhang, L., Zhang, G., & Zhang, H. (2014). Mapping and Spatial Analysis of Multiethnic Toponyms in Yunnan, China. *Cartography and Geographic Information Science*, 41(1), 86–99.

Wang, S. (1577/1773). *Qinding Siku Quanshu Jibu 6 Bieji: Yanzhou Xugao* [*Complete Books of the Four Repositories Collections 6 Chronological Collections: Continuation of Yanzhou Collections*] (Vol. 64). Beijing: W.P.

Wanjiru, M. W. & Matsubara, K. (2017). Street Toponymy and the Decolonisation of the Urban Landscape in Post-Colonial Nairobi. *Journal of Cultural Geography*, 34(1), 1–23.

Wanjiru-Mwita, M. & Giraut, F. (2020). Toponymy, Pioneership, and the Politics of Ethnic Hierarchies in the Spatial Organisation of British Colonial Nairobi. *Urban Science*, 4(1), 6.

Wheatley, P. (1961). *The Golden Khersonese: Studies in the Historical Geography of the Malay Peninsula before A.D. 1500*. Kuala Lumpur: University of Malaya Press.

Wideman, T. J. & Masuda, J. R. (2018). Assembling 'Japantown'? A Critical Toponymy of Urban Dispossession in Vancouver, Canada. *Urban Geography*, 39(4), 493–518.

Wynn, S. (2017). *The Surrender of Singapore: Three Years of Hell, 1942–45*. Barnsley: Pen & Sword Military.

Xie, W. & Xie, S. (2007). *Zhongguo Mingshan Shengshui Yinglian Jingxuan [Selected Couplets of Chinese Famous Mountains and Rivers]*. Xi'an: Shaanxi People Publishing House.

Xu, D. (2016). Islands' Metamorphoses: Two River Islands in Nanjing, China, as a Case Study in Historical Toponymy and Cartography. *Review of Historical Geography and Toponomastics*, 11(21–22), 47–56.

Xu, D. (2017). Five Newly Documented Village Names of Moso People: A Frontier Toponymic System. *Review of Historical Geography and Toponomastics*, 12(23–24), 37–44.

Yan, Q. (1986). *A Social History of the Chinese in Singapore and Malaya, 1800–1911*. Oxford: Oxford University Press.

Yeh, Y.-T. (2013). 'Erased Place Names' and Nation-Building: A Case Study of Singaporean Toponyms. In T.-L. Chu (Ed.), *Asia-Pacific Forum No. 59* (pp. 119–56). Taipei: Research Center for Humanities and Social Sciences, Academia Sinica.

Yeoh, B. S. A. (1992). Street Names in Colonial Singapore. *Geographical Review*, 82(3), 313–22.

Yeoh, B. S. A. (1996). Street-Naming and Nation-Building: Toponymic Inscriptions of Nationhood in Singapore. *Area*, 28(3), 298–307.

Yi, I. (2016). Cartographies of the Voice: Storying the Land as Survivance in Native American Oral Traditions. *Humanities*, 5(3), 62.

Yom, J. Y. S. & Cavallaro, F. (2020). Colonialism and Toponyms in Singapore. *Urban Science*, 4(4), 64.

Young, C. & Light, D. (2001). Place, National Identity and Post-Socialist Transformations: An Introduction. *Political Geography*, 20(8), 941–55.

Younger, J. (2020). Place Names, 10 July. Retrieved from http://people.ku.edu/~jyounger/LinearA/#10c.

Zde (2007). Engraving on a Mammoth Tusk, Map Gravettian. Retrieved from https://commons.wikimedia.org/wiki/File:Engraving_on_a_mammoth_tusk,_map,_Gravettian,_076872y.jpg.

Zelinsky, W. (2002). Slouching Toward a Theory of Names: A Tentative Taxonomic Fix. *Names*, 50(4), 243–62.

Zhang, J. (1999 [1773]). *Sichuan Tongzhi (Annals of Sichuan). Vol. 2 of Siku Quanshu - Shibu 11 Dili (Complete Books of the Four Repositories, History XI, Geography)* (Y. Ji, Ed.). Hong Kong: Digital Heritage Publishing Limited.

Zhao, F., Fu, Y., Luan, G., Zhang, S., Cai, J., Ding, J., Qian, J., & Xie, Z. (2020). Spatial-Temporal Characteristic Analysis of Ethnic Toponyms Based on Spatial Information Entropy at the Rural Level in Northeast China. *Entropy*, 22(4), 393.

Zhu, Z., Zhang, H., Zhao, J., Guo, X., Zhang, Z., Ding, Y., & Xiong, T. (2018). Using Toponyms to Analyse the Endangered Manchu Language in Northeast China. *Sustainability*, 10, 563.

Zoozaz1 (2021). File:Base Map of Singapore.png. Retrieved from https://commons.wikimedia.org/wiki/File:Base_Map_of_Singapore.png.

ZX95 (2012). File:Sandy Island on 1908 chart.jpg. Retrieved from https://commons.wikimedia.org/wiki/File:Sandy_Island_on_1908_chart.jpg.

# Index

CPSIA information can be obtained
at www.ICGtesting.com
Printed in the USA
LVHW020711260323
742605LV00008B/228